8th International Natural Language Generation Conference

(INLG 2014)

Including Proceedings of the INLG and SIGDIAL 2014 Joint Session

Philadelphia, Pennsylvania, USA
19-21 June 2014

ISBN: 978-1-63439-320-1

Printed from e-media with permission by:

Curran Associates, Inc.
57 Morehouse Lane
Red Hook, NY 12571

Some format issues inherent in the e-media version may also appear in this print version.

Printed by Curran Associates, Inc. (2014)

For permission requests, please contact the Association for Computational Linguistics at the address below.

Association for Computational Linguistics
209 N. Eighth Street
Stroudsburg, Pennsylvania 18360

Phone: 1-570-476-8006
Fax: 1-570-476-0860

acl@aclweb.org

Additional copies of this publication are available from:

Curran Associates, Inc.
57 Morehouse Lane
Red Hook, NY 12571 USA
Phone: 845-758-0400
Fax: 845-758-2634
Email: curran@proceedings.com
Web: www.proceedings.com

INLG 2014

Proceedings of the Eighth International Natural Language Generation Conference

Including

Proceedings of the INLG and SIGDIAL 2014 Joint Session

Organizers:
Margaret Mitchell, Kathleen McCoy, David McDonald, Aoife Cahill

19-21 June 2014
Philadelphia, PA, USA

The biennial meeting of the ACL Special Interest Group on Natural Language Generation (SIGGEN)

ARRIA

Microsoft Research

amazon

ETS

Listening. Learning. Leading.®

Order copies of this and other ACL proceedings from:

Association for Computational Linguistics (ACL)
209 N. Eighth Street
Stroudsburg, PA 18360
USA
Tel: +1-570-476-8006
Fax: +1-570-476-0860
acl@aclweb.org

ISBN 978-1-941643-22-8 (INLG 2014 Proceedings)
ISBN 978-1-941643-23-5 (INLG and SIGDIAL Joint Session 2014 Proceedings)

Introduction

Welcome to the Eighth International Natural Language Generation Conference (INLG 2014)! INLG is the biennial meeting of the ACL Special Interest Group on Natural Language Generation (SIGGEN). The INLG conference provides the premier forum for the discussion, dissemination, and archiving of research and results in the field of Natural Language Generation (NLG). Previous INLG conferences have been held in Ireland, the USA, Australia, the UK, and Israel. Prior to 2000, INLG meetings were held as international workshops with a history stretching back to 1983. In 2014, INLG is co-located with the 15th Annual SIGDIAL Meeting on Discourse and Dialogue (SIGDIAL 2014), in Philadelphia, Pennsylvania, USA.

The INLG 2014 program includes presentations of substantial, original, and previously unpublished results on all topics related to natural language generation. This year, INLG received 35 submissions (20 full papers, 12 short papers and 3 demo proposals) from 12 different countries. 10 submissions were accepted as full papers (8 presented orally, 2 as posters), 15 as short papers (4 presented orally, and 11 as posters), and 3 demos. 3 papers (2 long, 1 short) were accepted for a special joint session on generation and dialogue, included in this document. This marks the first year where researchers in SIGDIAL and SIGGEN will come together to discuss issues relevant to both communities. In addition, INLG 2014 includes a keynote address by Marilyn Walker (UCSC), who will talk about generating stories and answers to questions from narrative representations; and Chris Callison-Burch (UPenn), who will talk about large-scale paraphrasing for natural language generation.

The organizing committee would like to offer their thanks to our invited speakers for agreeing to join us and to the authors of all submitted papers. A conference like INLG would not happen without much help from many quarters: the organizers of the last two INLG conferences for sharing their wisdom, specifically, Barbara Di Eugenio (University of Illinois Chicago) for INLG 2012 and Ielka van der Sluis (Groningen) for INLG 2010; the SIGGEN board for allowing us to host the conference and for their assistance; Heather Blackman for administrative support and Denise Maurer for event planning; Verena Rieser, the sponsorship chair; Amanda Stent, for assistance with submissions and registration; Keelan Evanini, for help with local arrangements; and Priscilla Rasmussen at ACL for her enormous help, always extremely prompt and offered with cheerfulness. We have also received sponsorship from Arria, Amazon, Microsoft Research, and ETS, for which we are extremely grateful. Finally, we would like to welcome you to Philadelphia and hope that you have an enjoyable and inspiring visit!

Margaret Mitchell, Kathleen McCoy, David McDonald, and Aoife Cahill
INLG 2014 Co-Chairs

Organizers:

Margaret Mitchell, Microsoft Research (MSR)
Kathleen McCoy, University of Delaware
David McDonald, Smart Information Flow Technologies (SIFT)
Aoife Cahill, Educational Testing Service (ETS)

Sponsorship Chair:

Verena Rieser, Heriot-Watt University

Program Committee:

John Bateman, University of Bremen, Germany
Anja Belz, University of Brighton, UK
Stephan Busemann, DFKI GmbH, Germany
Nina Dethlefs, Heriot Watt University, UK
Leo Ferres, University Conception, Chili
Katja Fillippova, Google, Switzerland
Claire Gardent, CNRS/LORIA, France
Albert Gatt, University of Malta, Malta
Pablo Gervás, Universidad Complutense de Madrid, Spain
Raquel Hervás, Universidad Complutense de Madrid, Spain
Alistair Knott, University of Otago, New Zealand
Ioannis Konstas, University of Edinburgh, UK
Emiel Krahmer, Tilburg University, The Netherlands
Guy Lapalme, University of Montreal, Canada
Paul Piwek, The Open University, UK
Ehud Reiter, University of Aberdeen, UK
Verena Rieser, Heriot-Watt University, UK
Kristina Striegnitz, Union College, US
Mariët Theune, University of Twente, The Netherlands
Kees van Deemter, University of Aberdeen, UK
Ielka van der Sluis, University of Groningen, The Netherlands
Keith vander Linden, Calvin College, US
Jette Viethen, Macquarie University, Australia
Leo Wanner, Universitat Pompeu Fabra, Spain
Michael White, The Ohio State University, US
Sandra Williams, The Open University, UK
Luke Zettlemoyer, University of Washington, US

Invited Speakers:

Marilyn Walker, University of California, Santa Cruz
Chris Callison-Burch, University of Pennsylvania

Table of Contents

INLG Proceedings

INLG and SIGDIAL Joint Session Proceedings

A Case Study: NLG meeting Weather Industry Demand for Quality and Quantity of Textual Weather Forecasts

Somayajulu G Sripada, Neil Burnett and Ross Turner
Arria NLG Plc
{yaji.sripada,neil.burnett, ross.turner}@arria.com

John Mastin and Dave Evans
Met Office
{john.mastin, dave.evans}@metoffice.gov.uk

Abstract

In the highly competitive weather industry, demand for timely, accurate and personalized weather reports is always on the rise. In this paper we present a case study where Arria NLG and the UK national weather agency, the Met Office came together to test the hypothesis that NLG can meet the quality and quantity demands of a real-world use case.

1 Introduction

Modern weather reports present weather prediction information using tables, graphs, maps, icons and text. Among these different modalities only text is currently manually produced, consuming significant human resources. Therefore releasing meteorologists' time to add value elsewhere in the production chain without sacrificing quality and consistency in weather reports is an important industry goal. In addition, in order to remain competitive, modern weather services need to provide weather reports for any geo-location the end-user demands. As the quantity of required texts increases, manual production becomes humanly impossible. In this paper we describe a case study where data-to-text NLG techniques have been applied to a real-world use case involving the UK national weather service, the Met Office. In the UK, the Met Office provides daily weather reports for nearly 5000 locations which are available through its public website. These reports contain a textual component that is not focused on the geo-location selected by the end-user, but instead describes the weather conditions over a broader geographic region. This is done partly because the time taken to manually produce thousands of texts required would be in the order of weeks rather than minutes. In this case study a data-to-text NLG system was built to demonstrate that the site-specific data could be enhanced with site-specific text for nearly 5000 locations. This system, running on a standard desktop, was tested to produce nearly 15000 texts (forecasts for 5000 locations for 3 days into the future) in less than a minute. After internally assessing the quality of machine-generated texts for nearly two years, the Met Office launched the system on their beta site (http://www.metoffice.gov.uk/public/weather/forecast-data2text/) in December 2013 for external assessment. A screenshot of the forecast for London Heathrow on 5th March 2014 is shown in Figure 1. In this figure, the machine-generated text is at the top of the table. Ongoing work has extended the processing capabilities of this system to handle double the number of locations and an additional two forecast days. It has been found that the processing time scales linearly.

2 Related Work

Automatically producing textual weather forecasts has been the second favorite application for NLG, with 15 entries on Bateman and Zock's list of NLG application domains (the domain of medicine comes on top with 19 entries) [Bateman and Zock, 2012]. NLG applications in the weather domain have a long history. FOG was an early landmark NLG system in the domain of weather reports [Goldberg et al, 1994]. Working as a module of the Forecast Production Assistant (FPA), FOG was operationally deployed at Environment Canada to produce weather reports for the general public and also for marine users in both English and French. Using sampling and smoothing over space and time, FOG reduces raw data into a few significant events which are then organized and realized in textual form. MULTIMETEO is another industry deployed multi-lingual weather report generator [Coch 1998]. The focus of MULTIMETEO is 'interactive generation via knowledge administration'.

Proceedings of the 8th International Natural Language Generation Conference, pages 1–5,
Philadelphia, Pennsylvania, 19-21 June 2014. ©2014 Association for Computational Linguistics

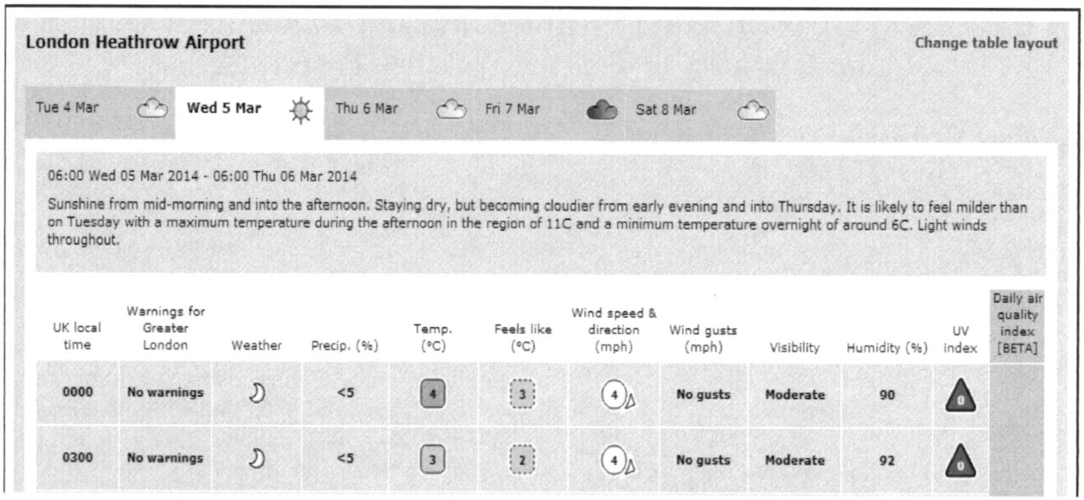

Figure 1. Screenshot of Text-Enhanced Five-day Weather Forecast for London Heathrow on 5 March 2014 showing only part of the data table

Expert forecasters post-edit texts (interactivity) in their native language and this knowledge is then reused (knowledge administration) for automatically generating texts in other languages. It is claimed that such interactive generation is better than using machine translation for multilingual outputs. SUMTIME-MOUSAM is yet another significant weather report generator that was operationally deployed to generate forecasts in English for oil company staff supporting oil rig operations in the North Sea [Sripada et al, 2003a]. Adapting techniques used for time series segmentation, this project developed a framework for data summarization in the context of NLG [Sripada et al, 2003b]. This time series summarization framework was later extended to summarizing spatio-temporal data in the ROADSAFE system [Turner et al, 2008]. ROADSAFE too was used in an industrial context to produce weather reports (including text in English and a table) for road maintenance in winter months. The NLG system reported in the current case study builds upon techniques employed by earlier systems, particularly SUMTIME-MOUSAM and ROADSAFE.

The main dimension on which the application described in this paper differs most from the work cited previously is the quantity of textual weather forecasts that are generated. Previous work has either focused on summarising forecast sites collectively (in the case of FOG and ROADSAFE), been limited in the number of sites forecast for (15 in the case of MULTIMETEO) or limited in geographic extent (SUMTIME-MOUSAM concentrated on oil rig operations in the North Sea). This aspect of the system, amongst others, posed a number of challenges discussed in Section 3.

3 System Description

For reasons of commercial sensitivity, the system description in this section is presented at an abstract level. At the architecture level, our system uses the Arria NLG Engine that follows the standard five stage data-to-text pipeline [Reiter, 2007]. The system integrates application specific modules with the generic reusable modules from the underlying engine. Input to the system is made up of three components:

1. Weather prediction data consisting of several weather parameters such as temperature, wind speed and direction, precipitation and visibility at three hourly intervals;
2. Daily summary weather prediction data consisting of average daily and nightly values for several weather parameters as above; and
3. Seasonal averages (lows, highs and mean) for temperature.

Because the system is built on top of the Arria NLG Engine, input data is configurable and not tied to file formats. The system can be configured to work with new data files with equivalent weather parameters as well as different forecast periods. In other words, the system is portable in principle for other use cases where site-specific forecasts are required from similar input data.

3.1 Expressing Falling Prediction Quality for Subsequent Forecast Days

As stated above, the system can be configured to generate forecast texts for a number of days into the future. Because prediction accuracy reduces going into the future, the forecast text on day 1 should be worded differently from subsequent days where the prediction is relatively more uncertain. An example output text for day 1 is shown in Figure 2 while Figure 3 shows the day 3 forecast. Note the use of 'expected' to denote the uncertainty around the timing of the temperature peak.

Staying dry and predominantly clear with only a few cloudy intervals through the night. A mild night with temperatures of 6C. Light winds throughout.

Figure 2. Example output text for day 1

Cloudy through the day. Mainly clear into the night. Highest temperatures expected during the afternoon in the region of 12C with a low of around 6C during the night. Light to moderate winds throughout.

Figure 3. Example output text for day 3

3.2 Lack of Corpus for System Development

A significant feature of the system development has been to work towards a target text specification provided by experts rather than extract such a specification from corpus texts, as is generally the case with most NLG system development projects. This is because expert forecasters do not write the target texts regularly; therefore, there is no naturally occurring target corpus. However, because of the specialized nature of the weather sublanguage (Weatherese), which has been well studied in the NLG community [Goldberg et al, 1994, Reiter et al 2005, Reiter and Williams 2010], it was possible to supplement text specifications obtained from experts. In addition, extensive quality assessment (details in section 3.4) helped us to refine the system output to the desired levels of quality.

3.3 Achieving Output Quantity

The main requirements of the case study have been 1) build a NLG capability that produces the quantity of texts required and 2) achieve this quantity without sacrificing the quality expected from the Met Office. As stated previously, the quantity requirement has been met by generating 15,000 texts in less than a minute, without need for high end computing infrastructure or parallelization. Figure 4 is a box plot showing character lengths of forecast texts for an arbitrary set of inputs. The median length is 177 characters. The outliers, with length 1.5 times the interquartile range (1.5 * 134 = 201 characters) above the upper quartile or below the lower quartile, relate to sites experiencing particularly varied weather conditions. Feedback on the appropriateness of the text lengths is discussed in Section 3.4.

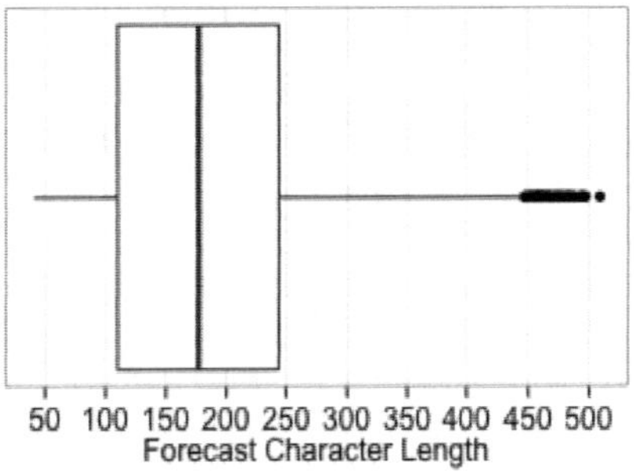

Figure 4. Boxplot of forecast character length

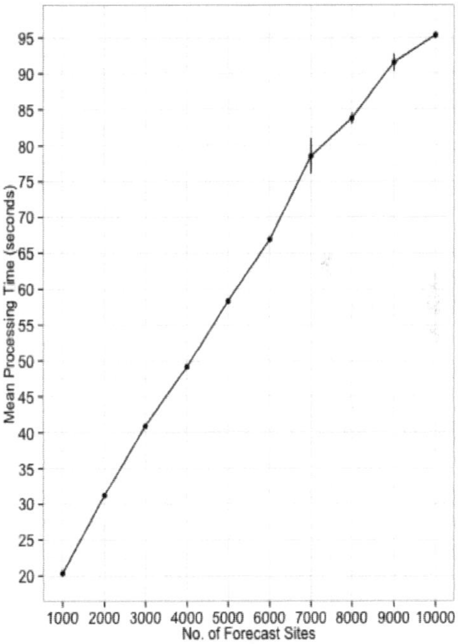

Figure 5. System Processing Time

The system has recently been extended to generate 50,000 texts without loss of performance. This extension has doubled the number of sites processed to 10,000 and extended the forecast to 5 days. It has also increased the geographic extent of the system from UK only to worldwide, discussed in Section 3.5. The plot in Figure 5 shows the relationship between processing time and the addition of new forecast sites. The results were obtained over 10 trials using a MacBook Pro 2.5 GHz Intel Core i5, running OS X 10.8 with 4GB of RAM.

3.4 Achieving Output Quality

Achieving the required text quality was driven by expert assessment of output texts that occurred over a period of two years. This is because experts had to ensure that the system output was assessed over the entire range of weather conditions related to seasonal variations over the course of a year. The following comment about the output quality made by a Met Office expert summarizes the internal feedback:

"They were very, very good and I got lots of verbal feedback to that affect from the audience afterwards. Looking back after the weekend, the forecasts proved to be correct too! I've been looking at them at other times and I think they're brilliant."

After successfully assessing the output quality internally, the Met Office launched the system on the Invent part of their website to collect end-user assessments. Invent is used by the Met Office to test new technology before introducing the technology into their workflows. With the help of a short questionnaire[1] that collects assessment of those end-users that use weather information for decision-making, quality assessment is ongoing. The questionnaire had three questions related to quality assessment shown in Figures 6-8. In the rest of the section we describe the results of this questionnaire based on 35 responses received between 1st January 2014 and 6th March 2014.

The first question shown in Figure 6 relates to assessing the usefulness of textual content in helping the end-user understand a weather report better. Out of the 35 respondents, 34 (97%) answered *'yes'* and 1 (3%) answered *'no'* for the question in Figure 6. The second question shown in Figure 7 relates to assessing if the text size is optimal for this use case. Here, out of the 35 respondents, 26 (74%) felt the text is *'about right'* size, 7 (20%) felt it is either *'too short'* or *'too long'* and 2 (6%) were *'unsure'*. The third question shown in Figure 8 relates to finding out if the end-user might want a forecast that includes textual content. Here, 32 (91%) wanted textual content while 3 (9%) did not want it.

[1] http://www.metoffice.gov.uk/invent/feedback

The Met Office is currently evaluating the new capability based upon the feedback received and how it can be applied to meet the demands of users across their portfolio of products.

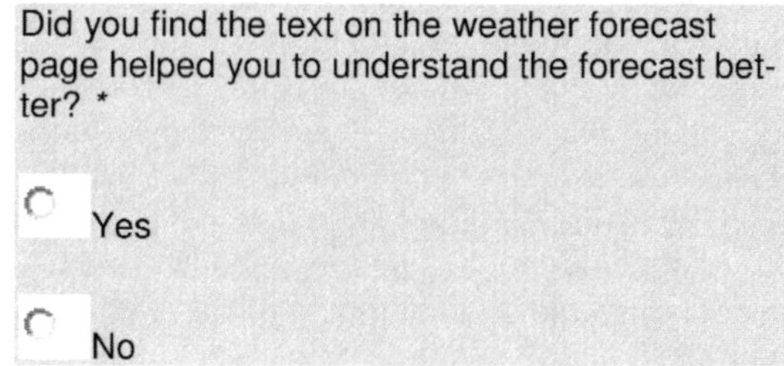
Did you find the text on the weather forecast page helped you to understand the forecast better? *

Yes

No

Figure 6. Question about textual content helping the end-user understand the forecast better

How did you find the text used? *

Too short

About right

Too long

Unsure / don't know

Figure 7. Question about length of the forecast text

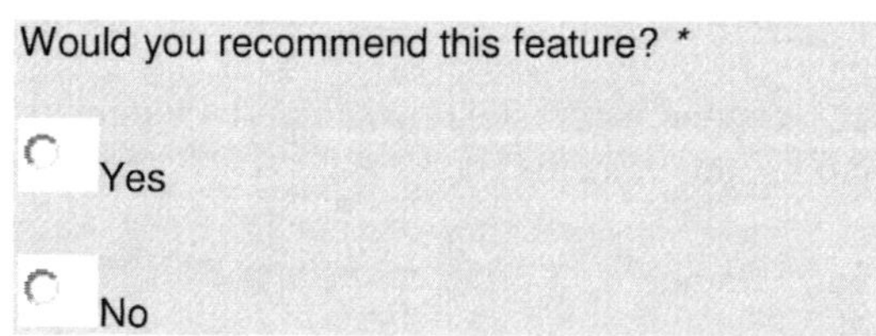
Would you recommend this feature? *

Yes

No

Figure 8. Question about the end-user's opinion on textual content as part of a weather report

The questionnaire also asked for free text comments. An example of one such comment is:

"Succinct and clear text. Contains all the important features and is well presented. Saves us having to summarise the visual descriptions ourselves (or rather helps to shape our conclusions about the 24 hour weather pattern)."

A big challenge during the development of such a system is providing quality assurance when generating such a large volume of texts. A number of automated checks had to be applied to the complete output during system testing as well as targeted sampling of input data to produce a representative sample of outputs for manual assessment.

3.5 Extending the Geographic Extent

Extending the scope of the system from UK-only sites to handling worldwide locations brings subtle challenges in addition to scaling the system, principally:

1. handling time zone changes; and
2. adapting to different climates.

In the case of point 1 above, time descriptions can become ambiguous where the sunrise and sunset time vary across geographies. Such times need to be carefully observed to avoid generating words such as "sunny" after dark. For point 2, general terminologies relating to description of temperatures cannot be universally applied across locations. For example, the meaning of terms such as "cool" differs at locations within the tropics versus locations north (or south) of 45 degrees of latitude.

4 Conclusion

We have presented a case study describing an application of NLG technology deployed at the Met Office. The system has been developed to meet the text production requirements for thousands of forecast locations that could not have been sustainable with human resources. The software can write a detailed five-day weather forecast for 10,000 locations worldwide in under two minutes. It would take a weather forecaster months to create the equivalent quantity of output.

In meeting the requirements of this particular use case a number of challenges have had to be met. Principally, these challenges have been focused upon processing speed and output text quality. While we have managed to achieve the required processing performance relatively quickly without the need for large amounts of computing resources or high-end computing infrastructure, ensuring the necessary output quality has been a longer process due to the high operating standards required and the high resource cost of quality assurance when delivering texts at such scale.

This application of NLG technology to site-specific weather forecasting has potential for a number of enhancements to the type of weather services that may be provided in the future, most notably the opportunity for very geographically localized textual forecasts that can be updated immediately as the underlying numerical weather prediction data is produced.

References

E. Goldberg, N. Driedger, and R. Kittredge. Using Natural-Language Processing to Produce Weather Forecasts. IEEE Expert, 9(2):45--53, 1994.

J. Coch. Interactive generation and knowledge administration in MultiMeteo. In Proceedings of the Ninth International Workshop on Natural Language Generation, pages 300--303, Niagara-on-the-lake, Ontario, Canada, 1998. software demonstration.

Bateman J and Zock M, (2012) Bateman/Zock list of NLG systems, http://www.nlg-wiki.org/systems/.

S. Sripada, E. Reiter, and I. Davy, (2003a) 'SumTime-Mousam: Configurable Marine Weather Forecast Generator', Expert Update, 6(3), pp 4-10, (2003)

S. Sripada, E. Reiter, J. Hunter and J. Yu (2003b). Generating English Summaries of Time Series Data using the Gricean Maxims. In Proceedings of KDD 2003, pp 187-196.

E. Reiter, S. Sripada, J. Hunter, J. Yu and Ian Davy (2005). Choosing Words in Computer-Generated Weather Forecasts. Artificial Intelligence. 167(1-2):137-169

E. Reiter (2007). An architecture for data-to-text systems, In ENLG 07, pp97-104.

Reiter, Ehud and Williams, Sandra (2010). Generating texts in different styles. In: Argamon, Shlomo; Burns, Kevin and Dubnov, Shlomo eds. The Structure of Style: Algorithmic Approaches to Manner and Meaning. Heidelberg: Springer, pp. 59–78

E. Reiter, S. Sripada, J. Hunter, J. Yu, and Ian Davy(2005). Choosing words in computer-generated weather forecasts. Artificial Intelligence. 167(1-2):137-169 (2005)

R. Turner, S. Sripada, E. Reiter, & I. Davy (2008). Using spatial reference frames to generate grounded textual summaries of geo-referenced data. Proceedings of the INLG 2008, Salt Fork, Ohio.

PatientNarr: Towards generating patient-centric summaries of hospital stays

Barbara Di Eugenio, Andrew D. Boyd, Camillo Lugaresi, Abhinaya Balasubramanian, Gail M. Keenan, Mike Burton, Tamara G. Rezende Macieira, Karen Dunn Lopez
University of Illinois at Chicago
Chicago, IL, USA

Carol Friedman
Columbia University
New York, NY, USA

Jianrong Li, Yves A. Lussier
University of Arizona
Tucson, AZ, USA

Abstract

PatientNarr summarizes information taken from textual discharge notes written by physicians, and structured nursing documentation. It builds a graph that highlights the relationships between the two types of documentation; and extracts information from the graph for content planning. SimpleNLG is used for surface realization.

1 Introduction

Every year, 7.9% of the US population is hospitalized (CDC, 2011). Patients need to understand what happened to them in the hospital, and what they should do after discharge. *PatientNarr* will ultimately be able to generate concise, lay-language summaries of hospital stays. We hypothesize that such summaries will help patients take care of themselves after they are discharged, and supplement current approaches to patient education, which is not always effective (Olson and Windish, 2010).

PatientNarr needs to summarize documentation that is currently **segregated by profession**; as a minimum, as *physician discharge notes* and as *nursing plans-of-care*. We contend that both sources are necessary to provide the patient with full understanding, also because much of the direct care provided by nurses will need to be continued following discharge (Cain et al., 2012).

In our case, PatientNarr summarizes data that is heterogeneous (textual for physician discharge notes, structured for nursing documentation). This paper describes the steps we have undetaken so far: (a) To demonstrate that physician and nurse documentations diverge, we map both to a graph, and study the relationships therein. This graph supports content planning. (b) We have developed the pipeline that extracts the information to be communicated, and renders it in English via SimpleNLG (Gatt and Reiter, 2009).

Related work. NLG and Summarization in the biomedical domain have been pursued for a few years (Di Eugenio and Green, 2010), but most work addresses health care personnel: to navigate cancer patients' medical histories (Hallett, 2008; Scott et al., 2013); to generate textual summaries describing a hospitalized infant for nurses (Portet et al., 2009); to generates reports of care for hand-off between emergency workers (Schneider et al., 2013). Most applications of NLG that target patients focus on behavioral changes (Reiter et al., 2003), or patient counseling (Green et al., 2011). Only few NLG systems attempt at generating personalized medical information from medical records or data (Williams et al., 2007; Mahamood and Reiter, 2011).

2 A motivating example

So far, we have gained access to 28 de-identified discharge notes of cardiology patients from the University of Illinois Hospital and Health Science System (UIHHSS). Figure 1 shows about 20% of the physician discharge notes for Patient 9. It is difficult to understand, not only because of jargon, but also because of ignorance of relevant domain relationships. Importantly, these notes do not talk about issues that are potentially important for the patient, like his state of mind, which are more often addressed by nurses. In our case, the nursing documentation is not textual, but entered via the HANDS tool, and stored in a relational database (Keenan et al., 2002). A tiny portion of the initial plan-of-care (POC) for Patient 9 is shown in Figure 2 (this nursing data is reconstructed, see Section 3). One POC is documented at every formal handoff (admission, shift change, or discharge). HANDS employs the NANDA-I taxon-

Proceedings of the 8th International Natural Language Generation Conference, pages 6–10,
Philadelphia, Pennsylvania, 19-21 June 2014.

Patient was admitted to Cardiology for new onset a fib in RVR. Was given an additional dose of diltazem 30mg po when first seen. Patient was started on a heparin drip for possible TEE and cardioversion. Overnight his HR was in the 100-110s; however did increase to 160s for which patient was given 120mg er of diltazem. HR improved; however, in the morning while awake and moving around, HR did increase to the 130-140s. Patient was given another dose of IV dilt 20mg. [...] Upon discharge was given two prescriptions for BP, HCTZ and losartan given LVH seen on echo. Patient was counseled on the risks of stroke and different options for anticoagulation. [...]

Figure 1: Excerpt from physician discharge notes (Patient 9)

omy of nursing diagnoses, represented by squares in Figure 2; the Nursing Outcomes Classification (NOC) – circles; and the Nursing Interventions Classification (NIC) – triangles (NNN, 2014). In Figure 2, *Acute Pain* is a diagnosis, and *Anxiety Level* and *Pain Level* (some of) its associated outcomes. *Anxiety Reduction* is an intervention associated with *Anxiety Level*; *Pain Management* and *Analgesic Administration* are interventions associated with *Pain Level*. A scale from 1 to 5 indicates the initial value associated with an outcome (i.e., the state the patient was in when s/he was admitted), the expected rating, and the actual rating at discharge. In Figure 2, the current level for *Pain Level* and *Anxiety Level* is 2 each, with an expected level of 5 at discharge, i.e., no pain/anxiety.

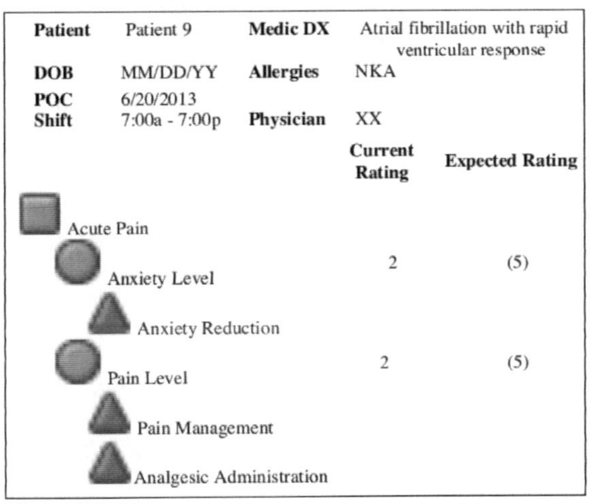
Patient: Patient 9 — Medic DX: Atrial fibrillation with rapid ventricular response
DOB: MM/DD/YY — Allergies: NKA
POC Shift: 6/20/2013 7:00a - 7:00p — Physician: XX

	Current Rating	Expected Rating
Acute Pain		
Anxiety Level	2	(5)
Anxiety Reduction		
Pain Level	2	(5)
Pain Management		
Analgesic Administration		

Figure 2: Excerpt from nursing documentation

Figures 1 and 2 suggest that physician and nursing documentations provide different perspectives on patients: e.g., *Anxiety* is not even mentioned in the discharge notes. One of the authors (a nursing student) wrote summaries for five of the 28 discharge summaries and their corresponding HANDS POCs – Figure 3 shows the summary for Patient 9. This initial round of human authoring was meant to provide some preliminary guidelines to generate automatic summaries. Please see Section 5 for our plans on obtaining a much larger quantity of more informed human-authored summaries.

3 Extracting relationships between physician notes and nursing data

To extract and relate information from our two sources, we rely on UMLS, MedLEE and HANDS. UMLS, the Unified Medical Language System (NLM, 2009), includes 2.6 million concepts (identified by Concept Unique Identifiers or CUIs) organized in a network. Importantly, many different medical and nursing terminologies have been incorporated into UMLS, including those used by HANDS (NANDA-I, NIC and NOC). UMLS provides mapping between their concepts and CUIs, via 8.6 million concept names and relationships between terminologies. Some relationships are of a hierarchical nature, where one concept is narrower than the other (e.g., Chest X-ray and Diagnostic radiologic examination).

MedLEE is a medical information extraction system (Friedman et al., 2004). In its semi-structured output, recognized entities are mapped to the corresponding CUI in UMLS.

HANDS has not been adopted at UIHHSS yet. Hence, we reconstructed HANDS POCs for those 28 patients on the basis of 40,661 cases collected at four hospitals where HANDS is in use. For each of the 28 patients, the same nursing student who authored the five summaries, selected similar cases, and used them to produce high-quality records consistent with actual nursing practice.

To relate physician and nursing documentations, we seed a graph with two sets of CUIs: those returned by MedLEE as a result of processing the physician discharge notes; and the CUIs corresponding to all the NANDA-I, NIC and NOC terms from the HANDS POCs. We then grow the graph by querying UMLS for the set of concepts related to each of the concepts in our set; the concepts that were not already part of the graph are then used to begin a new round of growth (we stop at round 2, to keep the time used by UMLS to answer, reasonable). From this graph, we keep the concepts that either belong to one of the

You were admitted with new onset of atrial fibrillation. You reported feeling weakness, chest pressure and increased shortness of breath. You reported acute pain and you were anxious. During your hospitalization you were treated with analgesics for your pain and pain management was performed by the nursing team. Your shortness of breath improved. Your decreased cardiac output was treated with medication administration and knowledge about cardiac precautions, hypertension management, your treatment regimen and the prescribed medication were taught to you by the nurses. A Transophageal Echocardiography was performed. You met the expected outcomes for your condition and you were discharged under the condition improved for your home. You have an appointment scheduled at Union Medical Center on [DATE] with Physician [DR.]. The list of your medications is attached to this discharge.

Figure 3: Human-authored summary (Patient 9)

source lists, or that are required to form a connection between a doctor-originated concept and a nurse-originated concept that would otherwise remain unconnected. All other concepts are removed. The result is a graph with several separate connected components, which correspond to clusters of related concepts occurring in the discharge notes or in the plans of care, or forming connections between the two sources.

We count distances in terms of relationships traversed, starting from the nursing concepts since they are fewer, and since path traversal is reversible.[1] Concepts can overlap; or be directly connected (distance one); or be directly connected through an intermediate concept (distance two). We do not consider distances beyond two. Table 1 shows results for our specific example, Patient 9, and average results across our 28 test cases. As we can see, there are very few concepts in common, or even at distance 1. Our results provide quantitative evidence for the hypothesis that physicians and nurses talk differently, not just as far as terminology is concerned, but as regards aspects of patient care. This provides strong evidence for our hypothesis that a hospitalization summary should include both perspectives.

4 Automatically generating the summary

In this baseline version of PatientNarr, we focused on understanding how the vital parameters have improved over time, the treatment given for improvement and the issues addressed during the process. The summary generated by PatientNarr for Patient 9 is shown in Figure 4. We extract information of interest from the graph obtained at the previous step; we couch it as features of phrasal constituents via the operations provided by the SimpleNLG API. SimpleNLG then assembles grammatical phrases in the right order, and helps in aggregating related sentences.

Since there are far fewer nursing than doctor concepts, we start from the NANDA-I codes, i.e., the diagnoses. The name associated in UMLS with the corresponding CUI is used. For each NANDA-I node, we highlight the treatments given (the NIC codes), e.g. see the sentence starting with *Acute onset pain was treated [...]* in Figure 4. For both diagnosis and treatments, we attempt to relate them to doctor's nodes. Specifically, we exploit the relationships in the UMLS ontology and include nodes in the graph we constructed that are at distance 1 or 2, and that are either doctor's nodes, or intermediate nodes that connect to a doctor's node. For example, in *Dysrhythmia management is remedy for tachycardia and Atrial Fibrillation, Dysrhythmia management* is a NIC intervention that is related to *Cardiac Arrhythmia*; in turn, *Cardiac Arrhythmia* is a direct hypernym of *tachycardia* and *Atrial Fibrillation* which were both extracted from the physician notes by MedLEE. *Cardiac Arrhythmia* was discovered by our graph building procedure, as described in Section 3.

We then highlight what improved during the hospital stay. As we mentioned earlier, the NOC codes (outcomes) are associated with a scale from 1 to 5 which indicates the initial value, the expected rating, and the actual rating at discharge. If the relative increase between admission and discharge encompasses more than 2 points on the scale, it is considered significant; if it encompasses 1 or 2 points, it is considered slight. In those cases in which more than one outcome is associated with a diagnosis, but improvement is not uniform, we include a cue "On the other hand". For Patient 9, in the last POC recorded just before discharge, *Anxiety Level* is up 2 points (to 4), whereas *Pain Level* is up 3. We also indicate to the patient if the final rating reached the rating that was initially hoped for; it did not for *Anxiety Level* (See the two sentences starting from *Pain level and Vi-*

[1] In UMLS, any relationship from concept A to concept B, has a corresponding relationship from B to A, not necessarily symmetric.

	# CUIs from Discharge Notes	# CUIs from Nursing POCs	# of common CUIs	# of CUI pairs at Distance 1	# of CUI pairs at Distance 2
Patient 9	83.00	28.00	0.00	3.00	13.00
Average	90.64	22.43	0.46	3.00	9.11

Table 1: Concept overlap in discharge notes and nursing POCs

You were admitted for atrial fibrillation with rapid ventricular response. Acute onset pain related to pain was treated with pain management, monitoring of blood pressure, temperature, pulse rate and respiratory rate and administration of analgesic. Pain level and vital signs have improved significantly and outcomes have met the expectations. On the other hand, level of anxiety has improved slightly. Cardiac Disease Self-Management, Disease Process (Heart disease), Hypertension Management, Cardiac Disease Management, Hypertension Management and Treatment Regimen were taught. Low Cardiac Output related to heart failure was treated with cardiac precautions, monitoring of blood pressure, temperature, pulse rate and respiratory rate, and dysrhythmia management. Dysrhythmia management is remedy for tachycardia and atrial fibrillation. As a result, cardiac pump effectiveness, cardiopulmonary status and cardiac tissue perfusion status have improved slightly. Actual Negative Breathing Pattern related to respiration disorders was treated with respiration monitoring. Respiratory Status has improved significantly. You have an appointment at Union Medical Center on DATE at TIME. The list of medication is attached to this discharge.

Figure 4: PatientNarr generated summary (Patient 9)

tal signs [...]. On the other hand, [...]). For the moment, we do not mention outcomes for which no improvement, or a setback, has been recorded.

The summary also includes: mentions of education that has been imparted; and reminders of future appointments and of medicines to be taken.

5 Future Work

The research described in this paper lays the foundations for our project, but clearly much work remains to be done. To start with, we plan to build a corpus of gold-standard summaries, in order to derive (semi-)automatic models of the information to be included from physician notes and from nursing documentation. The five human authored summaries we currently have at our disposal are not sufficient, neither in quality nor (obviously) in quantity. We intend to inform their generation via a number of focus groups with all stakeholders involved: patients, doctors and nurses. To start with, the five summaries we do have were presented to the Patient Advisory Board of an unrelated project. These two patients noted that all unfamiliar terms should be explained, and that what the patient should do to improve their health after discharge, should be included.

Secondly, we will generate lay language by taking advantage of resources such as the Consumer Health Vocabulary (Doing-Harris and Zeng-Treitler, 2011; CHV, 2013), which maps medical terms to plain-language expressions. Additionally, we will pursue more sophisticated extraction and rendering of rhetorical relationships among events and their outcomes (Mancini et al., 2007).

Last but not least, we will perform user studies, both controlled evaluation of our summaries while still at the development stage, and eventually longer-term assessments of whether our summaries engender better adherence to medications and better keeping of follow-up appointments, and ultimately, better health.

Acknowledgements

We thank three anonymous reviewers for their helpful comments. For partial financial support, we acknowledge award NPRP 5-939-1-155 from the Qatar National Research Fund, the UIC Department of Biomedical and Health Information Sciences, and the UIC Institute for Translational Health Informatics.

References

Carol H. Cain, Estee Neuwirth, Jim Bellows, Christi Zuber, and Jennifer Green. 2012. Patient experiences of transitioning from hospital to home: an ethnographic quality improvement project. *Journal of Hospital Medicine*, 7(5):382–387.

CDC. 2011. Hospital utilization (in non-federal short-stay hospitals). Centers for Disease Control and Prevention, http://www.cdc.gov/nchs/fastats/hospital.htm. Last accessed on 11/26/2013.

2013. Consumer Health Vocabulary Initiative.

http://www.layhealthinformatics.org/. Last accessed on 5/19/2014.

Barbara Di Eugenio and Nancy L. Green. 2010. Emerging applications of natural language generation in information visualization, education, and health-care. In Nitin Indurkhya and Fred J. Damerau, editors, *Handbook of Natural Language Processing, Second Edition*, chapter 23, pages 557–575. CRC Press, Taylor and Francis Group, Boca Raton, FL. ISBN 978-1420085921.

Kristina M. Doing-Harris and Qing Zeng-Treitler. 2011. Computer-assisted update of a consumer health vocabulary through mining of social network data. *Journal of Medical Internet Research*, 13(2).

C. Friedman, L. Shagina, Y. Lussier, and G. Hripcsak. 2004. Automated encoding of clinical documents based on natural language processing. *Journal of the American Medical Informatics Association*, 11(5):392.

Albert Gatt and Ehud Reiter. 2009. SimpleNLG: A realisation engine for practical applications. In *Proceedings of the 12th European Workshop on Natural Language Generation*, pages 90–93. Association for Computational Linguistics.

N. Green, R. Dwight, K. Navoraphan, and B. Stadler. 2011. Natural language generation of biomedical argumentation for lay audiences. *Argument and Computation*, 2(1):23–50.

C. Hallett. 2008. Multi-modal presentation of medical histories. In *IUI '08: Proceedings of the 13th International Conference on Intelligent User Interfaces*, pages 80–89, New York, NY, USA. ACM.

G.M. Keenan, J.R. Stocker, A.T. Geo-Thomas, N.R. Soparkar, V.H. Barkauskas, and J.A.N.L. Lee. 2002. The HANDS Project: Studying and Refining the Automated Collection of a Cross-setting Clinical Data set. *CIN: Computers, Informatics, Nursing*, 20(3):89–100.

Saad Mahamood and Ehud Reiter. 2011. Generating affective natural language for parents of neonatal infants. In *Proceedings of the 13th European Workshop on Natural Language Generation*, pages 12–21, Nancy, France, September. Association for Computational Linguistics.

Clara Mancini, Christian Pietsch, and Donia Scott. 2007. Visualising discourse structure in interactive documents. In *Proceedings of the Eleventh European Workshop on Natural Language Generation*, pages 89–92, Saarbrücken, Germany, June.

NLM. 2009. UMLS Reference Manual. Technical report, National Library of Medicine, September. http://www.ncbi.nlm.nih.gov/books/NBK9676/ (Last accessed on 12/09/2013).

2014. NNN: Knowledge-based terminologies defining nursing. http://www.nanda.org/nanda-i-nic-noc.html. (Last accessed on 5/19/2014).

Douglas P. Olson and Donna M. Windish. 2010. Communication discrepancies between physicians and hospitalized patients. *Archives of Internal Medicine*, 170(15):1302–1307.

François Portet, Ehud Reiter, Jim Hunter, Somayajulu Sripada, Yvonne Freer, and Cynthia Sykes. 2009. Automatic generation of textual summaries from neonatal intensive care data. *Artificial Intelligence*, 173:789–816, May.

Ehud Reiter, Roma Robertson, and Liesl Osman. 2003. Lessons from a failure: Generating tailored smoking cessation letters. *Artificial Intelligence*, 144:41–58.

Anne Schneider, Alasdair Mort, Chris Mellish, Ehud Reiter, Phil Wilson, and Pierre-Luc Vaudry. 2013. MIME - NLG Support for Complex and Unstable Pre-hospital Emergencies. In *Proceedings of the 14th European Workshop on Natural Language Generation*, pages 198–199, Sofia, Bulgaria, August. Association for Computational Linguistics.

Donia Scott, Catalina Hallett, and Rachel Fettiplace. 2013. Data-to-text summarisation of patient records: Using computer-generated summaries to access patient histories. *Patient Education and Counseling*, 92(2):153–159.

Sandra Williams, Paul Piwek, and Richard Power. 2007. Generating monologue and dialogue to present personalised medical information to patients. In *Proceedings of the Eleventh European Workshop on Natural Language Generation*, pages 167–170, Saarbrücken, Germany, June.

Using Conceptual Spaces to Model Domain Knowledge in Data-to-Text Systems

Hadi Banaee and Amy Loutfi
Center for Applied Autonomous Sensor Systems
Örebro University
Örebro, Sweden
{hadi.banaee, amy.loutfi}@oru.se

Abstract

This position paper introduces the utility of the conceptual spaces theory to conceptualise the acquired knowledge in data-to-text systems. A use case of the proposed method is presented for text generation systems dealing with sensor data. Modelling information in a conceptual space exploits a spatial representation of domain knowledge in order to perceive unexpected observations. This ongoing work aims to apply conceptual spaces in NLG for grounding numeric information into the symbolic representation and confronting the important step of acquiring adequate knowledge in data-to-text systems.

1 Introduction

Knowledge acquisition (KA) is important for building natural language generation (NLG) systems. Two KA techniques including corpus-based KA and structured expert-oriented KA have been previously studied for NLG systems in (Reiter et al., 2003) to improve the quality of acquired knowledge. Both techniques use rule-based approaches in order to enrich the similarities between generated texts and natural human-written texts. An important class of NLG frameworks which use a rule-based approach is data-to-text systems where a linguistic summarisation of numeric data is produced. The main architecture of data-to-text systems has been introduced by Reiter (2007) which includes the following stages: signal analysis, data interpretation, document planning, microplanning and realisation. Domain knowledge for these systems is formalised as a taxonomy or an ontology of information. In a data-to-text architecture, all the stages are using the provided taxonomy. In particular, the signal analysis stage extracts the information that is determined in taxonomies such as simple patterns, events, and trends. Also, the data interpretation stage abstracts information into the symbolic messages using the defined taxonomies.

Most recent data-to-text frameworks have been developed using Reiter's architecture with the addition of providing the taxonomies or ontologies corresponding to the domain knowledge. For instance, the work on summarising the gas turbine time series (Yu et al., 2007) has used expert knowledge to provide a taxonomy of the primitive patterns (i.e. spikes, steps, oscillations). Similarly, the systems related to the *Babytalk* project (Portet et al., 2009; Gatt et al., 2009; Hunter et al., 2012) have stored medically known observation (e.g. bradycardia) in local ontologies. In order to avoid generating ambiguous messages, these systems simplify the stored information in the taxonomies by using only the primitive changes interesting for the end users. The core of such systems is still based on this fact - that the content of the generated text is dependent on the richness of the domain knowledge in the provided taxonomies which are usually bounded by expert rules. This organised domain knowledge is usually an inflexible input to the framework which restricts the output of the stages in data-to-text architecture. For instance, the taxonomy in (Yu et al., 2007) does not allow the system to represent unexpected observations (e.g. wave or burst) out of the predefined domain knowledge. Likewise, in the medical domain, an unknown physiological pattern will be ignored if it does not have a corresponding entity in the provided ontology by expert. This limitation in data-to-text systems reveals the necessity of reorganising domain knowledge in order to span unseen information across the data.

This position paper introduces a new approach, inspired by the conceptual spaces theory, to model information into a set of concepts that can be used by data-to-text systems. The conceptual spaces

Proceedings of the 8th International Natural Language Generation Conference, pages 11–15,
Philadelphia, Pennsylvania, 19-21 June 2014.

theory creates a spatial model of concepts that represents knowledge or information. This theory presents a promising alternative to modelling the domain knowledge in taxonomies or ontologies, particularly when a data-driven analysis is to be captured in natural language. This paper outlines the notion of conceptual spaces and illustrates how it can be used in a use case. Section 2 reviews the theory of conceptual spaces and its notions. Section 3 presents the approach for applying the conceptual spaces in NLG frameworks. In Section 4, a simple application of the proposed method is shown. Finally, we address the challenges and outline our plans for future work.

2 On the Theory of Conceptual Spaces

The idea of conceptual spaces has been developed by Gärdenfors (2000) as a framework to represent knowledge at the conceptual level. A *conceptual space* is formed in geometrical or topological structures as a set of *quality dimensions* describing the attributes of information to be represented. For instance, a conceptual space might comprise dimensions such as width, weight, or saltiness. A *domain* is represented to be a set of interdependent dimensions which cannot logically be separated in a perceptual space. A typical example of a domain is 'colour' which can be defined through multi dimensions like hue, saturation, and brightness. *Properties* are the convex regions in a single domain describing the particular attributes of the domain. As an example, 'green' is a property corresponding to a region in the colour domain (Fig. 1, right). In natural language, properties are mostly associated with adjectives in a particular domain. A conceptual space contains a membership distance measure for each property within the domains which represents the regions occupied by the property and allows to depict the notion of similarity (Rickard et al., 2007).

Concepts are formed as regions in a conceptual space. In particular, a concept is represented as a set of related properties which might cover multiple domains together with information how these domains are correlated. For instance, the concept of 'apple' can be represented as regions in colour, size and taste domains (Fig. 1). The representation of concepts in space contains an assignment of weights to the domains or dimensions, in order to distinguish between similar concepts (Gärdenfors, 2004). In natural languages, concepts often correspond to nouns or describe verbs when time is involved as a dimension (Rickard et al., 2007).

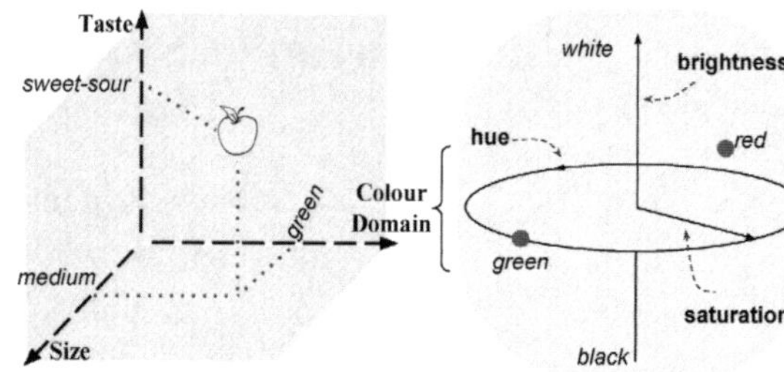

Figure 1: A typical example of a conceptual space to represent 'apple' concept.

The most representative instance of a concept is its *prototypical member* which is represented as an n-dimensional point in the concepts region. The conceptual space can be geometrically divided (e.g. using *Voronoi tessellation* (Gärdenfors, 2004)) to a set of categories corresponding to the prototypical members. *Objects* (such as instances, entities, or observations) in a conceptual space are identified in the concept regions which characterised as vectors of quality values. For example, a particular instance of 'apple' is depicted in Fig. 1 as a vector of properties <green, medium, sweet–sour>. An object contains a property depending on the nearness of its point to the defined region of the property. This notion leads to have a similarity measure within a domain to identify the properties of objects. *Similarity* is an essential notion in any conceptual space framework which is defined on individual domains. The geometrical representation of conceptual spaces provides the ability of using distance measures, which is missed in purely symbolic representations, to consider the similarity of concepts and instances.

3 Proposed Approach: Conceptual Spaces for Data-to-Text Systems

This section describes the usage of conceptual spaces for modelling numeric knowledge as concepts into a spatial representation. The proposed approach shows how to use conceptual space theory to reorganise the predefined taxonomies into a set of concepts in order to represent unexpected patterns. The idea consists of two phases, constructing a conceptual space corresponding to the taxonomy, and enhancing the regions in the space based on new observations. The general steps of the proposed approach are described as follows:

Step 1: Build the required taxonomy of observations and patterns in the same way as traditional data-to-text systems in order to provide a set of primitive information requirements using the expert-oriented, domain, or corpus-based knowledge. Primitive entities from these taxonomy will be the n-dimensional vectors of concepts in conceptual space.

Step 2: Initialise a conceptual space and determine its components, including quality dimensions, domains, and concepts corresponding to the domain knowledge and the context of data. Using similarity measures on the determined dimensions, the model is able to define the geometrical distance between each pair of vectors and identify the nearest concept for any point in space. By defining the applicable domains and dimensions, the conceptual space is able to characterise a vast range of interesting concepts, which may not be similar to the provided entities.

Step 3: Specify the ontological instances gathered in step one as concepts regions. This step grounds the primitive observations to a set of prototypical members as n-dimensional vectors in the created conceptual space. Also the space would be classified into a set of categories presenting the properties of the prototypical members. The main contribution of this approach is based on the fact - that by providing the semantic information as geometrical vectors, the model is spanned to conceptualise the information categories which enables calculating the similarities between knowledge entities like new (non-primitive) extracted patterns as new vectors in the space. However, a new entity could be 1) close to an existing prototypical member and placed in its geometrical category, or 2) an anomalous point and placed as a new prototype in the space.

Step 4: Rearrange the conceptual categories corresponding to the prototypical members by adding new instances to the model as new vector points. The symbolic properties of prototypical members in space are used to describe novel properties of unknown entities. When a new observation appears in space as a vector, it leads to reorganise the boundaries of concepts regions related to the new inserted member. The expanded space will provide more descriptive regions for unconsidered entities. It is notable that the provided domains and dimensions enables the conceptual space to grow with new entities which are event

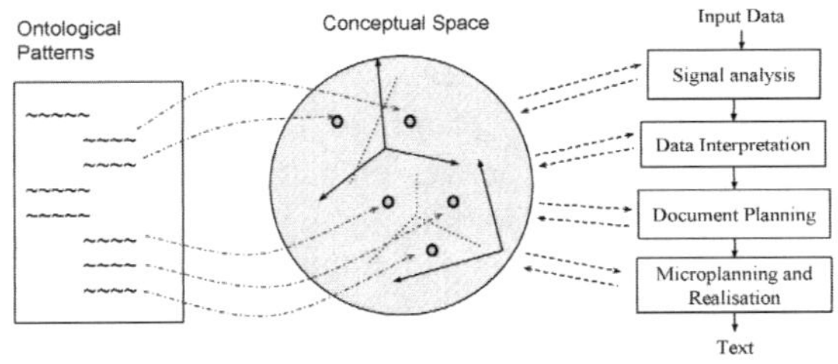

Figure 2: The conceptual space in data-to-text architecture as an alternative for ontological patterns.

sans association with existing categories.

Different stages of data-to-text architecture can be connected to the built conceptual space instead of their relations to the ontology. Specifically, pattern discovery in the signal analysis stage does not need to be limited to rules and domain constraints.

Data-to-text approaches which use ontologies for signal processing are able to apply probabilistic or fuzzy processes to map the patterns of data into the "*most likely*" concepts in ontology. However, one advantage of the proposed approach is that enables the system to represent new concepts that are non-relatively deviant cases, as well as covering intermediate patterns. So, any extracted information from data can be formalised in the conceptual space and then be characterised in a symbolic representation. Another advantage of this model is that the conceptual space assists the system to enrich the quality of represented messages in the final text with considering unseen, but interesting information for the end users. Fig. 2 depicts the conceptual space in relation with the stages of the data-to-text architecture.

4 Use Case: From Data Streams to Conceptual Representation

Knowledge extraction in data streams exploits the most informative observations (e.g. patterns and events) through the data (Rajaraman et al., 2011). In most of data-to-text systems, much attention has been given to the sensor data as the best indicator of data streams (e.g. weather sensor channels, gas turbine time series, and physiological data in body area networks). A robust text generation system for sensor data needs to provide a comprehensive information structure in order to summarise numeric measurements. Here, we explain how the proposed approach can apply to model the defined taxonomies in sensor data applications, particularly for gas turbine time series (Yu et al., 2007) and neonatal intensive care data (Gatt et al., 2009). The main challenge here is the definition of concepts and quality dimensions from non-sensible observations in time series data. However, a preliminary model is introduced as follows:

Based on the acquired knowledge in both systems, the patterns are categorised to 1) primitive disturbance shapes: spikes, steps, and oscillations, or 2) partial trends: rise, fall, and varying. These observations are associated with a set of attributes and descriptions for their magnitude, direction and/or speed (e.g. downward, upward, or rapidly, normally, etc.). A typical demonstration of taxonomies/ontologies in traditional data-to-text systems dealing with sensor data has been shown in Fig. 3-a. Our method exploits these structures to build an applicable conceptual space related to the acquired knowledge. It is worth noting that building the components of the conceptual spaces for different sensor data in other contexts would differ. To cover the observations in time series, two domains are defined: shape and trend domains. For the shape domain, the rules behind the definition of primitive events lead to determine quality dimensions. For instance, 'spike' is defined as "small time interval with almost same start and end, but big difference between max and min values". So, the spike concept can be characterised in the shape domain by quality dimensions: *time interval* (Δt), *start-end range* (Δse), and *min-max range* (Δmm). The prototypical member of spike concept can be represented as a vector of properties: v_1:<short Δt, small Δse, big Δmm>. Same dimensions can describe the steps and oscillations, shown in Fig. 3-b (top). For the trend domain, finding descriptive dimensions and properties is dependent on the selected features in the trend detection process (Banaee et al., 2013). Here, the provided quality dimensions for the trend domain include: *trend orientation* (α), and *trend duration* (Δd). As an example, 'sudden rise' concept can be represented as a region in the trend domain with a prototypical member vector v_2:<positive sharp α, short Δd>, shown in Fig. 3-b (bottom). The complex concepts can be spanned to multi domains with their properties regions. For instance, 'rapid upward spike' pattern is definable as a region in space, spanned in both shape and trend domains, which its representative vector has five property values in all dimensions like: v_3:<v_1, v_2>.

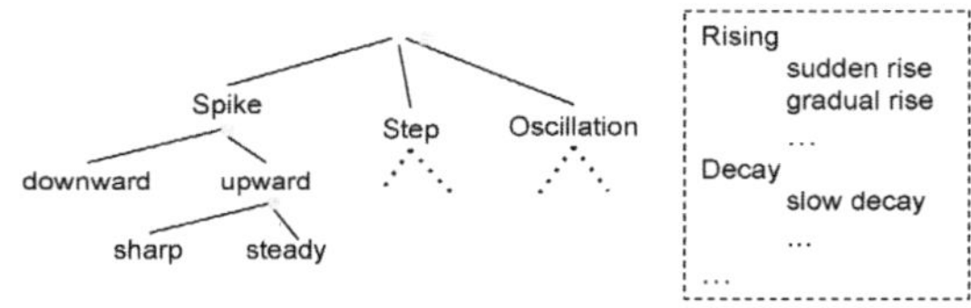

(a) Taxonomy and Ontology of Patterns

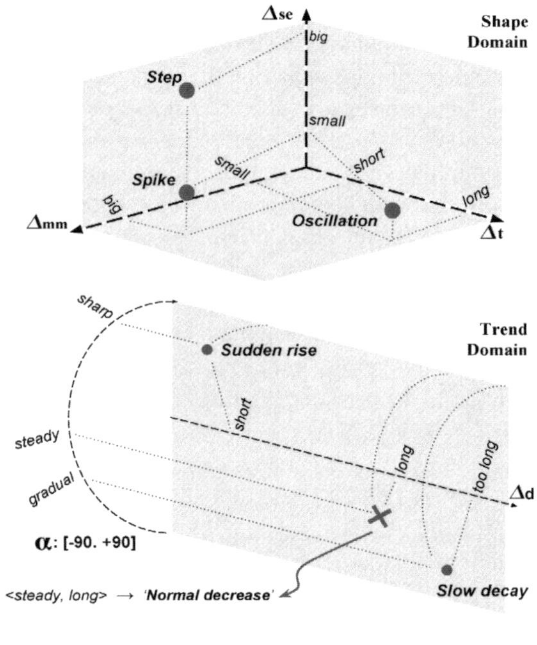

(b) Conceptual Space (Shape and Trend domains)

Figure 3: A conceptual space proposed for modelling domain knowledge in sensor data. a) Taxonomy and ontology of patterns, b) Shape domain and trend domain.

This modelling has an effect on signal analysing in that any unseen event and trend can be extracted and represented by finding the nearest prototypical instances in the corresponding vector space. Fig. 3-b (bottom) depicts an example of two points represented 'sudden rise' and 'slow decay' trends in the space. The location of a new instance in space, e.g. <steady, long> is computable by calculating geometrical distances of their properties, and consequently the corresponding descriptive symbols can be inferred as 'normal decrease'.

This use case focuses on event-based observations based on the shapes and trends of patterns in sensor data. Other contexts may be interested to represent other observations like repetitive rules, motifs and unexpected trends which need particular studies on how to model these issues in conceptual spaces and capture their properties.

5 Discussion and Conclusion

This position paper has presented the notion of conceptual spaces as an alternative approach to modelling domain knowledge in data-to-text systems. The next obvious steps are to use conceptual spaces in a NLG framework and experimentally validate their suitability for capturing data-driven events, patterns, etc. This paper has attempted to motivate the use of conceptual spaces in order to cope with information which cannot be accurately modelled by experts. Still, however, some remaining challenges are to be addressed. One challenge is determining a comprehensive set of domains and quality dimensions representing the acquired knowledge in a conceptual space. Another challenge is grounding concepts to linguistic description in order to provide a thorough symbolic description of quantitative vectors in the space. A further challenge is lexicalisation in modelling the conceptual spaces, which is related to choosing accurate words for the conceptual regions regarding to the semantic similarities for properties of the concepts, without using expert knowledge.

Acknowledgments

The authors of this work are partially supported by SAAPHO project: Secure Active Aging: Participation and Health for the Old (AAL-2010-3-035).

References

Ehud Reiter, Somayajulu G. Sripada, and Roma Robertson. 2003. Acquiring Correct Knowledge for Natural Language Generation. *Journal of Artificial Intelligence Research*, 18:491–516.

Ehud Reiter. 2007. An architecture for data-to-text systems. *ENLG'11: the Eleventh European Workshop on Natural Language Generation*, 97–104.

Jin Yu, Ehud Reiter, Jim Hunter, and Chris Mellish. 2007. Choosing the content of textual summaries of large time-series data sets. *Natural Language Engineering*, 13(1):25–49.

François Portet, Ehud Reiter, Albert Gatt, Jim Hunter, Somayajulu Sripada, Yvonne Freer, and Cindy Sykes. 2009. Automatic generation of textual summaries from neonatal intensive care data. *Artificial Intelligence*, 173(7):789–816.

Albert Gatt, François Portet, Ehud Reiter, Jim Hunter, Saad Mahamood, Wendy Moncur, and Somayajulu Sripada. 2009. From data to text in the neonatal intensive care unit: Using NLG technology for decision support and information management. *AI Communications*, 22(3):153–186.

James Hunter, Yvonne Freer, Albert Gatt, Ehud Reiter, Somayajulu Sripada, and Cindy Sykes. 2012. Automatic generation of natural language nursing shift summaries in neonatal intensive care: BT-Nurse. *Artificial Intelligence in Medicine*, 56(3):157–172.

Peter Gärdenfors. 2000. *Conceptual Spaces: The Geometry of Thought*. MIT Press.Cambridge, MA.

John T. Rickard, Janet Aisbett, and Greg Gibbon. 2007. Reformulation of the theory of conceptual spaces. *Information Sciences*, 177(21):4539–4565

Peter Gärdenfors. 2004. Conceptual spaces as a framework for knowledge representation. *Mind and Matter*, 2(2):9–27.

Anand Rajaraman, and Jeffrey D. Ullman 2011. *Mining of massive datasets*. Cambridge University Press.

H. Banaee, M. U. Ahmed, A. Loutfi 2013. A Framework for Automatic Text Generation of Trends in Physiological Time Series Data. *SMC'13: IEEE International Conference on Systems, Man, and Cybernetics*, 3876–3881.

Text simplification using synchronous dependency grammars: Generalising automatically harvested rules

M.A. Angrosh
Computing Science
University of Aberdeen, UK
angroshmandya@abdn.ac.uk

Advaith Siddharthan
Computing Science
University of Aberdeen, UK
advaith@abdn.ac.uk

Abstract

We present an approach to text simplification based on synchronous dependency grammars. Our main contributions in this work are (a) a study of how automatically derived lexical simplification rules can be generalised to enable their application in new contexts without introducing errors, and (b) an evaluation of our hybrid system that combines a large set of automatically acquired rules with a small set of hand-crafted rules for common syntactic simplification. Our evaluation shows significant improvements over the state of the art, with scores comparable to human simplifications.

1 Introduction

Text simplification is the process of reducing the linguistic complexity of a text, while still retaining the original information content and meaning. Text Simplification is often thought of as consisting of two components - syntactic simplification and lexical simplification. While syntactic simplification aims at reducing the grammatical complexity of a sentence, lexical simplification focuses on replacing difficult words or short phrases by simpler variants.

Traditionally, entirely different approaches have been used for lexical (Devlin and Tait, 1998; Biran et al., 2011; Yatskar et al., 2010; Specia et al., 2012) and syntactic simplification (Canning, 2002; Chandrasekar et al., 1996; Siddharthan, 2011; De Belder and Moens, 2010; Candido Jr et al., 2009). Recent years have seen the application of machine translation inspired approaches to text simplification. These approaches learn from aligned English and Simplified English sentences extracted from the Simple English Wikipedia (SEW) corpus (simple.wikipedia.org). However, even these approaches (Woodsend and Lapata, 2011; Wubben et al., 2012; Coster and Kauchak, 2011; Zhu et al., 2010) struggle to elegantly model the range of lexical and syntactic simplification operations observed in the monolingual simplification task within one framework, often differentiating between operation at leaf nodes of parse trees (lexical) and internal tree nodes (syntactic). The key issue is the modelling of context for application of lexical rules. While syntactic rules (for splitting conjoined clauses, or disembedding relative clauses) are typically not context dependent, words are typically polysemous and can only be replaced by others in appropriate contexts.

Our main contribution in this paper is to present a unified framework for representing rules for syntactic and lexical simplification (including paraphrase involving multiple words), and study for the first time how the definition of context affects system performance. A second contribution is to provide a substantial human evaluation (63 sentences and 70 participants) to evaluate contemporary text simplification systems against manually simplified output.

2 Related work

Text simplification systems are characterised by the level of linguistic knowledge they encode, and by whether their simplification rules are hand-crafted or automatically acquired from a corpus.

In recent times, the availability of a corpus of aligned English Wikipedia (EW) and Simple English Wikipedia (SEW) sentences has lead to the application of various "monolingual translation" approaches to text simplification. Phrase Based Machine Translation (PBMT) systems (Specia, 2010; Coster and Kauchak, 2011; Wubben et al., 2012) use the least linguistic knowledge (only word sequences), and as such are ill equipped to handle simplifications that require morphological changes, syntactic reordering or sentence splitting.

Zhu et al. (2010) in contrast present an approach based on syntax-based SMT (Yamada and

Proceedings of the 8th International Natural Language Generation Conference, pages 16–25,
Philadelphia, Pennsylvania, 19-21 June 2014.

Knight, 2001). Their translation model encodes probabilities for four specific rewrite operations on the parse trees of the input sentences: substitution, reordering, splitting, and deletion. Woodsend and Lapata (2011) propose quasi-synchronous tree substitution grammars (QTSG) for a similarly wide range of simplification operations as well as lexical substitution. Narayan and Gardent (2014) combine PMBT for local paraphrase with a syntactic splitting component based on a deep semantic representation. None of these systems model morphological information, which means some simplification operations such as voice conversion cannot be handled correctly.

Against this limitation, hand-crafted systems have an advantage here, as they tend to encode the maximum linguistic information. We have previously described systems (Siddharthan, 2010; Siddharthan, 2011) that can perform voice conversion accurately and use transformation rules that encode morphological changes as well as deletions, re-orderings, substitutions and sentence splitting. On the other hand, such hand-crafted systems are limited in scope to syntactic simplificatio as there are too many lexico-syntactic and lexical simplifications to enumerate by hand. We have also previously described how to construct a hybrid system that combines automatically derived lexical rules with hand-crafted syntactic rules within a single framework (Siddharthan and Mandya, 2014). We extend that work here by describing how such automatically learnt rules can be generalised.

3 Simplification using synchronous dependency grammars

We follow the architecture proposed in Ding and Palmer (2005) for Synchronous Dependency Insertion Grammars, reproduced in Fig. 1.

In this paper, we focus on the decomposition of a dependency parse into Elementary Trees (ETs), and the learning of rules to transduce a source ET to a target ET. We use the datasets of Coster and Kauchak (2011) and Woodsend and Lapata

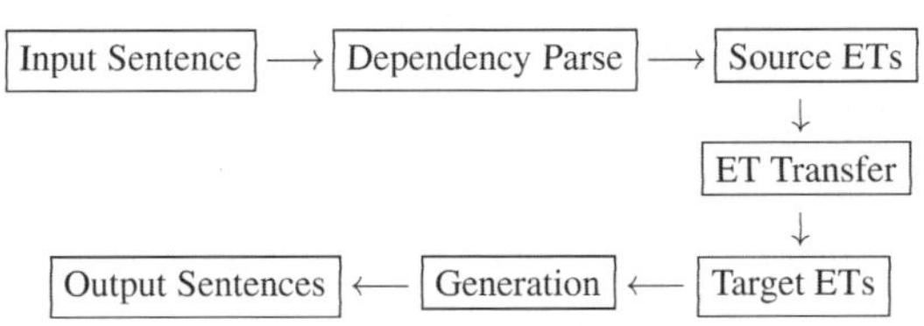

Figure 1: System Architecture

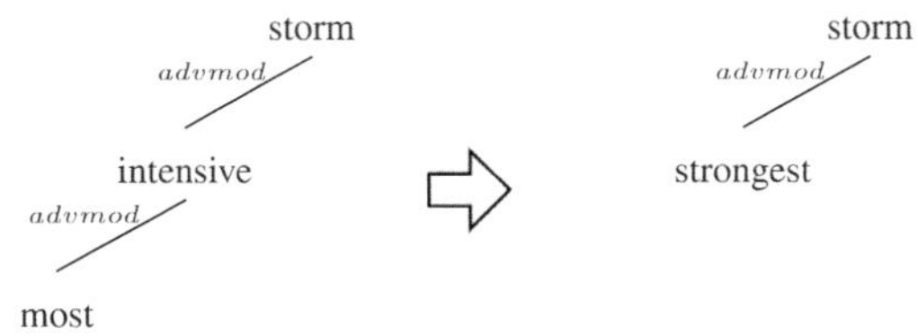

Figure 2: Transduction of Elementary Trees (ETs)

(2011) for learning rules. These datasets consist of ~140K aligned simplified and original sentence pairs obtained from Simple English Wikipedia and English Wikipedia. The rules are acquired in the format required by the RegenT text simplification system (Siddharthan, 2011), which is used to implement the simplification. This requires dependency parses from the Stanford Parser (De Marneffe et al., 2006), and generates output sentences from dependency parses using the generation-light approach described in (Siddharthan, 2011).

3.1 Acquiring rules from aligned sentences

To acquire a synchronous grammar from dependency parses of aligned English and simple English sentences, we just need to identify the differences. For example, consider two aligned sentences from the aligned corpus described in Woodsend and Lapata (2011):

1. (a) It was the second most intensive storm on the planet in 1989.
   (b) It was the second strongest storm on the planet in 1989.

An automatic comparison of the dependency parses for the two sentences (using the Stanford Parser) reveals that there are two typed dependencies that occur only in the parse of the first sentence, and one that occur only in the parse of the second sentence. Thus, to convert the first sentence into the second, we need to delete two dependencies and introduce one other. From this example, we extract the following rule:

RULE 1: MOST_INTENSIVE2STRONGEST

1. DELETE
   (a) advmod(?X0[intensive], ?X1[most])
   (b) advmod(?X2[storm], ?X0[intensive])
2. INSERT
   (a) advmod(?X2, ?X3[strongest])

The rule contains variables (?Xn), which can be forced to match certain words in square brackets.

Such deletion and insertion operations are central to text simplification, but a few other operations are also needed to avoid broken dependency links in the Target ETs. These are enumerated in (Siddharthan, 2011) and will not be reproduced here for shortage of space. By collecting such rules, we can produce a meta-grammar that can translate dependency parses in one language (English) into the other (simplified English). The rule above will translate "most intensive" to "strongest", in the immediate lexical context of "storm". For ease of presentation, we present the ET Transfer component as transformation rules, but this rule can also be presented as a transduction of elementary trees (Fig. 2).

3.2 Generalising rules

It is clear that the rule shown above will only be applied if three different words ("storm", "most" and "intensive") occur in the exact syntax specified on the left hand side of Figure 2. The rule is correct, but of limited use, for "most intensive" can be simplified to "strongest" only when it modifies the word "storm".

The modelling of lexical context is a particular weak point in previous work; for instance, Woodsend and Lapata (2011), in their quasi-synchronous tree substitution grammar, remove all lexical context for lexical simplification rules, to facilitate their application in new contexts. Similarly, phrase-based machine translation can default to lexical simplification using word level alignments if longer substrings from the input text are not found in the alignment table. However, as words can have different senses, lexical substitution without a lexical context model is error prone.

Our goals here are to enumerate methods to generalise rules, and to evaluate performance on unseen sentences. All the methods described are automated, and do not require manual effort.

Generalising from multiple instances: A single rule can be created from multiple instances in the training data. For example, if the modifier "extensive" has been simplified to "big" in the context of a variety of words in the ?X0 position, this can be represented succinctly as "?X0[networks, avalanches, blizzard, controversy]". Note that this list provides valid lexical contexts for application of the rule. If the word is seen in sufficient contexts, we make it universal by removing the list. Rule 2 below states that any of the words in "[extensive, large, massive, sizable, major, powerful, giant]" can be replaced by "big" in any lexical context ?X0, provided the syntactic context is an *amod* relation. To de-lexicalise context in this manner, each lexical substitution needs to have been observed in 10 different contexts. While not foolproof, this ensures that lexical context is removed only for common simplifications, which are more likely to be independent of context.

RULE 2: *2BIG

1. DELETE
   (a) amod(?X0, ?X1[extensive, large, massive, sizable, major, powerful, giant])
2. INSERT
   (a) amod(?X0, ?X2[big])

Reducing context size: Often, single lexical changes result in multiple relations in the INSERT and DELETE lists. Rule 3 shows a rule where the verb "amend" has been simplified to "change", in a context where the direct object is "Constitution" and there is an infinitive modifier relation to "proposals", using the auxiliary "to".

RULE 3: AMEND2CHANGE

1. DELETE
   (a) aux(?X0[amend], ?X1[to])
   (b) infmod(?X2[proposals], ?X0[amend])
   (c) dobj(?X0[amend], ?X3[Constitution])
2. INSERT
   (a) aux(?X4[change], ?X1)
   (b) infmod(?X2, ?X4)
   (c) dobj(?X4, ?X3)
3. MOVE
   (a) ?X0 ?X4

Rule 3 also shows the MOVE command created to move any other relations (edges) involving the node ?X0 to the newly created node ?X4. The MOVE list is automatically created when a variable (?X0) is present in the DELETE list but not in the INSERT list and ensures correct rule application in new contexts where there might be additional modifiers connected to the deleted word.

Rule 3 clearly encodes too much context. In such cases, we reduce the context by creating three rules, each with a reduced context of one relation (*aux*, *infmod* or *dobj*); for example:

RULE 3A: AMEND2CHANGE3

1. DELETE: dobj(?X0[amend], ?X1[Constitution])
2. INSERT: dobj(?X2[change], ?X1)
3. MOVE: ?X0 ?X2

In this paper, we generate rules with each possible lexical context, but one could filter out relations such as *aux* that provide a lexical context of a closed class word. The generalised Rule 3A makes clear the need for the MOVE operation, which is implemented in RegenT by rewriting ?X0 as ?X2 in the entire dependency parse after rule application. We will omit the MOVE command where it is not required to save space.

Extracting elementary trees: It is possible for the DELETE and INSERT lists to contain multiple simplification rules; i.e., multiple transductions over ETs (connected graphs). We need to ensure that each extracted rule contains a connected graph in the DELETE list. Where this is not the case, we split the rule into multiple rules. An example follows where three independent simplifications have been performed on a sentence:

4. (a) As a general rule , with an increase in elevation comes a decrease in temperature and an increase in precipitation .
   (b) As a normal rule , with an increase in height comes a decrease in temperature and an increase in rain .

The original extracted rule contains three relations with no variable in common:

RULE 4: INDEPENDENTELEMENTARYTREES

1. DELETE
   (a) amod(?X0[rule], ?X1[general])
   (b) prep_in(?X2[comes], ?X3[elevation])
   (c) prep_in(?X4[increase], ?X5[precipitation])
2. INSERT
   (a) amod(?X0, ?X6[normal])
   (b) prep_in(?X2, ?X7[height])
   (c) prep_in(?X4, ?X8[rain])

Relations with no variables in common belong to separate ETs, so we create three new rules:

RULE 4A
DELETE: amod(?X0[rule], ?X1[general])
INSERT: amod(?X0, ?X6[normal])

RULE 4B
DELETE: prep_in(?X2[comes], ?X3[elevation])
INSERT: prep_in(?X2, ?X7[height])

RULE 4C
DELETE: prep_in(?X4[increase], ?X5[precipitation])
INSERT: prep_in(?X4, ?X8[rain])

Removing lexical context from longer rules: While preserving lexical context is important to avoid meaning change in new contexts due to polysemy (this claim is evaluated in §3.5), it is unnecessary for longer rules involving more than one relation, as these tend to encode longer paraphrases with more standardised meanings. We thus remove the lexical context for rules involving multiple relations in the DELETE list[1].

3.3 Overview of extracted ruleset

In addition to the generalisation steps described above, we also automatically filtered out rules that were undesired for various reasons. As we use manually written rules in RegenT for common syntactic simplification (as described in Siddharthan (2011)), we filter out rules that involve dependency relations for passive voice, relative clauses, apposition, coordination and subordination. We also filter out rules with relations that are error-prone, based on a manual inspection. These involved single lexical changes involving the following dependencies: *det* and *num* (rules that change one determiner to another, or one number to another) and *poss* and *pobj* that mostly appeared in rules due to errorful parses. We also automatically filtered out errorful rules using the training set as follows: we applied the rules to the source sentence from which they were derived, and filtered out rules that did not generate the target sentence accurately. Finally, we restricted the number of relations in either the DELETE or INSERT list to a maximum of three, as longer rules were never being applied.

Tab. 1 shows how the filters and generalisation influence the number of rules derived involving 1–5 relations in each of the DELETE and INSERT lists. In addition, we also extract rules where the DELETE list is longer than the INSERT list; i.e., simplification that result in sentence shortening (e.g., Rule 1 in Section 3.1).

Tab. 2 provides details of the final number of filtered and generalised rules for different lengths of the DELETE and INSERT lists. The ruleset shown in Tab. 2 will henceforth be referred to as WIKI.

3.4 Generalising context with WordNet

To generalise the context of lexical simplification rules further, we now consider the use of WordNet

[1]Lexical context is defined as lexical specifications on variables occurring in both the DELETE and INSERT lists; i.e., words that are unchanged by the simplification.

DELETE	INSERT	IS	FS	GS
1	1	1111	593	4250
2	2	1051	357	171
3	3	1108	178	52
4	4	831	-	-
5	5	628	-	-

Table 1: Number of extracted rules where the INSERT and DELETE lists contain 1–5 relations (IS: initial set; FS: filtered set; GS: generalised set)

in expanding lexical context. The idea is that the lexical specification of context variables in rules can be expanded by identifying related words in WordNet. We propose to use Lin's similarity measure (Lin, 1998), an information content based similarity measure for our experiments as information content based measures are observed to perform better in deriving similar terms, in comparison to other methods (Budanitsky and Hirst, 2006). Lin's formula is based on Resnik's. Let $IC(c) = -log\, p(c)$ be the information content of a concept (synset) in WordNet, where $p(c)$ is the likelihood of seeing the concept (or any of its hyponyms) in a corpus. Resnik defines the similarity of two concepts c_1 and c_2 as $sim_{res}(c_1, c_2) = max_{c \in S(c_1,c_2)} IC(c)$, the IC of the most specific class c that subsumes both $c1$ and $c2$. Lin's formula normalises this by the IC of each class:

$$sim_{lin}(c_1, c_2) = \frac{2.sim_{res}(c_1, c_2)}{IC(c_1) + IC(c_2)}$$

Our next goal is to explore how the definition of lexical context impacts on a text simplification system.

3.5 Evaluation

To evaluate our work, we used the text simplification tool RegenT (Siddharthan, 2011) to apply different versions of the acquired rule sets to a test dataset. For example, consider the following rule shown in 6(a). This is the original rule extracted from the training data (cf. Tab. 2).

RULE 6(A): RULE-WIKI

1. DELETE
   (a) nsubjpass(??X0[adapted], ??X1[limbs])
2. INSERT
   (a) nsubjpass(??X0, ??X2[legs])

This rule is transformed to a no-context rule in 6(b), where words such as "adapted" that occur in both the DELETE and INSERT lists are removed entirely from the rule:

DELETE / INSERT	1	2	3	4	5
1 Relation	4250				
2 Relations	110	171			
3 Relations	91	165	52		
4 Relations	49	71	209	-	
5 Relations	24	44	80	-	-

Table 2: Details of rules derived with different length in DELETE and INSERT relations

RULE 6(B): NO-CONTEXT

1. DELETE
   (a) nsubjpass(??X0, ??X1[limbs])
2. INSERT
   (a) nsubjpass(??X0, ??X2[legs])

Finally the rule in 6(c), expands the context word "adapted" using WordNet classes with Lin's similarity greater than 0.1.

RULE 6(C): RULE-WITH-WORDNET0.1-CONTEXT

1. DELETE
   (a) nsubjpass(??X0[accommodated,adapted,adjusted, altered,assimilated,changed,complied, conformed,fited,followed,geared,heeded, listened,minded,moved,obeyed,oriented, pitched,tailored,varied],??X1[limbs])
2. INSERT
   (a) nsubjpass(??X0, ??X2[legs])

Evaluation of generalisability of rules: We expanded the context of rules derived from Wikipedia using various thresholds such as 0.1, 0.4 and 0.8 for Lin similarity measure and evaluated how many simplification operations were performed on the first 11,000 sentences from the dataset of Coster and Kauchak (2011). The details of rules applied on the test dataset, using different thresholds along with the Wiki-context and no-context rules are provided in Tab. 3. As seen, there is an increase in the application of rules with the decrease in threshold for Lin similarity measure. Removing the lexical context entirely results in an even larger increase in rule application. Next, we evaluate the correctness of rule application.

Evaluation of correctness of rule application: To test the correctness of the rule applications with

Rule Version	Rules	% Change
Wikicontext	7610	
WordNet context (0.8)	7870	3.41
WordNetcontext (0.4)	8488	11.85
WordNetcontext (0.1)	10715	40.80
Nocontext	31589	315.09

Table 3: Application of different versions of rules on test dataset (% change is the increase in the application of rules between Wiki-context and the corresponding version)

different rule sets, we performed a human evaluation to gauge how fluent and simple the simplified sentences were, and to what extent they preserved the meaning of the original. We compared three versions in this experiment: the original ruleset, the context expanded using $Sim_{Lin} >= 0.1$ (40% increase in rule applications) and with no lexicalised context (315% increase in rule applications). The goal is to identify a level of generalisation that increases rule application in new contexts without introducing more errors.

We used the first 11,000 sentences from the dataset of Coster and Kauchak (2011), the same dataset used for rule acquisition. We extracted at random 30 sentences where a simplification had been performed using the original ruleset. This gives an upper bound on the performance of the original Wikipedia-context ruleset, as these are all sentences from which the rules have been derived.

We then selected a further 30 sentences where a simplification had been performed using the WordNet-context (Lin=0.1), but not with the original ruleset. These are new applications of the generalised ruleset on sentences that it hasn't directly learnt rules from. Similarly, we selected a further 30 sentences where a simplification had been performed using the no-context ruleset, but not the Wikipedia-context or WordNet-context rulesets. Thus each set of 30 sentences contains new applications of the ruleset, as the lexical context is expanded, or abandoned completely.

This process gave us a total of 90 sentences to evaluate. We recruited participants through Amazon Mechanical Turk. Participants were filtered to be in the US and have an approval rating of 80%. These raters were shown 30 examples, each containing an original Wikipedia sentence followed by one of the simplified versions (WI, WN or NC). Order of presentation was random. For each such pair, raters were asked to rate each simplified version for fluency, simplicity and the extent to which it preserved the meaning of the original. The experiment provided 917 ratings for 90 sentences involving 28 raters. We used a Likert scale of 1–5, where 1 is totally unusable output, and 5 is the output that is perfectly usable.

The mean values and the standard deviation for fluency, simplicity and meaning preservation for sentences simplified using WordNet (Lin=0.1), Wiki and no context is shown in Tab. 4. As seen, the difference between the mean values for all three criteria of fluency, simplicity and meaning preservation between WordNet and Wiki version is very small as compared to simplified sentences with no-context rules. An analysis of variance (ANOVA) test was conducted to measure the effect of fluency, simplicity and meaning preservation for versions of simplified text.

Fluency: A one-way ANOVA conducted to evaluate fluency for versions of simplified text showed a highly significant effect of version (WN, WC, and NC) on the fluency score (F=51.54, p=$2\text{x}10^{-16}$). A Tukey's pairwise comparison test (Tukey's HSD, overall alpha level = 0.05) indicated significant difference between WI and NC and between WN and NC at $p = 0.01$. However, the difference between WN and WI was not significant at $p = 0.01$.

Simplicity: The ANOVA conducted to evaluate simplicity for different versions also showed a significant effect of version on the simplicity score (F=76.7, p=$2\text{x}10^{-16}$). A Tukey's pairwise comparison test (Tukey's HSD, overall alpha level = 0.05) indicated significant difference between WN and NC and WI and NC ($p < 0.01$). However, the difference between WN and WI was not significant at $p = 0.01$.

Meaning Preservation: The ANOVA conducted to evaluate meaning preservation for versions of simplified text also showed a highly significant effect of version on the meaning preservation score (F=17.22, p=$4.55\text{x}10^{-08}$). A Tukey's pairwise comparison test (Tukey's HSD, overall alpha level = 0.05) indicated significant difference between WN and NC and WI and NC ($p < 0.01$). However, the difference between WN and WI was not significant at $p = 0.01$.

This study suggests that there is no significant effect on accuracy of expanding the lexical context using WordNet (Lin=0.1), even though this results in an increase in rule application of 40%. The study also confirms that there is a sharp and

Rater	FLUENCY			SIMPLICITY			MEANING		
	WN	WI	NC	WN	WI	NC	WN	WI	NC
Mean	3.28	3.59	2.49	3.68	3.51	2.47	2.52	2.72	2.17
SD	1.38	1.31	1.44	1.32	1.28	1.34	1.12	1.11	1.27
Median	4	4	2	3	4	2	3	3	2

Table 4: Results of human evaluation of different versions of simplified text (WN: WordNet-context (Lin=0.1); WI: Wikipedia-context; NC: No-context)

significant drop in accuracy from removing lexical context altogether (the approach used by Wubben et al. (2012), for example). Next, we perform an evaluation of our hybrid text simplification system, that augments the existing RegenT system (Siddharthan, 2011), with its hand-written rules for syntactic simplification, with the automatically acquired lexicalised rules(the Lin=0.1 ruleset).

4 Hybrid text simplification system

The RegenT text simplification toolkit (Siddharthan, 2011) is distributed with a small hand crafted grammar for common syntactic simplifications: 26 hand-crafted rules for apposition, relative clauses, and combinations of the two; a further 85 rules handle subordination and coordination (these are greater in number because they are lexicalised on the conjunction); 11 further rules cover voice conversion from passive to active; 38 rules for light verbs and various cleft constructions; 99 rules to handle common verbose constructions described in the old GNU diction utility; 14 rules to standardise quotations.

The RegenT system does not have a decoder or a planner. It also does not address discourse issues such as those described in Siddharthan (2003a), though it includes a component that improves relative clause attachment based on Siddharthan (2003b). It applies the simplification rules exhaustively to the dependency parse; i.e., every rule for which the DELETE list is matched is applied iteratively (see Siddharthan (2011) for details).

We have created a hybrid text simplification system by integrating our automatically acquired rules (lexical context extended using WordNet for single change rules, and lexical context removed for longer rules) with the existing RegenT system as described above. This is sensible, as the existing manually written rules for syntactic simplification are more reliable than automatically extracted ones: They model morphological change, allowing for a linguistically accurate treatment of syntactic phenomenon such as voice change. The current work addresses a major limitation of hand-crafted text simplification systems—such systems restrict themselves to syntactic simplification, even though vocabulary plays a central role in reading comprehension. We hope that the methods described here can extend a hand-crafted system to create a hybrid text simplification system that is accurate as well as wide coverage. We next present a large scale manual evaluation of this hybrid system.

4.1 Evaluation

We performed a manual evaluation of how fluent and simple the text produced by our simplification system is, and the extent to which it preserves meaning.

Our system (henceforth, HYBRID) is compared to QTSG, the system by Woodsend and Lapata (2011) that learns a quasi-synchronous tree substitution grammar. This is the best performing system in the literature with a similar scope to ours in terms of the syntactic and lexical operations performed [2]. Further the two systems are trained on the same data. QTSG relies entirely on an automatically acquired grammar of 1431 rules. Our automatically extracted grammar has 5466 lexicalised rules to augment the existing manually written syntactic rules in RegenT.

We also compare the two systems to the manual gold standard SEW, and against the original EW sentences.

Data: We use the evaluation set previously used by several others (Woodsend and Lapata, 2011; Wubben et al., 2012; Zhu et al., 2010). This consists of 100 sentences from English Wikipedia (EW), aligned with Simple English Wikipedia (SEW) sentences. These 100 sentences have been excluded from our training data for rule acquisition, as is standard. Following the protocol of Wubben et al. (2012), we used all the sentences from the evaluation set for which both QTSG and

[2] The PBMT system of Wubben et al. (2012) reports better results than QTSG, but is not directly comparable because it does not perform sentence splitting, and also trains on a different corpus of news headlines.

Rater	FLUENCY				SIMPLICITY				MEANING			
	EW	SEW	QTSG	HYB	EW	SEW	QTSG	HYB	EW	SEW	QTSG	HYB
Mean	3.99	4.06	1.97	3.52	3.43	3.58	2.33	3.73	-	4.03	2.23	3.40
SD	0.94	1.00	1.24	1.24	1.07	1.22	1.26	1.30	-	1.02	1.23	1.18
Median	4	4	1	4	3	4	2	4	-	4	2	3

Table 5: Results of human evaluation of different simplified texts (EW: English Wikipedia; SEW: Simple English Wikipedia; QTSG: Woodsend and Lapata (2011) system; HYB: Our hybrid system)

HYBRID had performed at least one simplification (as selecting sentences where no simplification is performed by one system is likely to boost its fluency and meaning preservation ratings). This gave us a test set of 62 sentences from the original 100.

Method: We recruited participants on Amazon Mechanical Turk, filtered to live in the US and have an approval rating of 80%. These participants were shown examples containing the original Wikipedia sentence, followed by QTSG, HYBRID and SEW in a randomised manner. For each such set, they were asked to rate each simplified version for fluency, simplicity and the extent to which it preserved the meaning of the original. Additionally, participants were also asked to rate the fluency and simplicity of the original EW sentence. We used a Likert scale of 1–5, where 1 is totally unusable output, and 5 is output that is perfectly usable. The experiment resulted in obtaining a total of 3669 ratings for 62 sentences involving 76 raters.

Results: The results are shown in Tab. 5. As seen, our HYBRID system outperforms QTSG in all three metrics and is indeed comparable to the SEW version when one looks at the median scores. Interestingly, our system performs better than SEW with respect to simplicity, suggesting that the hybrid system is indeed capable of a wide range of simplification operations. The ANOVA tests carried out to measure significant differences between versions is presented below.

Fluency: A one-way ANOVA was conducted to evaluate fluency for versions of simplified text showed a highly significant effect of version (EW, SEW, QTSG, HYBRID) on the fluency score ($F=695.2$, $p<10^{-16}$). A Tukey's pairwise comparison test (Tukey's HSD, overall alpha level = 0.05) indicated significant differences between QTSG-EW; HYBRID-EW; HYBRID-QTSG; SEW-QTSG; SEW-HYBRID at $p = 0.01$.

Simplicity: A one-way ANOVA conducted to evaluate fluency for versions of simplified text showed a highly significant effect of version (EW, SEW, QTSG, HYBRID) on the simplicity score ($F=29.9$, $p<10^{-16}$). A Tukey's pairwise comparison test (Tukey's HSD, overall alpha level = 0.05) indicated significant differences between QTSG-EW; HYBRID-EW; HYBRID-QTSG; SEW-QTSG; all at $p<0.01$.

Meaning Preservation: A one-way ANOVA conducted to evaluate meaning preservation for versions of simplified text showed a highly significant effect of version (EW, SEW, QTSG, HYBRID) on the meaning preservation score ($F=578.1$, $p=2x10^{-16}$). A Tukey's pairwise comparison test (Tukey's HSD, overall alpha level = 0.05) indicated significant differences between QTSG-SEW; HYBRID-SEW; and HYBRID-QTSG all at $p<0.01$.

5 Conclusion

We have described a hybrid system that performs text simplification using synchronous dependency grammars. The grammar formalism is intuitive enough to write rules by hand, and a syntactic rule set is distributed with the RegenT system. The contributions of this paper are to demonstrate that the same framework can be used to acquire lexicalised rules from a corpus, and that the resultant system generates simplified sentences that are comparable to those written by humans.

We have documented how a grammar can be extracted from a corpus, filtered and generalised. Our studies confirm the benefits of generalising rules in this manner. The resultant system that combines this grammar with the existing manual grammar for syntactic simplification has outperformed the best comparable contemporary system in a large evaluation. Indeed our system performs at a level comparable to the manual gold standard in a substantial evaluation involving 76 participants, suggesting that text simplification systems are reaching maturity for real application.

Acknowledgements

This research is supported by an award made by the EPSRC; award reference: EP/J018805/1.

References

Or Biran, Samuel Brody, and Noemie Elhadad. 2011. Putting it simply: a context-aware approach to lexical simplification. In *Proceedings of the 49th Annual Meeting of the Association for Computational Linguistics: Human Language Technologies*, pages 496–501, Portland, Oregon, USA, June. Association for Computational Linguistics.

Alexander Budanitsky and Graeme Hirst. 2006. Evaluating wordnet-based measures of lexical semantic relatedness. *Computational Linguistics*, 32(1):13–47.

Arnaldo Candido Jr, Erick Maziero, Caroline Gasperin, Thiago AS Pardo, Lucia Specia, and Sandra M Aluisio. 2009. Supporting the adaptation of texts for poor literacy readers: a text simplification editor for brazilian portuguese. In *Proceedings of the Fourth Workshop on Innovative Use of NLP for Building Educational Applications*, pages 34–42. Association for Computational Linguistics.

Yvonne Canning. 2002. *Syntactic simplification of Text*. Ph.D. thesis, University of Sunderland, UK.

Raman Chandrasekar, Christine Doran, and Bangalore Srinivas. 1996. Motivations and methods for text simplification. In *Proceedings of the 16th International Conference on Computational Linguistics (COLING '96)*, pages 1041–1044, Copenhagen, Denmark.

William Coster and David Kauchak. 2011. Learning to simplify sentences using wikipedia. In *Proceedings of the Workshop on Monolingual Text-To-Text Generation*, pages 1–9. Association for Computational Linguistics.

Jan De Belder and Marie-Francine Moens. 2010. Text simplification for children. In *Prroceedings of the SIGIR workshop on accessible search systems*, pages 19–26.

M.C. De Marneffe, B. MacCartney, and C.D. Manning. 2006. Generating typed dependency parses from phrase structure parses. In *Proceedings of LREC*, volume 6, pages 449–454. Citeseer.

Siobhan Devlin and John Tait. 1998. The use of a psycholinguistic database in the simplification of text for aphasic readers. In J. Nerbonne, editor, *Linguistic Databases*, pages 161–173. CSLI Publications, Stanford, California.

Yuan Ding and Martha Palmer. 2005. Machine translation using probabilistic synchronous dependency insertion grammars. In *Proceedings of the 43rd Annual Meeting on Association for Computational Linguistics*, pages 541–548. Association for Computational Linguistics.

Dekang Lin. 1998. An information-theoretic definition of similarity. In *ICML*, volume 98, pages 296–304.

Shashi Narayan and Claire Gardent. 2014. Hybrid simplification using deep semantics and machine translation. In *Proc. of the 52nd Annual Meeting of the Association for Computational Linguistics.*

Advaith Siddharthan and Angrosh Mandya. 2014. Hybrid text simplification using synchronous dependency grammars with hand-written and automatically harvested rules. In *Proceedings of the 14th Conference of the European Chapter of the Association for Computational Linguistics*, pages 722–731, Gothenburg, Sweden, April. Association for Computational Linguistics.

Advaith Siddharthan. 2003a. Preserving discourse structure when simplifying text. In *Proceedings of the European Natural Language Generation Workshop (ENLG), 11th Conference of the European Chapter of the Association for Computational Linguistics (EACL'03)*, pages 103–110, Budapest, Hungary.

Advaith Siddharthan. 2003b. Resolving pronouns robustly: Plumbing the depths of shallowness. In *Proceedings of the Workshop on Computational Treatments of Anaphora, 11th Conference of the European Chapter of the Association for Computational Linguistics (EACL'03)*, pages 7–14, Budapest, Hungary.

Advaith Siddharthan. 2010. Complex lexico-syntactic reformulation of sentences using typed dependency representations. In *Proc. of the 6th International Natural Language Generation Conference (INLG 2010)*, pages 125–133. Dublin, Ireland.

Advaith Siddharthan. 2011. Text simplification using typed dependencies: a comparison of the robustness of different generation strategies. In *Proceedings of the 13th European Workshop on Natural Language Generation*, pages 2–11. Association for Computational Linguistics.

Lucia Specia, Sujay Kumar Jauhar, and Rada Mihalcea. 2012. Semeval-2012 task 1: English lexical simplification. In *Proceedings of the First Joint Conference on Lexical and Computational Semantics-Volume 1: Proceedings of the main conference and the shared task, and Volume 2: Proceedings of the Sixth International Workshop on Semantic Evaluation*, pages 347–355. Association for Computational Linguistics.

Lucia Specia. 2010. Translating from complex to simplified sentences. In *Proceedings of the Conference on Computational Processing of the Portuguese Language*, pages 30–39. Springer.

Kristian Woodsend and Mirella Lapata. 2011. Learning to simplify sentences with quasi-synchronous grammar and integer programming. In *Proceedings of the Conference on Empirical Methods in Natural Language Processing*, pages 409–420. Association for Computational Linguistics.

Sander Wubben, Antal van den Bosch, and Emiel Krahmer. 2012. Sentence simplification by monolingual machine translation. In *Proceedings of the 50th Annual Meeting of the Association for Computational Linguistics: Long Papers-Volume 1*, pages 1015–1024. Association for Computational Linguistics.

Kenji Yamada and Kevin Knight. 2001. A syntax-based statistical translation model. In *Proceedings of the 39th Annual Meeting on Association for Computational Linguistics*, pages 523–530. Association for Computational Linguistics.

Mark Yatskar, Bo Pang, Cristian Danescu-Niculescu-Mizil, and Lillian Lee. 2010. For the sake of simplicity: Unsupervised extraction of lexical simplifications from wikipedia. In *Human Language Technologies: The 2010 Annual Conference of the North American Chapter of the Association for Computational Linguistics*, pages 365–368. Association for Computational Linguistics.

Zhemin Zhu, Delphine Bernhard, and Iryna Gurevych. 2010. A monolingual tree-based translation model for sentence simplification. In *Proceedings of the 23rd international conference on computational linguistics*, pages 1353–1361. Association for Computational Linguistics.

A language-independent method for the extraction of RDF verbalization templates

Basil Ell
Karlsruhe Institute of Technology (KIT)
Karlsruhe, Germany
basil.ell@kit.edu

Andreas Harth
Karlsruhe Institute of Technology (KIT)
Karlsruhe, Germany
harth@kit.edu

Abstract

With the rise of the Semantic Web more and more data become available encoded using the Semantic Web standard RDF. RDF is faced towards machines: designed to be easily processable by machines it is difficult to be understood by casual users. Transforming RDF data into human-comprehensible text would facilitate non-experts to assess this information. In this paper we present a language-independent method for extracting RDF verbalization templates from a parallel corpus of text and data. Our method is based on distant-supervised simultaneous multi-relation learning and frequent maximal subgraph pattern mining. We demonstrate the feasibility of our method on a parallel corpus of Wikipedia articles and DBpedia data for English and German.

1 Introduction

Natural Language Generation (NLG) systems require resources such as templates (in case of template-based NLG) or rules (in case of rule-based NLG). Be it template-based or rule-based systems, these resources limit the variability and the domain-specificity of the generated natural language output and manual creation of these resources is tedious work.

We propose a language-independent approach that induces verbalization templates for RDF graphs from example data. The approach is language-independent since it does not rely on pre-existing language resources such as parsers, grammars or dictionaries.

Input is a corpus of parallel text and data consisting of a set of documents D and an RDF graph G, where D and G are related via a set of entities E where an entity can be described by a document in D and described by data in G. Output is a set of templates. Templates consist of a graph pattern that can be applied to query the graph and of a sentence pattern that is a slotted sentence into which parts of the query result are inserted. A template enables verbalization of a subgraph of G as a complete sentence.

An example is shown in Fig. 1.[1] The graph pattern GP can be transformed into a SPARQL query Q_{GP}. Querying the data graph G results in the graph G_{GP}. G_{GP} can be verbalized as an English (German) sentence S_{en} (S_{de}) using the sentence pattern SP_{en} (SP_{de}).

The approach employs the distant supervision principle (Craven and Kumlien, 1999; Bunescu and Mooney, 2007; Carlson et al., 2009; Mintz et al., 2009; Welty et al., 2010; Hoffmann et al., 2011; Surdeanu et al., 2012) from relation extraction: training data is generated automatically by aligning a database of facts with text; therefore, no hand-labeled data is required. We apply simultaneous multi-relation learning (Carlson et al., 2009) for text-data alignment and frequent maximal subgraph pattern mining to observe commonalities among RDF graph patterns.

Besides the general idea to allow for non-experts to assess information encoded in RDF, we envision application of these verbalization templates in three scenarios:

(1) In query interfaces to semantic databases, casual users - usually not capable of writing formal queries – specify their information needs using keywords (Lei et al., 2006; Thomas et al., 2007; Wang et al., 2008), questions in free-text or using a controlled language (Kaufmann et al., 2006; Cimiano et al., 2008; Wendt et al., 2012; Damljanovic et al., 2012), or forms (Hunter and Odat, 2011; Mendes

[1] Further examples and the evaluation material can be found on our website at http://km.aifb.kit.edu/sites/bridge-patterns/INLG2014

Proceedings of the 8th International Natural Language Generation Conference, pages 26–34,
Philadelphia, Pennsylvania, 19-21 June 2014.

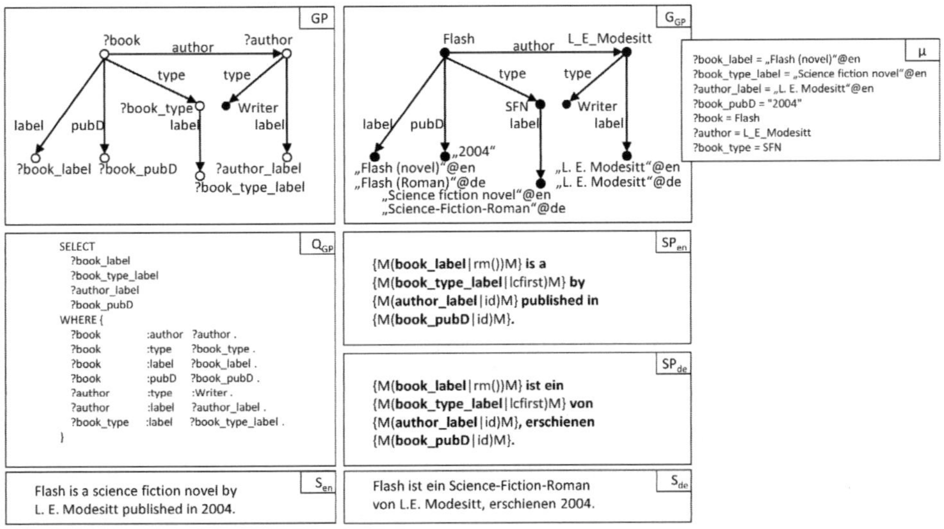

Figure 1: A template consists of a graph pattern GP and a sentence pattern SP. The graph pattern GP can be transformed into a SPARQL query Q_{GP}. A result of querying the data graph is the RDF graph G_{GP} with the list of solution mappings μ. This graph can be verbalized as an English sentence S_{en} using the English sentence pattern SP_{en} or as a German sentence S_{de} using the German sentence pattern SP_{de}. The modifiers, e.g. `lcfirst`, are explained in Table 1.

et al., 2008). The system queries an RDF database according to its interpretation of the input. Query results could be verbalized.

(2) Since the introduction of the Google Knowledge Graph,[2] when searching for an entity such as the city of Karlsruhe via Google, besides the search results shown on the left a table is displayed on the right which provides a short description of the entity taken from Wikipedia. While these descriptions are decoupled from data in the knowledge graph they could be generated automatically.

(3) The collaboratively-edited knowledge base Wikidata provides machine-readable data which can be used, e.g., by the Wikipedia. The Wikidata browsing interface *reasonator* currently explores the use of template-based NLG in order to provide human-readable descriptions of its entities.[3] Since the templates are created manually, currently only for few types of entities these verbalizations can be provided.

[2]`http://googleblog.blogspot.com/2012/05/introducing-knowledge-graph-things-not.html` (accessed 2014-03-20)

[3]See for example the page about Johann Sebastian Bach: `http://tools.wmflabs.org/reasonator/?q=Q1339` (accessed 2014-03-20)

1.1 Main contributions

We present an approach to induce RDF verbalization templates from a parallel text-data corpus. (1) The approach is distant-supervised, since it does not require labeled data but instead automatically aligns a database of facts with text by performing simultaneous multi-relation learning. (2) Hypotheses about a sentence's content are represented as an RDF graph pattern. Hypotheses graphs are reduced via frequent maximal subgraph pattern mining. (3) We introduce RDF verbalization templates consisting of a sentence pattern which includes modifiers and a graph pattern of unrestricted size. (4) Our approach does not use language resources such as parsers or dictionaries and is thus language independent and (5) does not depend on a certain ontology or domain. (6) The feasibility of the approach is validated for English and German given a large dataset which resulted in the induction of a large number of templates that are general in terms of enabling verbalization of numerous subgraphs in our dataset.

1.2 Definitions

- A **template** is a tuple (sp, gp) where sp is a sentence pattern and gp is a graph pattern. We denote the set of variables within a sentence pattern sp as $Var_{SP}(sp)$ and the set of variables within a graph pattern gp as $Var_{GP}(gp)$. A template (sp, gp) is *safe* if the set of variables within the sentence pattern is a subset of the set of variables within the graph pattern: $Var_{SP}(sp) \subseteq Var_{GP}(gp)$.

- A **sentence pattern** (SP) is a string that consists of terminals, variables, and modifiers. Within an SP a (var., mod.) tuple (v, m) is denoted as {`M(v|m)M`}. {`M(` and `)M`} serve as delimiters of a (var., mod.) tuple.
- A **graph pattern** is a set of triples patterns (s, p, o) where $s \in \mathcal{U} \cup \mathcal{V}$, $p \in \mathcal{U} \cup \mathcal{V}$, and $o \in \mathcal{U} \cup \mathcal{L} \cup \mathcal{V}$. $\mathcal{U}$ is a set of identifiers, $\mathcal{L}$ is a set of literals, and $\mathcal{V}$ is a set of variables.
- A **modifier** $m \in M$ is a function applicable to the value of a variable v - denoted by $m(v)$.

1.3 Template-based NLG

A template can be applied for Natural Language Generation as follows. Given an RDF data graph G and a template (sp, gp), a SPARQL SELECT query can be created: `SELECT PV WHERE` { gp' }. The list of projection variables `PV` is the list of variables $v \in Var_{SP}(sp)$. gp' is constructed by adding each triple pattern to gp'. An example of a query (Q_{GP}) created from a graph pattern (GP) is shown in Fig. 1.

Executing a query results in a solution sequence[4] which is a list of solution mappings $\mu{:}V \rightarrow \mathcal{T}$ from a set of variables V to a set of RDF terms $\mathcal{T} = \mathcal{U} \cup \mathcal{L}$. See Fig. 1 for an example of a solution mapping (μ).

For each non-terminal in sp representing a variable-modifier tuple (v, m), the modifier m is applied on $\mu(v)$ resulting in $m(\mu(v))$. Finally, the tuple (v, m), expressed as {`M(v|m)M`}, is replaced in sp with $m(\mu(v))$. After replacing each such tuple the sentence creation is complete.

2 Parallel corpus

Our approach requires a parallel corpus of text and data and consists of texts that describe entities in natural language and a data graph that semantically describes entities.

Formally, the parallel corpus consists of a set of entities E, a set of documents D, and an RDF data graph G. An entity can be described by a document in a certain language. The relation $document \subseteq E \times L \times D$ relates an (entity, language) tuple to a set of documents. $document(e, l)$ denotes the (potentially empty) set of documents that describe an entity $e \in E$ in language $l \in L$.

G is a set of triples (s, p, o) where $s, p \in \mathcal{U}$, and $o \in \mathcal{U} \cup \mathcal{L}$.

Each literal has a datatype, returned by the function *datatype*:$\mathcal{L} \rightarrow T$. Literals of type *string* can be language-tagged. The function $l_l{:}\mathcal{L} \rightarrow L$ returns the language $l_l(r) \in L$ for a literal $r \in \mathcal{L}$ if it exists. An entity can have a human-readable form which is a language-tagged literal. The relation $\lambda \subseteq E \times L \times \mathcal{L}$ relates an entity $e \in E$ to a (possibly empty) set of literals $\lambda(e, l) \subseteq \mathcal{L}$ in language $l \in L$. The property p_λ relates an entity with its label.

Each entity $e \in E$ occurs in the data graph. This means that G contains a triple (s, p, o) where $s{=}e$ or $o{=}e$.

3 Approach

Our approach consists of six steps:

1. For each entity $e \in E$ we collect sentences from documents about the entity that mention the entity.
2. For each sentence we align the sentence and the data graph by iteratively exploring the vicinity of the entity within the graph. This leads to a set of identified entities: entities that are believed to be mentioned within the sentence; and a set of observations. The subgraph of G that consists of all triples that contain an identified entity serves as an hypothesis graph: no fact that is not expressed in the subgraph is expressed in the sentence.
3. Each (sentence, identified entities, graph) triple is abstracted by replacing identified literals in the sentence and in the graph with variables and by replacing identified entities in the graph with variables. This step can lead to multiple distinct (sentence pattern, graph pattern) tuples for each sentence. This abstraction enables comparing different sentences that share the same sentence pattern after abstraction.
4. A set of (sentence pattern, graph patterns) tuples is built for each sentence pattern.
5. For each (sentence pattern, graph patterns) tuple the set of graph patterns is analyzed regarding their commonalities. This is realized via the frequent and maximal subgraph pat-

[4] We adopt the terminology from the SPARQL 1.1 Query Language documentation available at `http://www.w3.org/TR/2013/REC-sparql11-query-20130321/`.

tern extraction (fmSpan) algorithm which results in a set of graph patterns that are subgraph patterns to the input graph patterns.
6. Given the output of this algorithm and the abstracted sentences the templates are created.

3.1 Sentence collection

Given a language name l, a set of entities E, a set of documents D and an ordered list of modifiers M, for each entity $e \in E$ for each document $d \in document(e, l)$ (which describes e in language l) the document is split into a set of sentences. For each sentence that has an acceptable length (measured as the number of characters), for each label $x \in \lambda(e, l)$ and for each string modifier $m \in M_{string}$, we store the (sentence, entity, left, right, λ, matched) tuple if the modified label $m(x)$ matches the sentence. See Alg. 1.

Algorithm 1 Collect example sentences

```
procedure COLLECT EXAMPLE SENTENCES(l, E, D, M)
  for each e ∈ E do
    for each d ∈ document(e, l) ∈ D do
      for each s ∈ sentences(d, l_min, l_max) do
        for each x ∈ λ(e, l) do
          for each m ∈ M_string do
            if applicable(m, x) then
              (left, right, x') = MatchesLabel(s, x, m, "str")
              if (left, right, x') ≠ ∅ then
                Output (s, e, left, right, x, x', m)
                Continue with next sentence
```

Algorithm 2 MatchesLabel

```
procedure MATCHESLABEL(s, x, m, t)
  if t = "str" ∨ t ≠ "integer" then
    if length(x) ≥ 4 then
      if s matches (\W|^)\w{l_0, l_1}m(x)\w{r_0, r_1}(\W|$) then
        return (left, right, matched)
  else if t = integer then
    if s matches (\D|^)m(x)(\D|$) then
      return (left, right, matched)
  return ∅
```

In Alg. 2, $\backslash W$ denotes a non-word character (such as a blank), $\backslash D$ denotes a non-digit, $\backslash w$ denotes a word character[5] (such as "x"), $\backslash w\{a, b\}$ denotes a sequence of at least a word-characters and not more than b word characters, l_0 and l_1 are the minimum and maximum number of word characters that may appear on the left side of the modified string $m(x)$ between this string and a non-word character or the beginning of the sentence (^). r_0 and r_1 are the corresponding numbers regarding the right side of the modified string. \$ denotes the end of the sentence. In case of a match, the string that is matched by $\backslash w\{l_0, l_1\}$ is stored as *left*, the string that is matched by $\backslash w\{r_0, r_1\}$ is stored as *right* and the part that matches $m(x)$ is stored as *matched*. Note that *matched* can be different from $m(x)$ since the application of the modifier m to the string x can result in a regular expression that contains information for the matcher specifying that a part of the string needs to be matched case-insensitively.

Allowing a certain number of characters to be added to the left and to the right of a string has the intention to match even though prefixes and postfixes are added. For example, this allows to match "German" within its plural form "Germans" or to match "magic" within magician.

3.2 Sentence and data alignment

The sentence and the data graph are aligned by iteratively exploring the vicinity of an entity within the graph. This exploration is described by Alg. 3 which builds a set of observations *obs*. A member of this set is a 7-tuple where the first three members form a triple (entity, property, literal value), followed by the strings matched to the left and the right, the matched string and the modifier. Moreover, the algorithm creates a graph $graph \subseteq G$ consisting of all triples that contain an identified entity. Here, an entity e is identified if a modifier $m \in M$ exists such that an $x \in \lambda(e, l)$ exists such that the sentence matches $m(x)$. Output is the original sentence, the set of identified entities, the set of observations, and the subgraph.

Algorithm 3 Data Collection

```
procedure COLLECTDATA(s, e, lang, left, right, x, x', m)
  identified = ∅; todo = (e); done = ∅;
  graph = ∅; obs = {(e, p_l, x, left, right, x', m)}
  while todo ≠ ∅ do
    e ← todo.first
    todo ← todo\{e}; done ← done ∪ {e}
    for each (e, p, o) ∈ G do
      graph ← graph ∪ {(e, p, o)}
      if o is a literal then
        (l, r, o', m) = CL(s, o)
        if (l, r, o', m) ≠ ∅ then
          obs ← obs ∪ {(e, p, o, l, r, o', m)}
          if o = λ(e, lang) then
            identified ← identified ∪ {e}
      else if o is a URI then
        if o ∉ done ∧ o ∉ todo then
          todo.add(o)
    for each (e2, p, e) ∈ G do
      graph ← graph ∪ {(e2, p, e)}
      if e2 ∉ done ∧ o ∉ todo then
        todo.add(e2)
  Output (sentence, identified, obs, graph)
```

3.3 Sentence and graph abstraction

In the previous step, ambiguities may exist. For example, given two triples (e_1, p_1, v) and

[5] Note that word- and non-word characters are language-specific and may be defined for each language individually.

(e_2, p_2, v) where v is a literal value and the entities e_1 and e_2 are identified, if the value v is found in the sentence, then it cannot be resolved whether the sentence expresses the fact (e_1, p_1, v) or (e_2, p_2, v). Therefore, for each situation where a value appears in two distinct contexts or where values overlap (two values overlap if the intervals of their character positions overlap), the sentence and graph pattern is copied and on each copy another abstraction is performed thus leading to multiple abstractions per sentence. Alg. 4 iteratively creates all sentence abstractions given a language name l, a sentence S, and a set of observations *obs*. The function `poss` evaluates the set of observations that are still valid. The function `apply` replaces a string in a sentence with variable and modifier. Thereby, the *left* and *right* parts are added to the modifier. For an observation (e, p, o, l, r, o', m) the string concatenation $l+o'+r$ is replaced with $\{\mathtt{M}(v_i|\mathtt{m'})\mathtt{M}\}$. For each observation a new variable v_i is introduced. m' is a modifier to which the modifiers `+l(l)` and `+r(r)` are appended which denote that certain strings are added to the left and the right of the literal. The graph is abstracted by replacing the triple (e, p, o) with the triple pattern (e, p, v_1). After completely abstracting a sentence pattern, each identified entity is replaced by a variable; triples that do not contain any variable are removed.

Algorithm 4 Sentence abstraction

```
procedure ABSSENTENCE(l, S, obs)
  P ← poss(l, S, obs)
  if P = ∅ then
    Output(S)
  else
    O ← overlap(S, P)
    for each p ∈ P do
      if p ∉ O then
        S ← apply(S, p)
    if O = ∅ then
      Output(S)
    else
      for each p ∈ O do
        S' ← apply(S, p)
        AbsSentence(l, S', P)
```

3.4 Grouping

Given a set of (sp, gp) tuples, for each language we build groups of tuples where in each group the sentence patterns are pairwise equivalent when ignoring modifiers. Sentence patterns sp_i and sp_j are equivalent if either they are identical ($sp_i = sp_j$), or if an injective function $m{:}Var_{SP}(sp_i) \rightarrow Var_{SP}(sp_j)$ exists such that when each variable v in sp_i is replaced with $m(v)$, the resulting string sp'_i is identical to sp_j.

For each group the set of graph patterns is used as input for the algorithm presented in the following section.

3.5 Frequent maximal subgraph pattern extraction

Before we describe the *fmSpan* algorithm (fmSpan: Frequent Maximal Subgraph PAttern extractioN) we need to introduce our notation:

Two graph patterns gp_i and gp_j are *equivalent* ($gp_i = gp_j$) if an injective function $m{:}Var_{GP}(gp_i) \rightarrow Var_{GP}(gp_j)$ exists such that when each variable v in gp_i is replaced with $m(v)$, the resulting graph pattern gp'_i is identical to gp_j. A graph pattern gp_i is *subgraph pattern* to another graph pattern gp_j, denoted by $gp_i \subseteq^P gp_j$, if an injective function $m{:}Var_{GP}(gp_i) \rightarrow Var_{GP}(gp_j)$ exists such that when each variable v in gp_i is replaced with $m(v)$, resulting in gp'_i, each triple pattern in gp'_i is also a triple pattern in gp_j. Given a set of graph patterns $GP = \{gp_1, ..., gp_n\}$ and given a graph pattern x, the *coverage* of x regarding GP is the number of graphs in GP to which x is a subgraph pattern: $c(x, GP) := |\{gp_i \in GP | x \subseteq^P gp_i\}|$.

Given a set of graph patterns $I = \{gp_1, ..., gp_n\}$, from the set of all subgraph patterns $P = 2^{gp_1} \cup ... \cup 2^{gp_n}$ a set of graph patterns $K = \{gp_i, ..., gp_j\} \subseteq P$ is selected where:

1. for each $gp_k \in K$:
   (a) $c(gp_k, I) \geq min\_coverage$
   (b) $\neg\exists gp_l \in P : gp_k \neq gp_l \wedge gp_k \subseteq^P gp_l \wedge c(gp_l, I) \geq min\_coverage$
2. $\neg\exists gp_l \in P : c(gp_l, I) \geq min\_coverage \wedge (\neg\exists gp_m \in P : \neg(gp_m, gp_l) \wedge c(gp_m, I) \geq min\_coverage) \wedge gp_l \notin K$

This means that each member of K is sufficiently frequent (1a) and maximal (2b) and that every maximal graph pattern is contained in K (2).

3.6 Template creation

For each (sentence pattern, graph patterns) tuple the frequent maximal subgraph pattern mining is performed on the group of graph patterns which results in a set K of subgraph patterns. Each $k \in K$ is pruned with Alg. 5. Thereby, if a variable appears in a high number of triples that do not contain any other variable, then these triples are removed. After the pruning each $k \in K$ is then rejected if it is either not safe, not connected, or, when queried against G returns no results.

Algorithm 5 Graph-pattern pruning

```
1: procedure PRUNEGRAPHPATTERN(k)
2:   for each v ∈ Var_GP(k) do
3:     T ← {(s,p,o) ∈ k|(s = v ∧ o ∉ Var_GP(k)) ∨ (o = v ∧ s ∉ Var_GP(k))}
4:     if |T| > max_t then
5:       k ← k\T
```

Datatype	Modifier	Description
xsd:string	id	Does not change the string.
	lcfirst	Sets the first char to lower case if that char is upper case.
	ucfirst	Sets the first char to upper case if that char is lower case.
	case-i	Case-insensitive match
	rm()	If a string ends with a string in round braces, e.g. "Dublin (Ohio)", that part is cut off.
	-1r	Removes the rightmost char.
xsd:gYear	YYYY	Transforms a year value into a four-digit representation.
xsd:integer	integer_id	Does not change the integer.
	enInt_sep	Adds English thousands separators, e.g., *10,000*.
	deInt_sep	Adds German thousands separators, e.g., *10.000*.
xsd:date	enM,_D_Y	Result, e.g., *March, 22 2014*
	enD_M_Y	Result, e.g., *22 March 2014*
	deM_D,_Y	Result, e.g., *März 22, 2014*
	deD_M_Y	Result, e.g., *22. März 2014*

Table 1: List of modifiers per datatype

4 Experiments

We created a multilingual (English, German) parallel text-data corpus using data from DBpedia[6] and documents from the Wikipedia. The graph G consists of $88,708,622$ triples, the set of documents D consists of $4,004,478$ English documents and $716,049$ German documents. The corpus relations and functions are defined as follows:

- $document(e,l) :=$ $\{d|(e, \text{dbo:abstract}, "d"@l) \in G\}$.
- $\lambda(e,l) := \{v|(e, \text{rdfs:label}, "v"@l) \in G\}$
- The *datatype* of a literal `"r^^t"` is t.
- The language l_l of a literal `"d"@l` is l.

The modifiers we used in the experiment are given in Table 1.[7] Application of date and integer modifiers may also depend on the language of a sentence. On a value a list of modifiers can be applied. The list of string modifier lists is shown in Fig. 2. The table also shows how often each list of modifiers was applied during the abstraction of English and German sentences.

We created two sets of entities E_{en} (E_{de}): those for which an English (German) document exist that consists of at least 100 characters. E_{en} and E_{de} contain $3,587,146$ and $613,027$ entities, respectively. For each entity for each document we split the text into sentences using the Perl module *Lingua::Sentence*[8] and discarded sentences that do not end with a full stop, an exclamation mark, or a question mark or that were shorter (longer) than 50 (200) characters. We used the set of string modifiers presented in Fig. 2 to identify entities via occurrence of a modified version of their labels in a sentence. The results are $3,811,992$ ($794,040$) English (German) sentences.

Abstraction resulted in 3,434,108 (530,766) abstracted English (German) sentences where at least two entities are identified per sentence.

The group size histogram is displayed in Fig. 2.[9] The majority (90%) of all groups of English (German) sentences contain between 5 and 164 (5 and 39) sentences.

	groups ≥ 5	templates	all groups
en	4569	3816	686,687
de	2130	1250	269,551

Table 3: Number of groups with a cardinality ≥ 5, the number of induced templates and the number of all groups.

Table 3 gives for each language the number of groups that contain more than 5 graph patterns, the number of templates we induced, and the number of all groups. Results of the coverage evaluation $cov_t(G)$ are shown as a histogram in Fig. 3. It shows that for the majority of the templates a high number of subgraphs of G can be verbalized, which means that the templates are not fitted to only a small number of subgraphs: e.g. for 221 English templates verbalize between 10^5 and 10^6 subgraphs, each.

[6] `http://wiki.dbpedia.org/Downloads39` We used the files long_abstracts_en, long_abstracts_en-_uris_de, mappingbased_properties_en, raw_infobox_properties_en, article_categories_en, instance_types_en, labels_en, labels_en_uris_de, category_labels_en, and category_labels-_en_uris_de.

[7] Modifiers are only applied if their application to a literal modifies that literal. For example, if a string begins with a lower case character, then the *lcfirst* modifier is inapplicable.

[8] `http://search.cpan.org/~achimru/Lingua-Sentence-1.05`

[9] We cut off the long tail.

No	Modifier list	en	de	No	Modifier list	en	de	No	Modifier list	en	de
(1)	id	10,619,509	1,349,922	(9)	-1r	42,754	15,025	(17)	-1r, -1r, lcfirst	8430	90
(2)	lcfirst	141,865	868	(10)	-1r, lcfirst	7513	99	(18)	-1r, -1r, ucfirst	1020	5
(3)	ucfirst	11,018	8	(11)	-1r, ucfirst	875	4	(19)	-1r, -1r, case-i	733	92
(4)	case-i	295,593	16,351	(12)	-1r, case-i	863	50	(20)	rm(), -1r, -1r, lcfirst	0	0
(5)	rm()	2705	762	(13)	rm(), -1r, lcfirst	0	0	(21)	rm(), -1r, -1r, ucfirst	0	0
(6)	rm(), lcfirst	13	0	(14)	rm(), -1r, ucfirst	0	0	(22)	rm(), -1r, -1r, case-i	66	1
(7)	rm(), ucfirst	0	0	(15)	rm(), -1r, case-i	55	6				
(8)	rm(), case-i	50	0	(16)	-1r, -1r	39,113	11,632				

Table 2: List of lists of string modifiers and their number of applications

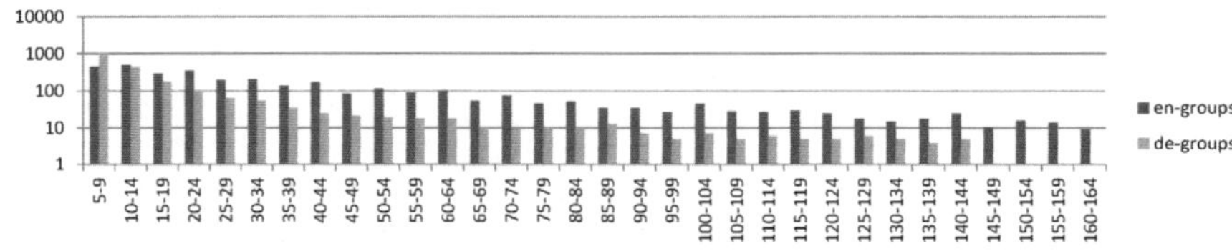

Figure 2: Histogram depicting how often sentence groups occurred with a particular size

5 Evaluation

We evaluate the results from the experiment described in the previous section along the dimensions *coverage*, *accuracy*, *syntactic correctness*, and *understandability* where the latter three are inspired by (Lester and Porter, 1997; Mellish and Dale, 1998; Reiter and Belz, 2009).

Coverage: we define $cov(t, G)$ of a template $t{=}(sp, gp)$ regarding a data graph G as the number of subgraphs of G that can be verbalized with that template i.e. match gp.

Accuracy: is measured in two parts:

1. The extent to which everything that is expressed in gp is also expressed in sp is measured for each triple pattern within the graph pattern on a 4-point scale: (1) *The triple pattern is explicitly expressed*, (2) *The triple pattern is implied*, (3) *The triple pattern is not expressed*, and (4) *Unsure*.

2. The extent to which the sp expresses information that is expr. in gp is measured on a 4-point scale: (1) *Everything is expressed*, (2) *Most things are expressed*, (3) *Some things are expressed*, and (4) *Nothing is expr.*.

Syntactic correctness: the degree to which the verb. is syntactically correct, in particular whether it adheres to English or German grammar: (1) The verb. is completely synt. correct. (2) The verb. is almost synt. correct. (3) The verb. presents some syntactical errors. (4) The verb. is strongly synt. incorrect.

Understandability: Adapted from (Nagao et al., 1985): (1) The meaning of the verb. is clear. (2) The meaning of the verb. is clear, but there are some problems in word usage, and/or style. (3) The basic thrust of the verb. is clear, but the evaluator is not sure of some detailed parts because of word usage problems. (4) The verb. contains many word usage problems, and the evaluator can only guess at the meaning. (5) The verb. cannot be understood at all.

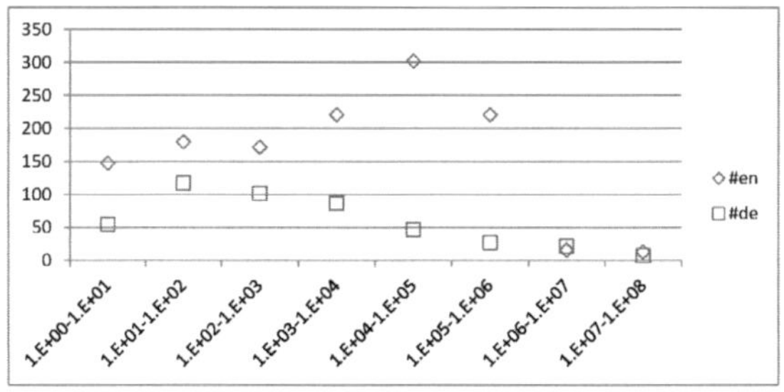

Figure 3: Histogram of the coverage $cov(t, G)$

We evaluated a random sample of 10 English and 10 German templates using a group of 6 evaluators which are experts in the fields of RDF and SPARQL and that are proficient in both English and German. Each template was evaluated by 3 experts, each expert evaluated 10 templates. For each template we retrieved a maximum of 100 subgraphs that matched the graph pattern, randomly selected 10 subgraphs and verbalized them. For each template an evaluator was asked to evaluate accuracy given the graph pattern and given the sentence pattern and, given the list of 10 verbalizations, to evaluate each sentence regarding syntactic correctness and understandability.

$cov(t, G)$ of all 5066 templates is shown in Fig. 3. For example, it shows that there are about 300 templates where each template can be used

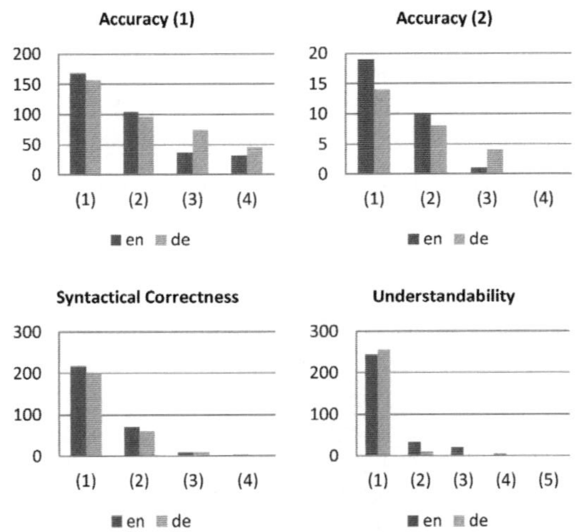

Figure 4: Evaluation results regarding accuracy, syntactical correctness, and understandability

to verbalize between 10^4 and 10^5 subgraphs of G. Results regarding the remaining dimensions are shown in Fig. 4. The values of the x-axes correspond to the scale of the respective dimension. The majority of the triple patterns are either explicitly or implicitly expressed in the sentence pattern. However, some triple patterns are not expressed in the sentence pattern. Syntactical correctness and understandability are mostly high.

6 Related work

(Welty et al., 2010) present *a technique for reading sentences and producing sets of hypothetical relations that the sentence may be expressing.* Given a parallel text-data corpus, entities identified as proper nouns in parsed sentences are replaced with variables. For each (pattern, set of relations) tuple for each sentence that matches this pattern it is counted in how many sentences that match this pattern a certain relation exists between the two entities identified in the sentence. This leads to positive weights assigned to patterns. Negative weights are assigned by applying patterns to sentences, identifying the entities and assigning a negative weight to the relation if the relation expressed by the pattern is not expressed in the data.

In contrast to this approach, our approach 1) does not require to parse input sentences 2) does not only regard relations between proper nouns, 3) constrains candidate entities to the vicinity of already identified entities. Moreover, 4) our approach takes into account the graph of entities identified in a sentence (hypothesis graphs) compared to sets of relations and can thus express multiple relations between entities.

(Duma and Klein, 2013) present an unsupervised approach to NLG template extraction from a parallel text-data corpus. Similar to our approach, text and data are aligned by identifying labels of entities in sentences. The search space is limited by only allowing to match entities that are directly linked to the entity a text is about. Sentences are abstracted by replacing the entity with the name of the property that links the entity with the entity the text is about thus limiting the depth of the graph to 1. Abstracted sentences are parsed and pruned by removing constituents that could not be aligned to the database and by removing constituents of certain classes and then post-processed using manually created rules.

(Gerber and Ngomo, 2011) present an approach to learning natural language representations of predicates from a parallel text-data corpus. For each predicate where a tuple of entities is identified in a sentence, the predicate's natural language representation is the string between the two entities, e.g. `'s acquisition of` for the predicate `subsidiary` and the sentence *Google's acquisition of Youtube comes as online video is really starting to hit its stride.* The main differences to our approach are 1) that we do not focus on learning how a single predicate is expressed but rather how a graph, consisting of multiple related entities, can be expressed in natural language and 2) that a relation between two entities is not only expressed by the string between two entities.

7 Conclusions

We have shown that verbalization templates can be extracted from a parallel text-data corpus in a distant-supervised manner – without the need for pre-existing language resources such as parsers, grammars or dictionaries – and that applying these templates for NLG leads to promising results. The main novelty is the application of frequent maximal subgraph pattern mining for the purpose of analyzing commonalities in sets of hypotheses graphs. Even though the approach is linguistically shallow, verbalizations are already syntactically mostly correct and understandable.

Acknowledgements

The authors acknowledge the support of the European Commission's Seventh Framework Programme FP7-ICT-2011-7 (XLike, Grant 288342).

References

Razvan Bunescu and Raymond Mooney. 2007. Learning to extract relations from the web using minimal supervision. In *Annual meeting-association for Computational Linguistics*, volume 45, pages 576–583.

Andrew Carlson, Justin Betteridge, Estevam R Hruschka Jr, and Tom M Mitchell. 2009. Coupling semi-supervised learning of categories and relations. In *Proceedings of the NAACL HLT 2009 Workshop on Semi-supervised Learning for Natural Language Processing*, pages 1–9. Association for Computational Linguistics.

P. Cimiano, P. Haase, J. Heizmann, M. Mantel, and R. Studer. 2008. Towards portable natural language interfaces to knowledge bases–The case of the ORAKEL system. *Data & Knowledge Engineering*, 65(2):325–354.

Mark Craven and Johan Kumlien. 1999. Constructing biological knowledge bases by extracting information from text sources. In Thomas Lengauer, Reinhard Schneider, Peer Bork, Douglas L. Brutlag, Janice I. Glasgow, Hans-Werner Mewes, and Ralf Zimmer, editors, *ISMB*, pages 77–86. AAAI.

D. Damljanovic, M. Agatonovic, and H. Cunningham. 2012. FREyA: An interactive way of querying Linked Data using natural language. In *The Semantic Web: ESWC 2011 Workshops*, pages 125–138. Springer.

Daniel Duma and Ewan Klein, 2013. *Generating Natural Language from Linked Data: Unsupervised template extraction*, pages 83–94. Association for Computational Linguistics, Potsdam, Germany.

Daniel Gerber and A-C Ngonga Ngomo. 2011. Bootstrapping the linked data web. In *1st Workshop on Web Scale Knowledge Extraction @ International Semantic Web Conference*, volume 2011.

Raphael Hoffmann, Congle Zhang, Xiao Ling, Luke Zettlemoyer, and Daniel S Weld. 2011. Knowledge-based weak supervision for information extraction of overlapping relations. In *Proceedings of the 49th Annual Meeting of the Association for Computational Linguistics: Human Language Technologies-Volume 1*, pages 541–550. Association for Computational Linguistics.

J. Hunter and S. Odat. 2011. Building a Semantic Knowledge-base for Painting Conservators. In *E-Science (e-Science)*, pages 173–180. IEEE.

E. Kaufmann, A. Bernstein, and R. Zumstein. 2006. Querix: A natural language interface to query ontologies based on clarification dialogs. In *International Semantic Web Conference (ISWC 2006)*, pages 980–981.

Yuangui Lei, Victoria Uren, and Enrico Motta. 2006. SemSearch: A Search Engine for the Semantic Web. pages 238–245. Springer.

J.C. Lester and B.W. Porter. 1997. Developing and empirically evaluating robust explanation generators: The KNIGHT experiments. *Comp. Linguistics*, 23(1):65–101.

C. Mellish and R. Dale. 1998. Evaluation in the conext of natural language generation. *Computer Speech and language*, 12(4):349–374.

P.N. Mendes, B. McKnight, A.P. Sheth, and J.C. Kissinger. 2008. TcruziKB: Enabling Complex Queries for Genomic Data Exploration. In *Semantic Computing, 2008*, pages 432–439.

Mike Mintz, Steven Bills, Rion Snow, and Dan Jurafsky. 2009. Distant supervision for relation extraction without labeled data. *Proceedings of the Joint Conference of the 47th Annual Meeting of the ACL and the 4th International Joint Conference on Natural Language Processing of the AFNLP: Volume 2 - ACL-IJCNLP 09*, pages 1003–1011.

Makoto Nagao, Jun-ichi Tsujii, and Jun-ichi Nakamura. 1985. The Japanese government project for machine translation. *Computational Linguistics*, 11(2-3):91–110.

E. Reiter and A. Belz. 2009. An investigation into the validity of some metrics for automatically evaluating natural language generation systems. *Computational Linguistics*, 35(4):529–558.

Mihai Surdeanu, Julie Tibshirani, Ramesh Nallapati, and Christopher D Manning. 2012. Multi-instance multi-label learning for relation extraction. In *Proceedings of the 2012 Joint Conference on Empirical Methods in Natural Language Processing and Computational Natural Language Learning*, pages 455–465. Association for Computational Linguistics.

E. Thomas, J.Z. Pan, and D. Sleeman. 2007. ONTOSEARCH2: Searching ontologies semantically. In *Proceedings of the OWLED 2007 Workshop on OWL: Experiences and Directions*, pages 70–72.

H. Wang, T. Tran, P. Haase, T. Penin, Q. Liu, L. Fu, and Y. Yu. 2008. SearchWebDB: Searching the Billion Triples. In *Billion Triple Challenge at the International Semantic Web Conference (ISWC 2008)*.

Chris Welty, James Fan, David Gondek, and Andrew Schlaikjer. 2010. Large scale relation detection. In *Proceedings of the NAACL HLT 2010 First International Workshop on Formalisms and Methodology for Learning by Reading*, pages 24–33. Association for Computational Linguistics.

M. Wendt, M. Gerlach, and H. Düwiger. 2012. Linguistic Modeling of Linked Open Data for Question Answering. *Interacting with Linked Data (ILD 2012)*, pages 75–86.

An ACG Analysis of the G-TAG Generation Process*

Laurence Danlos
Université Paris Diderot (Paris 7)
ALPAGE, INRIA Paris–Rocquencourt
Institut Universitaire de France, Paris, France
laurence.danlos@inria.fr

Aleksandre Maskharashvili and **Sylvain Pogodalla**
INRIA Villers-lès-Nancy, France
Université de Lorraine,
CNRS, LORIA, UMR 7503
Vandœuvre-lès-Nancy, France
aleksandre.maskharashvili@inria.fr
sylvain.pogodalla@inria.fr

Abstract

This paper presents an encoding of Generation-TAG (G-TAG) within Abstract Categorial Grammars (ACG). We show how the key notions of G-TAG have a natural interpretation in ACG, allowing us to use its *reversibility* property for text generation. It also offers solutions to several limitations of G-TAG.

1 Motivations

G-TAG (Danlos, 1998; Danlos, 2000) is a formalism based on the Tree Adjoining Grammar (TAG) formalism (Joshi et al., 1975; Joshi and Schabes, 1997) dedicated to text generation. It focuses on providing several notions to support useful data structures, such as g-derivation trees or lexical databases, to effectively relate a surface form (a derived tree or a string) to a conceptual representation. An actual implementation in ADA was first provided for French (Meunier, 1997), and it has recently been implemented in the .NET framework as the EasyText NLG system and is operational at Kantar Media, a French subsidiary company of TNS-Sofres (Danlos et al., 2011).

The G-TAG proposal can be seen as a result of the observation of the mismatch between the derivation tree notion of TAG and the expected semantic dependencies (Schabes and Shieber, 1994) from a generation perspective. Several approaches that extend the derivation tree notion of TAG have been proposed to overcome this difficulty. Other approaches showed that the derivation trees still could be used without additional modifications. Such approaches rely on unification (Kallmeyer and Romero, 2004; Kallmeyer and Romero, 2007) or a functional approach to TAG (Pogodalla, 2004; Pogodalla, 2009)[1] based on Abstract Categorial Grammars (ACG) (de Groote, 2001). The latter is *intrinsically reversible*: the grammars and the algorithms are the same for parsing and for generation.

We propose then to study G-TAG under the ACG perspective. We show that the key notion of g-derivation tree naturally express itself in this framework. The surface form construction from a conceptual representation can then use the general algorithms of ACG, the very same ones that can be used in parsing to analyze mildly context sensitive languages (TAG generated language, LCFRS) (de Groote and Pogodalla, 2004), following (Kanazawa, 2007)'s proposal here applied to give an ACG account of G-TAG. We do not consider here the G-TAG treatment of preferences between the different realizations of the same input. Similarly, we do not consider the generation of pronouns used in G-TAG and we will work on integrating a theory of generation of referring expressions.

2 Sketching G-TAG

G-TAG deals with the *How to say it?* task of generation. The input is a conceptual representation. A G-TAG grammar includes *elementary* trees, as any TAG grammar. But it also makes *g-derivation* trees primary objects, relating them to the elementary trees and considering them as pivot to the conceptual representation level.

Conceptual Representation G-TAG conceptual representation makes use of notions as *second order relation*, *first order relation* and *thing*. Second order relations have two arguments which are *relations* (either first or second order ones) and typically correspond to discourse relations,

*This work has been supported by the French agency Agence Nationale de la Recherche (ANR-12-CORD-0004).

[1]Synchronous approaches (Nesson and Shieber, 2006) are similar in many respects, as shown in (Storoshenk and Frank, 2012).

Proceedings of the 8th International Natural Language Generation Conference, pages 35–44,
Philadelphia, Pennsylvania, 19-21 June 2014. ©2014 Association for Computational Linguistics

whereas first order relations have *things* as their arguments. While (Danlos, 2000) uses reified formulas of a logical conceptual representation language as G-TAG inputs, it can also be represented as a higher-order logical formula (Meunier, 1997) or as a SDRT-like formula (Danlos et al., 2001). We follow here this presentation. Equation (1) exemplifies an input that could be realized as *Jean a passé l'aspirateur pour être récompensé par Marie. Puis il a fait une sieste* (John has vacumed in order to be rewarded by Mary. Then he took a nap).

$$\texttt{SUCCESSION}(\texttt{GOAL}(\texttt{VACUUMING}(\texttt{Jean}), \texttt{REWARDING}(\texttt{Marie}, \texttt{Jean})), \texttt{NAPPING}(\texttt{Jean})) \quad (1)$$

G-TAG Lexical Database A lexical entry of G-TAG corresponds to a lemma. For each lexical entry (i.e. lemma) there is a set of TAG elementary trees which corresponds to it. Among the TAG elementary trees that correspond to a given lexical entry, there is the canonical representative, and all the other representatives are represented by adding features to the canonical representative. For example, if the lexical entry is to love, then the canonical representative will be the active form of the verb to love. Then the passive alternation is represented by adding a feature [+passive] to to love. Moreover, all the lexical entries attached to a concept (such as SUCCESSION) belong to a same *lexical base*. So for a concept, there can be a lexical entry describing verbal realizations of the concept. These realizations can correspond to the active or to the passive forms, etc. There can also be a lexical entry which corresponds to nominal realizations, etc.

G-Derivation Trees A TAG derivation tree can be seen as a record of the substitutions and adjunction occurring during a TAG analysis. The same is true for g-derivation tree. However, while TAG derivation trees are considered as a by-product, with inflected anchors, G-TAG derivation trees are first class structures that are combined in order to reflect the conceptual input. To abstract from the surface form and from the derived tree they can relate to, they don't correspond to inflected forms but bear features that are used in a post-processing step. Complex g-derivation trees are built by going through the dynamic selection process of a lexical item from the set of appropriate candidates for a given concept. So contrary to TAG derivation trees, they are not fully instantiated trees: their arguments are represented by variables whose lexicalization are not carried out yet.

G-Derived Trees A g-derivation tree defines a unique g-derived tree corresponding to it. This correspondance is maintained all along the realization process and a post-processing module outputs the surface representation (text) from the g-derived tree. In addition to inflecting forms using the feature values it can make some rewriting to propose *different versions* of the initial text. In this particular sense, g-derived tree corresponds to possibly multiple text outputs generated by the post-processing module.

3 The G-TAG Generation Process

Let us assume the input of Equation 1. The G-TAG process starts by lexicalizing relations that have the widest scope in the conceptual representation: typically second order relations, then first order relations, and things.[2] Back to the example, we first lexicalize the second order relation SUCCESSION. Several items are associated with this relation: après (after), avant (before), ensuite (afterwards), auparavant (beforehand), puis (then), etc. Each of them has two arguments, however, some of them produce texts comprising two or more sentences, like ensuite(afterwards); some of them can produce either two sentence texts or one sentence text, while others produce only one sentence. For instance, *Jean a passé l'aspirateur. Ensuite, il a fait une sieste* (John has vacuumed. Afterwards, he took a nap) is a two sentences text while *John a fait une sieste après avoir passé l'aspirateur* (John took a nap after having vacuumed) is a one sentence text. For this reason, items describing the arguments or the result of second order relations have features expressing the following constraints: $(+\mathrm{T}, +\mathrm{S})$ indicates it is a text (two ore more sentences); $(+\mathrm{S})$ indicates it is either a single sentence or a text; $(-\mathrm{T}, +\mathrm{S})$ indicates it is a sentence (not a text). Every second order relation has three features: one for output, and two for inputs. [3]

[2]Correctness of the process is ensured because the grammars don't contain auxiliary trees that would reverse the predication order. (Danlos, 2000) argues such cases don't occur in technical texts, the first target of G-TAG. We don't elaborate on this point since the ACG approach we propose remove this constraint for free.

[3]In G-TAG, any discourse connective has exactly two arguments. A discussion about this point is provided in (Dan-

Let us assume that the G-TAG g-derivation tree ensuite$(+\mathrm{T}, +\mathrm{S})$ belonging to the lexical database associated with the concept `SUCCESSION` is first chosen, resulting in a text rather than a sentence (illustrated by the leftmost g-derivation tree of Figure 1 . The process then tries to realize its two arguments. The first one involves the `GOAL` relation that can be realized either by pour (in order to) or by pour que (so that), as exemplified by the rightmost g-derivation trees of Figure 1. Both have features $(-\mathrm{T}, +\mathrm{S})$ for the inputs (i.e. arguments) and return a tree labeled at the root by $(-\mathrm{T}, +\mathrm{S})$.

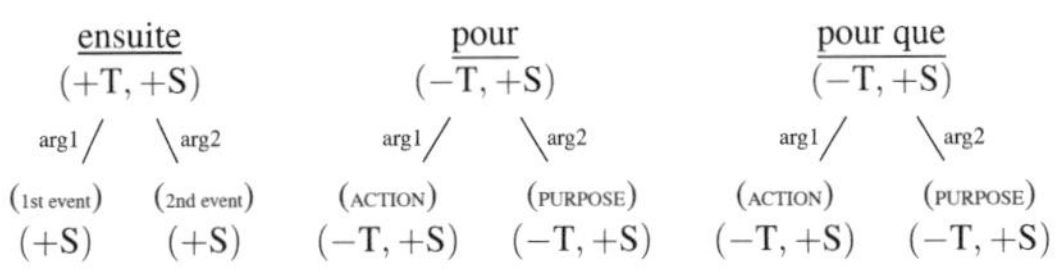

Figure 1: G-derivation trees samples

Despite pour and pour que bearing the same features, the syntactic trees corresponding to pour and pour que are quite different. For pour que S substitution nodes can be substituted by two tensed sentences, while pour takes a finite sentence and a "sentence" in the infinitive form without any nominal subject. Figure 2 shows the associated elementary trees. Selecting one or the other during the generation process restricts the possible realizations for the arguments. This is enforced by a feature associated to the elementary tree, namely the (+reduc-subj) feature as shown in Fig. 3. Again, we may assume that G-TAG selects pour,

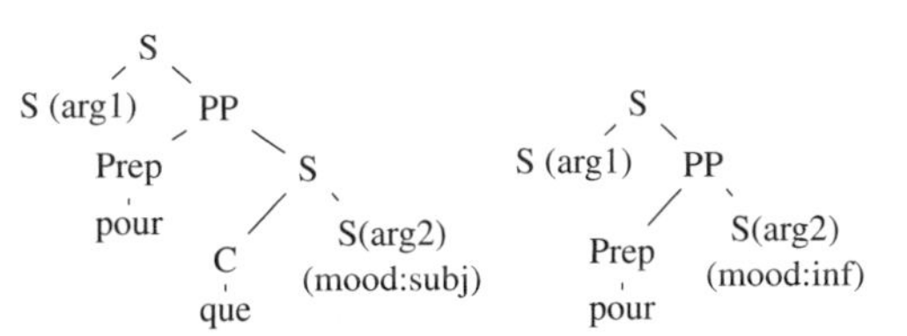

Figure 2: Elementary trees of *pour que* (so that) and *pour* (in order to)

which will enforce, because of the associated elementary trees, that the subject of the first and the second arguments are the same. Afterwards, we need to lexicalize these two arguments with a common subject `Jean`. From a semantic point of view, the agent of `VACUUMING` has to be the beneficiary of `REWARDING` (the rewardee). `VACUUMING` can only be lexicalized as passer-l'aspirateur (run-the-vacuum-cleaner), while there are several lexicalization options for the `REWARDING`: récompenser (to reward), donner-récompense (to give-reward), and recevoir-récompense (to receive-reward). Let us notice that donner-récompense does not meet the constraint on a shared subject as it cannot have the rewardee as its subject[4]. The remaining options are: recevoir-récompense, whose canonical representation has the rewardee as subject; and récompense whose passive construction has the rewardee as subject. s Assuming a choice of récompenser[+passive],[5] the lexicalizations of the arguments of the first order relations remain. As `Marie` occurs only once and in subject position, it can only be lexicalized as *Marie*. On the other hand, `Jean` three times: one will be the implicit subject of the subordinate, then as argument of `VACUUMING` and `NAPPING`. Therefore it can be either lexicalized in both of the cases as Jean, or Jean and the pronoun il (*he*). In G-TAG, there are some post-processing rules that take care of the generation of referring expressions, but not in a really principled way so we do not demonstrate them here. We assume a lexicalization by Jean in both cases. Figure 3 shows the g-derivation tree associated with the input of Equation 1 and Fig. 4 show the unique resulting (non-flected) derived tree. The post-processing modules then outputs: *Jean a passé l'aspirateur pour être récompensé par Marie. Ensuite, il a fait une sieste.* (John vacuumed in order to be rewarded by Mary. Afterwards, he took a nap.)

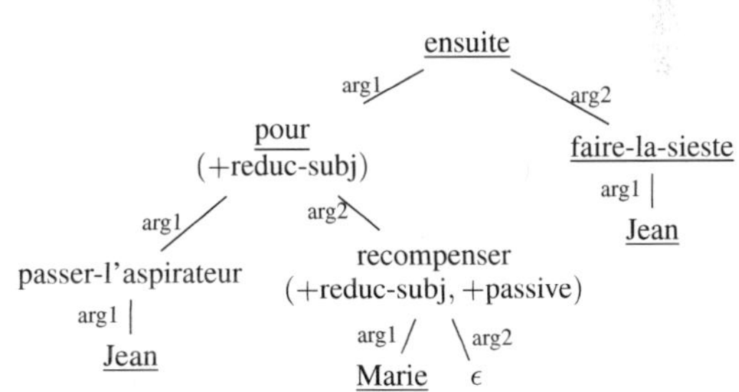

Figure 3: Fully instantiated g-derivation tree

4 ACG Definition

Abstract Categorial Grammars (ACGs) (de Groote, 2001) are a type theo-

los, 2000).

[4]It lacks passivation in French and there is no form equivalent to: John was given a reward by Mary.

[5]Of course, all these branching points offer several realizations of the same entry. But for explanatory purposes, we describe only one at each step.

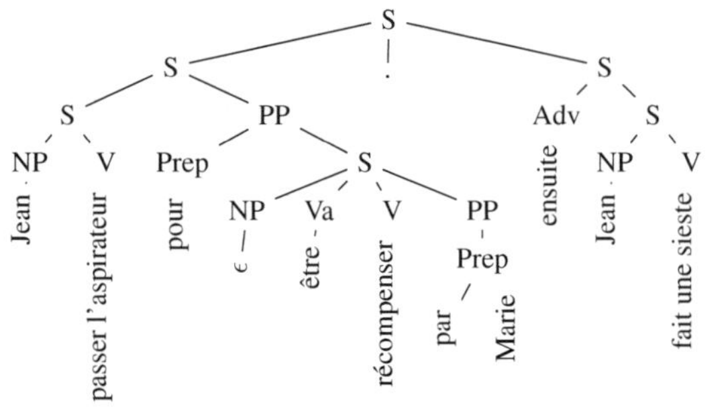

Figure 4: Non-inflected derived tree

retical framework that is able to encode several grammatical formalisms (de Groote and Pogodalla, 2004). An ACG defines two languages: the abstract one and the object one. The abstract level describe the admissible parse structures and a *lexicon* maps these structures to the ones we observe at the object level (strings for surface forms, logical formulas for semantic forms). In all cases, the considered languages are sets of λ-terms that generalize string and tree languages.

Definition. *A* higher-order linear signature *(also called a* vocabulary*) is defined to be a triple* $\Sigma = \langle A, C, \tau \rangle$*, where:*

- *A is a finite set of atomic types (also noted* A_Σ*),*
- *C is a finite set of constants (also noted* C_σ*),*
- *and* τ *is a mapping from C to* $\mathscr{T}_A$ *the set of types built on A:* $\mathscr{T}_A ::= A | \mathscr{T}_A \to \mathscr{T}_A$ *(also noted* $\mathscr{T}_\Sigma$*).*

Given a higher-order linear signature Σ*,* $\Lambda(\Sigma)$ *is the set of* λ*-terms built on* Σ*, and for* $t \in \Lambda(\Sigma)$ *and* $\alpha \in \mathscr{T}_\Sigma$ *such that t has type* α*, we note* $t :_\Sigma \alpha$ *(the* Σ *subscript is omitted when obvious from the context).*

Definition. *An* abstract categorial grammar *is a quadruple* $\mathscr{G} = \langle \Sigma, \Xi, \mathscr{L}, s \rangle$ *where:*

1. Σ *and* Ξ *are two higher-order linear signatures, which are called the* abstract vocabulary *and the* object vocabulary*, respectively;*
2. $\mathscr{L} : \Sigma \longrightarrow \Xi$ *is a lexicon from the abstract vocabulary to the object vocabulary. It is a homomorphism that maps types and terms built on* Σ *to types and terms built on* Ξ *as follows:*
   - *if* $\alpha \to \beta \in \mathscr{T}_\Sigma$ *then* $\mathscr{L}(\alpha \to \beta) = \mathscr{L}(\alpha) \to \mathscr{L}(\beta)$
   - *if* $x \in \Lambda(\Sigma)$ *(resp.* $\lambda x.t \in \Lambda(\Sigma)$ *and* $t\,u \in \Lambda(\Sigma)$*) then* $\mathscr{L}(x) = x$ *(resp.* $\mathscr{L}(\lambda x.t) = \lambda x.\mathscr{L}(t)$ *and* $\mathscr{L}(t\,u) = \mathscr{L}(t)\,\mathscr{L}(u)$*)*

   It is then enough to define $\mathscr{L}$ *on the atomic types and on the constants of* Σ *to define it on all types and terms, provided that for any constant* $c : \alpha$ *of* Σ *we have* $\mathscr{L}(c) : \mathscr{L}(\alpha)$*. We note* $t :=_{\mathscr{G}} u$ *if* $\mathscr{L}(t) = u$ *and omit the* $\mathscr{G}$ *subscript if obvious from the context.*
3. $s \in \mathscr{T}_\Sigma$ *is a type of the abstract vocabulary, which is called the* distinguished type *of the grammar.*

Table 1 provides an ACG example $\mathscr{G}_{\textit{d-ed trees}}$ where the abstract typed constants of $\Sigma_{der\theta}$ encode the combinatorial properties of the associated (through the lexicon $\mathscr{L}_{\textit{d-ed trees}}$) elementary trees.

Definition. *The* abstract language *of an ACG* $\mathscr{G} = \langle \Sigma, \Xi, \mathscr{L}, s \rangle$ *is* $\mathcal{A}(\mathscr{G}) = \{t \in \Lambda(\Sigma) \,|\, t :_\Sigma s\}$

The object language *of the grammar* $\mathcal{O}(\mathscr{G}) = \{t \in \Lambda(\Xi) \,|\, \exists u \in \mathcal{A}(\mathscr{G}).\, t = \mathscr{L}_G(u)\}$

For instance, the term $C_{\mathsf{reward}}\, I_{\mathsf{S}}\, I_{\mathsf{v}}\, C_{\mathsf{Mary}}\, C_{\mathsf{Jean}} : \mathsf{S} \in \mathscr{G}_{\textit{d-ed trees}}$, and its image, the derived tree for *Marie récompense Jean* (Mary rewards John).

It is important to note that, from a purely mathematical point of view, there is no structural difference between the abstract and the object vocabulary: both are higher-order signatures. This allows for combining ACGs in different ways:

- by having a same abstract vocabulary shared by several ACGs: this can be used to make two object terms (for instance a string and a logical formula) share the same underlying structure. $\mathscr{G}_{\textit{d-ed trees}}$ and $\mathscr{G}_{Log}$ in Fig. 5 illustrate such a composition.
- by making the abstract vocabulary of one ACG the object vocabulary of another ACG, allowing for the control of the admissible structures of the former by the latter. $\mathscr{G}_{yield}$ and $\mathscr{G}_{\textit{d-ed trees}}$ in Fig. 5 illustrate such a composition.

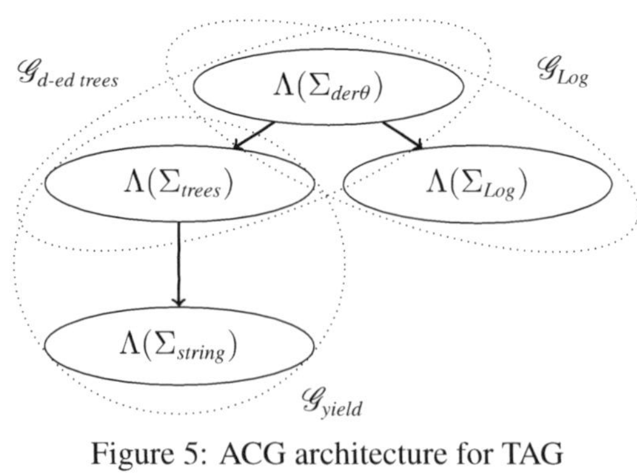

Figure 5: ACG architecture for TAG

Crucial to our analysis is that ACG parsing of a term u amounts to finding an abstract term t such that $t{:=}\,u$, no matter whether u represents a string, a tree, or a logical formula. This can be done in polynomial time for ACGs whose abstract constant types are at most of order 2: second order ACGs as (Kanazawa, 2007) shows.[6] The result relies on a reduction of the parsing problem to Datalog querying where the term to be parsed is stored in a database. Interestingly, this database can represent a set of terms (Kanazawa, 2011, Section 4.2) and the query reduces to checking whether at least one of them can be retrieved. This allows the query associated with a term representing a logical formula to extend to all the terms that are equivalent modulo the associativity and the commutativity of the conjunction.

5 ACG Encoding

5.1 TAG as ACG

Because ACG considers both the abstract language and the object language, the encoding of TAG into ACG makes (abstract) terms representing derivation trees primary. The encoding uses two ACGs $\mathscr{G}_{\textit{d-ed trees}} = \langle \Sigma_{\textit{der}\theta}, \Sigma_{\textit{trees}}, \mathscr{L}_{\textit{d-ed trees}}, \mathsf{S}\rangle$ and $\mathscr{G}_{\textit{yield}} = \langle \Sigma_{\textit{trees}}, \Sigma_{\textit{string}}, \mathscr{L}_{\textit{yield}}, \tau\rangle$.

We exemplify the encoding[7] of a TAG analyzing (2) in Fig. 6.[8]

(2) *Marie récompense ensuite Jean*
Mary rewards then John

This sentence is usually analyzed in TAG with a derivation tree where the adverb adjoins at the v node.

The three higher-order signatures are:

$\Sigma_{\textit{der}\theta}$: Its atomic types include S, v, np, S_A, v_A... where the X types stand for the categories X of the nodes where a substitution can occur while the X_A types stand for the categories X of the nodes where an adjunction can occur. For each elementary tree $\gamma_{\textit{lex. entry}}$ it contains a constant $C_{\textit{lex. entry}}$ whose type is based on the adjunction and substitution sites as Table 1 shows. It additionally contains constants $I_X : X_A$ that are meant to provide a fake auxiliary tree on adjunction sites where no adjunction actually takes place in a TAG derivation.

$\Sigma_{\textit{trees}}$: Its unique atomic type is τ the type of trees. Then, for any X of arity n belonging to the ranked alphabet describing the elementary trees of the TAG, we have a constant $X_n : \overbrace{\tau \multimap \cdots \multimap \tau}^{n \text{ times}} \multimap \tau$

$\Sigma_{\textit{string}}$: Its unique atomic type is σ the type of strings. The constants are the terminal symbols of the TAG (with type σ), the concatenation $+ : \sigma \multimap \sigma \multimap \sigma$ and the empty string $\varepsilon : \sigma$.

Table 1 illustrates $\mathscr{L}_{\textit{d-ed trees}}$.[9] $\mathscr{L}_{\textit{yield}}$ is defined as follows:

- $\mathscr{L}_{\textit{yield}}(\tau) = \sigma$;
- for $n > 0$, $\mathscr{L}_{\textit{yield}}(X_n) = \lambda x_1 \cdots x_n . x_1 + \cdots + x_n$;
- for $n = 0$, $X_0 : \tau$ represents a terminal symbol and $\mathscr{L}_{\textit{yield}}(X_0) = X$.

Then, the derivation tree, the derived tree, and the yield of Fig. 6 are represented by:

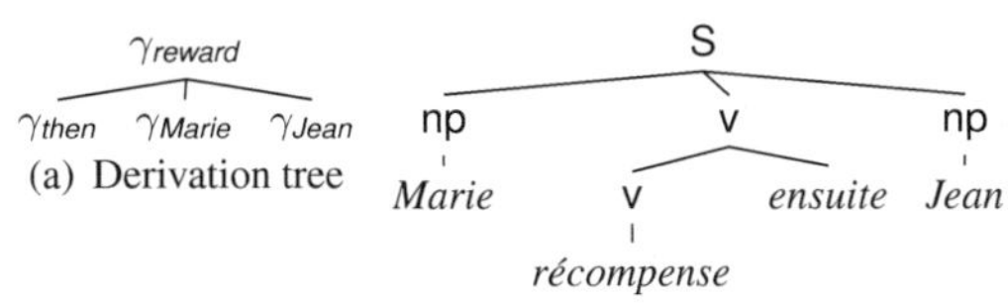

(a) Derivation tree

(b) Derived tree

Figure 6: *Marie récompense ensuite Jean*

$\gamma_5 = C_{\textit{reward}}\ I_{\mathsf{S}}\ (C^{\mathsf{V}}_{\textit{then}}\ I_{\mathsf{S}})\ C_{\textit{Marie}}\ C_{\textit{Jean}}$

$\mathscr{L}_{\textit{d-ed trees}}(\gamma_5)$
$= \mathsf{S}_3\ (\mathsf{np}_1\ \textit{Marie})$
$(\mathsf{v}_2\ (\mathsf{v}_1\ \textit{récompense})\ \textit{ensuite})\ (\mathsf{np}_1\ \textit{Jean})$

$\mathscr{L}_{\textit{yield}}(\mathscr{L}_{\textit{d-ed trees}}(\gamma_5)) = \textit{Marie} + \textit{récompense} + \textit{ensuite} + \textit{Jean}$

5.2 G-TAG as ACG

In order to model G-TAG in ACG, first we need to design the abstract signature $\Sigma_{\textit{g-der}\theta}$ in which we can have entries for G-TAG. This entries will reflect the ideology that G-TAG is based on. For instance, in G-TAG discourse level words like *ensuite* can take as its arguments texts and sentences and produces text. In order to model this, we introduce types S and T. Then, we can define $D^{SS}_{\textit{then}}$: $\mathsf{S} \multimap \mathsf{S} \multimap \mathsf{T}$, which means that $D^{SS}_{\textit{then}}$ has takes two arguments of type S and returns a result of type T. As in G-TAG, *ensuite* can take two

[6]It actually extends this result to *almost* linear object terms where variables with atomic type can be duplicated, as it commonly happens at the semantic level.

[7]This corresponds to the systematic encoding of (Pogodalla, 2009) of TAG and its semantics into ACG.

[8]We follow the grammar of (Abeillé, 2002).

[9]With $\mathscr{L}_{\textit{d-ed trees}}(X_A) = \tau \multimap \tau$ and for any other type X, $\mathscr{L}_{\textit{d-ed trees}}(X_A) = \tau$.

Abstract constants of $\Sigma_{der\theta}$	Their images by $\mathscr{L}_{d\text{-}ed\ trees}$	The corresponding TAG trees
$C_{Jean} : \mathsf{np}$	$c_{Jean} \begin{array}{l} : \tau \\ = \mathsf{np}_1\ Jean \end{array}$	$\gamma_{Jean} =$ np (Jean)
$C^{\mathsf{v}}_{then} : \mathsf{v}_A \multimap \mathsf{v}_A$	$c^{\mathsf{v}}_{then} \begin{array}{l} : (\tau \multimap \tau) \multimap (\tau \multimap \tau) \\ = \lambda^o vx.v\ (\mathsf{v}_2\ x ensuite) \end{array}$	$\gamma_{then} =$ v (v^* *ensuite*)
$C_{reward} : \begin{array}{c} \mathsf{S}_A \multimap \mathsf{v}_A \multimap \mathsf{np} \\ \multimap \mathsf{np} \multimap \mathsf{S} \end{array}$	$c_{reward} \begin{array}{l} : \begin{array}{l} (\tau \multimap \tau) \multimap (\tau \multimap \tau) \multimap \tau \\ \multimap \tau \multimap \tau \end{array} \\ = \lambda^o avso.a\ (\mathsf{S}_3\ s\ (v\ (\mathsf{v}_1\ récompense))\ o) \end{array}$	$\gamma_{reward} =$ S (np v(*récompense*) np)
$I_X : X_A$	$\lambda x.x : \tau \multimap \tau$	

Table 1: A TAG as an ACG: $\mathscr{L}_{d\text{-}ed\ trees}$ and $\mathscr{L}_{log.sem}$ lexicons

texts as arguments and return text as well, we need to do have another entry for modeling this fact. This makes us to introduce another constant D^{TT}_{then}: $\mathsf{T} \multimap \mathsf{T} \multimap \mathsf{T}$. For the same kind of reason, we introduce following constants: D^{ST}_{then}: $\mathsf{S} \multimap \mathsf{T} \multimap \mathsf{T}$, D^{TS}_{then} and $\mathsf{T} \multimap \mathsf{S} \multimap \mathsf{T}$. Other relations, like *auparavant* is modeled in the same way as *ensuite* in $\Sigma_{g\text{-}der\theta}$.

Apart from *ensuite* and *auparavant*, there are connectives as *avant* (before) and *après* (after) that need to be modeled differently from *ensuite*. Indeed, while *ensuite* results in a text, placing side by side a text and a sentence separated with a period, *avant* and *après* in French combine in a single sentence a (full) clause and an infinitive clause with an implicit subject: the one of the first clause. It is clear that in order to type *avant* and *après* in the $\Sigma_{g\text{-}der\theta}$ signature, one should use a type which schematically looks as $\ldots \multimap \mathsf{S}$. On the other hand, one needs to give the exact type to them. Despite that in TAG and G-TAG *avant* and *après* take two sentential arguments (labelled by S), the second argument bears a feature indicating it lacks the subject and that the latter has to be shared with the first sentence. For instance: *Jean a fait une sieste après avoir passé l'aspirateur* (John took a nap after having vacuumed), here the subject of *avoir passé l'aspirateur* (having vacuumed) is *Jean*, which comes from the sentence Jean a fait une sieste (John took a nap). So, *Jean a fait une sieste* (John took a nap) can be seen as a sentence whose subject is shared by another sentence as well. In order to model this point, we use following type: $\mathsf{Sws} \multimap \mathsf{Sh} \multimap \mathsf{np} \multimap \mathsf{S}$. Indeed, the Sws and the Sh types correspond to the type of sentences missing a subject. Furthermore, we need to model *pour* and *pour que*, which were introduced in order to lexicalize the GOAL relation in G-TAG. First, let us have a look at *pour que*. It can take as its arguments two complete (from a syntax point of view) sentences and results in a sentence as in: *Il travaille pour que vous puissiez manger*. So, $D_{pour\ que}$, which is an entry corresponding to *pour que*, can be assigned a $\mathsf{S} \multimap \mathsf{S} \multimap \mathsf{S}$ type. The syntactic difference between *pour que* and *pour* was highlighted in Section 3: *pour* takes as arguments a complete sentence and an infinitive form of a sentence missing a subject whose subject comes from the first argument. Thus, in this case, similarly to case of *avant* and *après*, *pour* has to be modeled as an entry that has type $\mathsf{Sws} \multimap \mathsf{Sinf} \multimap \mathsf{np} \multimap \mathsf{S}$, where Sinf stands for the type of an infinitive form of a clause missing a subject. We also need to deal with encoding different forms of a verb. For instance, récompenser has an active and a passive form. In G-TAG derivation, both of them can be encountered. In order to model this fact, two different entries are introduced: one for the passive form and one for the active form, which is the canonical construction for récompenser. So, we need to have two distinct entries $D^{passive}_{recompense}$ and $D^{active}_{recompense}$, and both of them have type $\mathsf{S}_A \multimap \mathsf{v}_A \multimap \mathsf{np} \multimap \mathsf{np} \multimap \mathsf{S}$. Moreover, (Danlos, 2000) poses the problem that G-TAG cannot handle a text where the adverb adjoin at the v node rather than on the S node as in: *Jean a passé l'aspirateur. Il a ensuite fait une sieste* (John vacuumed. He *then* took a nap.) According to (Danlos, 2000) modelling such text production requires a formalism more powerful than TAG. In the ACG framework, this observations translates into defining an entry $D^{\mathsf{v}}_{then} : \mathsf{S} \multimap (\mathsf{v}_A \multimap \mathsf{S}) \multimap \mathsf{T}$ in $\Sigma_{g\text{-}der\theta}$ which is third order and that is, as such, beyond the TAC into ACG encoding (that only requires second-order types).[10] This also offers a

[10]Currently, there is no theoretical complexity result for parsing such ACG fragments. However, in this particu-

general mechanism for providing constants encoding adverbial connectives with two arguments as in discourse grammars such as D-STAG (Danlos, 2011), but contrary to D-LTAG where one of the arguments is anaphorically given from the preceding discourse (Webber, 2004).

G-Derivation Trees to Derivation Trees We translate terms of $\Sigma_{g\text{-}der\theta}$, which correspond to g-derivation trees, into the TAG derivation tree language defined on $\Sigma_{der\theta}$ using the lexicon $\mathscr{L}_{der\text{-}der}$ of Table 2. It is interesting to see how to inter-

$$
\begin{aligned}
\mathscr{L}_{der\text{-}der}(\mathsf{S}) &= \mathscr{L}_{der\text{-}der}(\mathsf{T}) = \mathscr{L}_{der\text{-}der}(\mathsf{Sws}) \\
&= \mathscr{L}_{der\text{-}der}(\mathsf{Sinf}) = \mathscr{L}_{der\text{-}der}(\mathsf{Sh}) \\
&= \mathsf{S} \\
\mathscr{L}_{der\text{-}der}(\mathsf{S}_A) &= \mathsf{S}_A \\
\mathscr{L}_{der\text{-}der}(\mathsf{v}_A) &= \mathsf{v}_A \\
\mathscr{L}_{der\text{-}der}(\mathsf{np}) &= \mathsf{np} \\
\mathscr{L}_{der\text{-}der}(I_{\mathsf{S}}) &= I_{\mathsf{S}} \\
\mathscr{L}_{der\text{-}der}(I_{\mathsf{v}}) &= I_{\mathsf{v}}
\end{aligned}
$$

Table 2: The $\mathscr{L}_{der\text{-}der}$ lexicon

pret D^{V}_{then}: $\mathsf{S} \multimap (\mathsf{v}_A \multimap \mathsf{S}) \multimap \mathsf{T}$ into $\Sigma_{der\theta}$. For this reason, we introduce in $\Sigma_{der\theta}$ the following constant: $Ⓢ_2 : \mathsf{S} \multimap \mathsf{S} \multimap \mathsf{S}$ that allows for combining two sentences with a period. Now, it is possible to translate D^{V}_{then} into $\Sigma_{der\theta}$ as follows: $\mathscr{L}_{der\text{-}der}(D^{\mathsf{V}}_{then}) = \lambda^o S_1\, S_2. Ⓢ_2\; S_1 (S_2\, C^{\mathsf{V}}_{then})$. It means that D^{V}_{then} is interpreted as performing both the operation of combining two sentences with a period and the adjunction of *ensuite* on the v node of the second sentence.

G-Derived Trees as Interpretation of G-Derivation Trees As soon as g-derivation trees as term built on $\Sigma_{g\text{-}der\theta}$ are interpreted as term built on $\Sigma_{der\theta}$, we can map them to derived trees. Thus, by composing the two lexicons $\mathscr{L}_{der\text{-}der}$ and $\mathscr{L}_{d\text{-}ed\ trees}$ we can get directly from G-TAG into derived trees

5.3 From G-TAG to Montague Style Semantics Using ACGs

(Pogodalla, 2009) defines a signature Σ_{Log} and a lexicon $\mathscr{L}_{Log}$ from $\Sigma_{der\theta}$ to Σ_{Log}. The entries in Σ_{Log} have Montague like semantics. The lexicon translates a derivation tree into a corresponding formula. We will use the same kind of semantic language for conceptual representations. In other words, our language will produce the formulas that are used in the conceptual representation of G-TAG, while we will stick to the Montague style translations from syntax to semantics.

So, we define a signature Σ_{conrep} of conceptual representation that is similar to the one of (Pogodalla, 2009). Σ_{conrep} defines two atomic types e and t and constants such as: **j**, **m** ... of type e, the constant **REWARD** of type $e \multimap e \multimap t$, the constant **CLAIM** of type $e \multimap t \multimap t$ and the constant **SEEM** of type $t \multimap t$. Moreover, we have constants **SUCC**, **GOAL** of type $t \multimap t \multimap t$.

We are able to translate $\Sigma_{g\text{-}der\theta}$ into Σ_{conrep} with the help of the lexicon $\mathscr{L}_{der\text{-}con}$. The lexicon $\mathscr{L}_{der\text{-}con}$ is extension of the lexicon defined in (Pogodalla, 2009), because we are adding to the domain (i.e. abstract language) the constants that are not in the $\Sigma_{der\theta}$.

$$
\begin{aligned}
\mathscr{L}_{der\text{-}con}(\mathsf{S}) &= \mathscr{L}_{der\text{-}con}(\mathsf{T}) = t \\
\mathscr{L}_{der\text{-}con}(\mathsf{v}_A) &= (e \rightarrow t) \multimap (e \rightarrow t) \\
\mathscr{L}_{der\text{-}con}(\mathsf{S}_A) &= t \multimap t \\
\mathscr{L}_{der\text{-}con}(\mathsf{np}) &= (e \rightarrow t) \multimap t \\
\mathscr{L}_{der\text{-}con}(D_{jean}) &= \lambda^o P.P(\mathbf{j}) \\
\mathscr{L}_{der\text{-}con}(D^{ST}_{then}) &= \mathscr{L}_{der\text{-}con}(D^{SS}_{then}) \\
&= \mathscr{L}_{der\text{-}con}(D^{ST}_{then}) \\
&= \mathscr{L}_{der\text{-}con}(D^{TS}_{then}) \\
&= \mathscr{L}_{der\text{-}con}(D^{TT}_{then}) \\
&= \lambda s_2 s_1 . \mathbf{SUCC}\; s_2\; s_1 \\
\mathscr{L}_{der\text{-}con}(D^{ST}_{bef.}) &= \mathscr{L}_{der\text{-}con}(D^{SS}_{bef.}) \\
&= \mathscr{L}_{der\text{-}con}(D^{ST}_{bef.}) \\
&= \mathscr{L}_{der\text{-}con}(D^{TS}_{bef.}) \\
&= \mathscr{L}_{der\text{-}con}(D^{TT}_{bef.}) \\
&= \lambda^o\, s_1 s_2 .\, \mathbf{SUCC}\; s_2\; s_1 \\
\mathscr{L}_{der\text{-}con}(D_{rewards}) &= \lambda^o s\; a\; O\; S.s(S(a(\lambda^o x.O(\lambda^o y. \\
&\qquad (\mathbf{REWARD}\; x\; y))))
\end{aligned}
$$

Note that the interpretation of np is $[\![\mathsf{np}]\!] = (e \rightarrow t) \multimap t$, using a non-linear implication (but almost linear). Typically, the sharing of the subject by the two clauses related by *pour* or *avant de* induces non linearity.

The Sinf, Sh, and Sws types all are interpreted as $[\![\mathsf{np}]\!] \multimap [\![\mathsf{S}]\!] = ((e \rightarrow t) \multimap t) \multimap t$ as they denote clauses lacking a subject. Then we translate the constants D_{pour}, $D_{\text{après}}$, and D_{avant} in the following way:

$$
\begin{aligned}
&\mathscr{L}_{der\text{-}con}(D_{pour}) = \\
&\quad \lambda^o s_1 . \lambda^o s_2 . \lambda^o N.N(\lambda x.(\mathbf{GOAL}(s_1(\lambda P.P\; x)) \\
&\qquad\qquad (s_2(\lambda P.P\; x))))
\end{aligned}
$$

$$
\begin{aligned}
&\mathscr{L}_{der\text{-}con}(D_{apres}) = \\
&\quad \lambda^o s_1 . \lambda^o s_2 . \lambda^o N.N(\lambda x.(\mathbf{SUCC}(s_1(\lambda P.P\; x)) \\
&\qquad\qquad (s_2(\lambda P.P\; x))))
\end{aligned}
$$

lar case, we could use a second-order—and polynomial—encoding of multi-component TAG into ACG.

$$\mathscr{L}_{\textit{der-con}}(D_{\textsf{avant}}) = \lambda^{o} s_1.\lambda^{o} s_2.\lambda^{o} N.N(\lambda x.(\mathbf{SUCC}(s_2(\lambda P.P\ x))(s_1(\lambda P.P\ x))))$$

5.4 The G-TAG Process as a Morphism Composition

We exemplify the whole process using the term $T_0 = \mathbf{SUCC}(\mathbf{VAC}(\mathbf{jean}), \mathbf{REWARD}(\mathbf{marie}, \mathbf{jean}))$ of type t.[11] The terms representing the g-derivation trees that generate this conceptual representation are the antecedents of T_o by $\mathscr{L}^{-1}_{\textit{der-con}}$: $\mathscr{L}^{-1}_{\textit{der-con}}(T_0) = \{t_1, \dots, t_8\}$ that all are of type T. They are given in Figure 7. Each of these retrieved terms $t_1, \dots, t_8$ are then mapped to terms representing TAG derivation trees, i.e. built on $\Sigma_{der\theta}$ via the lexicon $\mathscr{L}_{\textit{der-der}}$. They can be can in turn be interpreted as syntactic derived trees via the lexicon $\mathscr{L}_{\textit{d-ed trees}}$, and the latter can be interpreted as strings using the lexicon $\mathscr{L}_{\textit{yield}}$. So from T_0 we can have eight surface forms: $\mathscr{L}_{\textit{yield}}(\mathscr{L}_{\textit{d-ed trees}}(\mathscr{L}_{\textit{der-der}}(t_i))), i \in [1, 8]$. Let us show this process on the example of t_5[12]. It illustrates the generation of the example (3).[13]

(3) *Jean* *a passé l'aspirateur.* *Marie*
John vacuumed. Mary
a récompensé *ensuite* *Jean.*
rewarded afterwards John.

$$\mathscr{L}_{\textit{der-der}}(t_5) = \text{Ⓢ}_2\ (C_{\textsf{vac}} I_{\mathsf{S}} I_{\mathsf{V}} C_{\textsf{jean}})(C_{\textsf{reward}} I_{\mathsf{S}} C^{\mathsf{V}}_{\textsf{then}} C_{\textsf{marie}} C_{\textsf{jean}})$$

$$\mathscr{L}_{\textit{d-ed trees}}(\mathscr{L}_{\textit{der-der}}(t_5) = \mathsf{S}_3\ (\mathsf{S}_2\ (\mathsf{np}_1\ \textit{Jean})(\mathsf{v}_1\ \textit{a passé l'aspirateur}))$$

$$.$$

$$(\mathsf{S}_3(\mathsf{np}_1\ \textit{Marie})(\mathsf{v}_2\ (\mathsf{v}_1\ \textit{a récompensé})\ \textit{ensuite})(\mathsf{np}_1\ \textit{Jean}))$$

And the surface forms is given by composing the interpretations:

$$\mathscr{L}_{\textit{yield}}(\mathscr{L}_{\textit{d-ed trees}}(\mathscr{L}_{\textit{der-der}}(t_5)) = \textit{Jean} + \textit{a passé} + \textit{l'aspirateur} + . + \textit{Marie} + \textit{a recompensé} + \textit{ensuite} + \textit{Jean}$$

[11]The associated conceptual input is a simplified version of the conceptual input of Equation 1 without the `GOAL` concept and a replacement of the `NAP` one by the `REWARDING` one.

[12]t_5 is such that $\mathscr{L}_{\textit{der-der}}(t_5) = \gamma_5$ and the term γ_5 was used as example at Section 5.1.

[13]For sake of simplicity we assume the adverb adjoins on the whole auxiliary+verb phrase rather than only on the auxiliary as it would be in French.

$$
\begin{aligned}
t_1 &= D^{SS}_{\textsf{then}}(D_{\textsf{vac}} I_{\mathsf{S}} I_{\mathsf{V}} D_{\textsf{jean}})(D_{\textsf{reward}} I_{\mathsf{S}} I_{\mathsf{V}} D_{\textsf{marie}} D_{\textsf{jean}})\\
t_2 &= D^{SS}_{\textsf{then}}(D_{\textsf{vac}} I_{\mathsf{S}} I_{\mathsf{V}} D_{\textsf{jean}})(D^{\text{passive}}_{\textsf{reward}} I_{\mathsf{S}} I_{\mathsf{V}} D_{\textsf{marie}} D_{\textsf{jean}})\\
t_3 &= D^{SS}_{\textsf{bef.}}(D_{\textsf{reward}} I_{\mathsf{S}} I_{\mathsf{V}} D_{\textsf{marie}} D_{\textsf{jean}})(D_{\textsf{vac}} I_{\mathsf{S}} I_{\mathsf{V}} D_{\textsf{jean}})\\
t_4 &= D^{SS}_{\textsf{bef.}}(D^{\text{passive}}_{\textsf{reward}} I_{\mathsf{S}} I_{\mathsf{V}} D_{\textsf{jean}} D_{\textsf{marie}})(D_{\textsf{vac}} I_{\mathsf{S}} I_{\mathsf{V}} D_{\textsf{jean}})\\
t_5 &= D^{\mathsf{V}}_{\textsf{then}}(D_{\textsf{vac}} I_{\mathsf{S}} I_{\mathsf{V}} D_{\textsf{jean}})(\lambda^{o} a.D_{\textsf{reward}}\ I_{\mathsf{S}}\ a\ D_{\textsf{marie}} D_{\textsf{jean}})\\
t_6 &= D^{\mathsf{V}}_{\textsf{then}}(D_{\textsf{vac}} I_{\mathsf{S}} I_{\mathsf{V}} D_{\textsf{jean}})(D^{\text{passive}}_{\textsf{reward}} I_{\mathsf{S}} I_{\mathsf{V}} D_{\textsf{jean}} D_{\textsf{marie}})\\
t_7 &= D_{\textsf{after}}(D^{\text{sws}}_{\textsf{vac}} I_{\mathsf{S}} I_{\mathsf{V}})(D_{\textsf{receive-rew.}} I_{\mathsf{S}} I_{\mathsf{V}} D_{\textsf{jean}}) D_{\textsf{marie}}\\
t_8 &= D_{\textsf{bef.}}(D^{\text{sws}}_{\textsf{vac}} I_{\mathsf{S}} I_{\mathsf{V}})(D_{\textsf{receive-rew.}} I_{\mathsf{S}} I_{\mathsf{V}} D_{\textsf{jean}}) D_{\textsf{marie}}
\end{aligned}
$$

Figure 7: Antecedents of T_0 by $\mathscr{L}_{\textit{der-con}}$

6 Related Work

We can only quickly mention two related pieces of work. On the one hand, (Gardent and Perez-Beltrachini, 2010) also takes advantage of the formal properties underlying the tree language of derivation trees to propose a generation process using TAG grammars. On the other hand, (Nakatsu and White, 2010) also includes discourse relations in the grammar with *Discourse Combinatory Categorial Grammar* and a type-theoretical framework to provide a text (rather than sentence) generation process.

7 Conclusion

This paper shows how G-TAG can be encoded as ACG. It relies on the fact that both G-TAG and the encoding of TAG within ACG make the derivation tree a primary notion. Then we can benefit from the polynomial reversibility of the ACG framework. It also offers a generalization of the process to all kinds of adjunctions, including the predicative ones. It also offers a new insight on discourse grammars for the adverbial connective encoding (Danlos, 2011). Note that contrary to an important part of G-TAG that offers a way (based on a semantic and a linguistic analysis) to rank the different realizations of a conceptual representation, we do not deal here with such preferences. As syntactic ambiguity treatment is not usually part of the syntactic formalism, we prefer the "realization ambiguity" treatment not to be part of the generation formalism. Finally, a crucial perspective is to integrate a theory of generation of referring expressions relying on type-theoretical approaches to dynamics semantics (de Groote, 2006; de Groote and Lebedeva, 2010) that would ensure a large compatibility with the ACG framework.

References

[Abeillé2002] Anne Abeillé. 2002. *Une grammaire électronique du français*. Sciences du langage. CNRS Éditions.

[Danlos et al.2001] Laurence Danlos, Bertrand Gaiffe, and Laurent Roussarie. 2001. Document sructuring à la SDRT. In Helmut Horacek, Nicolas Nicolov, and Leo Wanner, editors, *Proceedings of the ACL 2001 Eighth European Workshop on Natural Language Generation (EWNLG)*. http://aclweb.org/anthology/W/W01/W01-0803.pdf.

[Danlos et al.2011] Laurence Danlos, Frédéric Meunier, and Vanessa Combet. 2011. EasyText: an operational NLG system. In *ENLG 2011, 13th European Workshop on Natural Language Generation*, September. http://hal.inria.fr/inria-00614760/en/.

[Danlos1998] Laurence Danlos. 1998. G-TAG : Un formalisme lexicalisé pour la génération de textes inspiré de TAG. *Traitement Automatique des Langues*, 39(2). http://hal.inria.fr/inria-00098489.

[Danlos2000] Laurence Danlos. 2000. G-TAG: A lexicalized formalism for text generation inspired by tree adjoining grammar. In Anne Abeillé and Owen Rambow, editors, *Tree Adjoining Grammars: Formalisms, Linguistic Analysis, and Processing*, pages 343–370. CSLI Publications.

[Danlos2011] Laurence Danlos. 2011. D-STAG: a formalism for discourse analysis based on SDRT and using synchronous TAG. In Philippe de Groote, Markus Egg, and Laura Kallmeyer, editors, *14th conference on Formal Grammar - FG 2009*, volume 5591 of *LNCS/LNAI*, pages 64–84. Springer. http://dx.doi.org/10.1007/978-3-642-20169-1_5.

[de Groote and Lebedeva2010] Philippe de Groote and Ekaterina Lebedeva. 2010. Presupposition accommodation as exception handling. In *Proceedings of the SIGDIAL 2010 Conference*, pages 71–74, Tokyo, Japan, September. Association for Computational Linguistics. http://www.aclweb.org/anthology/W/W10/W10-4313.

[de Groote and Pogodalla2004] Philippe de Groote and Sylvain Pogodalla. 2004. On the expressive power of Abstract Categorial Grammars: Representing context-free formalisms. *Journal of Logic, Language and Information*, 13(4):421–438. http://hal.inria.fr/inria-00112956.

[de Groote2001] Philippe de Groote. 2001. Towards Abstract Categorial Grammars. In *Association for Computational Linguistics, 39th Annual Meeting and 10th Conference of the European Chapter, Proceedings of the Conference*, pages 148–155. http://aclweb.org/anthology/P/P01/P01-1033.pdf.

[de Groote2006] Philippe de Groote. 2006. Towards a montagovian account of dynamics. In Masayuki Gibson and Jonathan Howell, editors, *Proceedings of Semantics and Linguistic Theory (SALT) 16*. http://elanguage.net/journals/index.php/salt/article/view/16.1/1791.

[Gardent and Perez-Beltrachini2010] Claire Gardent and Laura Perez-Beltrachini. 2010. RTG based surface realisation for TAG. In *Proceedings of the 23rd International Conference on Computational Linguistics (COLING 2010)*, pages 367–375, Beijing, China, August. Coling 2010 Organizing Committee. http://www.aclweb.org/anthology/C10-1042.

[Joshi and Schabes1997] Aravind K. Joshi and Yves Schabes. 1997. Tree-adjoining grammars. In G. Rozenberg and A. Salomaa, editors, *Handbook of formal languages*, volume 3, chapter 2. Springer.

[Joshi et al.1975] Aravind K. Joshi, Leon S. Levy, and Masako Takahashi. 1975. Tree adjunct grammars. *Journal of Computer and System Sciences*, 10(1):136–163.

[Kallmeyer and Romero2004] Laura Kallmeyer and Maribel Romero. 2004. LTAG semantics with semantic unification. In *Proceedings of TAG+7*, pages 155–162.

[Kallmeyer and Romero2007] Laura Kallmeyer and Maribel Romero. 2007. Scope and situation binding for LTAG. *Research on Language and Computation*, 6(1):3–52. http://dx.doi.org/10.1007/s11168-008-9046-6.

[Kanazawa2007] Makoto Kanazawa. 2007. Parsing and generation as datalog queries. In *Proceedings of the 45th Annual Meeting of the Association of Computational Linguistics (ACL)*, pages 176–183. http://www.aclweb.org/anthology/P/P07/P07-1023.

[Kanazawa2011] Makoto Kanazawa, 2011. *Parsing and generation as Datalog query evaluation*. Under review. http://research.nii.ac.jp/~kanazawa/publications/pagadqe.pdf.

[Meunier1997] Frédéric Meunier. 1997. *Implantation du formalisme de génération G-TAG*. Ph.D. thesis, Université Paris 7 — Denis Diderot.

[Nakatsu and White2010] Crytal Nakatsu and Michael White. 2010. Generating with discourse combinatory categorial grammar. *Linguistic Issues in Language Technology*, 4(1). http://elanguage.net/journals/index.php/lilt/article/view/1277/871.

[Nesson and Shieber2006] Rebecca Nesson and Stuart M. Shieber. 2006. Simpler TAG semantics through synchronization. In *Proceedings of the 11th Conference on Formal Grammar*, Malaga, Spain, 29–30 July. CSLI Publications.

http://cslipublications.stanford.edu/FG/2006/nesson.pdf.

[Pogodalla2004] Sylvain Pogodalla. 2004. Computing Semantic Representation: Towards ACG Abstract Terms as Derivation Trees. In *Proceedings of TAG+7*, pages 64–71. http://hal.inria.fr/inria-00107768.

[Pogodalla2009] Sylvain Pogodalla. 2009. Advances in Abstract Categorial Grammars: Language Theory and Linguistic Modeling. ESSLLI 2009 Lecture Notes, Part II. http://hal.inria.fr/hal-00749297.

[Schabes and Shieber1994] Yves Schabes and Stuart M. Shieber. 1994. An alternative conception of tree-adjoining derivation. *Computational Linguistics*, 20(1):91–124. http://aclweb.org/anthology/J/J94/J94-1004.pdf.

[Storoshenk and Frank2012] Dennis Ryan Storoshenk and Robert Frank. 2012. Deriving syntax-semantics mappings: node linking, type shifting and scope ambiguity. In *Proceedings of TAG+11*, pages 10–18.

[Webber2004] Bonnie Webber. 2004. D-LTAG: Extending :exicalized TAG to discourse. *Cognitive Science*, 28:751–779. http://dx.doi.org/0.1207/s15516709cog2805_6.

A Template-based Abstractive Meeting Summarization: Leveraging Summary and Source Text Relationships

Tatsuro Oya, Yashar Mehdad, Giuseppe Carenini, Raymond Ng
Department of Computer Science
University of British Columbia, Vancouver, Canada
{toya, mehdad, carenini, rng}@cs.ubc.ca

Abstract

In this paper, we present an automatic abstractive summarization system of meeting conversations. Our system extends a novel multi-sentence fusion algorithm in order to generate abstract templates. It also leverages the relationship between summaries and their source meeting transcripts to select the best templates for generating abstractive summaries of meetings. Our manual and automatic evaluation results demonstrate the success of our system in achieving higher scores both in readability and informativeness.

1. Introduction

People spend a vast amount of time in meetings and these meetings play a prominent role in their lives. Consequently, study of automatic meeting summarization has been attracting peoples' attention as it can save a great deal of their time and increase their productivity.

The most common approaches to automatic meeting summarization have been extractive. Since extractive approaches do not require natural language generation techniques, they are arguably simpler to apply and have been extensively investigated. However, a user study conducted by Murray *et al.* (2010) indicates that users prefer abstractive summaries to extractive ones. Thereafter, more attention has been paid to abstractive meeting summarization systems (Mehdad *et al.* 2013; Murray *et al.* 2010; Wang and Cardie 2013). However, the approaches introduced in previous studies create summaries by either heavily relying on annotated data or by fusing human utterances which may contain grammatical mistakes. In this paper, we address these issues by introducing a novel summarization approach that can create readable summaries with less need for annotated data. Our system first acquires templates from human-authored summaries using a clustering and multi-sentence fusion algorithm. It then takes a meeting transcript to be summarized, segments the transcript based on topics, and extracts important phrases from it. Finally, our system selects templates by referring to the relationship between human-authored summaries and their sources and fills the templates with the phrases to create summaries.

The main contributions of this paper are: 1) The successful adaptation of a word graph algorithm to generate templates from human-authored summaries; 2) The implementation of a novel template selection algorithm that effectively leverages the relationship between human-authored summary sentences and their source transcripts; and 3) A comprehensive testing of our approach, comprising both automatic and manual evaluations.

We instantiate our framework on the AMI corpus (Carletta *et al.,* 2005) and compare our summaries with those created from a state-of-the-art systems. The evaluation results demonstrate that our system successfully creates informative and readable summaries.

2. Related Work

Several studies have been conducted on creating automatic abstractive meeting summarization systems. One of them includes the system proposed by Mehdad *et al.*, (2013). Their approach first clusters human utterances into communities (Murray *et al.*, 2012) and then builds an entailment graph over each of the latter in order to select the salient utterances. It then applies a semantic word graph algorithm to them and creates abstractive summaries. Their results show some improvement in creating informative summaries.

Proceedings of the 8th International Natural Language Generation Conference, pages 45–53,
Philadelphia, Pennsylvania, 19-21 June 2014.

However, since they create these summaries by merging human utterances, their summaries are still partially extractive.

Recently, there have been some studies on creating abstract summaries of specific aspects of meetings such as decisions, actions and problems (Murray *et al.* 2010; Wang and Cardie, 2013). These summaries are called the *Focused Meeting Summaries* (Carenini *et al.*, 2011).

The system introduced by Murray *et al.* first classifies human utterances into specific aspects of meetings, e.g. decisions, problem, and action, and then maps them onto ontologies. It then selects the most informative subsets from these ontologies and finally generates abstractive summaries of them, utilizing a natural language generation tool, simpleNLG (Gatt and Reiter, 2009). Although their approach is essentially focused meeting summarization, after creating summaries of specific aspects, they aggregate them into one single summary covering the whole meeting.

Wang and Cardie introduced a template-based focused abstractive meeting summarization system. Their system first clusters human-authored summary sentences and applies a Multiple-Sequence Alignment algorithm to them to generate templates. Then, given a meeting transcript to be summarized, it identifies a human utterance cluster describing a specific aspect and extracts all summary-worthy relation instances, i.e. indicator-argument pairs, from it. Finally, the templates are filled with these relation instances and ranked accordingly, to generate summaries of a specific aspect of the meeting.

Although the two approaches above are both successful in creating readable summaries, they rely on much annotated information, such as dialog act and sentiment types, and also require the accurate classification of human utterances that contain much noise and much ill-structured grammar.

Our approach is inspired by the works introduced here but improves on their shortcomings. Unlike those of Murray *et al.* (2010) and Wang and Cardie (2013), our system relies less on annotated training data and does not require a classifier. In addition, our evaluation indicates that our system can create summaries of the entire conversations that are more informative and readable than those of Mehdad *et al.*(2013).

3. Framework

In order for summaries to be readable and informative, they should be grammatically correct and contain important information in meetings. To this end, we have created our framework consisting of the following two components: 1) An off-line template generation module, which generalizes collected human-authored summaries and creates templates from them; and 2) An on-line summary generation module, which segments meeting transcripts based on the topics discussed, extracts the important phrases from these segments, and generate abstractive summaries of them by filling the phrases into the appropriate templates. Figure 1 depicts our framework. In the following sections, we describe each of the two components in detail.

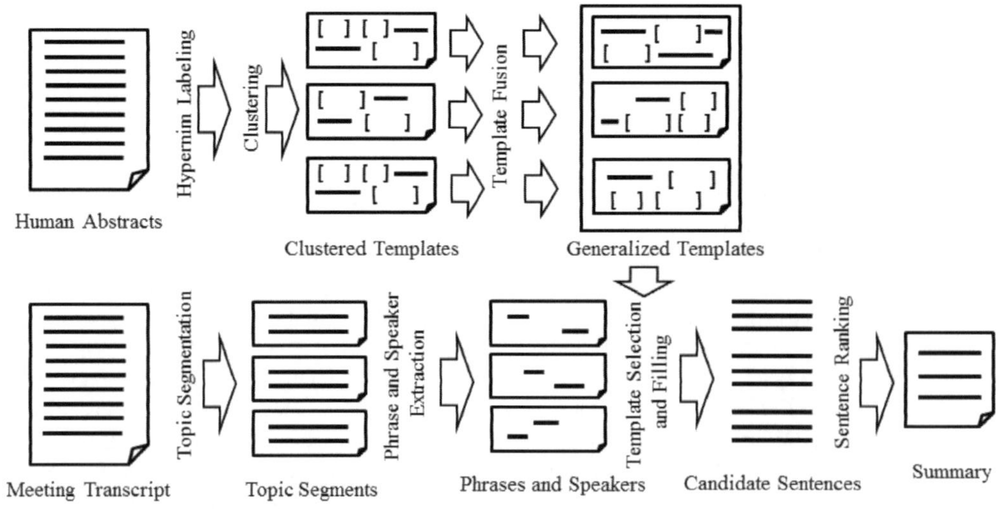

Figure 1: Our meeting summarization framework. Top: off-line Template generation module. Bottom: on-line Summary Generation module.

3.1 Template Generation Module

Our template generation module attempts to satisfy two possibly conflicting objectives. First, templates should be quite specific such that they accept only the relevant fillers. Second, our module should generate generalized templates that can be used in many situations. We assume that the former is achieved by labeling phrases with their hypernyms that are not too general and the latter by merging related templates. Based on these assumptions, we divide our module into the three tasks: 1) Hypernym labeling; 2) Clustering; and 3) Template fusion.

3.1.1 Hypernym Labeling

Templates are derived from human-authored meeting summaries in the training data. We first collect sentences whose subjects are meeting participant(s) and that contain active root verbs, from the summaries. This is achieved by utilizing meeting participant information provided in the corpus and parsing sentences with the Stanford Parser (Marneffe *et al.,* 2006). The motivation behind this process is to collect sentences that are syntactically similar. We then identify all noun phrases in these sentences using the Illinois Chunker (Punyakanok and Roth, 2001). This chunker extracts all noun phrases as well as part of speech (POS) for all words. To add further information on each noun phrase, we label the right most nouns (the head nouns) in each phrase with their hypernyms using WordNet (Fellbaum, 1998). In WordNet, hypernyms are organized into hierarchies ranging from the most abstract to the most specific. For our work, we utilize the fourth most abstract hypernyms in light of the first goal discussed at the beginning of Section 3.1, i.e. not too general. For disambiguating the sense of the nouns, we simply select the sense that has the highest frequency in WordNet.

At this stage, all noun phrases in sentences are tagged with their hypernyms defined in WordNet, such as "artifact.n.01", and "act.n.02", where n's stands for nouns and the two digit numbers represent their sense numbers. We treat these hypernym-labeled sentences as templates and the phrases as blanks.

In addition, we also create two additional rules for tagging noun phrases: 1) Since the subjects of all collected sentences are meeting participant(s), we label all subject noun phrases as "speaker"; and 2) If the noun phrases consist of meeting specific terms such as "the meeting" or "the group", we do not convert them into blanks. These two rules guarantee the creation of templates suitable for meetings.

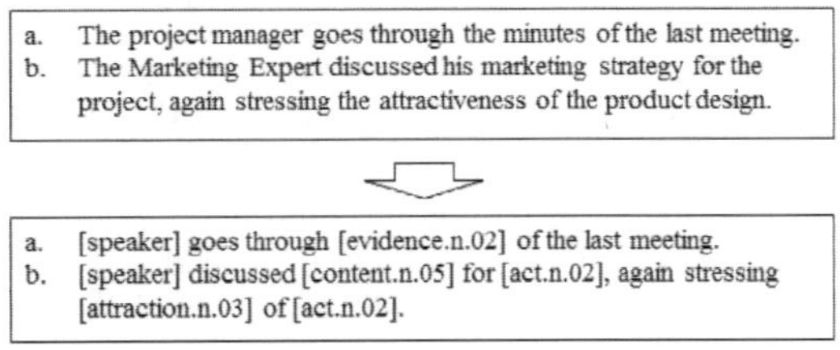

Figure 2: Some examples of hypernym labeling task

3.1.2 Clustering

Next, we cluster the templates into similar groups. We utilize root verb information for this process assuming that these verbs such as "discuss" and "suggest" that appear in summaries are the most informative factors in describing meetings. Therefore, after extracting root verbs in summary sentences, we create fully connected graphs where each node represents the root verbs and each edge represents a score denoting how similar the two word senses are. To measure the similarity of two verbs, we first identify the verb senses based on their frequency in WordNet and compute the similarity score based on the shortest path that connects the senses in the hypernym taxonomy. We then convert the graph into a similarity matrix and apply a Normalized Cuts method (Shi and Malik, 2000) to cluster the root verbs. Finally, all templates are organized into the groups created by their root verbs.

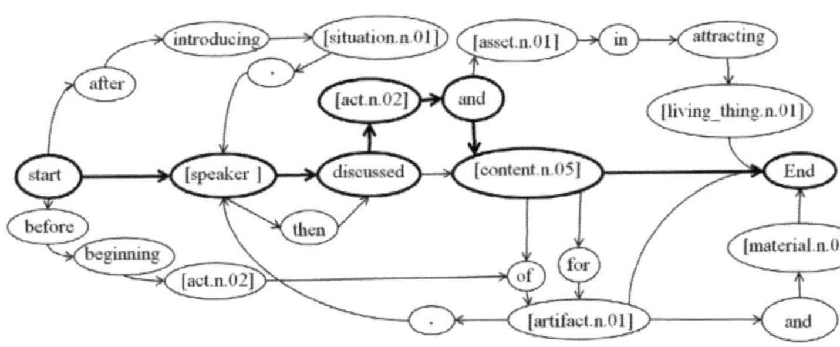

Figure 3: A word graph generated from related templates and the highest scored path (shown in bold)

3.1.3 Template Fusion

We further generalize the clustered templates by applying a word graph algorithm. The algorithm was originally proven to be effective in summarizing a cluster of related sentences (Boudin and Morin, 2013; Filippova, 2010; Mehdad *et al.*, 2013). We extend it so that it can be applied to templates.

Word Graph Construction

In our system, a word graph is a directed graph with words or blanks serving as nodes and edges representing adjacency relations.

Given a set of related templates in a group, the graph is constructed by first creating a start and end node, and then iteratively adding templates to it. When adding a new template, the algorithm first checks each word in the template to see if it can be mapped onto existing nodes in the graph. The word is mapped onto a node if the node consists of the same word and the same POS tag, and no word from this template has been mapped onto this node yet. Then, it checks each blank in the template and maps it onto a node if the node consists of the same hypernym-labeled blank and no blank from this template has been mapped onto this node yet.

When more than one node refer to the same word or blank in the template, or when more than one word or blank in the template can be mapped to the same node in the graph, the algorithm checks the neighboring nodes in the current graph as well as the preceding and the subsequent words or blanks in the template. Then, those word-node or blank-node pairs with higher overlap in the context are selected for mapping. Otherwise, a new node is created and added to the graph. As a simplified illustration, we show a word graph in Figure 3 obtained from the following four templates.

- After introducing [situation.n.01], [speaker] then discussed [content.n.05] .
- Before beginning [act.n.02] of [artifact.n.01], [speaker] discussed [act.n.02] and [content.n.05] for [artifact.n.01] .
- [speaker] discussed [content.n.05] of [artifact.n.01] and [material.n.01] .
- [speaker] discussed [act.n.02] and [asset.n.01] in attracting [living_thing.n.01] .

Path Selection

The word graph generates many paths connecting its start and end nodes, not all of which are readable and cannot be used as templates. Our aim is to create concise and generalized templates. Therefore, we create the following ranking strategy to be able to select the ideal paths. First, to filter ungrammatical or complex templates, the algorithm prunes away the paths having more than three blanks; having subordinate clauses; containing no verb; having two consecutive blanks; containing blanks which are not labeled by any hypernym; or whose length are shorter than three words. Note that these rules, which were defined based on close observation of the results obtained from our development set, greatly reduce the chance of selecting ill-structured templates. Second, the remaining paths are reranked by 1) A normalized path weight and 2) A language model learned from hypernym-labeled human-authored summaries in our training data, each of which is described below.

1) Normalized Path Weight

We adapt Filippova (2010)'s approach to compute the edge weight. The formula is shown as:

$$w(e_{i,j}) = \frac{\frac{\mathrm{freq(i)} + \mathrm{freq(j)}}{\sum_{p \in P} \mathrm{diff}(p,i,j)^{-1}}}{\mathrm{freq(i)} \times \mathrm{freq(j)}}$$

where $e_{i,j}$ is an edge that connects the nodes i and j in a graph, *freq(i)* is the number of words and blanks in the templates that are mapped to node i and *diff(p,i,j)* is the distance between the offset positions of nodes i and j in path p. This weight is defined so that the paths that are informative and that contain salient (frequent) words are selected. To calculate a path score, *W(p)*, all the edge weights on the path are summed and normalized by its length.

2) Language Model

Although the goal is to create concise templates, these templates must be grammatically correct. Hence, we train an n-gram language model using all templates generated from the training data in the hypernym labeling stage. Then for each path, we compute a sum of negative log probabilities of n-gram occurrences and normalize the score by its length, which is represented as *H(p)*.

The final score of each path is calculated as follows:

$$\mathrm{Score(p)} = \alpha \times \mathrm{W(p)} + \beta \times \mathrm{H(p)}$$

where α and β are the coefficient factors which are tuned using our development set. For each group of clusters, the top ten best scored paths are selected as templates and added to its group.

As an illustration, the path shown in bold in Figure 3 is the highest scored path obtained from this path ranking strategy.

3.2 Summary Generation Module

This section explains our summary generation module consisting of four tasks: 1) Topic segmentation; 2) Phrase and speaker extraction; 3) Template selection and filling; and 4) Sentence ranking.

3.2.1 Topic Segmentation

It is important for a summary to cover all topics discussed in the meeting. Therefore, given a meeting transcript to be summarized, after removing speech disfluencies such as "uh", and "ah", we employ a topic segmenter, LCSeg (Galley *et al.*, 2003) which create topic segments by observing word repetitions.

One shortcoming of LCSeg is that it ignores speaker information when segmenting transcripts. Important topics are often discussed by one or two speakers. Therefore, in order to take advantage of the speaker information, we extend LCSeg by adding the following post-process step: If a topic segment contains more than 25 utterances, we subdivide the segment based on the speakers. These subsegments are then compared with one another using cosine similarity, and if the similarity score is greater than that of the threshold (0.05), they are merged. The two numbers, i.e. 25 and 0.05, were selected based on the development set so that, when segmenting a transcript, the system can effectively take into account speaker information without creating too many segments.

3.2.2 Phrase And Speaker Extraction

All salient phrases are then extracted from each topic segment in the same manner as performed in the template generation module in Section 3.1, by: 1) Extracting all noun phrases; and 2) Labeling each phrase with the hypernym of its head noun. Furthermore, to be able to select salient phrases, these phrases are subsequently scored and ranked based on the sum of the frequency of each word in the segment. Finally, to handle redundancy, we remove phrases that are subsets of others.

In addition, for each utterance in the meeting, the transcript contains its speaker's name. Therefore, we extract the most dominant speakers' name(s) for each topic segment and label them as "speaker". These phrases and this speaker information will later be used in the template filling process. Table 1 below shows an example of dominant speakers and high scored phrases extracted from a topic segment.

Dominant speakers
Project Manager (speaker) Industrial Designer (speaker)
High scored phrases (hypernyms)
the whole look (appearance.n.01) the company logo (symbol.n.01) the product (artifact.n.01) the outside (region.n.01) electronics (content.n.05) the fashion (manner.n.01)

Table 1: Dominant speakers and high scored phrases extracted from a topic segment

3.2.3 Template Selection and Filling

In terms of our training data, all human-authored abstractive summary sentences have links to the subsets of their source transcripts which support and convey the information in the abstractive sentences as illustrated in Figure 4. These subsets are called communities. Since each community is used to create one summary sentence, we hypothesize that each community covers one specific topic.

Thus, to find the best templates for each topic segment, we refer to our training data. In particular, we first find communities in the training set that are similar to the topic segment and identify the templates derived from the summary sentences linked to these communities.

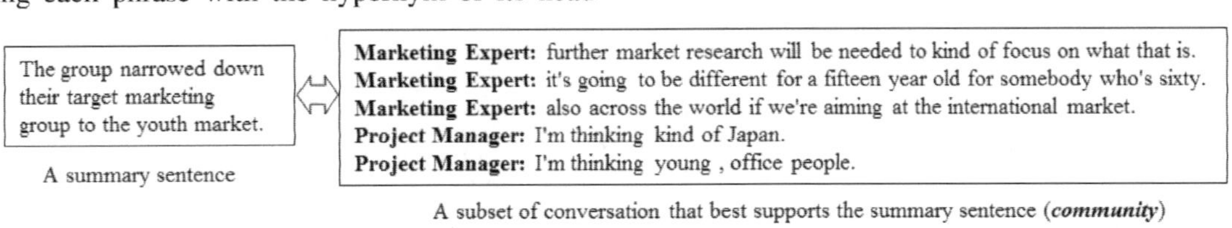

Figure 4: A link from an abstractive summary sentence to a subset of a meeting transcript that conveys or supports the information in the abstractive sentence

This process is done in two steps, by: 1) Associating the communities in the training data with the groups containing templates that were created in our template generation module; and 2) Finding templates for each topic segment by comparing the similarities between the segments and all sets of communities associated with the template groups. Below, we describe the two steps in detail.

1) Recall that in the template generation module in Section 3.1, we label human-authored summary sentences in training data with hypernyms and cluster them into similar groups. Thus, as shown in Figure 5, we first associate all sets of communities in the training data into these groups by determining to which groups the summary sentences linked by these communities belong.

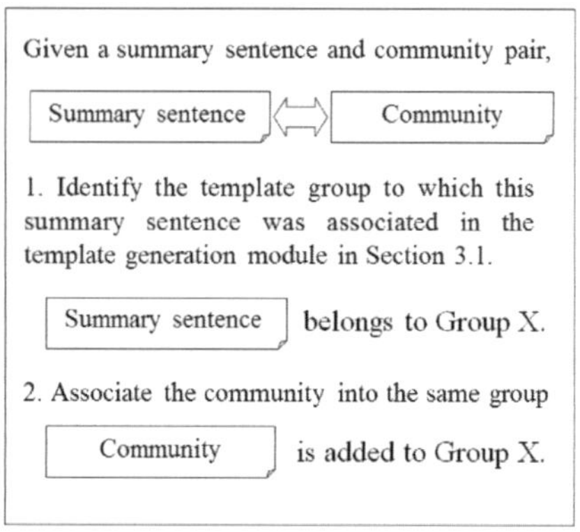

Figure 5: An example demonstrating how each community in training data is associated with a group containing templates

2) Next, for each topic segment, we compute average cosine similarity between the segment and all communities in all of the groups.

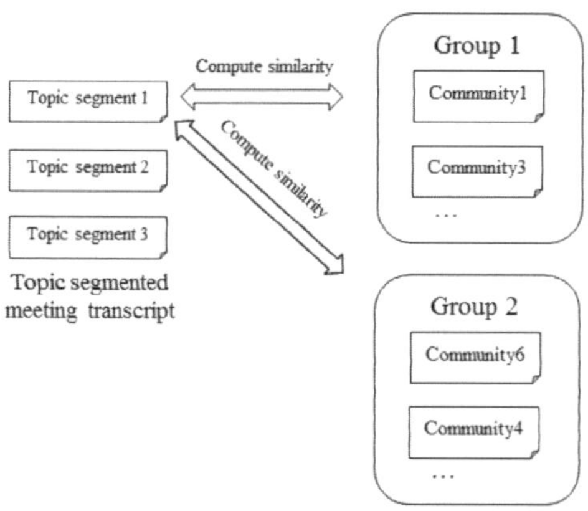

Figure 6: Computing the average cosine similarities between a topic segment and all sets of com munities in each group

At this stage, each community is already associated with a group that contains ranked templates. In addition, each segment has a list of average-scores that measures how similar the segment is to the communities in each group. Hence, the templates used for each segment are decided by selecting the ones from the groups with higher scores.

Our system now contains for each segment a set of phrases and ideal templates, both of which are scored, as well as the most dominant speakers' name(s). Thus, candidate sentences are generated for each segment by: first, selecting speakers' name(s), then selecting phrases and templates based on their scores; and finally filling the templates with matching labels. Here, we limit the maximum number of sentences created for each topic segment to 30. This number is defined so that the system can avoid generating sentences consisting of low scored phrases and templates. Finally, these candidate sentences are passed to our sentence ranking module.

3.2.4 Sentence Ranking

Our system will create many candidate sentences, and most of them will be redundant. Hence, to be able to select the most fluent, informative and appropriate sentences, we create a sentence ranking model considering 1) Fluency, 2) Coverage, and 3) The characteristics of the meeting, each of which are summarized below:

1) Fluency

We estimate the fluency of the generated sentences in the same manner as in Section 3.1.3. That is, we train a language model on human-authored abstract summaries from the training portions of meeting data and then compute a normalized sum of negative log probabilities of n-gram occurrences in the sentence. The fluency score is represented as *H(s)* in the equation below.

2) Coverage

To select sentences that cover important topics, we give special rewards to the sentences that contain the top five ranked phrases.

3) The Characteristics of the Meeting

We also add three additional scoring rules that are specific to the meeting summaries. In particular, these three rules are created based on phrases often used in the opening and closing of meetings in a development set: 1) If sentences derived from the first segment contain the words "open" or "meeting", they will be rewarded; 2) If sentences derived from the last segment contain the words "close" or "meeting", the sentences will again be rewarded; and 3) If sentences not derived from the first or last segment contains the words "open" or "close", they will be penalized.

The final ranking score of the candidate sentences is computed using the follow formula:

$$\mathrm{Score}(s) = \alpha \mathrm{H}(s) + \sum_{i=1}^{5} \beta_i \mathrm{R}_i(s) + \sum_{i=1}^{3} \gamma_i \mathrm{M}_i(s)$$

where, $R_i\ (s)$ is a binary that indicates whether the top i ranked phrase exists in sentence s; $M_i\ (s)$ is also a binary that indicates whether the i th meeting specific rule can be met for sentence s; and α, β_i and γ_i are the coefficient factors to tune the ranking score, all of which are tuned using our development set.

Finally, the sentence ranked the highest in each segment is selected as the summary sentence, and the entire meeting summary is created by collecting these sentences and sorting them by the chronological order of the topic segments.

4. Evaluation

In this section, we describe an evaluation of our system. First, we describe the corpus data. Next, the results of the automatic and manual evaluations of our system against various baseline approaches are discussed.

4.1 Data

For our meeting summarization experiments, we use manually transcripted meeting records and their human-authored summaries in the AMI corpus. The corpus contains 139 meeting records in which groups of four people play different roles in a fictitious team. We reserved 20 meetings for development and implemented a three-fold cross-validation using the remaining data.

4.2 Automatic Evaluation

We report the F1-measure of ROUGE-1, ROUGE-2 and ROUGE-SU4 (Lin and Hovy, 2003) to assess the performance of our system. The scores of automatically generated summaries are calculated by comparing them with human-authored ones.

For our baselines, we use the system introduced by Mehdad *et al.* (2013) (FUSION), which creates abstractive summaries from extracted sentences and was proven to be effective in creating abstractive meeting summaries; and TextRank (Mihalcea and Tarau, 2004), a graph based sentence ranker that is suitable for creating extractive summaries. Our system can create summaries of any length by adjusting the number of segments to be created by LCSeg. Thus, we create summaries of three different lengths (10, 15, and 20 topic segments) with the average number of words being 100, 137, and 173, respectively. These numbers generally corresponds to human-authored summary length in the corpus which varies from 82 to 200 words.

Table 2 shows the results of our system in comparison with those of the two baselines. The results show that our model significantly outperforms the two baselines. Compared with FUSION, our system with 20 segments achieves about 3 % of improvement in all ROUGE scores. This indicates that our system creates summaries that are more lexically similar to human-authored ones. Surprisingly, there was not a significant change in our ROUGE scores over the three different summary lengths. This indicates that our system can create summaries of any length without losing its content.

Models	*Rouge-1*	*Rouge-2*	*Rouge-SU4*
TextRank	21.7	2.5	6.5
FUSION	27.9	4.0	8.1
Our System 10 Seg.	28.4	6.7	10.1
Our System 15 Seg.	30.6	**6.8**	10.9
Our System 20 Seg.	**31.5**	6.7	**11.4**

Table 2: An evaluation of summarization performance using the F1 measure of ROUGE-1 2, and SU4

4.3 Manual Evaluation

We also conduct manual evaluations utilizing a crowdsourcing tool[1]. In this experiment, our system with 15 segments is compared with FUSION, human-authored summaries (ABS) and, human-annotated extractive summaries (EXT).

After randomly selecting 10 meetings, 10 participants were selected for each meeting and given instructions to browse the transcription of the meeting so as to understand its gist. They were then asked to read all different types of summaries described above and rate each of them on a 1-5 scale for the following three items: 1) The summary's overall quality, with "5" being the best and "1" being the worst possible quality; 2) The summary's fluency, ignoring the capitalization or punctuation, with "5" indicating no grammatical mistakes and "1" indicating too many; and 3) The summary's informativeness, with "5" indicating that the summary covers all meeting content and "1" indicating that the

[1] http://www.crowdflower.com/

summary does not cover the content at all.

The results are described in Table 3. Overall, 58 people worldwide, who are among the most reliable contributors accounting for 7 % of overall members and who maintain the highest levels of accuracy on test questions provided in pervious crowd sourcing jobs, participated in this rating task. As to statistical significance, we use the 2-tail pairwise t-test to compare our system with the other three approaches. The results are summarized in Table 4.

Models	*Quality*	*Fluency*	*Informativeness*
Our System	**3.52**	**3.69**	**3.54**
ABS	3.96	4.03	3.87
EXT	3.02	3.16	3.30
FUSION	3.16	3.14	3.05

Table 3: Average rating scores.

Models Compared	*Quality (P-value)*	*Fluency (P-value)*	*Informativeness (P-value)*
Our System vs. ABS	0.000162	0.000437	0.00211
Our System vs. FUSION	0.00142	0.0000135	0.000151
Our System vs. EXT.	0.000124	0.0000509	0.0621

Table 4: T-test results of manual evaluation

As expected, for all of the three items, ABS received the highest of all ratings, while our system received the second highest. The t-test results indicate that the difference in the rating data is statistically significant for all cases except that of informativeness between ours and the extractive summaries. This can be understood because the extractive summaries were manually created by an annotator and contain all of the important information in the meetings.

From this observation, we can conclude that users prefer our template-based summaries over human-annotated extractive summaries and abstractive summaries created from extracted salient sentences. Furthermore, it demonstrates that our summaries are as informative as human-annotated extractive ones.

Finally, we show in Figure 7 one of the summaries created by our system in line-with a human-authored one.

5. Conclusion and Future Work

In this paper, we have demonstrated a robust abstractive meeting summarization system. Our approach makes three main contributions. First, we have proposed a novel approach for generating templates leveraging a multi-sentence fusion algorithm and lexico-semantic information. Second, we have introduced an effective template selection method, which utilize the relationship between human-authored summaries and their source transcripts. Finally, comprehensive evaluation demonstrated that summaries created by our system are preferred over human-annotated extractive ones as well as those created from a state-of-the-art meeting summarization system.

The current version of our system uses only hypernym information in WordNet to label phrases. Considering limited coverage in WordNet, future work includes extending our framework by applying a more sophisticated labeling task utilizing a richer knowledge base (e.g., YAGO). Also, we plan to apply our framework to different multi-party conversational domains such as chat logs and forum discussions.

Human-Authored Summary
The project manager opened the meeting and had the team members introduce themselves and describe their roles in the upcoming project. The project manager then described the upcoming project. The team then discussed their experiences with remote controls. They also discussed the project budget and which features they would like to see in the remote control they are to create. The team discussed universal usage, how to find remotes when misplaced, shapes and colors, ball shaped remotes, marketing strategies, keyboards on remotes, and remote sizes. team then discussed various features to consider in making the remote.

Summary Created by Our System with 15 Segment
project manager summarized their role of the meeting . user interface expert and project manager talks about a universal remote . the group recommended using the International Remote Control Association rather than a remote control . project manager offered the ball idea .user interface expert suggested few buttons . user interface expert and industrial designer then asked a member about a nice idea for The idea . project manager went over a weak point . the group announced the one-handed design . project manager and industrial designer went over their remote control idea . project manager instructed a member to research the ball function . industrial designer went over stability point .industrial designer went over definite points .

Figure 7: A comparison between a human-authored summary and a summary created by our system

Acknowledgements

We would like to thank all members in UBC NLP group for their comments and UBC LCI group and ICICS for financial support.

References

Florian Boudin and Emmanuel Morin. 2013. Keyphrase Extraction for N-best Reranking in Multi-Sentence Compression. In *Proceedings of the*

2013 Conference of the North American Chapter of the Association for Computational Linguistics: Human Language Technologies (NAACL-HLT 2013), 2013.

Giuseppe Carenini, Gabriel Murray, and Raymond Ng.

2011. Methods for Mining and Summarizing Text Conversations. *Morgan Claypool.*

J. Carletta, S. Ashby, S. Bourban, M. Flynn, M. Guillemot, T. Hain, J. Kadlec, V. Karaiskos, W. Kraaij, M. Kronenthal, G. Lathoud, M. Lincoln, A. Lisowska, I. McCowan, W. Post, D. Reidsma, and P. Wellner. 2005. The AMI meeting corpus: A pre-announcement. In *Proceeding of MLMI 2005*, Edinburgh, UK, pages 28–39.

Christiane Fellbaum 1998. *WordNet, An Electronic Lexical Database.* The MIT Press. Cambridge, MA.

Katja Filippova. 2010. Multi-sentence compression: finding shortest paths in word graphs. In *Proceedings of the 23rd International Conference on Computational Linguistics, COLING '10*, pages 322–330, Stroudsburg, PA, USA. Association for Computational Linguistic

Michel Galley, Kathleen McKeown, Eric Fosler-Lussier and Hongyan Jing. 2003. Discourse segmentation of multi-party conversation. In *Proceedings of the 41st Annual Meeting of the Association for Computational Linguistics (ACL 2003)*. 562–569. Sapporo, Japan.

Albert Gatt and Ehud Reiter. 2009. SimpleNLG: a Realisation Engine for Practical Applications. In *ENLG'09: Proceedings of the 12th European Workshop on Natural Language Generation*, pages 90–93, Morristown, NJ, USA. Association for Computational Linguistics.

Ravi Kondadadi, Blake Howald and Frank Schilder. 2013. A Statistical NLG Framework for Aggregated Planning and Realization. In *Proceeding of the Annual Conferene for the Association of Computational Linguistic (ACL 2013).*

Marie-Catherine de Marneffe, Bill MacCartney and Christopher D. Manning. 2006. Generating Typed Dependency Parses from Phrase Structure Parses. In *Proceedings of the Fifth International Conference on Language Resources and Evaluation (LREC'06).*

Yashar Mehdad, Giuseppe Carenini, Frank Tompa. 2013. Abstractive Meeting Summarization with Entailment and Fusion. In *Proceedings of the 14th European Natural Language Generation (ENLG - SIGGEN 2013)*, Sofia, Bulgaria.

Rata Mihalcea and Paul Tarau 2004. TextRank: Bringing order into texts. In *Proceedings of the 2004 Conference on Empirical Methods in Natural Language Processing*, July.

Gabriel Murray, Giuseppe Carenini, and Raymond T. Ng. 2010. Generating and validating abstracts of meeting conversations: a user study. In *INLG 2010*.

Gabriel Murray, Giuseppe Carenini and Raymond Ng. 2012. Using the Omega Index for Evaluating Abstractive Community Detection, *NAACL 2012, Workshop on Evaluation Metrics and System Comparison for Automatic Summarization*, Montreal, Canada.

Vasin Punyakanok and Dan Roth. 2001. The Use of Classifiers in Sequential Inference. *NIPS (2001)* pp. 995-1001.

Jianbo Shi and Jitendra Malik. 2000. Normalized Cuts & Image Segmentation. *IEEE Trans. of PAMI*, Aug 2000.

David C. Uthus and David W. Aha. 2011. Plans toward automated chat summarization. In *Proceedings of the Workshop on Automatic Summarization for Different Genres, Media, and Languages, WASDGML'11*, pages 1-7, Stroudsburg, PA, USA. Association for Computational Linguistics.

Lu Wang and Claire Cardie. 2013. Domain-Independent Abstract Generation for Focused Meeting Summarization. In *ACL 2013*.

Liang Zhou and Eduard Hovy. 2005. Digesting virtual "geek" culture: The summarization of technical internet relay chats. In *Proceedings of the 43rd Annual Meeting of the Association for Computational Linguistics (ACL'05)*, pages 298-305, Ann Arbor, Michigan, June. Association for Computational Linguistics.

A Hybrid Approach to Multi-document Summarization of Opinions in Reviews

Giuseppe Di Fabbrizio
Amazon.com*
Cambridge, MA - USA
pino@difabbrizio.com

Amanda J. Stent
Yahoo! Labs
New York, NY - USA
stent@labs.yahoo.com

Robert Gaizauskas
Department of Computer Science
University of Sheffield, Sheffield - UK
R.Gaizauskas@sheffield.ac.uk

Abstract

We present a hybrid method to generate summaries of product and services reviews by combining natural language generation and salient sentence selection techniques. Our system, STARLET-H, receives as input textual reviews with associated rated topics, and produces as output a natural language document summarizing the opinions expressed in the reviews. STARLET-H operates as a hybrid abstractive/extractive summarizer: using extractive summarization techniques, it selects salient quotes from the input reviews and embeds them into an automatically generated abstractive summary to provide evidence for, exemplify or justify positive or negative opinions. We demonstrate that, compared to extractive methods, summaries generated with abstractive and hybrid summarization approaches are more readable and compact.

1 Introduction

Text summarization is a well-established area of research. Many approaches are *extractive*, that is, they select and stitch together pieces of text from the input documents (Goldstein et al., 2000; Radev et al., 2004). Other approaches are *abstractive*; they use natural language generation (NLG) techniques to paraphrase and condense the content of the input documents (Radev and McKeown, 1998). Most summarization methods focus on distilling *factual* information by identifying the input documents' main topics, removing redundancies, and coherently ordering extracted phrases or sentences. Summarization of *sentiment-laden text* (e.g., product or service reviews) is substantially different from the traditional text summarization task: instead of presenting facts, the summarizer must present the range of opinions and the consensus opinion (if any), and instead of focusing on one topic, the summarizer must present information about multiple aspects of the target entity.

*This work was conducted when in AT&T Labs Research

In addition, traditional summarization techniques discard redundancies, while for summarization of sentiment-laden text, similar opinions mentioned multiple times across documents are crucial indicators of the overall strength of the sentiments expressed by the writers (Ku et al., 2006).

Extractive summaries are linguistically interesting and can be both informative and concise. Extractive summarizers also require less engineering effort. On the other hand, abstractive summaries tend to have better coverage for a particular level of conciseness, and to be less redundant and more coherent (Carenini et al., 2012). They also can be constructed to target particular discourse goals, such as summarization, comparison or recommendation. Although in theory, it is possible to produce user-targeted extractive summaries, user-specific review summarization has only been explored in the context of abstractive summarization (Carenini et al., 2012).

Current systems for summarizing sentiment-laden text use information about the attributes of the target entity (or entities); the range, mean and median of the ratings of each attribute; relationships between the attributes; and links between ratings/attributes and text elements in the input documents (Blair-Goldensohn et al., 2008). However, there is other information that no summarizer currently takes into account. This includes temporal features (in particular, depending on how old the documents are, products and services evaluated features may change over time) and social features (in particular, social or demographic similarities or relationships between document authors and the reader of the summary). In addition, there is an essential contradiction at the heart of current review summarization systems: the system is authoring the review, but the opinions contained therein are really attributable to one or more human authors, and those attributions are not retained in the review summary. For example, consider the extractive summary generated with STARLET-E (Di Fabbrizio et al., 2013): *"Delicious. Can't wait for my next trip to Buffalo. GREAT* <u>*WINGS*</u>*. I have rearranged business trips*

Proceedings of the 8th International Natural Language Generation Conference, pages 54–63,
Philadelphia, Pennsylvania, 19-21 June 2014.

so that I could stop in and have a helping or two of their wings". We were seated promptly and the staff was courteous.

The summary is generated by selecting sentences from reviews to reflect topics and rating distributions contained in the input review set. Do the two sentences about wings reflect one (repeated) opinion from a single reviewer, or two opinions from two separate reviewers? The ability to attribute subjective statements to known sources can make them more trustworthy; conversely, in the absence of the ability to attribute, a reader may become skeptical or confused about the content of the review summary. We term this summarization issue *opinion holder attribution*.

In this paper we present STARLET-H, a *hybrid* review summarizer that combines the advantages of the abstractive and extractive approaches to summarization and implements a solution to the opinion holder attribution problem. STARLET-H takes as input a set of reviews, each review of which is labeled with aspect ratings and authorship. It generates *hybrid abstractive/extractive* reviews that: 1) are informative (achieve broad coverage of the input opinions); 2) are concise and avoid redundancy; 3) are readable and coherent (of high linguistic quality); 4) can be targeted to the reader; and 5) address the opinion holder attribution problem by directly referring to reviewers authorship when embedding phrases from reviews. We demonstrate through a comparative evaluation of STARLET-H and other review summarizers that hybrid review summarization is preferred over extractive summarization for readability, correctness, completeness (achieving broad coverage of the input opinions) and compactness.

2 Hybrid summarization

Most NLG research has converged around a "consensus architecture" (Reiter, 1994; Rambow and Korelsky, 1992), a pipeline architecture including the following modules: 1) **text planning**, which determines how the presentation content is selected, structured, and ordered; 2) **sentence planning**, which assigns content to sentences, inserts discourse cues to communicate the structure of the presentation, and performs sentence aggregation and optionally referring expression generation; and 3) **surface realization**, which performs lexical selection, resolves syntactic issues such as subject-verb and noun-determiner agreement, and assigns morphological inflection to produce the final grammatical sentence. An abstractive summarizer requires the customization of these three modules. Specifically, the text planner has to select and organize the information contained in the input reviews to reflect the rating distributions over the aspects discussed by the reviewers. The sentence planner must perform aggregation in such a way as to optimize summary length without confusing the reader, and insert discourse cues that reveal the discourse structure underlying the summary. And, finally, the surface realizer must select the proper domain lexemes to express positive and negative opinions.

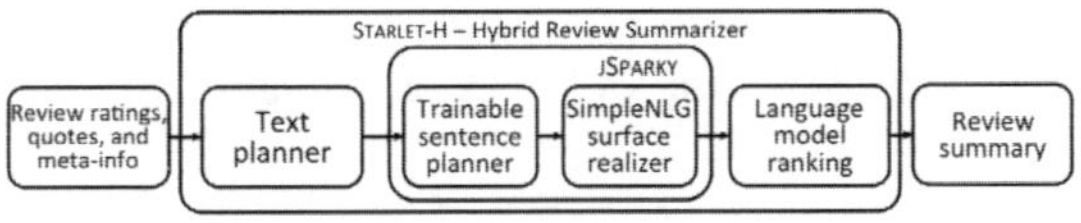

Figure 1: STARLET-H hybrid review summarizer architecture

Figure 1 shows the architecture we adopted for our STARLET-H hybrid review summarizer. We use a generate-and-select approach: the decisions to be made at each stage of the NLG process just outlined are complex, and because they are not truly independent of each other, a generate-and-rank approach may be best (allowing each component to express alternative 'good' choices and choosing the best combination of these choices at the end). Our text planner is responsible for analyzing the input text reviews, extracting per-attribute rating distributions and other meta-data from each review, and synthesizing this information to produce one or more discourse plans. Our sentence planner, JSPARKY – a freely-available toolkit (Stent and Molina, 2009) – can produce several candidate sentence plans and their corresponding surface realizations through SimpleNLG (Gatt and Reiter, 2009). The candidate summaries are ranked by calculating their perplexity with a language model trained over a large number of sentences from additional restaurant reviews collected over the Web.

2.1 Data

STARLET-H uses review data directly, as input to summarization, and indirectly, as training data for statistical models and for lexicons for various stages of the summarization process.

For training data, we used two sets of labeled data: one for the restaurant domain and the other for the hotel domain. Both corpora include manually created sentence-level annotations that identify: 1) opinion targets – phrases referring to domain-relevant aspects that are the targets of opinions expressed by the reviewer; 2) opinion phrases – phrases expressing an opinion about an entity, and its polarity (positive or negative); and 3) opinion groups – links between opinion phrases and their opinion targets. Additionally, sentences satisfying the properties of quotable sentence mentioned in Section 3 were labeled as "quotable". Table 1 summarizes the overall statistics of the two corpora. The annotated corpora included the following rated aspects: *Atmosphere, Food, Service, Value*, and *Overall* for the Restaurant domain, and *Location, Rooms, Service, Value*, and *Overall* for the Hotel domain[1].

Table 1: Quote-annotated dataset statistics

Dataset	**RQ4000**	**HQ4000**	
Domain	Restaurant	Hotel	Total
Reviews	484	404	888
Sentences	4,007	4,013	8,020
Avg sentences / review	8.28	9.93	9.03

2.2 Text planning

Reviews present highly structured information: each contains an (implicit or explicit) rating of one or more aspects of a target entity, possibly with justification or evidence in the form of examples. The rich information represented in these ratings – either directly expressed in reviews or extracted by an automatic rating prediction model – can be exploited in several ways. Our text planner receives as input a set of text reviews with associated per-aspect ratings, and for each review proceeds through the following analysis steps:

Entity description Extracts basic information to describe the reviewed entity, e.g., the name and location of the business, number of total and recent reviews, review dates and authors, etc.

Aspect distribution categorization Categorizes the rating distribution for each aspect of the reviewed entity as one of four types: 1) positive – most of the ratings are positive; 2) negative – most of the ratings are negative; 3) bimodal – most of the ratings are equally distributed into positive and negative values; 4) uniform – ratings are uniformly distributed across the rating scale.

[1]Some examples from the annotated corpus are available at the following address `http://s286209735.onlinehome.us/starlet/examples`

Quote selection and attribution Classifies each sentence from the reviews using a quote selection model (see Section 3), which assigns to each sentence an aspect, a rating polarity (positive/negative) and a confidence score. The classified sentences are sorted by confidence score and a candidate quote is selected for each aspect of the target entity that is explicitly mentioned in the input reviews. Each quote is stored with the name of the reviewer for correct authorship attribution. Note that when the quote selection module is excluded, the system is an abstractive summarizer, which we call STARLET-A.

Lexical selection Selects a lexicon for each aspect based on its rating polarity and its assigned rating distribution type. Lexicons are extracted from the corpus of annotated opinion phrases described in Di Fabbrizio et al. (2011).

Aspect ordering Assigns an order over aspects using aspect ordering statistics from our training data (see Section 2.4), and generates a discourse plan, using a small set of rhetorical relations organized into summary templates (see below).

2.3 Sentence planning

The STARLET-H sentence planner relies on rhetorical structure theory (RST) (Mann and Thompson, 1989). RST is a linguistic framework that describes the structure of natural language text in terms of the *rhetorical* relationships organizing textual units. Through a manual inspection of our training data, we identified a subset of six RST relations that are relevant to review summarization: *concession, contrast, example, justify, list*, and *summary*. We further identified four basic RST-based summary templates, one for each per-aspect rating distribution: mostly positive, mostly negative, uniform across all ratings, and bimodal (e.g., both positive and negative). These summary templates are composed by the text planner to build summary discourse plans. The JSPARKY sentence planner then converts input discourse plans into sentence plans, performing sentence ordering, sentence aggregation, cross-sentence reference resolution, sentence tense and mode (passive or active), discourse cue insertion, and the selection of some lexical forms from FrameNet (Baker et al., 1998) relations.

Figure 2 illustrates a typical RST template representing a positive review summary and corresponding text output generated by JSPARKY. For each aspect of the considered domain, the sentence plan strategy covers a variety of opinion distribu-

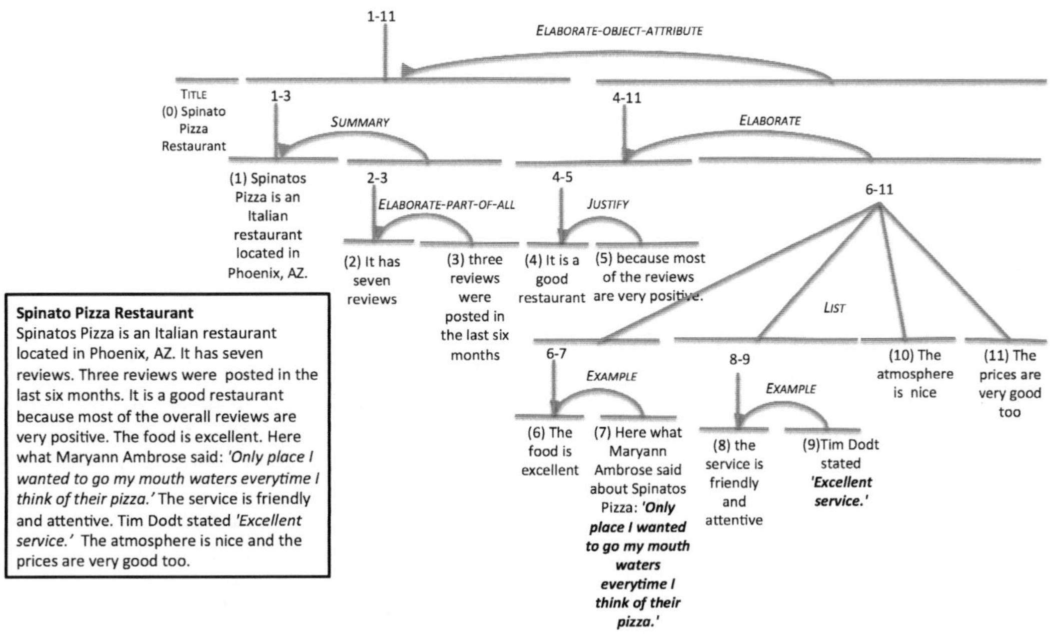

Figure 2: Example of RST structure generated by the text planner for mostly positive restaurant reviews

tion conditions (e.g., positive, negative, bimodal, and uniform), and provides alternative RST structures when the default relation is missing due to lack of data (e.g., missing quotes for a specific aspect, missing information about review distribution over time, missing type of cuisine, and so on). The sentence template can also manage lexical variations by generating multiple options to qualify a specific pair of aspect and opinion polarity. For instance, in case of very positive reviews about restaurant atmosphere, it can provide few alternative adjective phrases (e.g., great, wonderful, very warm, terrific, etc.) that can be used to produce more summary candidates (over-generate) during the final surface realization stage.

2.4 Ordering aspects and polarities

The discourse structure of a typical review consists of a summary opinion, followed by a sequence of per-aspect ratings with supporting information (e.g., evidence, justification, examples, and concessions). The preferred sequence of aspects to present in a summary depends on the specific review domain, the overall polarity of the reviews, and how opinion polarity is distributed across the reviewed aspects. Looking at our training data, we observed that when the review is overall positive, positively-rated aspects are typically discussed at the beginning, while negatively-rated aspects tend to gather toward the end. The opposite order seems predominant in the case of negative reviews. When opinions are mixed, aspect ordering strategies are unclear. To most accurately model aspect ordering, we trained weighted finite state transducers for the restaurant and hotel domains using our training data. Weighted finite state transducers (WFSTs) are an elegant approach to search large feature spaces and find optimal paths by using well-defined algebraic operations (Mohri et al., 1996). To find the optimal ordering of rated aspects in a domain, the text planner creates a WFST with all the possible permutations of the input sequence of aspects, and composes it with a larger WFST trained from bigram sequences of aspects extracted from the relevant domain-specific review corpus. The best path sequence is then derived from the composed WFST by applying the Viterbi decoding algorithm. For instance, the sequence of aspects and polarities represented by the string: `value-n service-p overall-n food-n atmosphere-n`[2] is first permuted in all the different possible sequences and then converted into a WFST. Then the permutation network is fully composed with the larger, corpus-trained WFST. The best path is extracted by dynamic programming, producing the optimal sequence `service-p value-n overall-n atmosphere-n food-n`.

[2]We postfix the aspect label with a '-p' for positive and with '-n' for negative opinion

2.5 Lexical choice

It can be hard to choose the best opinion words, especially when the summary must convey the different nuances between "good" and "great" or "bad" and "terrible" for a particular aspect in a particular domain. For our summarization task, we adopted a simple approach. From our annotated corpora, we mined both positive and negative opinion phrases with their associated aspects and rating polarities. We sorted the opinion phrases by frequency and then manually selected from the most likely phrases adjective phrases that may correctly express per-aspect polarities. We then split positive and negative phrases into two levels of polarity (i.e., strongly positive, weakly positive, weakly negative, strongly negative) and use the number of star ratings to select the right polarity during content planning. For bimodal and uniform polarity distributions, we manually defined a customized set of terms. Sample lexical terms are reported in Table 2.

3 Quote selection modeling

There are several techniques to extract salient phrases from text, often related to summarization problems, but there is a relatively little work on extracting *quotable sentences* from text (Sarmento and Nunes, 2009; De La Clergerie et al., 2009) and none, to our knowledge, on extracting quotes from sentiment-latent text. So, what does make a phrase quotable? What is a proper quote definition that applies to review summarization? We define a *sentiment-laden quotable phrase* as a text fragment with the following characteristics: **attributable** – clearly ascribable to the author; **compact and simple** – it is typically a relatively short phrase (between two and twenty words) which contains a statement with a simple syntactic structure and independent clauses; **self-contained** its meaning is clear and self-contained, e.g., it does not include pronominal references to entities outside its scope; **on-topic** – it refers to opinion targets (i.e., aspects) in a specific domain; **sentiment-laden** – it has one or two opinion targets and an unambiguous overall polarity. Example quotable phrases are presented in Table 3.

Table 3: Example of quotes from restaurant and hotel domains

```
'Everyone goes out of their way to make sure you
are happy with their service and food.'
'The stuffed mushrooms are the best I've ever had
as was the lasagna.'
'Service is friendly and attentive even during
the morning rush.'
'I've never slept so well away from home loved
the comfortable beds.'
'The price is high for substandard mattresses
when I pay this much for a room.'
```

To automatically detect quotes from reviews, we adopted a supervised machine learning approach based on manually labeled data. The classification task consists of classifying both aspects and polarity for the most frequent aspects defined for each domain. Quotes for the aspect `food`, for instance, are split into positive and negative classification labels: `food-p` and `food-n`, respectively. We identify quotable phrases and associate them with aspects and rating polarities all in one step, but multi-step approaches could also be used (e.g., a configuration with binary classification to detect quotable sentences followed by another classification model for aspect and polarity detection).

3.1 Training quote selection models

We used the following features for automatic quote selection: **ngrams** – unigrams, bigrams, and trigrams from the input phrases with frequency higher than three; **binned number of words** – we assumed a maximum length of twenty words per sentence and created six bins, five of them uniformly distributed from one to twenty, and the sixth including all the sentences of length greater than twenty words; **POS** – unigrams, bigrams, and trigrams for part of speech tags; **chunks** – unigrams, bigrams, and trigrams for shallow parsed syntactic chunks; **opinion phrases** – a binary feature to keep track of the presence of positive and negative opinion phrases as defined in our annotated review corpora. In our annotated data only the most popular aspects are well represented. For instance, `food-p` and `overall-p` are the most popular positive aspects among the quotable sentences for the restaurant domain, while quotes on `atmosphere-n` and `value-n` are scarce. The distribution is even further skewed for the hotel domain; there are plenty of quotes for `overall-p` and `service-p` and only 13 samples (0.43%) for `location-n`. To compensate for the broad variation in the sample population, we used *stratified sampling* methods to divide the data into more balanced testing and training data We generated 10-fold stratified training/test sets. We experimented with three machine learning algorithms: MaxEnt, SVMs with linear kernels, and SVMs with polynomial kernels. The MaxEnt learning algorithm produced statistically better classification results than the other algorithms when used with uni-

Table 2: Summarizer lexicon for most frequent adjective phrases by aspect and polarity

Domain	Restaurant				Hotel				
Aspect	positive	very positive	negative	very negative	Aspect	positive	very positive	negative	very negative
atmosphere	nice, good, friendly, comfortable	great, wonderful, very warm, terrific	ordinary, depressing	really bad	location	good, nice, pleasant	amazing, awesome, excellent, great	bad, noisy, gloomy	very bad, very bleak, very gloomy
food	good, delicious, pleasant, nice, hearty, enjoyable	great, excellent, very good, to die for, incredible	very basic, unoriginal, uninteresting, unacceptable, sub-standard, poor	mediocre, terrible, horrible, absolutely horrible	rooms	comfortable, decent, clean, good	amazing, awesome, gorgeous	average, basic, subpar	terrible, very limited, very average
overall	good, quite enjoyable, lovely	wonderful, terrific, very nice	bad, unremarkable, not so good	absolutely terrible, horrible, pretty bad	overall	great, nice, welcoming	excellent, superb, perfect	average, nothing great, noisy	quite bad, awful, horrible
service	attentive, friendly, pleasant, courteous	very attentive, great, excellent, very friendly	inattentive, poor, not friendly, bad	extremely poor, horrible, so lousy, awful	service	friendly, great, nice, helpful, good	very friendly, great, excellent, very nice	average, basic, not that great	very bad, dreadful
value	reasonable, fair, good value	very reasonable, great	not that good, not worthy	terrible, outrageous	value	great, nice, good, decent	very good, wonderful, perfectly good	not good	not very good

gram features. This confirmed a general trend we have previously observed in other text classification experiments: with relatively small and noisy datasets, unigram features provide better discriminative power than sparse bigrams or trigrams, and MaxEnt methods are more robust when dealing with noisy data.

3.2 Quote selection results

Table 4 reports precision, recall and F-measures averaged across 10-fold cross-validated test sets with relative standard deviation. The label `nq` identifies non-quotable sentences, while the other labels refer to the domain-specific aspects and their polarities. For the quote selection task, precision is the most important metric: missing some potential candidates is less important than incorrectly identifying the polarity of a quote or substituting one aspect with another. The text planner in STARLET-H further prunes the quotable phrases by considering only the quote candidates with the highest scores.

Table 4: Quote, aspect, and polarity classification performances for the restaurant domain

	Precision	Recall	F-measure
atmosphere-n	0.233	0.080	0.115
atmosphere-p	0.589	0.409	0.475
food-n	0.634	0.409	0.491
food-p	0.592	0.634	0.612
nq	0.672	0.822	0.740
overall-n	0.545	0.275	0.343
overall-p	0.555	0.491	0.518
service-n	0.699	0.393	0.498
service-p	0.716	0.563	0.626
value-n	0.100	0.033	0.050
value-p	0.437	0.225	0.286
Hotel	**Precision**	**Recall**	**F-measure**
location-n	-	-	-
location-p	0.572	0.410	0.465
nq	0.678	0.836	0.748
overall-n	0.517	0.233	0.305
overall-p	0.590	0.492	0.536
rooms-n	0.628	0.330	0.403
rooms-p	0.667	0.573	0.612
service-n	0.517	0.163	0.240
service-p	0.605	0.500	0.543
value-n	-	-	-
value-p	0.743	0.300	0.401

4 Evaluation

Evaluating an abstractive review summarizer involves measuring how accurately the opinion content present in the reviews is reflected in the summary and how understandable the generated content is to the reader. Traditional multi-document summarization evaluation techniques utilize both qualitative and quantitative metrics. The former require human subjects to rate different evaluative characteristics on a Likert-like scale, while the latter relies on automatic metrics such as ROUGE (Lin, 2004), which is based on the common number of n-grams between a peer, and one or several gold-standard reference summaries.

4.1 Evaluation materials

To evaluate our abstractive summarizer, we used a qualitative metric approach and compared four review summarizers: 1) the open source MEAD system, designed for extractive summarization of general text (Radev et al., 2004); 2) STARLET-E, an extractive summarizer based on KL-divergence and language modeling features that is described in Di Fabbrizio et al. (2011); 3) STARLET-A, the abstractive summarizer presented in this paper, *without* the quote selection module; and 4) the hybrid summarizer STARLET-H.

We used the Amazon Mechanical Turk[3] crowd-

[3] `http://www.mturk.com`

sourcing system to post subjective evaluation tasks, or HITs, for 20 restaurant summaries. Each HIT consists of a set of ten randomly ordered reviews for one restaurant, and four randomly ordered summaries of reviews for that restaurant, each one accompanied by a set of evaluation widgets for the different evaluation metrics described below. To minimize reading order bias, both reviews and summaries were shuffled each time a task was presented.

4.2 Evaluation metrics

We chose to carry out a qualitative evaluation in the first instance as n-gram metrics, such as ROUGE, are not necessarily appropriate for assessing abstractive summaries. We asked each participant to evaluate each summary by rating (using a Likert scale with the following rating values: 1) Not at all; 2) Not very; 3) Somewhat; 4) Very; 5) Absolutely) the following four summary criteria: **readability** – a summary is readable if it is easy to read and understand; **correctness** – a summary is correct if it expresses the opinions in the reviews; **completeness** – a summary is complete if it captures the whole range of opinions in the reviews; **compactness** – a summary is compact if it does not repeat information.

4.3 Evaluation procedure

We requested five evaluators for each HIT. To increase the chances of getting accurate evaluations, we required evaluators to be located in the USA and have an approval rate of 90% or higher (i.e., have a history of 90% or more approved HITs). Manual examinations of the evaluation responses did not show evidence of tampered data, but statistical analysis showed unusually widely spread rating ranges. We noticed that most evaluators only evaluated one or two HITs; this may imply that they tried a few HITs and then decided not to continue because they found the task too long or the instructions unclear. We then re-opened the evaluation and directly contacted three additional evaluators, explaining in detail the instructions and the evaluation scales. For consistency, we asked these evaluators to complete the evaluation for all HITs. In our analysis, we only included the five evaluators (two from the first round of evaluation, and three from the second) who completed all HITs. For each evaluation metric, the five workers evaluated each of the 20 summaries, for a total of 100 ratings. Table 5 shows an example output of the four summarization methods for a single set of restaurant review documents.

Table 5: Example of MEAD-based, extractive, abstractive and hybrid summaries from the restaurant domain

MEAD Summary a truly fun resturant everyone who like spicy food should try the rattoes and for a mixed drink the worm burner really good food and a fun place to meet your friends. We were attracted by the great big frog on the exterior of the building and the fun RAZZOO S logo during a trip to the mall. it was great the waitress was excellent very prompt and courteous and friendly to all a real complement to razzoo 's way of service her name was Tabitha. The best spicy food restaurant with great server and fast service.
Extractive summary Eat there every chance i get. We ve been going here for years. Their crawfish etoufee is the BEST. And such an awesome value for under 10. Excellent as always. Some of the best food in the area. I use to work at Razzoo s. It was hard to leave. The people are great and so is the food. I still go in there and miss it more everytime. I Love Loney. It was great. Our server was great and very observant. Try the Chicken Tchoupitoulas.
Abstractive summary Razzoo's Cajun Cafe in Concord, NC is an American restaurant. It has nine reviews. It had three very recent reviews. It is an awesome, American restaurant. It has many very positive reviews. It has an excellent atmosphere and and has always exceptional service.
Hybrid summary Razzoo's Cajun Cafe in Concord, NC is an American restaurant. It has nine reviews. It had three very recent reviews. It is an awesome, American restaurant. It has many very positive reviews. First it has a great price. Angela Haithcock says ``And such an awesome value for under 10''. Second it has always exceptional service and for instance Danny Benson says ``it was great the waitress was excellent very prompt and courteous and friendly to all a real complement to razzoo's way of service her name was Tabitha''. Third it has an excellent atmosphere. Last it has amazing food. Scott Kern says ``Some of the best food in the area''.

4.4 Evaluation results and discussion

The evaluation results are presented in Table 6. Each evaluation metric is considered separately. Average values for STARLET-E, STARLET-A and STARLET-H are better than for MEAD across the board, suggesting a preference for summaries of sentiment-laden text that take opinion into account. To validate this hypothesis, we first computed the non-parametric Kruskal-Wallis statistic for each evaluation metric, using a chi-square test to establish significance. The results were not significant for any of the metrics.

However, when we conducted pairwise Wilcoxon signed-rank tests considering two summarization methods at a time, we found some significant differences ($p < 0.05$). As predicted,

Table 6: Qualitative evaluation results

	MEAD	Starlet-E	Starlet-A	Starlet-H
Readability	2.95	3.17	3.64	3.74
Completeness	2.88	3.29	3.290	3.58
Compactness	3.07	3.35	3.80	3.58
Correctness	3.26	3.48	3.59	3.72

MEAD perform substantially worse than both STARLET-A and STARLET-H on readability, correctness, completeness, and compactness. STARLET-A and STARLET-H are also preferred over STARLET-E for readability. While STARLET-A is preferred over STARLET-E for compactness (the average length of the abstractive reviews was 45.05 words, and of the extractive,102.30), STARLET-H is preferred over STARLET-E for correctness, since the former better captures the reviewers opinions by quoting them in the appropriate context. STARLET-A and STARLET-H achieve virtually indistinguishable performance on all evaluation metrics. Our evaluation results accord with those of Carenini et al. (2012); their abstractive summarizer had superior performance in terms of content precision and accuracy when compared to summaries generated by an extractive summarizer. Carenini et al. (2012) also found that the differences between extractive and abstractive approaches are even more significant in the case of controversial content, where the abstractive system is able to more effectively convey the full range of opinions.

5 Related work

Ganesan et al. (2010) propose a method to extract salient sentence fragments that are both highly frequent and syntactically well-formed by using a graph-based data structure to eliminate redundancies. However, this approach assumes that the input sentences are already selected in terms of aspect and with highly redundant opinion content. Also, the generated summaries are very short and cannot be compared to a full-length output of a typical multi-document summarizer (e.g., 100-200 words). A similar approach is described in Ganesan et al. (2012), where very short phrases (from two to five words) are collated together to generate what the authors call *ultra-concise* summaries.

The most complete contribution to evaluative text summarization is described in Carenini et al. (2012) and it closely relates to this work. Carenini et al. (2012) compare an extractive summarization system, MEAD* – a modified version of the open source summarization system MEAD (Radev et al., 2004) – with SEA, an abstractive summarization system, demonstrating that both systems perform equally well. The SEA approach, although better than traditional MEAD, has a few drawbacks. Firstly, the sentence selection mechanism only considers the most frequently discussed aspects, leaving the decision about where to stop the selection process to the maximum summary length parameter. This could leave out interesting opinions that do not appear with sufficient frequency in the source documents. Ideally, all opinions should be represented in the summary according to the overall distribution of the input reviews. Secondly, Carenini et al. (2012) use the absolute value of the sum of positive and negative contributions to determine the relevance of a sentence in terms of opinion content. This flattens the aspect distributions since sentences with very negative or very positive polarity or with numerous opinions, but with moderate polarity strengths, will get the same score, regardless. Finally, it does not address the opinion holder attribution problem leaving the source of opinion undefined. In contrast, STARLET-H follows reviews aspect rating distributions both to select quotable sentences and to summarize relevant aspects. Moreover, it explicitly mentions the opinion source in the embedded quoted sentences.

6 Conclusions

In this paper, we present a hybrid summarizer for sentiment-laden text that combines an overall abstractive summarization method with an extractive summarization-based quote selection method. This summarizer can provide the readability and correctness of abstractive summarization, while addressing the opinion holder attribution problem that can lead readers to become confused or misled about who is making claims that they read in review summaries. We plan a more extensive evaluation of STARLET-H. Another potential area of future research concerns the ability to personalize summaries to the user's needs. For instance, the text planner can adapt its communicative goals based on polarity orientation – a user can be more interested in exploring in detail negative reviews – or it can focus more on specific (user-tailored) aspects and change the order of the presentation accordingly. Finally, it could be interesting to customize the summarizer to provide an overview of what is available in a specific geographic neighborhood and compare and contrast the options.

References

Collin F. Baker, Charles J. Fillmore, and John B. Lowe. The Berkeley FrameNet Project. In *Proceedings of the 17th International Conference on Computational Linguistics - Volume 1*, COLING '98, pages 86–90, Stroudsburg, PA, USA, 1998. Association for Computational Linguistics. doi: 10.3115/980451.980860. URL `http://dx.doi.org/10.3115/980451.980860`.

Sasha Blair-Goldensohn, Kerry Hannan, Ryan McDonald, Tyler Neylon, George Reis, and Jeff Reynar. Building a Sentiment Summarizer for Local Service Reviews. In *NLP in the Information Explosion Era*, 2008.

Giuseppe Carenini, Jackie Chi Kit Cheung, and Adam Pauls. Multi-Document Summarization of Evaluative Text. *Computational Intelligence*, 2012.

Éric De La Clergerie, Benoît Sagot, Rosa Stern, Pascal Denis, Gaëlle Recourcé, and Victor Mignot. Extracting and Visualizing Quotations from News Wires. In *Language and Technology Conference*, Poznan, Pologne, 2009. Projet Scribo (pôle de compétitivité System@tic).

Giuseppe Di Fabbrizio, Ahmet Aker, and Robert Gaizauskas. STARLET: Multi-document Summarization of Service and Product Reviews with Balanced Rating Distributions. In *Proceedings of the 2011 IEEE International Conference on Data Mining (ICDM) Workshop on Sentiment Elicitation from Natural Text for Information Retrieval and Extraction (SENTIRE)*, Vancouver, Canada, december 2011.

Giuseppe Di Fabbrizio, Ahmet Aker, and Robert Gaizauskas. Summarizing On-line Product and Service Reviews Using Aspect RatingDistributions and Language Modeling. *Intelligent Systems, IEEE*, 28(3):28–37, May 2013. ISSN 1541-1672. doi: 10.1109/MIS.2013.36.

Kavita Ganesan, ChengXiang Zhai, and Jiawei Han. Opinosis: A Graph-Based Approach to Abstractive Summarization of Highly Redundant Opinions. In *Proceedings of the 23rd International Conference on Computational Linguistics*, COLING '10, pages 340–348, Stroudsburg, PA, USA, 2010. Association for Computational Linguistics.

Kavita Ganesan, ChengXiang Zhai, and Evelyne Viegas. Micropinion Generation: An Unsupervised Approach to Generating Ultra-concise Summaries of Opinions. In *Proceedings of the 21st international conference on World Wide Web*, WWW '12, pages 869–878, New York, NY, USA, 2012. ACM.

Albert Gatt and Ehud Reiter. SimpleNLG: A Realisation Engine for Practical Applications. In *Proceedings of the 12th European Workshop on Natural Language Generation*, ENLG '09, pages 90–93, Stroudsburg, PA, USA, 2009. Association for Computational Linguistics.

Jade Goldstein, Vibhu Mittal, Jaime Carbonell, and Mark Kantrowitz. Multi-document Summarization by Sentence Extraction. In *Proceedings of the 2000 NAACL-ANLP Workshop on Automatic summarization - Volume 4*, pages 40–48, Stroudsburg, PA, USA, 2000. Association for Computational Linguistics.

Lun-Wei Ku, Yu-Ting Liang, and Hsin-Hsi Chen. Opinion Extraction, Summarization and Tracking in News and BlogCorpora. In *Proceedings of AAAI-2006 Spring Symposium on Computational Approaches to Analyzing Weblogs*, 2006.

Chin-Yew Lin. ROUGE: A Package for Automatic Evaluation of summaries. In *Proc. ACL workshop on Text Summarization Branches Out*, page 10, 2004.

William C. Mann and Sandra A. Thompson. Rhetorical Structure Theory: A Theory of Text Organization. In Livia Polanyi, editor, *The Structure of Discourse*. Ablex, Norwood, NJ, 1989.

Mehryar Mohri, Fernando Pereira, and Michael Riley. Weighted Automata in Text and Speech Processing. In *ECAI-96 Workshop*, pages 46–50. John Wiley and Sons, 1996.

Dragomir Radev, Timothy Allison, Sasha Blair-Goldensohn, John Blitzer, Arda Çelebi, Stanko Dimitrov, Elliott Drabek, Ali Hakim, Wai Lam, Danyu Liu, Jahna Otterbacher, Hong Qi, Horacio Saggion, Simone Teufel, Michael Topper, Adam Winkel, and Zhu Zhang. MEAD – A Platform for Multidocument Multilingual Text Summarization. In *Conference on Language Resources and Evaluation (LREC)*, Lisbon, Portugal, May 2004.

Dragomir R. Radev and Kathleen R. McKeown. Generating natural language summaries from multiple on-line sources. *Computational Linguistiscs*, 24(3):470–500, September 1998. ISSN 0891-2017.

Owen Rambow and Tanya Korelsky. Applied Text Generation. In *Proceedings of the Third Conference on Applied Natural Language Processing*, pages 40–47, Trento, Italy, 1992. Association for Computational Linguistics. 31 March - 3 April.

Ehud Reiter. Has a Consensus NL Generation Architecture Appeared, and is it Psychologically Plausible? In David McDonald and Marie Meteer, editors, *Proceedings of the 7th. International Workshop on Natural Language generation (INLGW '94)*, pages 163–170, Kennebunkport, Maine, 1994.

Luis Sarmento and Sérgio Nunes. Automatic Extraction of Quotes and Topics from News Feeds. In *4th Doctoral Symposium on Informatics Engineering (DSIE09)*, 2009.

Amanda Stent and Martin Molina. Evaluating Automatic Extraction of Rules for Sentence Plan Construction. In *Proceedings of the SIGDIAL 2009 Conference: The 10th Annual Meeting of the Special Interest Group on Discourse and Dialogue*, SIGDIAL '09, pages 290–297, Stroudsburg, PA, USA, 2009. Association for Computational Linguistics.

Adapting Graph Summaries to the Users' Reading Levels

Priscilla Moraes, Kathleen McCoy and Sandra Carberry
Department of Computer and Information Sciences
University of Delaware, Newark, Delaware, USA
[pmoraes | mccoy | carberry]@udel.edu

Abstract

Deciding on the complexity of a generated text in NLG systems is a contentious task. Some systems propose the generation of simple text for low-skilled readers; some choose what they anticipate to be a "good measure" of complexity by balancing sentence length and number of sentences (using scales such as the D-level sentence complexity) for the text; while others target high-skilled readers. In this work, we discuss an approach that aims to leverage the experience of the reader when reading generated text by matching the syntactic complexity of the generated text to the reading level of the surrounding text. We propose an approach for sentence aggregation and lexical choice that allows generated summaries of line graphs in multimodal articles available online to match the reading level of the text of the article in which the graphs appear. The technique is developed in the context of the SIGHT (Summarizing Information Graphics Textually) system. This paper tackles the micro planning phase of sentence generation discussing additionally the steps of lexical choice, and pronominalization.

1 Introduction

Multimodal documents from online popular media often contain information graphics that augment the information found in the text. These graphics, however, are inaccessible to blind users. The SIGHT system is an ongoing project that proposes methods of making this information accessible to visually impaired users by generating a textual summary capturing the high-level message of the graphic along with visually distinctive features. Figure 1 shows an example of an information graphic found in popular media. This graphic ostensibly conveys that there was a change in the trend of ocean levels, which is first stable until about 1940 and then rising through 2003. Earlier work on the system (Wu, Carberry, Elzer, & Chester, 2010) is able to infer this high-level message given a representation of the graphic.

Nevertheless, a generated summary should convey more than just the intended message. It should provide important visual features that jump out at a person who views the graphic (such as the fluctuation in the data values as seen in the graph in Figure 1). The set of remarkable features is different for different graphics. Previous work of ours (Moraes, Carberry, & McCoy, 2013) presents methods that capture these most important features and allow the composition of customized summaries for each graph. Thus, given a graphic, our previous work has resulted in a system that can produce a set of propositions to include in its summary. In this paper, we turn to the subsequent phases of generation: given a set of propositions, how these propositions should be realized such that the resultant text is adapted to the user's reading level and thus is coherent and understandable.

Therefore, this work presents novel strategies that have been deployed in the text generation phase of the SIGHT system applied to line graphs. It describes the micro planning phase, emphasizing sentence aggregation, lexical choice and pronominalization. The contribution of this work is the provision of coherent and concise textual summaries that narrate line graphs' high-level content to visually impaired users through approaches that rely on 1) making the right wording choices and 2) making appropriate syntactical decisions in order to achieve a desired reading level for the generated text.

Previous work in generation assumes a particular level of complexity for all texts created. Our hypothesis is that the graph's summary should vary depending on the user's reading level. Although one could explicitly inquire about the user's reading level, this would be intrusive and

Proceedings of the 8th International Natural Language Generation Conference, pages 64–73,
Philadelphia, Pennsylvania, 19-21 June 2014. ©2014 Association for Computational Linguistics

would detract from the overall experience. Thus we hypothesize that the level of complexity of the article in which the graph appears roughly equates with the user's reading level --- that is, users generally choose articles that are at their own reading comfort level. Therefore, our approach is to generate summaries that reflect the reading level of the accompanying article. Not only will such summaries be coherent and understandable to the user, but also the summary should fit seamlessly into the user's reading of the article.

The decision to match the text complexity of the generated text to that of the article's text was inspired by results of an experiment performed with college students aiming to evaluate the content determination output. In the experiment, sentences were generated for each proposition selected by the system. Comments made by the subjects revealed that the simplest possible text was not easier to understand. Rather, it caused them confusion and discomfort when reading it. Based on these results, we decided to tackle the problem of deciding on the text complexity of automatically generated text by following the same syntactical complexity of the surrounding text, by reading level. In addition, we use word frequencies to select more common lexical items to compose summaries of lower reading levels.

The next section presents the background and motivation for our work. Section 3 discusses some related work concerned with text generation and simplification. Section 4 presents our proposed approach to text generation that adapts the output to the reading level of the surrounding text. Section 5 shows some examples of text generated in different grade level groups. Section 6 shows our preliminary evaluation and it is followed by some conclusions and ideas for future work in Section 7 and 8, respectively.

2 Background

The approaches presented in this work are deployed in the context of the SIGHT system. The system is concerned with providing access to information graphics present in multimodal documents from popular media such as the graphic in Figure 1. For this graphic, the content selection module[1] (Moraes et al., 2013) chooses the following propositions for inclusion in the initial summary:

- graph type (line graph);
- entity being measured (annual difference from Seattle's 1899 sea level, in inches);
- the intended message of the graphic (changing trend: stable then rising);
- the high fluctuation of the data values;
- the description of the individual segments of the graphic;
- the initial value (annotated end point);
- the ending value (annotated end point).

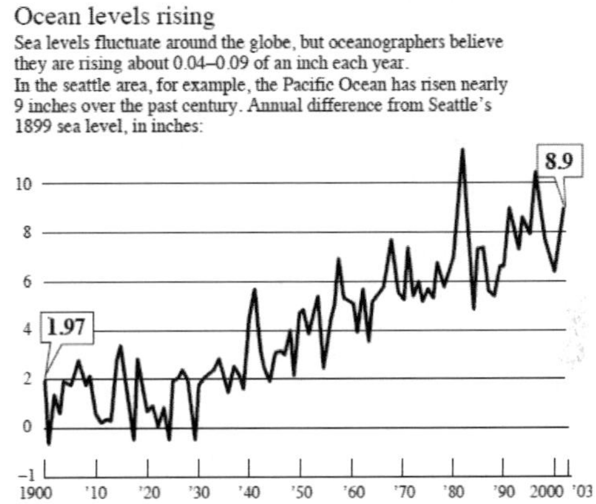

Figure 1: Example of a graphic that has a Changing Trend as its intended message and presents out-standing visual features (volatility and annotations on end points).

These propositions are not necessarily selected in this listed order, nor in the order they will be mentioned in the summary. They are selected based on their overall importance in the context of the graphic since the content selection framework is based on an adapted version of a centrality-based algorithm. Once these propositions are selected, an overarching organizational strategy must be chosen to decide on the most appropriate ordering. Our system gives most importance to the overall intended message of the graphic and thus this will be mentioned first. Next, a description of the features of the individual trend(s) will be provided. Finally, summary information about the whole graph will be given. The system must make further decisions when the graph conveys more than one trend (such as the graph in Figure 1). For such cases, the system must further decide whether to organize the description of the trends (1) by the trends themselves – e.g. either in left to right order - when no trend is considered more important than the others; or (2) by importance – when a trend has a

[1] The content selection module has been presented in a previous paper and is outside the scope of this paper.

greater set of features selected for the discourse or it composes a candidate intended message, which augments the intended message (Moraes et al., 2013). In the latter case, if a piece of the graphic (trend) has significantly more features selected, meaning that it possesses a higher number of visually outstanding features, it will be described first, then followed by the other trends. The organization of the sentences is a separate step that happens prior to the realization phase, which is the focus here, and will not be discussed further in this paper.

Having the set of ordered propositions selected, the question that arises is how to realize this information to the user. The most straightforward way of realizing the summary would be to realize each proposition as a single sentence. This strategy was applied in an evaluation experiment (briefly described next) that aimed to test the preciseness of the content selection framework. The experiment presented the subjects with line graphs and their correspondent generated initial summaries (the propositions were properly ordered for this experiment). Subjects were asked whether or not the most important information about the graphic was part of the summary and whether the summary presented unnecessary or redundant information. They were also offered the opportunity to provide additional comments.

For the experiment, the initial summary for the graphic in Figure 1 was the following:

```
The image shows a line graph. The line graph is highly volatile. The line graph presents the number of annual difference from Seattle's 1899 sea level, in inches. The line graph shows a trend that changes. The changing trend consists of a stable trend from 1900 to 1928 followed by a rising trend through 2003. The first segment is the stable trend. The stable trend has a starting value of 1.97 inches. The second segment is the rising trend. The rising trend has an ending value of 8.9 inches.
```

Although the experiment was intended to evaluate the content present in the summaries, various comments addressed the syntactical construction of the text. These comments highlighted the lack of aggregation and pronominalization. For instance, a common theme of the comments was that some of the information could be "combined" and presented more succinctly.

All the participants of the experiment were graduate students. These results showed that more sophisticated readers *prefer* text that is more sophisticated. This finding pointed to the necessity of an aggregation step before the delivery of the summaries. However, questions arose concerning how much aggregation to do, how to measure aggregation to choose one strategy over another, or to decide on a desired level of aggregation.

To answer the above questions, we decided to examine the text complexity of the text surrounding the graphic --- that is, the text from the article in which the graph appears. We presume that this text complexity equates with the user's reading level and thus summaries at this level of complexity will be understandable and coherent to the users. This approach seemed to be the best way of customizing the text complexity of the summaries in order to tailor summaries to individual users.

3 Related Work

Research on generating text concerned with low-skilled users has been conducted by (Williams & Reiter, 2004, 2005a, 2005b, 2008; Williams, Reiter, & Osman, 2003). As stated by (Williams & Reiter, 2005b), most NLG systems generate text for readers with good reading ability. Thus, they developed a system called *SkillSum* which adapts its output for readers with poor literacy after assessing their reading and numeracy skills. Their results show that, for these target readers, the micro planning choices made by *SkillSum* enhanced readability. (Siddharthan, 2003) proposes a regeneration phase for syntactical text simplification in order to preserve discourse structure "aiming to make the text easier to read for some target group (like aphasics and people with low reading ages) or easier to process by some program (like a parser or machine translation system). (J. Carroll et al., 1999) presents a text simplification methodology to help language-impaired users. (Rello & Baeza-Yates, 2012) investigates dyslexic errors on the Web and (Rello, Baeza-Yates, Bott, & Saggion, 2013) propose a system that uses lexical simplification to enhance readability and understandability of text for people with dyslexia. They help users to understand the text by offering as options the replacement of more complicated lexical items by simpler vocabulary. They performed experiments with people with no visual impairments and with people with dyslexia and concluded that the system improved readability for the users with dyslexia and improved comprehensibility for users with no visual impairments. Experiments performed with blind users and the usability of a system that provides access to charts and graphs is presented by (Ferres, Lindgaard, Sumegi, & Tsuji, 2013).

Other NLG systems make decisions on text complexity based on available scales such as the D-level sentence complexity (Covington, He, Brown, Naci, & Brown, 2006). One example is presented in (Demir et al., 2010) where tree structures are built representing all the possible ways sentences can be aggregated and the choice of the tree tries to balance the number of sentences, their D-level complexity, and the types of relative clauses.

Although text simplification is crucial to target low-skilled readers and users with language disabilities, our experiment with college students showed that the simplest text was rather unpleasant to read for them. We therefore propose a technique that focuses on adjusting the generated text to the reading level of the surrounding text. Thus, our system should satisfy both high-level and low-level readers.

4 Aggregation and Text Complexity

The initial summaries generated by the system are composed of individual sentences that were realized from atomic concept units. Since we use a bottom-up approach when selecting content, in order to achieve different text complexity levels, a sentence aggregation step is needed. The aggregation module is in charge of merging propositions that describe an entity, creating a more complex sentence that will encompass the information selected that describes the referring expression.

The approach proposed by (Wilkinson, 1995) presents the aggregation process divided in two major steps: semantic grouping and sentence structuring. Although they are interdependent, both are needed in order to achieve aggregation in a text. Initiatives on automatic aggregation (or only semantic grouping) of text using learning techniques also exist. (Barzilay, 2006), (Bayyarapu, 2011), (Walker, Rambow, & Rogati, 2001) are some examples of learning aggregation rules and grouping constrains in order to aggregate text. (Demir, 2010) presents a mechanism in which each proposition is a single node tree which can be realized as a sentence and attempts to form more complex trees by combining trees in such a way so that the more complex tree (containing multiple propositions) can still be realized as a single sentence. In order to decide which tree is the best one to be realized, Demir's work applies the revised D-level sentence complexity scale, which measures the syntactic complexity of a sentence according to its syntactic structure.

Although learning methodologies are innovative, they strive to train the algorithms in order to choose the best text plan based in a specific task or environment (defined by the training data and the decision of which plan is the "best" given the human subjects' judgments). Our contention is that a given sentence plan can be perfectly suitable in one context and, at the same time, be ineffective in another one, making the choice of the best text plan a variable. For this reason, we decided to take into consideration the article reading level when choosing the text plan that will be used to design the aggregation of summaries generated by our system. This approach allows the summary of the line graph to fit coherently within the article's text. Text plans, in the context of this work, refer to the different set of rules that are followed in order to aggregate propositions before the realization phase. Each text plan decides how propositions related to a given entity should be combined in order to produce sentences.

4.1 Reading Level Assessment

Much effort has been devoted to developing automated approaches for assessing text complexity. Some examples are the use of support vector machines (Schwarm & Ostendorf, 2005) in order to find topical texts at a given reading level. Another approach is the use of statistical language models (Collins-Thompson & Callan, 2005; Collins-Thompson & Callan, 2004) for predicting reading difficulty. The combination of vocabulary and grammatical features in order to predict reading difficulty for first and second language texts is the object of study in (Heilman, Collins-Thompson, Callan, & Eskenazi, 2007).

(Sheehan, Kostin, Futagi, & Flor, 2010) developed a system called *SourceRater* (now named *TextEvaluator*), which considers features of text that go beyond syntactical features. The authors list a set of dimensions of text that influences in a text reading complexity. These dimensions are: Spoken vs. Written Language, Academic Orientation, Syntactic Complexity, Narrative Style, Overt Expression of Persuasion, Vocabulary Difficulty, and Negation. They divide texts into literary and informational in order to assess these features and their impact in reading difficulty after finding that these styles have substantial differences. They evaluate their technique by comparing their results with assessments done using Flesh-Kincaid reading level assessment (Kincaid, Fishburne, Rogers, & Chissom, 1975) applied to text categorized into grade levels by the Common Core Standards ("Common Core State Standards Initiative," 2014).

Another tool, Coh-Metrix (Graesser et al., 2004), was designed to analyze text on measures of cohesion, language and readability. This evaluator also categorizes the input text into one of Scientific, Narrative or Informational and it considers features such as cohesion relations, user world knowledge, language, and discourse characteristics besides syntactical features such as word and sentence length when assessing the text complexity.

To generate text that complies with a given reading level, we consider that a common, well-know, widely-used metric such as Flesch-Kincaid or SMOG (Laughlin, 1969) will suffice for providing input to the text planning phase of our system. To assure the usefulness of this metric in our context, we evaluated the similarity between assessments done by Flesch-Kincaid and SMOG and assessments made by *TextEvaluator*. For this comparison, we used 55 articles from our corpus[2]. The results showed that for only 20 percent of the articles was the reading level assessment provided by Flesch-Kincaid and SMOG different from the text complexity classification done by *TextEvaluator*. From these results, we concluded that simple reading assessments such as Flesch-Kincaid and SMOG would suffice for guiding the choice of syntactical text complexity in our generated summaries.

4.2 Generating Summaries for Different Reading Levels

When generating the initial summaries of line graphs, our system creates different text plans for each group of grade levels (each group comprises two or more grade levels starting at the 5th grade) and applies the appropriate one depending upon the assessed reading level of the text in the article containing the graphic.

Because the summary is not long enough to be exact when determining its reading level (since longer texts result in more accurate assessment of their reading level), we decided not to create one text plan for each grade level. Instead, we have created five grade level groups and each one comprises two or more grades. For each group of grade levels, we define a text plan that increases a sentence syntactic structure complexity as the grade gets higher. We define a text plan for summaries that can range between grades 5 (inclusive) and 7 (exclusive), another text plan for grades between 7 (inclusive) and 9 (excusive). A third text plan is defined for grades 9 inclusive and 11 (exclusive), one for 11 (inclusive) and 13 (exclusive) and, finally, another one for grades greater than or equal to 13 (college level).

The content selection framework, as mentioned earlier, defines the content of a given summary dynamically. Due to this fact, the amount of information (or the number of propositions) selected for inclusion in a summary varies per graphic. Our intention is to make sure that the reading level of the summaries generated by our system do not exceed the reading level of their respective article's text. It is admissible, however, for the summary to have a slightly lower reading level than the one from the text.

The organization phase, which is a previous step, divides the set of propositions produced by the content selection module into three groups: 1) propositions that comprise an introduction containing the high-level message of the graphic, 2) propositions that detail the individual trends of the graph, and 3) propositions that convey computational information about the overall graph. Thus, from the set of selected propositions, the text plan of a given group defines rules on Noun Phrase (NP) density and lexical choice. When describing an entity, attributes of this entity can be added to the NP as modifiers using either adjectives e.g. "*a steep rising trend*", conjunctions e.g., "*the rising trend is steep and volatile*" or relative clauses e.g. "*a rising trend, which is steep*". When the modifier of an NP is a Verb Phrase (VP), it is combined using a relative clause e.g., "*the line graph, which presents the number of jackets sold in 2013...*" VPs can be modified by adverbs e.g., "*the falling trend is very steep*". The text plans applies rules within sets of propositions that are grouped hierarchically. Within these major groups, propositions can only be aggregated if they belong to the same

[2] Our Digital Library contains multimodal articles collected from popular media. It is available at http://ir.cis.udel.edu/~moraes/udgraphs

entity. The decision of using one syntactic structure over the other is currently based on discourse strategies. The complexity added by a relative clause over the one added by an adjective, for example, is the focus of current investigation (more details in Section 8) and will be considered when choosing one construction over another.

4.3 Lexical Choice

Most of the work on text simplification and readability assessment considers lexicalization a crucial aspect for readability and comprehensibility. (Rello, Baeza-Yates, Bott, & Saggion, 2013) presents a system that increases the understandability and readability of text by helping users understand the text by replacing complex words with more common ones in the lexicon. (Laughlin, 1969) states that longer and more precise words are usually harder to understand.

This led us to use more common words at lower grade levels to increase the chance of the text being easily understood by the reader. For this, we use the Word Frequency Data from the Corpus of Contemporary American English (Davies, 2008). Precise and specific words (which are less frequently used) that describe visual features of line graphs such as *volatility* and *steepness* are replaced by other words or expressions that are more commonly used but still carry the same meaning, such as *"peaks and valleys"* or *"ups and downs"*. The experiment presented in Section 6 corroborates this claim, showing that college level students were comfortable with the use of such lexical items whereas fifth graders complained about them and asserted they did not know their meanings. Future work concerns the use of lexical items categorized by reading levels (details in Section 8).

4.4 Pronominalization

Another important feature is the pronominalization of referring expressions. This technique avoids reintroduction of entities every time they are mentioned. The experiment mentioned in Section 2 showed that the reintroduction of entities or the repetition of referring expressions (when a pronoun could be used) in fact jeopardized the understanding of some passages in the summaries. The participants would usually complain that a given summary was confusing because it could be "better presented" and they would additionally provide us with comments regarding the reintroduction of the referring expressions. From these results, we concluded that it would be valuable to include a pronominalization step in the aggregation phase so that even the summaries that are at a lower grade level would not repeat the referring expression when using multiple non aggregated sentences.

The propositions chosen by the content selection framework contain the information about their memberships (features such as volatility and steepness point to the segment of the graphic they belong to). This membership information is the clue used to define discourse focus. Our work follows the approach applied in the TEXT system (McKeown, 1992), in which pronouns are used in order to refer to the entity being focused in subsequent sentences. Also inspired by the work presented by (McCoy & Strube, 1999) our system makes use of other anaphoric expressions besides pronouns, such as "the trend" or "the graph". These alternative anaphoric expressions are used to reintroduce entities when the discourse focus changes. The following example shows the use of pronouns and the reintroduction of the entity in the last set of propositions. The entities that are in focus in each sentence are underlined and the referring expressions are bolded.

The <u>image</u> shows a line graph. The <u>line graph</u> presents the number of cumulative, global unredeemed frequent-flier miles. **It** conveys a rising trend from 1999 to 2005. **It** has a starting value of 5.5. **It** has an ending value of 14.2. **The graph** shows an overall increase of 8.7.

The last sentence changes the focus back to the overall graph. Even though the entity *line graph* was already mentioned, the focus had changed to the entity *rising trend*, so when the focus returns to the entity *line graph*, the system makes use of a definite reference to reintroduce it.

5 Examples of Summaries Generated for Different Reading Levels

Below are examples of some of the summaries that our system generates for the graph in Figure 1 at different reading levels. Their assessed reading levels provided by SMOG are also shown[3]. The summaries in these examples are also pro-

[3] These results were obtained from using a tool available in the GNU project Style and Diction (FSF, 2005).

nominalized. The pronominalization phase is described in Section 4.4.

Summary for Grades > 5 and <= 7

```
The image shows a line graph. The line graph has ups and downs. It presents the number of annual difference from Seattle's 1899 sea level, in inches. It conveys a changing trend. It consists of a stable trend from 1900 to 1928 followed by a rising trend through 2003. The first segment is the stable trend. It has a starting value of 1.97 inches. The second segment is the rising trend. It has an ending value of 8.9 inches.
(SMOG 4.8)
```

Summary for Grades > 11 and <= 13

```
The image shows a highly volatile line graph, which presents the number of annual difference from Seattle's 1899 sea level, in inches, in addition to conveying a changing trend that consists of a stable trend from 1900 to 1928 followed by a rising trend through 2003. The first segment is the stable trend that has starting value of 1.97 inches. The second segment is the rising trend that has ending value of 8.9 inches.
(SMOG 10.0)
```

The assessed reading level of these passages are below the maximum threshold due to the limited number of propositions selected by the content determination algorithm.

6 Evaluation

This work on aggregation was motivated by the evaluation described in Section 2, which was intended to evaluate the content selection phase of the system. Much to our surprise, many of the comments indicated that the summaries were difficult to read because they lacked aggregation! This result caused us to implement the work presented here. Our first evaluation therefore replicated our first experiment where, instead of using a simple sentence for each proposition, sentences were aggregated to reflect a 7th – 9th grade reading level (the level slightly lower than the median of the articles collected for our corpus).

Table 1 compares the results of these two initial experiments. The results[4] show a dramatic drop in the comments related to issues with aggregation. From this preliminary experiment results, we felt encouraged to pursue the generation of summaries suited to grade levels.

	Number of Subjects	**Number of Responses**	**Number of complaints**
Experiment 1	16	201	22
Experiment 2	29	331	4

Table 1. Comparison of results from preliminary experiment.

Our second experiment targeted our generation of grade-level appropriate text. In this experiment, we wished to judge whether readers at different reading levels would prefer texts generated by our system aimed at their reading level. We therefore recruited two groups of participants: (1) students from a fifth grade elementary school in the area and (2) undergraduate students in an introductory CS course at a university.

Participants were presented with 2 summaries from each of 5 different graphs. One of the summaries was generated to be at a 5th – 7th grade reading level and the other at a 11th – 13th grade reading level. The participants were asked to select the summary they liked the best and to provide comments on what they did not like in either summary.

Table 2 shows the results of this experiment. Five students from 5th grade and thirty-four freshmen college students were recruited to participate. From these results we can see that, in fact, the majority in both groups preferred the grade-level appropriate summary. For the freshmen college students, the fact that the subjects were almost evenly split on their choices, even though they are at the same grade level, was expected. This shows that reading preferences may vary even among people from same age/grade level. Since there were subjects who preferred simple to complex text, we can assume that reading skills can vary even within a grade level group. Our contention is that readers who prefer simple text would read venues that use simple text structure and syntax. That is where our ap-

[4] The number of complaints presented in Table 1 are concerned only with syntactical issues.

proach plays an even better role when looking into the surrounding text the user is reading. Following this approach, instead of assessing or asking the user which level they are in, gives us more chances of being successful at producing text that will be more appropriate to each user.

Analyzing the results on the choices of the opposite summary to their target group, we noticed that there was an agreement amongst subjects regarding the type of the graph. Kids who showed a preference for the complex text, for example, did so only for graphics describing a simple trend, therefore having a small amount of information an making it easy for them to follow.

Some college students who chose the simpler summary provided comments that showed to be independent of the reading level decisions of the system. Some subjects pointed that a default connective applied by the realizer ("in addition to") was making the summary complicated to read. That can actually be the cause of the choice for the simple summary, and not necessarily the amount of aggregation. To address this, we consider that changing the connective to a more common one (e.g. "and") would make the text more fluid.

From these results, we conclude that, indeed, adapting the generated text to the complexity of text commonly read by a user is a promising path to follow. An experiment where we provide the subjects with the article accompanying the graph and ask them to choose the summary that they believe fits the text complexity of the summary is intended and planned as future work. We have initiated investigation in some automated ways of generating text within these different grade level groups and we discuss it further in Section 8.

	Chose Summaries for 5th – 7th Grades (%)	**Chose Summaries for 11th - 13th Grades (%)**
5th grade	80	20
Freshmen students	47	53

Table 2. Results from experiment measuring choices of summaries in different reading levels.

7 Conclusion

Most NLG systems available today generate text that focus on specific target readers. Some of them focus on text generation for low-skilled readers, while others generate text for high-skilled readers. In this work, we presented an approach that offers a solution that attends to the needs of readers at different grade levels.

Our system generates initial summaries of line graphs available in popular media, so visually impaired users can have access to the high-level message these resources carry. Our contention is that users read articles from venues that they feel comfortable with reading. Therefore, we assert that generating summaries that fit the text complexity of the overall article leverages the quality of the generated text. We showed an approach that uses Flesch-Kincaid and SMOG reading assessments in order to determine the syntactical complexity of the generated text. From the experiments performed, we conclude that pursuing the generation of natural language text that fits the reading level of the surrounding text is promising.

8 Path Forward

Investigation on more automated ways of deciding on how to aggregate propositions is the next step to take. Our current aggregation method relies on templates for each group. We anticipate some techniques to learn how different text constructions can affect reading measures and then using them when choosing an adjective over a relative clause for increasing the NP density and use of passive voice, for example. This would allow the aggregation phase to be easily applied to NLG systems in different contexts.

Another important point is the choice of lexical items by reading level or age. We plan on investigating how the usage of word frequency by age/grade level (Carroll, 1972) might help achieving a more appropriate summary for a given grade level. Then, the lexical items that are listed as common to the target grade reading level would be applied in their respective context.

Some comments provided on the second experiment described in Section 6 were that it was not so easy to understand long sentences on which values and dates were also present. This aspect deserves investigation on acquiring numeracy skills along with reading skills as clues to assess the best text complexity to present. Research that assess numeracy and literacy skills of users is presented by (Williams & Reiter, 2008).

From the accessibility prospective, an experiment with blind users is anticipated. We intend to evaluate the effect of generating text in different reading levels for people with visual and/or reading impairments.

References

Barzilay, R. (2006). *Aggregation via set partitioning for natural language generation.* Paper presented at the In HLT-NAACL.

Bayyarapu, H. S. (2011). *Efficient algorithm for Context Sensitive Aggregation in Natural Language generation.* Paper presented at the RANLP.

Carroll, J. B. (1972). A New Word Frequency Book. *Elementary English, 49*(7), pp. 1070-1074.

Collins-Thompson, K., & Callan, J. (2005). Predicting Reading Difficulty with Statistical Language Models. *J. Am. Soc. Inf. Sci. Technol., 56*(13), 1448-1462.

Collins-Thompson, K., & Callan, J. P. (2004). *A Language Modeling Approach to Predicting Reading Difficulty.* Paper presented at the HLT-NAACL.

Common Core State Standards Initiative. (2014). Retrieved 2014-01-09, from http://www.corestandards.org/

Covington, M., He, C., Brown, C., Naci, L., & Brown, J. (2006). *How Complex is that Sentence? A Proposed Revision of the Rosenberg and Abbeduto D-Level Scale.* Paper presented at the Research Report, Artificial Intelligence Center, University of Georgia.

Davies, M. (2008). Word frequency data: Corpus of Contemporary American English.

Demir, S. (2010). *Sight for visually impaired users: Summarizing information graphics textually.* University of Delaware.

Demir, S., Oliver, D., Schwartz, E., Elzer, S., Carberry, S., McCoy, K. F., & Chester, D. (2010). Interactive SIGHT: textual access to simple bar charts. *New Rev. Hypermedia Multimedia, 16*, 245-279.

Ferres, L., Lindgaard, G., Sumegi, L., & Tsuji, B. (2013). Evaluating a Tool for Improving Accessibility to Charts and Graphs. *ACM Trans. Comput.-Hum. Interact., 20*(5), 28:21-28:32.

FSF. (2005). Style and Diction GNU project. from www.gnu.org/software/diction

Graesser, A. C., McNamara, D. S., Louwerse, M. M., Cai, Z., Dempsey, K., Floyd, Y., . . . Correspondence, F. Y. (2004). *Coh-Metrix: Analysis of text on cohesion and language.* Paper presented at the M. Louwerse Topics in Cognitive Science.

Heilman, M., Collins-Thompson, K., Callan, J., & Eskenazi, M. (2007). *Combining Lexical and Grammatical Features to Improve Readability Measures for First and Second Language Texts.* Paper presented at the HLT-NAACL.

Kincaid, J. P., Fishburne, R. P., Rogers, R. L., & Chissom, B. S. (1975). Derivation of New Readability Formulas (Automated Readability Index, Fog Count and Flesch Reading Ease Formula) for Navy Enlisted Personnel.

Laughlin, G. H. M. (1969). SMOG Grading-a New Readability Formula. *Journal of Reading, 12*(8), pp. 639-646.

McCoy, K., & Strube, M. (1999). *Generating Anaphoric Expressions: Pronoun or Definite Description?* Paper presented at the ACL WORKSHOP ON DISCOURSE AND REFERENCE STRUCTURE.

McKeown, K. (1992). *Text Generation*: Cambridge University Press.

Moraes, P. S., Carberry, S., & McCoy, K. (2013). *Providing access to the high-level content of line graphs from online popular media.* Paper presented at the Proceedings of the 10th International Cross-Disciplinary Conference on Web Accessibility, Rio de Janeiro, Brazil.

Rello, L., Baeza-Yates, R., Bott, S., & Saggion, H. (2013). *Simplify or Help?: Text Simplification Strategies for People with Dyslexia.* Paper presented at the Proceedings of the 10th International Cross-Disciplinary Conference on Web Accessibility, New York, NY, USA.

Rello, L., & Baeza-Yates, R. A. (2012). The presence of English and Spanish dyslexia in the Web. *The New Review of Hypermedia and Multimedia, 18*(3), 131-158.

Schwarm, S. E., & Ostendorf, M. (2005). *Reading Level Assessment Using Support Vector Machines and Statistical Language Models.* Paper presented at the Proceedings of the 43rd Annual Meeting on Association for Computational Linguistics, Stroudsburg, PA, USA.

Sheehan, K. M., Kostin, I., Futagi, Y., & Flor, M. (2010). Generating automated text complexity classifications that are aligned with targeted text complexity standards.

Walker, M. A., Rambow, O., & Rogati, M. (2001). *SPoT: a trainable sentence planner.* Paper presented at the Proceedings of the second meeting of the North American Chapter of the Association for Computational Linguistics on Language technologies, Stroudsburg, PA, USA.

Wilkinson, J. (1995). Aggregation in Natural Language Generation: Another Look.

Williams, S., & Reiter, E. (2008). Generating basic skills reports for low-skilled readers*. *Natural Language Engineering, 14*(4), 495-525.

Wu, P., Carberry, S., Elzer, S., & Chester, D. (2010). *Recognizing the intended message of line graphs.* Paper presented at the Proceedings of the 6th international conference on

Diagrammatic representation and inference, Berlin, Heidelberg.

Experimental Design to Improve Topic Analysis Based Summarization

John E. Miller
Computer & Information Sciences
University of Delaware
Newark, DE 19711
jmiller@udel.edu

Kathleen F. McCoy
Computer & Information Sciences
University of Delaware
Newark, DE 19711
mccoy@udel.edu

Abstract

We use efficient screening experiments to investigate and improve topic analysis based multi-document extractive summarization. In our summarization process, topic analysis determines the weighted topic content vectors that characterize the corpora, and then Jensen-Shannon divergence extracts sentences that best match the weighted content vectors to assemble the summaries. We use screening experiments to investigate several control parameters in this process, gaining better understanding of and improving the topic analysis based summarization process.

1 Introduction

We use efficient experimental design to investigate and improve topic analysis based multiple document extractive summarization. Our process proceeds in two steps: Latent Dirichlet Analysis (LDA) topic analysis determines the topics that characterize the multi-document corpus, and Jensen-Shannon divergence selects sentences from the corpus. This process offers many potential control settings for understanding and improving the summarization process.

Figure 1 shows topic analysis with corpus input, control settings, and product outputs of topics and probability estimates of topic compositions and document mixtures. There are controls for document preparation (headlines) and analysis (number of topics, initial α and β, number of iterations, and whether to optimize α and β in process).

Figure 2 shows summarization with corpus and topic inputs, control settings, and the text summarization product. There are controls for extraction of sentences (Extract α and JSD Divisor) and for composing the summary (Order policy).

Topic analysis has become a popular choice for text summarization as seen in Text Analysis Conferences (TAC, 2010; TAC, 2011) with individual team reports (Delort and Alfonseca, 2011; Lui et al., 2011; Mason and Charniak, 2011). Nenkova and McKeown (2012; 2011) included topic analysis among standard methods in their surveys of text summarization methodologies. Haghighi and Vanderwende (2009) explored extensions of LDA topic analysis for use in multiple document summarization tasks. Yet there are many control settings that can affect summarization that have not been explicitly studied or documented, and that are important for reproducing research results.

In this text summarization pilot study, we experiment with several control settings. As in Mason and Charniak (2011) we do a general rather than guided summarization. Our primary contribution is illustrating the use of efficient experimental design on control settings to help understand and improve the text summarization process. We enjoy some success in this endeavor even as we are surprised by some of our results.

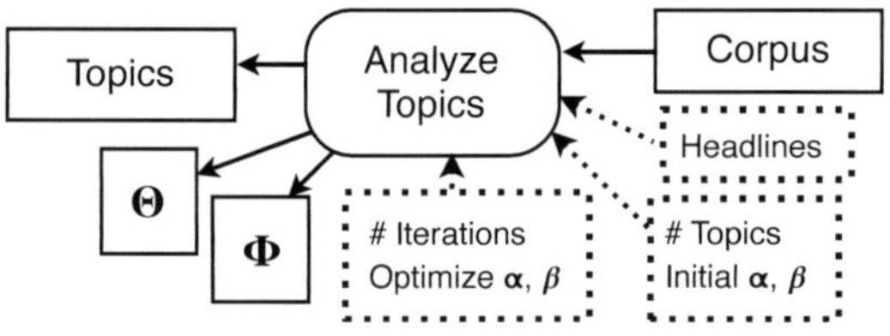

Figure 1: Topic Analysis

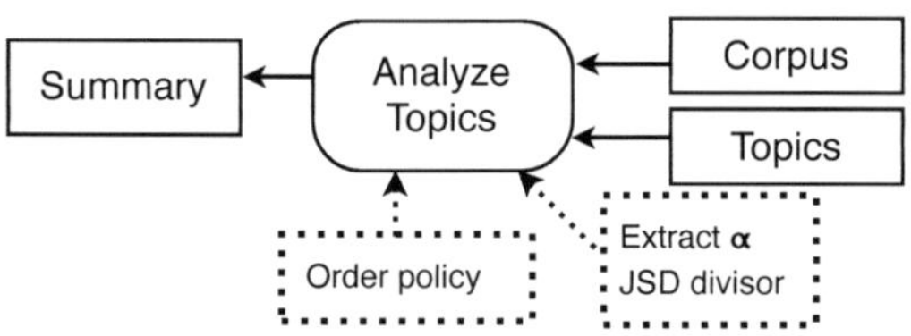

Figure 2: Text Summarization

Proceedings of the 8th International Natural Language Generation Conference, pages 74–82,
Philadelphia, Pennsylvania, 19-21 June 2014. ©2014 Association for Computational Linguistics

2 Technical Background

2.1 LDA Topic Analysis

LDA topic analysis uses a per document bag of words approach to determine topic compositions of words and document mixtures of topics. Analysis constructs topic compositions and document mixtures by assigning words to topics within documents. Weighted topic compositions can then be used as a basis for selecting the most informative text to include in summarizations.

LDA topic analysis is based on a generative probabilistic model. Document mixtures of topics are generated by a multinomial distribution, Θ, and topic compositions of words are generated by a multinomial distribution, Φ. Both Θ and Φ in turn are generated by Dirichlet distributions with parameters α and β respectively. Figure 3 (Steyvers and Griffiths, 2007) shows a corpus explained as the product of topic word compositions (Φ) and document topic mixtures (Θ).

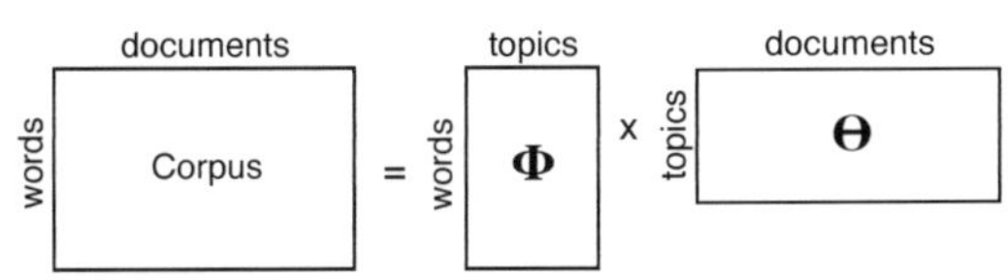

Figure 3: Topic Model

The joint distribution of words and topics (Griffiths and Steyvers (2004)) is given by $P(\boldsymbol{w}, \boldsymbol{z}) = P(\boldsymbol{w}|\boldsymbol{z})P(\boldsymbol{z})$ where in generating a document the topics are generated with probability $P(\boldsymbol{z})$ and the words given the topics are generated with probability $P(\boldsymbol{w}|\boldsymbol{z})$. Here

$$P(\boldsymbol{w}|\boldsymbol{z}) = \left(\frac{\Gamma(\beta_{\bullet})}{\Gamma(\beta)^{V}}\right)^{Z} \prod_{z=1}^{Z} \frac{\prod_{v} \Gamma(n_{zv} + \beta)}{\Gamma(n_{z\bullet} + \beta_{\bullet})}, \tag{1}$$

where n_{zv} is the number of times word v occurs in topic z, $n_{z\bullet}$ is the number of times topic z occurs, $\beta_{\bullet}$ is the sum of the β scalar over all word types, and $\Gamma(\,)$ is the gamma function (Knuth, 2004), and

$$P(\boldsymbol{z}) = \left(\frac{\Gamma(\alpha_{\bullet})}{\Gamma(\alpha)^{Z}}\right)^{D} \prod_{d=1}^{D} \frac{\prod_{z} \Gamma(n_{zd} + \alpha)}{\Gamma(n_{\bullet d} + \alpha_{\bullet})}, \tag{2}$$

where n_{zd} is the number of times topic z occurs in document d, $n_{\bullet d}$ is the number of times document d occurs, and $\alpha_{\bullet}$ is the sum of αs over topics.

Analysis reverses the generative model. Given a corpus, topic analysis identifies weighted topic word compositions and document topic mixtures from the corpus. We assign topics to words in the training corpus using Gibbs sampling (Gelman et al., 2004) where each word is considered in turn in making the topic assignment. We monitor training progress by $\log P(\boldsymbol{w}, \boldsymbol{z})$ where a greater $\log P(\boldsymbol{w}, \boldsymbol{z})$ indicates better fit. After sufficient iterations through the corpus the $\log P(\boldsymbol{w}, \boldsymbol{z})$ typically converges to steady state.

Analysis products are topic determinations for the corpus as well as weighted estimates of topic word compositions Φ and document topic mixtures Θ. The α and β priors are optimized (re-estimated) during training and the asymmetric α which varies by topic can be used as a measure of topic importance in our summarization step.

The topic analysis implementation used in this pilot study borrows from the UMass Mallet topic analysis (McCallum, 2002).

2.2 Jensen-Shannon Divergence

From the topic word compositions and optimized αs, we form a weighted aggregate vector of the prominent topics, and select sentences from the corpus that have minimal divergence from the aggregate topic. *The operating assumption is that the aggregate topic vector adequately represents the content of an ideal summary.* So the closer to *zero* divergence from the aggregate topic, the closer we are to the ideal summary.

We seek to minimize the Jensen-Shannon Divergence, $JSD(C||T)$, a symmetric Kullback-Liebler (KL) divergence, between the extractive summary content, C, and the aggregate topic, T, using a greedy search method of adding at each pass through the corpus the sentence that most reduces the divergence. Haghighi and Vanderwende (2009) made similar use of KL divergence in their *Topic Sum* method.

In preliminary studies, this minimize JSD criterion seemed to give overly long sentences because the greedy method favored the greatest reduction in JSD regardless of the length of the sentence. This affected readability and rapidly used up all available target document size. Therefore we modified the greedy search method to consider sentence length as well.[1]

[1]Global optimization of $JSD(C||T)$ could address both of these issues; we will investigate this option in a future effort.

In selecting each new sentence we seek to maximize the reduction in divergence corrected for sentence length

$$\frac{(JSD(C_{t-1}||T) - JSD(S_t, C_{t-1}||T))}{function(length(S_t))}, \quad (3)$$

where S_t is the sentence under consideration and C_{t-1} is the content from the previously completed iterations, and the function of length of S_t, is either the constant 1 (i.e. no correction for sentence length) or $\sqrt{length(S_t)}$.

3 Pilot Study Using TAC 2010 Samples

Our goal is to investigate and optimize factors that impact multi-document extractive summarization. We hope to subsequently extend our findings and experience to abstractive summarization as well.

For our pilot, we've chosen summarization of the 2010 Text Analysis Conference (2010) sample themes, which are conveniently available and of a manageable size. The three sample themes are from different summarization categories out of a total of 46 news themes over five different categories, with 10 original and 10 follow-up news reports each. In the original TAC 2010 task, participants were asked to do focused queries varying with the summarization category. In our pilot we perform an undirected summarization of the original news reports.

NIST provides 4 model summaries for each news theme annotated for the focused summary, and we use these model summaries in scoring our extractive summarizations.[2] We also include a measure of fluency in our assessment.

Our document summarization task is then: multiple document extractive summarization using 10 documents of less than 250 words each to construct summaries of 100 words.

3.1 Preliminary Results of Topic Analysis

Topic analysis is such a complex methodology that it makes sense to fix some parameters before using it in the summarization process.

We use the commonly accepted initial α value of 1 for each topic giving a sum of α values equal to the number of topics. Later, we experiment with a single individual topic initial α value, but we always maintain an initial α sum equal to the number of topics. Likewise we use the scalar β value 0.1 typical of a modest number of word types (less than 1000 in this study).

In prior studies, we found that re-estimating α and β frequently adds little cost to topic analysis and drives better and more rapid convergence. We optimize α and β every 5 iterations, starting at iteration 50.

How Many Topics to Use

The number of topics depends on the problem itself. The problem of size of $\approx$ 2000 words per news theme would indicate a number of topics between 3 and 20 as adequate to explain document word use where the $log(|Corpus|)$ is the minimum and $\sqrt{|Corpus|}$ is the maximum number of topics to use (Meilă, 2007).

A common way to select the correct number of topics is to optimize $\log P(\boldsymbol{w})$ on held-out documents, where greater log likelihoods indicate a better number of topics. While it would be impractical to do such a study for each news theme or each document summary, it is reasonable to do so on a few sample themes and then generalize to similar corpora. We look at log likelihood for 3, 5, and 10 topics using the TAC 2010 sample themes. As there are only 10 documents for each theme, we use the TAC 2010 update documents as held-out documents for calculating the log likelihoods.

Topic word distributions, Φ, from training are used to infer document mixtures, Θ, on the held-out data, and the log $P(\boldsymbol{w})$ is calculated (Teh et al., 2007) as:

$$P(\boldsymbol{w}) = \prod_{d,i}\left(\sum_{z}\frac{n_{zw_i}+\beta}{n_{z\bullet}+\beta_{\bullet}}\frac{n_{zd}+\alpha}{n_{\bullet d}+\alpha_{\bullet}}\right), \quad (4)$$

where the sum is over all possible topics for a given word and the product is over all documents and words.

Table 1 shows mean log likelihoods for the news themes at 3, 5 and 10 topics each. There is little practical difference between the log likelihood measures even though the 3 topic model has a significantly lower log likelihood ($p < 0.05$) than the 5 and 10 topic models. We assess topic quality more directly to see which model is better.

3 Topics	5 Topics	10 Topics
-6.00	-5.97	-5.96

Table 1: Held-out Log Likelihood Number Topics.

[2] Comparison of our summarization results versus the TAC 2010 task will necessarily be imprecise given the differences in focus of our pilot study from TAC 2010.

Useful topic quality measures are:

Importance measured by number of documents (or optimized αs). Low importance topics, with very few documents related to a topic, indicate that we have more topics than necessary. While not a fatal flaw, the topic model may be over fit.

Coherence measured as a log sum of co-occurrence proportions of each topic's high frequency words across multiple documents (Mimno et al., 2011). The more negative the coherence measure, the poorer the coherence. A few poor coherence topics is not fatal, but the topic model may be over fit.

Similarity to other topics measured by cosine distance between topic vectors is undesirable. The more similar the topics, the more difficult it is to distinguish between them. Many similar topics makes it difficult to discriminate among topics over the corpus.

Reviewing the document quality for 3, 5 and 10 topics we find:

- More low importance topics in 10 versus 5 and 3 topic models,
- Somewhat better topic coherence in 3 and 5 topic models,
- Undesirable greater topic similarity for the 3 versus 5 versus 10 topic models.

We choose the 10 topic model giving higher priority to the problem of undesirable topic similarity, recognizing that we may get some unimportant or less coherent topics. As our summarization process only uses the most important topics for the aggregate topic, the occasional unimportant and less coherent topic should not matter.

Document Preparation

Document cleaning removed all HTML, as well as all header information not related to the articles themselves; document dates, references, and headlines were saved for use in the document summarization step. Document headlines were optionally folded into the document text. Stop words were removed and remaining words lemmatized for topic analysis.

4 Design of Experiments

As our information about the various controls in the process and the expected results is fairly rudimentary, we use efficient screening experimental designs to evaluate several factors at the same time with a minimum number of trials. We define the factors (control parameters) in our experiment, the dependent variables we will measure, and finally select the screening design itself.

Most of the process of topic analysis will remain fixed such as the use of 10 topics, initial α sum of 10, initial scalar β of 0.1, optimization of α and β every 5 iterations and 500 total iterations before saving the final topic vector weights and corresponding topic alphas.

From our experimentation we hope to find:

- Factors impacting dependent variables,
- Gross magnitude of impact on dependent variables,
- Factors to followup with in more detail.

4.1 Experimental Factors

In screening experiments, we chose factors about which we have crude information, and which we think could impact intermediate or final product results. To learn as much as possible about factor effects, we choose to vary them between default and extreme settings or between two extremes where we hope to see some positive impact.

Our experimental factors are:

Save headline text as part of document preparation (Yes, No). Headlines often contain important summary information. We test to see if such information improves summaries.

Single fixed α proportion of the α sum (*, 0.5). Topic analysis typically selects (weights) a few important topic vectors with substantial proportions of the α sum. We want to see if biasing selection of a *single* important vector at a 0.5 proportion of the α sum improves summaries versus unbiased α weighting (*).

Aggregate topic policy as a proportion of the α sum for selecting the topic aggregate used in summarization (0.5, 0.75). We order topics based on the optimized (re-estimated) αs and aggregate topics summing and weighting by the αs until we reach the aggregate topic policy proportion. We want to see which policy (0.5 or 0.75) proportion of the α sum results in better summaries.

JSD divisor to use with iterative greedy search for sentences (ONE, SQRT). Prior work shows the JSD Divisor impacts the length of sentences selected. We test the impact on the summaries themselves.

Order policy for constructing the summary from selected sentences (DATE-DOC, SALIENCE-DOC). Ordering sentences by news report date or by salience as measured by reduction in JSD should impact the fluency of summaries.

4.2 Dependent Variables

We want readable and informative text that summarizes content of the input documents in the allowable space. We measure several intermediate process variables as well as evaluate the summaries themselves.

Intermediate measures include:

- Initial selected sentence Jensen-Shannon divergence from the aggregate topic. The first sentence selected should substantially reduce divergence.
- Final selected sentence Jensen-Shannon divergence from the aggregate topic. Divergence close to zero would indicate broad coverage of the aggregate topic; it may be related to summary content.
- Number of topics in the aggregate topic.
- Average sentence length. This should be impacted by the JSD divisor; it may be related to summary fluency.

ROUGE (Lin, 2011) is a package for automatic evaluation of summaries that compares system produced summaries to model (gold standard) summaries and reports statistics such as R-2, bi-gram co-occurrence statistics between system and model summaries, and SU4, skip bi-gram co-occurrence statistics where word pairs no more than 4 words apart may also be counted as bigrams. The R-2 and SU4 are automated content measures reported for TAC 2010, and the gold standard summaries are readily available for the samples topics. We use ROUGE R-2 and SU4 as reliable dependent measures and for comparison to TAC 2010 results.

We add a simple measure of fluency focused on across sentence issues. The fluency score starts at a value of 5 and then subtracts: 1 for each *non sequitur* or obvious out of order sentence, $1/2$ for each missing co-reference, non-informative, ungrammatical, or redundant sentence. For sentences of less than 20 words, when more than one penalty applies only the most severe penalty is applied, so as not to penalize the same short phrase multiple times. Scoring is done by one of the authors without knowing the combination of experimental factors of the summary (blind scoring).

Summary measures thus include: ROUGE R-2, ROUGE SU4, and Fluency.

4.3 Select Experimental Design

Screening designs focus on detecting and assessing main effects and optionally low order interaction effects. When all experimental factors are continuous, center points may also be included in some designs. In subsequent stages of experimentation, when factors have been reduced to a minimum, one can use more fine grained factor settings to better map the response surface for those factors. Two common families of screening designs (Montgomery, 1997) are:

Two level fractional factorial Uses a power of $1/2$ fraction of a full two level factorial design. For example, instead of running all possible combinations of 5 factors (i.e. 32 trials), you could choose a $1/2$ or even $1/4$ fraction of the design, based on how many experiments you can run and how much confounding you are willing to accept between main effects and various interaction effects. The $1/2$ fraction of a 5 factor design would result in 16 trials being run with the main effects estimated clear of any 2-way or 3-way interactions.

Plackett-Burman These screening designs are available in multiples of 4 trials and can have as many factors as the number of trials less one. Main effects are confounded with all other effects in the Plackett-Burman design and so not estimable, but the confounding is spread evenly among all main effects rather than concentrated in specific interactions as in the fractional factorial.

We've chosen the 12 run Plackett-Burman design with 5 factors and 6 degrees of freedom from the unassigned (dummy) factors available to estimate error. Assuming sparsity of effects (or equivalently invoking the Pareto principal), there will likely only be a few critical factors explaining much of the variation in dependent variables.

Table 2 shows the resulting Plackett-Burman design excluding dummy factors.

Run	Fixed Alpha	Aggr Topic	JSD Div	Order	Head Line
1	.5	.75	ONE	SAL	YES
2	*	.75	SQRT	DATE	YES
3	.5	.5	SQRT	SAL	NO
4	*	.75	ONE	SAL	YES
5	*	.5	SQRT	DATE	YES
6	*	.5	ONE	SAL	NO
7	.5	.5	ONE	DATE	YES
8	.5	.75	ONE	DATE	NO
9	.5	.75	SQRT	DATE	NO
10	*	.75	SQRT	SAL	NO
11	.5	.5	SQRT	SAL	YES
12	*	.5	ONE	DATE	NO

Table 2: Plackett-Burman 12 DOE.

5 Experimental Results

We analyze our experiment using conventional analysis of variance (ANOVA) and show tables of means for the various experimental conditions. As this is a screening experiment, we treat a p-value < 0.20 as *informative* and consider the corresponding factor worth further consideration. To save space, only significant p-values are reported rather than the full ANOVAs.

5.1 Intermediate Measures

Number of topics in the aggregate topic is directly impacted by the AggrTopic setting; we simply report the mean number of topics selected by AggrTopic value (Table 3). The 1.0 average number of topics for AggrTopic set to 0.5 indicates that only *one* topic was ever selected for the aggregate topic at this setting. This implies that the most important topic always had an α proportion > 0.50 of the α sum even when the FixedAlpha setting was * (for unbiased α weighting). This is unexpected in that we thought the most important topic α determined by topic analysis would be more variable and show some α values with proportions less than 0.5 of the α sum.

Aggr Topic	Number Topics
0.50	1.00
0.75	4.55

Table 3: Average Number Topics.

Average sentence length in the summary may be affected by any of the independent variables except sentence order policy. JSD Divisor has a dramatic impact ($p < 0.0001$) and AggrTopic a modest impact ($p < 0.01$) on average sentence length. Using a divisor of ONE in the JSD based sentence selection results in much longer sentences while using AggrTopic of 0.5 results in shorter sentences (Table 4).

Aggr Topic	Sentence Length	JSD Divisor	Sentence Length
0.5	20.3	ONE	26.8
0.75	23.9	SQRT	17.4

Standard Error of the mean = 0.78

Table 4: Average Sentence Length.

Initial selected sentence Jensen-Shannon divergence (JSD) should be affected directly by JSD Divisor in iterative sentence selection, but may also be affected by any of the other independent variables except for sentence order policy. AggrTopic and JSD Divisor strongly impact initial sentence JSD ($p < 0.00005$).

The table of JSD initial sentence means by AggrTopic and JSD Divisor is revealing (Table 5). The JSD for the initial sentence selected is lower for AggrTopic of 0.5. We observed above that only *one* topic is selected for the aggregate topic when AggrTopic is 0.5. Thus we achieve a lower divergence of the initial sentence from the aggregate topic when the aggregate is composed of only *one* topic. For initial sentence JSD, aggregating topics seems ineffective.

Similarly a JSD Divisor of ONE gives a lower initial divergence than using the SQRT as the divisor. The interpretation is problematic here in that a divisor of ONE seems to give lower initial divergence because it selects longer sentences, which means that less space remains in the summary to select other sentences minimizing total divergence.

Aggr Topic	JSD Initial	JSD Divisor	JSD Initial
0.5	0.665	ONE	0.658
0.75	0.735	SQRT	0.742

Standard Error of the mean = 0.0056

Table 5: Average Initial JSD.

Table 6 shows the impact of AggrTopic and JSD Divisor together on the JSD for the initial sentence. There is still the issue of whether using a JSD Divisor of ONE is appropriate given the effect on the remaining summary size, but the effects appear additive.

Aggr Topic	JSD Divisor	JSD initial
0.50	ONE	0.627
0.50	SQRT	0.703
0.75	ONE	0.690
0.75	SQRT	0.780

Standard Error of the mean = 0.0080

Table 6: Average Initial JSD.

Final sentence Jensen-Shannon Divergence (JSD) may be affected by any but the sentence order policy variable. AggrTopic ($p < 0.00001$) and JSD Divisor ($p < 0.001$) strongly impact the final sentence JSD; there is also a possible effect from including headlines in the summary ($p < 0.1$). The effect of the JSD Divisor has reversed from the initial JSD; using a divisor of ONE results here in a *less desirable* higher divergence for the final sentence. The AggrTopic effect is about the same as for initial JSD divergence; a single dominant topic seems more effective than using an aggregate topic.

Aggr Topic	JSD Final	JSD Divisor	JSD Final
0.5	0.422	ONE	0.487
0.75	0.513	SQRT	0.448

Standard Error of the mean = 0.0047

Table 7: Average Initial JSD.

Impact of AggrTopic and JSD Divisor together on the JSD for the initial sentence (Table 8) seems additive.

Aggr Topic	JSD Divisor	JSD final
0.50	ONE	0.437
0.50	SQRT	0.407
0.75	ONE	0.537
0.75	SQRT	0.490

Standard Error of the mean = 0.0066

Table 8: Average Final JSD.

5.2 Product Measures

Based on the analysis of intermediate measures, it would seem that using a JSD Divisor of the SQRT and selecting only the dominant topic gives less divergence from the aggregate topic. However, we have to be careful here in drawing conclusions based on intermediate variables; selecting only the dominant topic may result in reduced divergence, but this does not necessarily mean that the dominant topic is representative of good summaries.

We examine product variables to provide direct support in our study, and so we ask how ROUGE R-2 and SU4, and fluency evaluations vary with the experimental factors. This pilot studies unguided summarization of initial stories from the 3 sample news themes from 3 separate categories. While results are not directly comparable with those of the full TAC 2010 test corpus, we will use the TAC 2010 results as a reference point versus our own results. The average of all experiments are reported along with the TAC 2010 results (Table 9). Our ROUGE R-2 and SU4 performance seems reasonable showing results better than the baseline but not as good as the best system.

Reference System	R-2	SU4
Baseline - Lead sentences	5.4	8.6
Baseline - MEAD†	5.9	9.1
Best System	9.6	13.0
Pilot Average	6.7	10.1
Pilot Minimum	5.6	8.7
Pilot Maximum	8.1	11.9

†Text summarization system (Radevet al., 2004)

Table 9: TAC 2010 ROUGE Scores.

ROUGE R-2 results show no significant impact from our experimental factors. This is disappointing as it gives us no handle on how to improve performance.

ROUGE SU4 shows a modest impact for AggrTopic ($p < 0.025$) and the possible impact of JSD Divisor ($p < 0.20$). Note that we dropped Order and FixedAlpha factors from the model; Order because it can only effect sentence order and FixedAlpha because the most important α determined automatically by topic analysis did not vary much from the 0.5 FixedAlpha. A benefit of dropping terms from the model is that we have more dummy factors to estimate error.

The ROUGE SU4 means (Table 10) show the same pattern as for the JSD final sentence, but the differences are not as clear cut. Box and whiskers plots for AggrTopic and JSD Divisor (Figures 4 and 5) offer more insight into the AggrTopic and JSD Divisor effects.

There is a clear distinction between AggrTopic

Aggr Topic	ROUGE SU4	JSD Divisor	ROUGE SU4
0.5	10.75	ONE	9.70
0.75	9.48	SQRT	10.53

Standard Error of the mean = 0.32

Table 10: Average ROUGE SU4.

levels 0.5 and 0.75 with better results at the 0.5 level, except for an outlier value of 9.1. Investigation shows no data coding error and nothing special about the experimental conditions other than if uses a JSD Divisor of ONE which also gives lower SU4 scores. The box and whiskers plots for JSD Divisor effects also suggest a positive effect for JSD Divisor of SQRT, but the whiskers overlap the boxes indicating no strong effect.

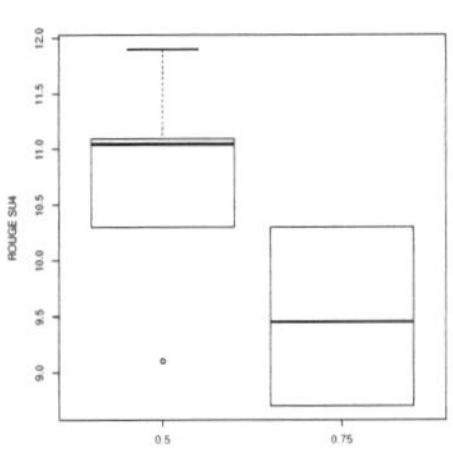

Figure 4: ROUGE SU4 by Aggr Topic

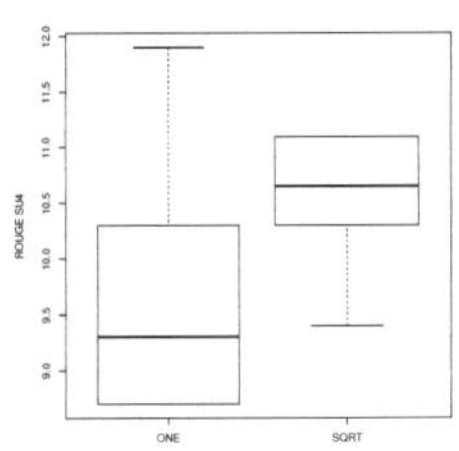

Figure 5: ROUGE SU4 by JSD Divisor

We had speculated that the final sentence divergence might be related to some of the end product measures. Indeed, we find that JSD final sentence is strongly inversely related to ROUGE SU4 as shown by regression analysis (Table 11). While the residual error of 0.73 indicates that we can only reliably predict ROUGE SU4 within 1.5 units (for averages of 3 trials), this is still important. A 0.1 reduction in final sentence divergence corresponds on the average to a 1.4 unit increase in ROUGE SU4.

	Estimate	StdErr	t	Pr(>|t|)
Intercept	16.865	1.934	8.721	~0.0
JSDfinal	-14.435	4.112	-3.510	0.006

Residual standard error: 0.73 on 10 degrees of freedom

F-statistic: 12.32 on 1 and 10 DF, p-value: 0.0056

Table 11: Regression - ROUGE SU4.

We thought *Simple Fluency* would show an effect for sentence order policy and maybe other factors. Analysis shows an effect for JSD Divisor ($p < 0.05$) and possible effects of Order policy and Head lines ($p < 0.20$).

Fluency means (Table 12) show that fluency is better for JSD Divisor ONE. From our experience of scoring Fluency, this would seem to be because the fewer and longer sentences with JSD Divisor of ONE offer fewer chances for disfluencies. The better Fluency with DATE ordering likely comes from fewer out of order or *non sequitur* sentences, and the better Fluency with NO headlines likely results from fewer short ungrammatical headlines as part of the text.

JSD Div	Fluency	Order	Fluency	Head Lines	Fluency
ONE	3.95	DATE	3.80	NO	3.80
SQRT	3.33	SAL	3.47	YES	3.47

Standard Error of the mean = 0.16

Table 12: Average Fluency.

6 Summary and Discussion

Our pilot studied topic analysis based multi-document extractive summarization using the 2010 TAC sample topics. Our experimental design process identified control factors with their default and extreme settings, defined intermediate and final product dependent measures, designed the experiment, ran, and analyzed the experiment.

We identified an intermediate variable, final selected sentence divergence, that could be used as a stand-in for the product content measure, ROUGE SU4. We found that using a single dominant topic, instead of an aggregate topic, and using a divisor of the square root of sentence length in sentence selection, improved final sentence divergence and ROUGE SU4. However, using a divisor of one in sentence selection improved fluency of summaries which is at odds with the benefit of using square root of sentence length to improve content.

Our planned experimentation has made obvious and objective the process of describing and improving our extractive summarization process. It is an extremely useful process and furthermore a process that when documented permits sharing of results and even duplicating of results by others working in this area.

References

Jean-Yves Delort and Enrique Alfonseca. 2011. Description of the Google Update Summarizer. *2011 TAC Proceedings.*

Andrew Gelman, John B. Carlin, Hal S. Stern, and Donald B. Rubin. 2004. *Bayesian Data Analysis.* Chapman and Hall/CRC, New York, USA.

Tom L. Griffiths and Mark Steyvers. 2004. Finding Scientific Topics. *PNAS*, 101(Suppl. 1):5228-5235.

Aria Haghighi and Lucy Vanderwalde. 2009. Exploring Content Models for Multi-Document Summarization. *2009 NACL Conference*, HLT Proceedings:362-370.

Donald E. Knuth. 1997. *The Art of Computer Programming*, Volume 1 (Fundamental Algorithms). Addison Wesley, New York, USA.

Chin-Yew Lin. 204. ROUGE: A Package for Automatic Evaluation of Summaries. *ACL 2004* Proceedings of Workshop: Text Summarization Branches Out.

Hongyan Liu, Pingan Liu, Wei Heng, and Lei Li. 2011. The CIST Summarization System at TAC 2011. *2011 TAC Proceedings.*

Dragomir Radev, Timothy Allison, Sasha Blair-Goldensohn, John Blitzer, Arda Celebi, Stanko Dimitrov, Elliott Drabek, Ali Hakim, Wai Lam, Danyu Liu, Jahna Otterbacher, Hong Qi, Horacio Saggion, Simone Teufel, Michael Topper, Adam Winkel, and Zhu Zhang. 2004. MEAD — A platform for multidocument multilingual text summarization. *Conference on Language Resources and Evaluation LREC, Lisbon, Portugal, (May 2004).*

Rebecca Mason and Eugene Charniak. 2011. BLLIP at TAC 2011: A General Summarization System for a Guided Summarization Task. *2011 TAC Proceedings.*

Andres K. McCallum. 2002. MALLET: A Machine Learning for Language Toolkit. http://mallet.cs.umass.edu.

Marina Meilă. 2007. Comparing Clusterings – an information based distance. *J. Multivariate Analysis*, 98(5):873-895.

David Mimno, Hanna M. Wallach, Edmund Talley, Miriam Leenders, and Andrew McCallum. 2011. Optimizing Semantic Coherence in Topic Models. *2011 EMNLP Conference*, Proceedings:262-272.

Douglas C. Montgomery. 1997. *Design and Analysis of Experiments.* John Wiley and Sons, New York, USA.

Ani Nenkova and Kathleen McKeown. 2011. Automatic Summarization. *Foundations and Trends in Information Retrieval*, 5(2-3):1003-233.

Ani Nenkova and Kathleen McKeown. 2012. A Survey of Text Summarization Techniques. *Mining Text Data.* In Charu C. Aggarwal and ChengXiang Zhai (eds.) Springer.

Mark Steyvers and Tom Griffiths. 2007. Probabilisitic Topic Models. *Latent Semantic Analysis: A road to Meaning.* In T. Landauer, S. D. McNamara & W. Kintsch (eds.) Laurence Erlbaum.

Task Analysis Conference 2010 – Summarization Track. 2010. http://www.nist.gov/tac/2010/Summarization/.

Task Analysis Conference 2011 – Summarization Track. 2011. http://www.nist.gov/tac/2011/Summarization/.

Yee Whye Teh, Dave Newman, and Max Welling. 2007. Collapsed Variational Inference for HDP. *Advances in Neural Information Processing Systems*:1481-1488.

Towards a Description of Symbolic Maps

Daniel Couto Vale
SFB/TR8 Spatial Cognition
University of Bremen
danielvale@uni-bremen.de

Elisa Vales
SFB/TR8 Spatial Cognition
University of Bremen
evales@uni-bremen.de

Rumiya Izgalieva
SFB/TR8 Spatial Cognition
University of Bremen
rumiya@uni-bremen.de

Abstract

Symbolic resources for text synthesis and text analysis are typically created and stored separately. In our case, we have a KPML-resource (Nigel) and a CCG for English. In this paper, we argue that reversing efficient resources such as ours cannot in general be achieved. For this reason, we propose a symbolic map that can be converted automatically into both synthesis- and analysis-oriented resources. We show that completeness of description can only be achieved by such a map while efficiency concerns can only be tackled by the directed rules of task-oriented resources not because of the current state of the art, but because reversing task-oriented symbolic resources is impossible in principle.

1 Introduction

Currently, symbolic resources guiding text analysis and text synthesis are created and stored separately. Several researchers have attempted to use the same resource for both tasks (Kasper, 1988; Neumann, 1991; Neumann and van Noord, 1992; Strzalkowski, 1994; O'Donnell, 1994; Pulman, 1995; Klarner, 2005) motivated by the fact that this would not only be cognitively more plausible but also allow translation at a semantic level, integration of new words from analysis into synthesis, reduction of costs in engineering as well as making it easier to share information among research groups of different fields.

The resources we currently use in human-robot interaction in English are also separate: a KPML-resource (Nigel) and a CCG. The specialty about Nigel and our CCG is that they share not only the same kind of semantics, but also the same mapping between symbolic and semantic structures. Here 'symbolic structure' is understood as KPML's 'structure' and CCG's 'sign', and corresponds to 'grammatical constructions' of cognitive semantics (Lakoff, 1987), to 'linguistic mediation' of truth-reference semantics (Smith and Brogaard, 2003), and to 'wording' of systemic functional linguistics (Matthiessen, 1995; Matthiessen and Halliday, 1999; Matthiessen and Halliday, 2004; Halliday and Matthiessen, 2014).

In this paper, we shall review the available directed rules that constitute the resources in KPML and OpenCCG and argue that they are useful in their respective tasks – either synthesis or analysis, – but are either unsuitable or not competitive for the inverse task.

Aiming not at reversibility but at reusability, we propose to create a map between symbolic and semantic structures that can be compiled into both synthesis-oriented and analysis-oriented resources. With this approach, we aim at separating concerns, so that efficiency can be tackled by the directed rules of task-oriented resources and completeness of description by a less efficient uncompiled shared symbolic map.

2 Irreversibility of Current Resources

In computational linguistics, approaches to text processing can be divided into statistical and categorial according to the usage of graded or binary relations between inputs and outputs of processing. Approaches can also be divided depending on whether the textual content is a representation of something else (symbolic) or whether it is a representation of the text itself (non-symbolic). In this sense, approaches that have a semantic structure as input or output are symbolic and those that make use of a syntactic tree whose composite-component relations do not match the ones of semantics are not. The present work falls into the symbolic subset. Although our initial attempt is categorial, the ideas presented here can be used in statistical approaches as well, provided that these approaches are symbolic in nature.

Looking from the perspective of the philosophy of language, in the last 50 years, computational efforts in categorial symbolic text processing have converged on one single notion of a symbolic map. In such a notion, both symbolic (lexical or grammatical) and semantic structures play an essential role in deciding which analytical and synthetic hypotheses are to be taken further or discarded. On the text synthesis front, systemic networks were used by both KOMET and Penman engines as directed rules for text synthesis. Those engines were later unified into the KOMET-Penman Multilingual

Engine (KPML Engine) (Bateman, 1995a; Bateman, 1995b; Bateman, 1996; Bateman, 1997). On the text analysis front, typed-feature unification was developed and implemented in engines for a family of highly lexicalised grammatical frameworks (HLG). Combinatory Categorial Grammars (CCG) (Steedman, 1987; Steedman, 1996; Steedman, 1998; Steedman and Baldridge, 2011) are a special type of HLG that reduce the task of text analysis to accepting or rejecting hypotheses of both symbolic and semantic composition during functional unification. KPML and OpenCCG are then only candidates for consideration because they allow the implementation of a shared symbolic map. In other words, a pair of engines that support such a map is a necessary and sufficient condition for the reusability scheme we propose.

In the following, we shall review the grammatical notions embedded in the resources for KPML and OpenCCG in order to support our argumentation that reversibility of such directed resources is not to be achieved.

2.1 Resources for KPML

According to the KPML documentation (Bateman, 1996) and our own inspection of Nigel, resources for KMPL may contain three kinds of realisation operations: structural (insert, conflate, expand), linear (partition, order, order-at-front, order-at-end), and inter-rank (preselect, agreement, classify, outclassify, inflectify, lexify).

Below symbolic structure, textual tokens are produced by morphological realisation operators of two kinds: one for selecting token copies (preselect-substance, preselect-substance-as-stem, preselect-substance-as-property), and one for modifying them (morphose).

These realisation operators are bundled in wording 'patterns' that are linked to classes of wordings (grammatical features). The typology arising from these classes is used as a network of options (network of grammatical systems) among structure kinds. The selection of a structure kind of a system is done by a decision tree (chooser). Each decision in the decision tree is achieved by inspecting (inquiry) a semantic and lexical specification for a text. The decision tree contains not only decisions (ask) but also mappings from lexical/semantic constituents to functions of symbolic constituents (identify, copyhub, choose, pledge, termpledge). Values can be associated with a function (concept, modification-specification, terms, term).

Finally, there are four ways to produce a token in KPML. Three of them consist of selecting a word and selecting its form with a form class. The actual token production is left to a morphological component. Two word selection strategies are: selecting a word grammatically (lexify, classify, outclassify) and selecting a word associated with a particular conceptual value (term-resolve-id). A mapping between concepts and words is provided either by concept-word links (annotate-concept) or by embedding word specifications into what would otherwise be a pure semantic specification (lex). A distinct mapping function between the intersection of form classes and word pattern indexes is implemented in LISP for every linguistic resource. At the morphological level, a token is produced by selecting a token model and applying any necessary morphological modifications to it (preselect-substance, preselect-substance-as-stem, preselect-substance-as-property, morphose).

Therefore, as with any other categorial text synthesiser, KPML traverses a network of options among progressively finer types of structures and makes choices between different structure types depending on semantical and lexical restrictions. Its speciality comes not from the general approach, but from the amount and quality of detailed linguistic knowledge applied to the synthesis of text in Nigel, which makes Nigel a good option for our applications that demand natural utterances. This is also the main reason why so many attempts have been made to use Nigel for text analysis.

2.2 Resources for OpenCCG

OpenCCG, as for any other engine using chart parsing, relies on the assumption that a hypothesised structure is only to be considered if it is part of a structure for the whole input text. This assumption of syntagmatic holism was first formulated by Frege (1884) and Wittgenstein (1921; 1922). Chart parsing with CCGs goes beyond: both syntagmatic and paradigmatic holisms are to be enforced, i.e. semantic fitting is used as a filter for analytical hypotheses as well. Such a paradigmatic holism was first formulated by Davidson (1967).

OpenCCG is an engine for analysing texts with CCGs (Steedman and Baldridge, 2011; Bozşahin et al., 2005). It classifies word forms into categories according to their affordances of combining with other word forms and structures in the process of building up larger structures and construing meaning. In this process, the empty slots of semantic frames, associated with a word, are filled up by the semantic values of the structures that the word form combines with.

Only complete symbolic and semantic structures that represent the whole text are kept by the text analyser (although incomplete structures may also be retrieved for online text processing).

There are two kinds of combinatory categories: the complete (atomic) does not combine with any other structure; the incomplete (complex) has either a frame with empty slots or is missing word parts, so it combines with other structures for semantic or symbolic completion.

Incomplete categories of symbolic structures are turned into a complete category by the OpenCCG engine whenever a structure that is combinable with a preceding or following structure of a certain kind is preceded or followed by a structure of this kind. Slashes \, | and / indicate that a structure of a combinatory category is combinable with a structure that respectively precedes it, is adjacent to it, or follows it. For instance, the structure of *saw* holding a two-slot frame in the clause *Mary saw John* can be said to belong to the category Clause\Mention/Mention, because it expects a complete mention (Mention) of the sensed thing after it and a complete mention (Mention) of the senser before it. The resulting structure after combination is a complete clause (Clause).

In addition, slashes come in four different generalities: they may allow no composition (·), only harmonic compositions (◇), only crossing compositions (×) or any composition (•).

The smallest structures in OpenCCG are word forms. Word forms (morph entries) map a token pattern (word) to a word id (stem), a combinatory category tag (pos), the meaning of the word (class), and a list of form classes (fs-macros) and slot fillers (lf-macros). This terminal mapping is equivalent to the map from grammatical functions to lexical and semantical structures in KPML.

2.3 KPML-Analysis and CCG-Synthesis

Kay (1979; 1985) developed the Functional Unification Grammar (FUG) and Kasper (1988) used FUG for exploring text analysis with Nigel. Analysing a clause took about 1 minute (currently approx. 500ms assuming 120-times faster processors) and analysing a complex clause took several minutes. Kasper concluded grammars needed to be "tuned" and augmented for the inverse task, but also that some information would be superfluous and counterproductive for either text synthesis or text analysis. Following Kasper, O'Donnell (1994) reduced the descriptive complexity of Nigel to create a text analyser. After this, Henschel (1995; 1997) attempted to analyse text with the full Nigel grammatical description again by abstracting an open-world typology from a systemic network and compiling the Nigel resource completely for the first time into a typed-feature-structure resource. However, the resource was unusable for practical text analysis. When reviewing these previous attempts, Bateman (2008) pointed out that the conception of systemic-functional resources alone, as it is, cannot support effective automatic text analysis due to fundamental theoretical concerns. That is, the paradigmatic organisation of the systemic-functional approach raises an enormous search space problem when used for text analysis because the network does not have information about which grammatical feature is relevant for any given text token. If one uses such a network for analysing text, one needs to produce a complete set of all possible intersections of grammatical features in order to predict all supported analyses, which is the solution provided by Kasper and by Henschel. Bateman shows that this is computationally intractable for the full version of Nigel's noun group and Nigel's clause.

On the CCG side, broad-coverage surface realisation has also been attempted (White et al., 2007; Rudnick, 2010). In order for a CCG to work for text synthesis, it was enriched with a customised semantics. The resulting search space was still too large and, for this reason, a search heuristic was applied using n-grams, pos-tags, supertags, and semantic values for evaluation of paths. The realisation achieved promising scores with a time-limit of 15 seconds when trained over the CCGBank – a derivation corpus with the same sentences as the Penn TreeBank – and tested over the same sentences.

However, the decision of synthesising a text with a search heuristic is a consequence of the fact that the used resource does not hold all the information necessary for a guided search algorithm for text synthesis. The reason for this is also of a theoretical nature. Once structural information is embedded in word forms, combinatory categories and type changes, it is impossible to take this information back out of them and repack it in a network of options without counting on two essential constructs for synthesis: on the one side, semantic composition and semantic paradigms and, on the other side, a paradigmatic organisation of classes of structure provided by disjunct unions of structure classes (systems). CCGs do not and could not, for efficiency reasons, rely on logical disjunctions, which are essential for text synthesis.

To make the consequences of this limitation more clear, let us take an example of how combinatory operators are declared in resources for OpenCCG (abbreviations: C = Clause, M = Mention, f = Figure, e = Element):

– danced (*I danced*)
– stopped dancing (*I stopped dancing*)
– started dancing (*I started dancing*)
(C[mode-2]:f\M:e0) => (C[mode-ø]:f\M:e0)
@f<hasTense>e1:Past

– am here (*I am here*)
(C[mode-1]:f\M:e0) => (C[mode-ø]:f\M:e0)
@f:State(<hasTense>e1:Present)

– am (*I am dancing*)
am := (C[mode-ø]:f\M:e0)/(C[mode-6]:f\M:e0)
@f:Change(<hasTense>e1:Present)

– will (*I will dance*)
will := (C[mode-ø]:f\M:e0)/(C[mode-4]:f\M:e0)
@f<hasTense>e1:Future

– stopped (*I stopped dancing*)
stopped := (C[mode-2]:f\M:e0)/(C[mode-6]:f\M:e0)
@f<hasPhase>e1:Stop

– started (*I started dancing*)
started := (C[mode-2]:f\M:e0)/(C[mode-6]:f\M:e0)
@f<hasPhase>e1:Start

Simplified extract of our CCG-resource

The above combinatory categories and type-changes cover different semantic contributions, which are not automatically organisable into systems of symbolic and semantic classes. First, the resource for OpenCCG does not have the information that Past, Present, and Future constitute a semantic disjunction of TENSE and that Start and Stop belong to a distinct semantic disjunction of PHASE. Moreover, the resource does not have the information that finite clauses have tense and that non-finite clauses do not, so that it could decide which system to traverse for each kind of clause. And, finally, we cannot guarantee that an inspection of the figure type happens before the selection of 1) the present auxiliary *am* in *I am dancing* representing a change in the present and 2) the present form *am* of the process of Being in *I am here* (instead *I am being here*) representing a present state. This incapability of grouping contrasting options and of conditioning and ordering systems within a network demands a search algorithm with backtracking. Because of the computational costs of backtracking, it also demands a search heuristic as engineering solution.

3 Symbolic Map

We acknowledge the unsuitability of task-oriented resources for the inverse tasks of synthesis and analysis and shall tackle the issues of bridging a paradigmatic text synthesis and a syntagmatic text analysis at a theoretical level. We propose to describe a symbolic-semantic map that can be compiled into task-oriented resources for separate engines (concretely here: KPML and OpenCCG): a scheme that falls into the Reusability Scheme A (reversibility type) of Klarner (2005) (see Figure 1). In our case, this reusability scheme applies to both grammar and lexicon.

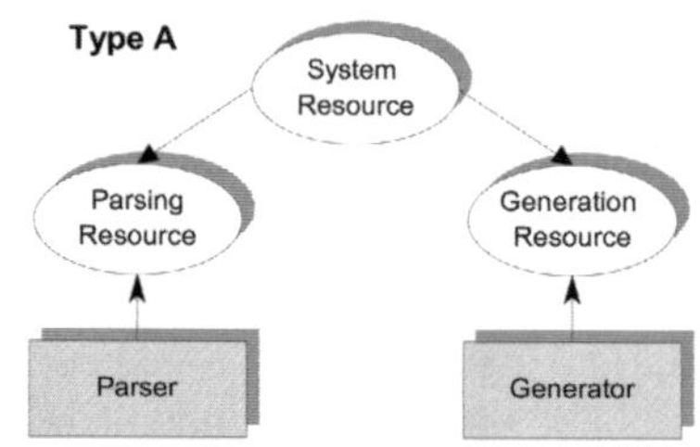

Figure 1. Reusability Scheme

In our argumentation, we shall propose a reformulation of Nigel as a description in OWL of a symbolic map that supports the proposed compilation. Moving from specific to general, we shall point out which mapping strategies can be used and show that every descriptive region of Nigel is representable in such a map.

3.1 Sketch

Bateman (2008) has sketched how an automatic text analysis with systemic-functional theory ('systemic parse') needs to look. It needs a functional description for sequences of text tokens, including the necessary information both for assigning grammatical features to structures and for identifying composites on a sequence of constituents. Such a symbolic map, we shall see, needs to account for the systemic-functional trinocular view of symbolic systems: from above, from below and from around. Moreover, it also needs to account for two different affordances required for a classification of structures: one that organises disjoint classes as a system of grammatical features for text synthesis and another that organises the same disjunctions as restrictions for the combination of incomplete structures in text analysis. The former organisation moves all information of structure into the grammatical network, whereas the latter organisation moves it into word forms.

In the reusability scheme of our new resource, we keep the structural information out of the systemic network and out of the word forms. It is stored in a symbolic map that allows us to pack it into the two task-oriented resources, i.e. into the systemic network for text synthesis and into word forms/type changes for text analysis. We have chosen to represent this information in Description Logic (OWL-DL) since both the typology embedded in a systemic network for KPML and the typology of features in the types file for OpenCCG can be derived from such descriptions.

3.2 Trinocular View

When classifying symbolic units, we not only conceive of them as patterns for recognition and for expression (from below), but also as bricks for building up a whole with given parts and for selecting parts for a planned whole (from around), and also as devices for construing meaning and for realising it (from above). Therefore, all classes of symbols in our symbolic map will be defined based on their affordances as patterns, bricks, and devices. So our approach is different from that of Henschel (1995; 1997) not only in the fact that we will not extract a typology in description logic from a systemic network (in fact, we will do the opposite), but also in the fact that each structure will be specified in our description as three particulars: one classified from above, one from around, and one from below. The classification from above is convertible into KPML-inquiries, the classification from around is convertible to preselectable grammatical features in KPML, and the classification from below is related to groups of realisation statements in KPML. The definitions of brick classes and of pattern classes are responsible for their functions as meaning-making devices (see Figure 2). In the following, we discuss how these concepts are operationalised for CCG.

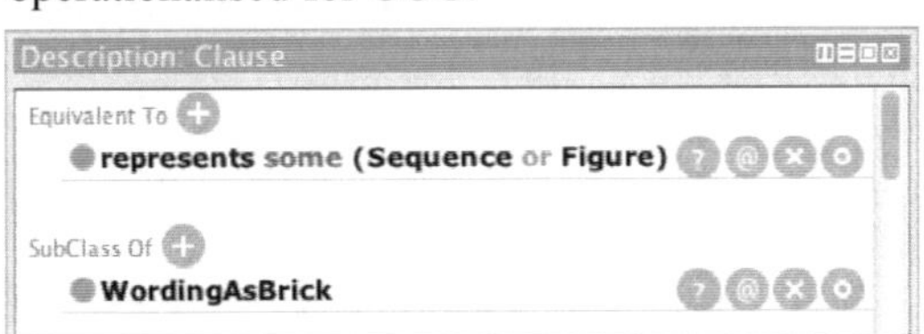

Figure 2. Description of Clause in Protégé

3.3 Word vs Form vs Copy

Moving bottom up in the creation of a descriptive theory, we define a token as a segment of text that matches a continuous pattern (of phonemes or graphemes) suitable for both recognition or expression.

Looking from above, a choice of tokens in a token sequence such as *helped…out* in *he helped me out* represents one single semantic value and is here understood as corresponding to a single word, namely HelpOut.

Looking from around, a word form – that of which a text token is a copy – is defined as composing a particular word and belonging to a particular form class. For the word HelpOut, there are two tokens and therefore two forms, one of them being that of *helped* and the other one being that of *out* in *he helped me out*.

3.4 Pattern vs Brick vs Device

At the leaves of the semantic dependency structure are the semantic values of words and at the corresponding leaves of the symbolic structure are not words, but the forms of words. In this sense, a particular word form is related to three notions: 1) a particular pattern that is used for recognising and producing tokens (copy), 2) a device for realising and construing meaning (word), and 3) a brick for construing larger symbolic structures (form). At this point, we have a triplicity of composition. While a brick is part of a larger symbolic structure, its semantic value is part of a larger semantic structure and its physical pattern is recognisable or produceable in a larger text. In KPML, a semantic structure is specified externally and the correspondence between symbolic and semantic compositionality is guaranteed by the restriction of attaching either the same semantic structure or parts of it to the parts of its corresponding symbolic structure. In OpenCCG, the same compositionality is guaranteed by applying the λ-function of an incomplete constituent to the values of complete constituents (category application) or by composing the λ-functions of two chained incomplete constituents (combinatory rules).

Moreover, symbolic compositionality is linear in nature. As reflected in both KPML and OpenCCG, the position of symbolic constituents may be fixed in relation to other constituents while the semantic constituents cannot. For instance, the position of *nice* in relation to *day* in *have a nice day* is typically realised with the operation "order Epithet:nice Classifier:day" in KPML while it is embedded in the word categories "nice:Classifier/Classifier" and "day:Classifier" in OpenCCG.

4 Target: Nigel coverage

We shall propose a map for every structure class covered by Nigel by tackling the theoretical issues.

4.1 Terms

In Nigel, form classes are used for selecting particular forms of a word while in a CCG they are used for limiting the applicability of the category of a matched token. Usually the form selection and its applicability are related to either role or agreement restrictions.

In the Nigel grammar, some word classes are defined for automatically creating tokens from the stem of a word such as the verb classes "es-ed" for verbs such as *wish* (*wishes*, *wished*). For indicating the existence of irregular patterns, there are word classes such as "irr". There are also word classes which are used for controlling the selection of a token index based on a set of form classes (or inflectional features) such as "inflectable", "noun", and "verb". All of these word classes together belong to morphology because they are meant to guide the selection of token models and their modifications into the patterns to print out or recognise. With such classes, Nigel is able to reduce the description of a word to a short code such as the following:

```
<Word id="Arrive">
  <Class name="Process" />
  <Class name="EndingWith-e-es-ed-ing" />
  <SampleMap>
    <Sample name="stem" value="arrive" />
  </SampleMap>
</Word>
```

Sample 1. Word Arrive

We store the classes of copies, forms, and words in a lexical ontology together with their relations. In this way, we are able to generate the same systemic network for the rank of word in KPML and, at the same time, all word forms and word form classes for OpenCCG.

In addition, there are word classes used as criteria for selecting words in Nigel. These are the grammatical – or closed-class – words. For them, there is a number of different selecting criteria which are better explained at the ranks where these selections are made (clause, phrase, or group).

In CCG, the morphological entries are not words, but forms. As in KPML, forms have a word identifier (stem), inflectional/agreement classes (macros), they have an attribute for form applicability (pos) and may have an additional semantic value in case of lexical words (class). Therefore, the word exemplified in Sample 1, can be compiled via ontological reasoning into the following structure:

```
<entry word="arrive"   stem="Arrive" class="Arrive"
     macros="@mode-1 @mention-1 @base @Arrive" />
<entry word="arrives"  stem="Arrive" class="Arrive"
     macros="@mode-1 @mention-2 @base @Arrive" />
<entry word="arrive"   stem="Arrive" class="Arrive"
     macros="@mode-1 @mention-3 @base @Arrive" />
<entry word="arrived"  stem="Arrive" class="Arrive"
     macros="@mode-2 @mention-1 @base @Arrive" />
[…]
```

Sample 2. Forms of Word Arrive in CCG

A sample word ontology and the java code for generating resources can be found at https://github.com/DanielCoutoVale/SymbolicMap.

4.2 Composites

In the beginning of every traversal of the systemic network, a symbolic structure is classified either as a clause, a group or phrase, a word or a morpheme. By listing all preselectable classes, we came to the conclusion that there is a fine-grained rank region that includes not only clauses, phrases, groups, and words, but subtypes of these. Clauses are either complexes or simplexes, either dependent or independent. Phrases and groups can be either a nominal group, a quantity group, a quality group, an adverbial group or a prepositional phrase. These subtypes can have further specifications that we shall call here, for simplification, clause mode and noun group case. At this point, below the preselectable classes, it is possible to propose a composite structure whose further specification is exclusively semantical and lexical in nature and whose fitting is governed exclusively by the compositionality of the semantic structure. This possibility was also noticed by Henschel in her final remarks (Henschel, 1997).

At this point of the traversal, for each particular class of structure, there is a semantic correspondent. *Sequences* are realised by clause complexes, *Figures* by clause simplexes, *Elements* by phrases and groups. Subtypes of *Elements* are realised by subtypes of phrases and groups: *Circumstances* by prepositional phrases and adverbial groups, *Things* by noun groups, *Qualities* by adjectival groups, *Quantities* by quantity groups. Finally, *Elements* have two other subtypes: *Processes* and *Modalities*, which occupy respectively the heads of clauses and phrases (see Figure 3).

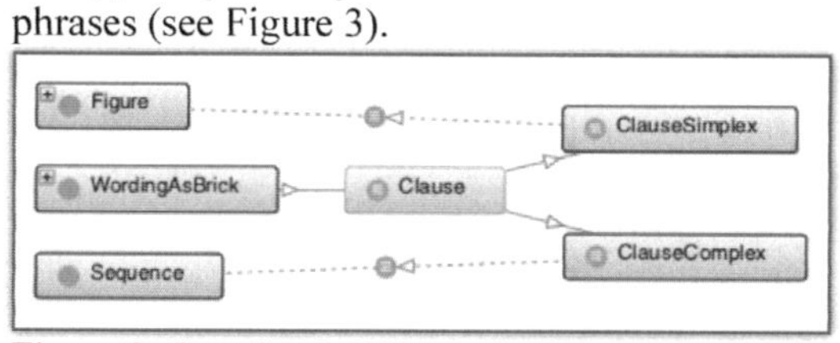

Figure 3. OntoGraf of Clause in Protégé

Since we need to allow changing the type of complete structures into combinable constituents of larger structures during text analysis, a description of symbolic systems must store more information than Nigel at this point. How these type-changes are achieved shall be explained in the following.

4.3 Adjuncts

Type changing in OpenCCG provides a way to implement the separation between pattern, brick, and device. For instance, this operator allows us to create simple rules for *very*

(Qualification/Qualifier) and *nice* (Qualifier) to result in the complete structure of *very nice* (Qualification). Then, by adding the possibility of changing the type Qualification into Classifier/Classifier, we are able to turn the category of this symbolic structure into an adjunct for the classifier *wine* (Classifier) in *this is a very nice wine*. At the same time, we still allow it to be a complement of the process *is* (Clause\Mention/Qualification) in *this wine is very nice*.

4.4 Grammatical Word Selection

In addition to the currently defined semantic elements, the semantic specification of Nigel also contains properties for answering semantic queries. These semantic queries embed a typology of *deictics*, of *tense*, and of *phase* inside of the systemic network. In order to embed these typologies into word forms, the semantic types must be moved to the semantic ontology. For instance, the meaning of *the* in KPML is that it is a 'nonselective', 'nontypic', 'nominal', and 'specific' instantiation of a 'class' of 'non-interactants'. The grammatical feature of *the* is a subtype of all these other features. During text analysis, *the* can be assigned the corresponding grammatical feature while the supertypes of this feature can be inferred with an ontology after the analysis.

4.5 Specification

In Nigel, there are systems whose features are realised either by selecting a unit/form class or by creating a head/tail structure. Tense is an example of this. On the one hand, positive future is realised by adding *will* (T0-head) and selecting the infinitive form for the head of the remaining verbal group (T0-tail) such as *make* in *it will make sense*. On the other hand, positive present is realised by selecting the present form for the head of the verbal group (T0-atom) such as *makes* in *it makes sense*. Therefore, for each region in each rank that creates a specification of clauses, phrases, or groups, we need to have either a head-tail structure or an atom for KPML. The respective corresponding structures for OpenCCG would be an incomplete category or a type-change.

4.6 Complements

Circumstance complements such as *of Mary* in *in front of Mary* create no new challenges for description. Figure complements, on the other hand, do. The clause, as the representation of a figure (state or event), is a symbolic structure whose constituents represent the elements of a semantic figure. Nigel adds the representative functions of clause constituents in the traversal of a figure typology. Each level of the typology decides whether a semantic role is present or not in the figure and therefore if a constituent must have the function of such a role. Roles include those of actor, actee, senser, sensum, sayer, target, verbiage, carrier, attribute, identified, identifier among others. Semantic roles and their presence for a given figure type are stored outside the system in a separate typology (GUM-3) (Bateman et al., 2010). The correspondent of the transitivity region in OpenCCG would be the mapping of logical variables to the diamond modes of a figure node as specified in the XML below:

```
<satop nomvar="SimpleAction">
    <diamond mode="hasProcess">
        <nomvar name="Process"/>
    </diamond>
    <diamond mode="hasActor">
        <nomvar name="Actor"/>
    </diamond>
</satop>
```

Sample 3. Logical Form in OpenCCG

Which process words can be used in each figure type need not be defined in KPML because both the figure type (SimpleAction, AffectingAction, etc.) and the process type (Running, Jumping, Singing, Seeing, etc.) are defined in the semantic specification that is passed to KPML as an input for text synthesis. This mapping from process types to figure types is necessary in OpenCCG and, therefore, process words need to be assigned process types so that SimpleActionProcesses are associated with a derivation family that has a medium/ actor, and so that AffectingActionProcesses are associated with a derivation family that has an agent/actor and a medium/goal, and so on. The whole set of rules involving transitivity can be automatically derived from a typology of figures both for KPML and for OpenCCG that includes such process classes.

In addition, in KPML, voice is implemented by mapping the transitive functions described above (actor, actee, recipient, senser, sensum, sayer, target...) to a smaller set of ergative functions (agent, medium, beneficiary). For example, the clause *the duke gave my aunt the teapot* has *the duke* as actor, *my aunt* as recipient and *the teapot* as goal in the transitive structure and *the duke* as agent, *my aunt* as beneficiary, and *the teapot* as medium in the ergative structure. For each figure type, there is a mapping of specific transitive functions to ergative functions. The ergative functions are the ones that get mapped to the subject, the direct(-object) and the indirect(-object) functions depending on the voice (agent-receptive voice, medium-receptive voice, and beneficiary-receptive voice). To implement a similar voice construct in OpenCCG, we propose a strategy of moving the mapping of transitive-ergative functions to a secondary step of reasoning after text analysis (example in https://github.com/DanielCoutoVale/SymbolicMap). After doing this, the actual voice structure can be implemented with categories such as Clause\Mention/Mention/Mention/Process for the auxiliary word *was* in *the teapot was given by the duke to my aunt* and with the type changing rule Process –> Clause\Mention/Mention/Mention applied to the Process *gave* in *the duke gave my aunt a teapot*. Which category or rule to apply depends on the ergative functions of each figure type – e.g. figures with a medium and no agent do not have a "passive" form. Culmination – the choice between *the teapot was given my aunt by the duke* and *the teapot was given by the duke to my aunt* – was realised in OpenCCG together with voice.

5 Evaluation

For evaluation, we targeted the only real challenge in the relation between Nigel and our CCG (clause complements) by creating a simple symbolic map with two ranks (clause and mention), with three figure types, three voices and two culminations (complements). This resource was compiled into a systemic network and into combinatory categories and type change rules successfully. Text synthesis and text analysis work as intended, that is, algorithmically without backtracking. For instance, the automatically generated CCG gives the correct standard analysis for *the duke gave my aunt the teapot* according to SFG as seen in the Table 1:

the duke	*gave*	*my aunt*	*the teapot*
Actor	Process	Recipient	Goal
Agent		Beneficiary	Medium

Table 1. Analysis for *the duke* as subject

For utterances such as *my aunt was given the teapot by the duke* see Tables 2-3, two hypotheses of analysis are given by CCG. Both analyses are correct if only symbolic and semantic compositionality is taken into account. An analysis, according to which the teapot receives someone's aunt (Table 3), can only be discarded when knowledge about the world (and not about language) is applied.

my aunt	*was*	*given*	*the teapot*	*by the duke*
Recipient		Process	Goal	Actor
Beneficiary			Medium	Agent

Table 2. Analysis 1 for *my aunt* as subject

my aunt	*was*	*given*	*the teapot*	*by the duke*
Goal		Process	Recipient	Actor
Medium			Beneficiary	Agent

Table 3. Analysis 2 for *my aunt* as subject

The compilation speed for OpenCCG word forms is very slow: one second per word form on a computer with 2.6 Ghz processor. The compilation of OpenCCG combinatory categories, type changing rules, KPML lexicon and network, on the other hand, is efficient. Once compiled, the speed of text analysis is that of a regular hand-written resource for OpenCCG and is equivalent in size and quality through code inspection.

6 Conclusion

In this paper, we have shown that task-oriented resources for KPML and OpenCCG do not contain the necessary information for doing the inverse task and that their directed rules cannot encode the information that is necessary for the resources to become reversible.

Therefore, we have adopted a third strategy of creating a completely descriptive map between symbolic and semantic structures that can be compiled into a systemic network and into combinatory categories and type changing rules.

Our evaluation has shown that the approach is sound and is able to solve previously identified issues on a theoretical level. However, we are still unsure about the amount of engineering resources that would be needed in order to complete the same coverage of Nigel within such a paradigm. Nevertheless, from the pilot study undertaken, the approach appears promising.

Acknowledgements

We gratefully acknowledge the support of the Deutsche Forschungsgemeinschaft (DFG) through the Collaborative Research Center SFB/TR8 Spatial Cognition.

References

John A. Bateman. 1995a. Basic technology for multilingual theory and practise: the KPML development enviroment. In *Proceedings of the Workshop on Multilingual Text Generation IJCAI-95*, pages 1–12. Montreal.

John A. Bateman. 1995b. KPML: the KOMET-Penman Multilingual Linguistic Resource Development Environment. In *Proceedings of the Fifth European Workshop on Natural Language Generation*, pages 219–222. Leiden.

John A. Bateman. 1996. *KPML Development Environment*. GMD-Forschungszentrum Informationstechnik GmbH, Sankt Augustin.

John A. Bateman. 1997. Enabling technology for multilingual natural language generation: the KPML development environment. *Natural Language Engineering*, 3(1):15–55.

John A. Bateman. 2008. Systemic-functional linguistics and the notion of linguistic structure: unanswered questions, new possibilities. *Meaning in context implementing intelligent applications of language studies*, pages 24–58. Continuum, London/New York.

John A. Bateman, Joana Hois, Robert Ross, and Thora Tenbrink. 2010. A linguistic ontology of space for natural language processing. *Artificial Intelligence*, 174(14):1027–1071.

Cem Bozşahin, Geert-Jan Kruijff, and Michael White. 2005. *Specifying Grammars for OpenCCG: A Rough Guide*. Retrieved from http://www.metu.edu.tr/~bozsahin/nli/ceng563/link/grammars-rough-guide.pdf

Donald Davidson. 1967. Truth and Meaning. *Synthese*, 17(1):304–323.

Friedrich Ludwig Gottlob Frege. 1884. *Grundlagen der Arithmetik: eine logisch mathematische Untersuchung über den Begriff der Zahl*. Wilhelm Köbner, Breslau.

Michael A.K. Halliday and Christian M.I.M. Matthiessen. 2014. *Halliday's Introduction to Functional Grammar*, 4th edition. Routledge, London/New York.

Renate Henschel. 1995. Traversing the Labyrinth of Feature Logics for a Declarative Implementation of Large Scale Systemic Grammars. Retrieved from http://www.elsnet.org/publications/clnlp95

Renate Henschel. 1997. Compiling Systemic Grammar into Feature Logic Systems. Retrieved from http://citeseerx.ist.psu.edu/viewdoc/download?doi=10.1.1.52.3153&rep=rep1&type=pdf

Robert T. Kasper. 1988. An experimental parser for systemic grammars. In *Proceedings of the Twelfth International Conference on Computational Linguistics*, pages 309–312, Budapest.

Martin Kay. 1979. Functional Grammar. In *Proceedings of the Berkeley Linguistics Society*. pages 142–158, Berkeley.

JP Martin Kay. 1985. Parsing in functional unification grammar. *Natural Language Parsing*. Cambridge University Press, Cambridge, UK.

Martin Klarner. 2005. Reversibility and re-usability of resources in NLG and natural language dialog systems. In *Proceedings of the Tenth European Workshop on Natural Language Generation*, pages 185-190. Aberdeen.

George Lakoff. 1987. *Women, fire and dangerous things: what categories reveal about the mind*. University of Chicago Press, Chicago.

Christian M.I.M. Matthiessen. 1995. *Lexicogrammatical cartography: english systems*. International Language Sciences Publishers, Tokyo.

Christian M.I.M. Matthiessen and Michael A.K. Halliday. 1999. *Construing experience through meaning: a language-based approach to cognition*. Continuum, London/New York.

Christian M.I.M. Matthiessen and Michael A.K. Halliday. 2004. *An introduction to functional grammar*, 3rd edition. Oxford University Press, New York.

Günter Neumann. 1991. A bidirectional model for natural language processing. In *Proceedings of the Fifth Conference on European chapter of the Association for Computational Linguistics*, pages 245–250, Berlin.

Günter Neumann and Gertjan van Noord. 1992. Self-monitoring with reversible grammars. In *Proceedings of the Fourteenth International Conference on Computational Linguistics*, pages 700–706, Nantes.

Michael O'Donnell. 1994. *Sentence analysis and generation: a systemic perspective*. Ph.D. thesis, University of Sydney, Sydney.

Stephen G. Pulman. 1995. Review of Reversible Grammar in Natural Language Processing. In *Computational Linguistics*, 21:269–271.

Alex Rudnick. 2010. *Review: realization with CCG*. Retrieved from http://www.cs.indiana.edu/~alexr/nonpubs/alexr-ccg-generation.pdf

Barry Smith and Berit Brogaard. 2003. A Unified Theory of Truth and Reference. *Logique et Analyse,* 43:1–46.

Mark Steedman. 1987. Combinatory grammars and parasitic gaps. *Natural Language and Linguistic Theory*, 5(3):403–439.

Mark Steedman. 1996. *A very short introduction to CCG*. Retrieved from http://www.inf.ed.ac.uk/teaching/courses/nlg/readings/ccgintro.pdf

Mark Steedman. 1998. Categorial Grammar. *The MIT Encyclopedia of Cognitive Sciences*, pages 1–9. MIT Press, Cambridge, MA.

Mark Steedman and Jason Baldridge. 2011. Combinatory Categorial Grammar. *Non-Transformational Syntax*, pages 181–224. Blackwell, Oxford, UK.

Tomek Strzalkowski. 1994. Reversible Grammar. *Reversible Grammar in Natural Language Processing*, pages xiii–xxi. Springer Science +Business Media, Dordrecht.

Michael White, Rajakrishnan Rajkumar, and Scott Martin. 2007. Towards broad coverage surface realization with CCG. In *Proceedings of the Workshop on Using Corpora for NLG Language Generation and Machine Translation*, pages 22-30, Brighton.

Lugwig Josef Johann Wittgenstein. 1921. Logisch-Philosophische Abhandlung. *Annalen der Naturphilosophie*, 14:185-262.

Lugwig Josef Johann Wittgenstein. 1922. *Tractatus Logico-Philosophicus*. Kegan Paul, Trench Trubner & Co, London.

Adapting SimpleNLG for Brazilian Portuguese realisation

Rodrigo de Oliveira
Department of Computing Science
University of Aberdeen
Aberdeen, UK, AB24 3UE
rodrigodeoliveira@abdn.ac.uk

Somayajulu Sripada
Department of Computing Science
University of Aberdeen
Aberdeen, UK, AB24 3UE
yaji.sripada@abdn.ac.uk

Abstract

This paper describes the ongoing implementation and the current coverage of SimpleNLG-BP, an adaptation of SimpleNLG-EnFr (Vaudry and Lapalme, 2013) for Brazilian Portuguese.

1 Introduction

Realisation is the last step in natural language generation (NLG) systems, so the goal of a realisation engine is to output text. SimpleNLG is a Java library that employs morphological, syntactic and orthographical operations on non-linguistic input to output well-formed sentences in English. SimpleNLG-EnFr (Vaudry and Lapalme, 2013) is an adaptation of SimpleNLG for French. This paper describes the current state of SimpleNLG-BP[1], an adaptation of SimpleNLG-EnFr for realisation in Brazilian Portuguese.

2 Recycling SimpleNLG-EnFr

To implement SimpleNLG-BP, we opted to extend SimpleNLG-EnFr instead of the original SimpleNLG. The main reason was the linguistic phenomenon of preposition contraction, which is what happens in *da mesa* (*of the table*): *da* is the fusion of *de* (*of*) with *a* (the.FEM.SNG). Because preposition contraction happens in French but not in English, we simply adapted the algorithm in SimpleNLG-EnFr to suit Brazilian Portuguese.

3 Coverage of SimpleNLG-BP

As of submission date of this paper (May 23, 2014), almost all efforts in implementing SimpleNLG-BP focused on morphological operations, as described in *Moderna Gramática Portuguesa* (Bechara, 2009). However, a testbed of 43 instances including full sentences in non-interrogative form and isolated phrases could be successfully generated by SimpleNLG-BP.

[1]The source code for SimpleNLG-BP can be found at https://github.com/rdeoliveira/simplenlg-en-fr-pt .

3.1 Morphology

Morphological operations in the current state of SimpleNLG-BP tackle 3 phrase types: noun phrases, preposition phrases and verb phrases.

3.1.1 Pluralisation of nouns

Pluralisation rules in Brazilian Portuguese normally add a final *-s* to nouns, but word-internal modifications may also be applied, depending on the word's stress, last vowel and/or ending. Possible noun endings in Brazilian Portuguese are: *-l*, *-m*, *-n*, *-r*, *-s*, *-x*, *-z* and vowels. SimpleNLG-BP currently includes all pluralisation rules for nouns ending in *-m*, *-r*, *-s*, *-x* or most vowels, but only some rules for endings *-l*, *-n*, *-z* and *-ão*. The pluralisation algorithm will still attempt to pluralise any string, which is useful to handle neologisms.

3.1.2 Preposition contraction

Similar to French, Brazilian Portuguese provides a morphophonological mechanism to contract words in preposition phrases. The prepositions that undergo contraction are *a* (*by*, *to*), *em* (*in*, *or*, *at*), *de* (*from*, *of*) and *por* (*through*, *by*) – or preposition complexes ending in those, such as *atrás de* (*behind*) or *em frente a* (*in front of*). When these precede a determiner or adverb, preposition and following item combine to form a single word. Take *as* (*the*.FEM.PLR), for instance. If it appears in a preposition phrase after *a*, *em*, *de* or *por*, the result will be *às*, *nas*, *das* and *pelas*, respectively. Note that *desde* (*since*) ends with *-de* but does not undergo contraction. The same applies for *contra* (*against*) and *para* (*to*, *for*); both end in *-a* but do not undergo contraction.

Proceedings of the 8th International Natural Language Generation Conference, pages 93–94,
Philadelphia, Pennsylvania, 19-21 June 2014.

3.1.3 Verb conjugation

English systematically combines all 3 tenses – past, present and future – to perfective and/or progressive aspects. This gives English a total of 12 possible combinations for the same verb, person and number. Subjunctive or imperative moods are of little concern to English, since base forms of verbs are usually identical to non-indicative forms.

Brazilian Portuguese may be said to express the same number of tenses, aspects and moods. In practice, this does not apply. Perfectiveness in Brazilian Portuguese traditional grammars is seen as a 3-element set – perfective, imperfective and pluperfective – which apply only to the past tense. English uses perfectiveness across all 3 tenses (*had done*, *have done*, *will have done*). Moreover, subjunctive forms in Brazilian Portuguese are morphologically distinct from indicative forms. Conditional is not built by adding an unchangeable auxiliary (e.g. *would*), but by morphology as well. Finally, infinitive forms of verbs may be conjugated or not. Thus, it was more practical to implement tense in SimpleNLG-BP as a 10-element set – past, present, future, imperfect, pluperfect, conditional, subjunctive present, subjunctive imperfect, subjunctive future and personal infinitive – where each tense may already pack some sense of aspect and mood.

Nevertheless, we implement aspect as a separate 3-element set, to be optionally declared as verb features, in order to trigger verb periphrasis formation. Modern Brazilian Portuguese uses verb periphrases extensively; e.g. the periphrastic form *tinha feito* (*had done*) is normally used instead of the single-verb form *fizera* (also *had done*). SimpleNLG-BP associates *ter* (*have*) to perfectiveness and *estar* (*be*) to progressiveness, thereby resembling the grammar of English and preserving most of the optional verb-phrase features used in the original SimpleNLG. Additionally, we included *prospectiveness* in the aspect set (as suggested by Bechara (2009) pp. 214-215) to generate periphrases that express future by means of the auxiliary *ir* (*go*). With a 3-element aspect set and a 10-element tense set, SimpleNLG-BP is able to build 80 different forms[2] for the same verb, person and number. Additionally, negative, passive and modalised verb phrases are also supported. Modals generate prepositions automatically, if required, such as *dar* (be able to) and *acabar* (end), whose prepositions are *para* and *de* respectively.

[2]Even though 22 of these don't seem to be used by Brazilian Portuguese speakers.

As far as subject-verb agreement, if the verb to be conjugated exists in the default lexicon file, the final string is simply retrieved; if not, a conjugation algorithm attempts to inflect the verb. For SimpleNLG-BP, we compiled an XML lexicon file out of DELAF_PB (Muniz, 2004), an 880,000-entry lexicon of inflected words in Brazilian Portuguese. The original file became too large at first – 1,029,075 lines, 45.4MB – which turned out to be an issue. A default run of SimpleNLG compiles the default lexicon file *a priori* to store it in memory, so a single run (e.g. 1 test case) took an average of 2.5 seconds, just to build the lexicon onto memory. Since an inefficiency of that dimension can be prohibitive in some practical contexts, we compiled a smaller list of 57 irregular verbs in Brazilian Portuguese plus personal pronouns, which became only 4,075-line long (167KB) and takes only 0.17 seconds for compilation in average. SimpleNLG-BP includes both the lexicon file and the lexicon compiler, if one wishes to modify the default lexicon.

4 Summary

We described SimpleNLG-BP, an ongoing adaptation of SimpleNLG for Brazilian Portuguese, which currently supports noun pluralisation, preposition contractions and verb conjugation, and includes a lexicon file and a lexicon compiler.

Acknowledgements

The first author of this paper thanks Arria/Data2Text Limited for funding his doctoral research at the University ofAberdeen.

References

Evanildo Bechara. 2009. *Moderna Gramática Portuguesa*. Nova Fronteira & Lucerna, Rio de Janeiro, 37 edition.

Marcelo Caetano Martins Muniz. 2004. A construção de recursos lingüístico-computacionais para o português do Brasil: o projeto Unitex-PB. Master's thesis, USP.

Pierre-Luc Vaudry and Guy Lapalme. 2013. Adapting SimpleNLG for bilingual English-French realisation. In *14th European Conference on Natural Language Generation*, pages 183–187, Sofia, Bulgaria.

Generating Summaries of Line Graphs

Priscilla Moraes, Gabriel Sina, Kathleen McCoy and Sandra Carberry
Department of Computer and Information Sciences
University of Delaware, Newark, Delaware, USA
[pmoraes | gsina | mccoy | carberry]@udel.edu

Abstract

This demo presents a Natural Language Generation (NLG) system that generates summaries of informational graphics, specifically simple line graphs, present in popular media. The system is intended to capture the high-level knowledge conveyed by the graphic and its outstanding visual features. It comprises a content selection phase that extracts the most important content of the graphic, an organization phase, which orders the propositions in a coherent manner, and a realization phase that uses the text surrounding the article to make decisions on the choice of lexical items and amount of aggregation applied to the propositions to generate the summary of the graphic.

1 Introduction

Multimodal documents from online popular media often contain information graphics that augment the information found in the text. These graphics, however, are inaccessible for visually impaired users or in environments where the image cannot be processed/displayed. Our system captures the high-level content of the graphic and produces a textual summary that conveys it. Figure 1 shows the system architecture.

The first step is the identification of the presence of a graphical image in the web page by a Browser Helper Object (BHO) (Elzer et al., 2007). If a graphic is present on the web page, the Graphical Information Extraction Module (VEM) (Chester & Elzer, 2005) is triggered by the BHO in order to extract the data from the image. The VEM then produces an XML representation of the graphic that is used by the Intention Recognition Module (IRM) for simple bar charts (Elzer, Green, Carberry, & Hoffman, 2006), simple line graphs (Wu, Carberry, Elzer, & Chester, 2010) and grouped bar charts (R. Burns, Carberry, & Elzer, 2010; R. Burns, Carberry, & Schwartz, 2013; R. J. Burns, 2013). The XML representation of the graphic, along with the intended message identified by the IRM, is sent to the Generation Module (GM), which produces a textual summary of the most important content presented in the graphic. The system produces an initial summary and follow-up responses for simple bar charts (Demir, Carberry, & Elzer, 2009; Demir, Carberry, & McCoy, 2008) and this demo presents the GM for simple line graphs.

This demo focuses on presenting the generation phase of the system. For that, we will demonstrate the generation of summaries in the context of a digital library that is available online[1] and that contains information graphics collected from online popular media, along with the articles containing the graphics. In addition, we have included hand-generated XML representations for the graphics (the current VEM is not fully robust). For each article that contains a graph, the user can choose to have access to the generated summary by clicking on the "Generate summary" button (highlighted in Figure 2). Figure 2 shows a screenshot on which the graph shown in Figure 3 has its article featured.

For accessibility projects that may use our system (applications developed for visually impaired users, for example), the application might use a combination of key strokes to allow user interaction. The module of the system that is the focus of this demo is the Generation Module.

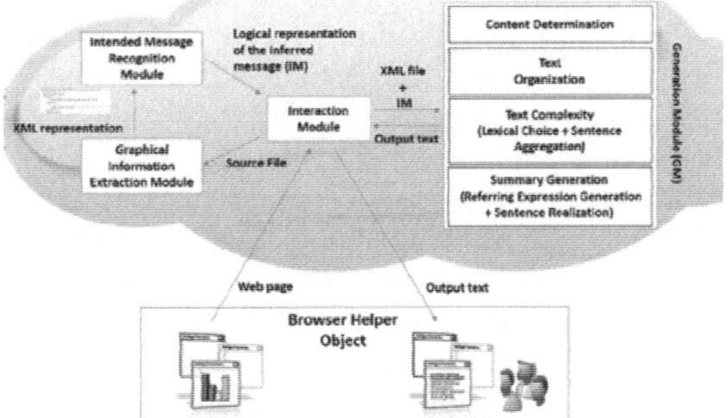

Figure 1: System Architecture

[1] http://ir.cis.udel.edu/~moraes/udgraphs

Proceedings of the 8th International Natural Language Generation Conference, pages 95–98,
Philadelphia, Pennsylvania, 19-21 June 2014.

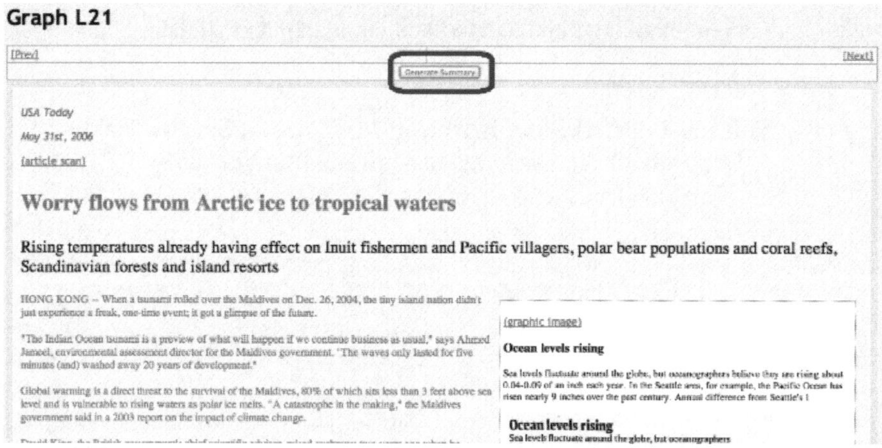

Figure 2: Digital library screenshot where we have added summary generation functionality.

2 Generation Module

For generating summaries of line graphs, the first step is the selection of content. In order to select the most important features of the line graph that should be conveyed in the summary, the system represents the intended message and the visual features identified by a human subject experiment (Greenbacker, Carberry, & McCoy, 2011) using a graph. A centrality-based algorithm, which is an adapted version of PageRank (Page, Brin, Motwani, & Winograd, 1999), is then implemented to select the most important information (represented as nodes in the graph). This implementation allows semantic relationships between propositions to be represented on the edges of the graph. The core of the content selection framework is to detect present outstanding visual features in the graphic, along with its intended message, in order to select nodes. Details in the content selection phase are available in the work presented at (P. S. Moraes, Carberry, & McCoy, 2013).

The next phase is the organization of the selected content. The organization phase works by ordering the selected propositions such that the delivered summary is fluent and coherent. The summaries are organized having an introduction section, a detailed section and a conclusion. The introduction consists of overall information about the line graph (the type of the graph, the entity being measured, the volatility of the graph and its intended message). The identified trends are described in the detail section. For this part of the summary, pieces of the graphic that outstand due to its visual features may be described first, being followed by other trends. Finally, the conclusion section of the summary presents computational information about the graphic (overall value and rate change, time span of the graphic, maximum and minimum points and dates when they occur). The strategies on organizing the summaries are described in (P. Moraes, McCoy, & Carberry, 2014).

The last step of the Generation Module is the aggregation of propositions into more complex sentences. This decision is usually left to the designer's choice on how much aggregation to perform when generating text. Some systems are designed to generate simple text for people with low reading abilities (Williams & Reiter, 2005a). As stated by (Williams & Reiter, 2005b), most NLG systems available generate text for high-skilled users. Our system generates line graph summaries that fit the reading level of the article in which the line graph appears. We contend that users generally read articles from venues they feel comfortable with reading. In this manner, we intrinsically assess the user's reading level without needing to actively survey it.

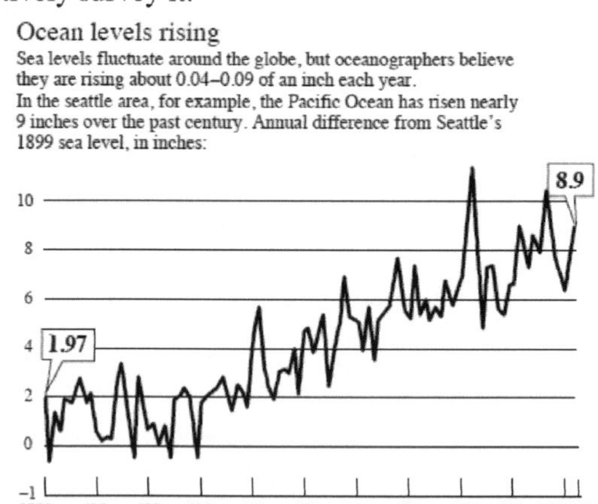

Figure 3: A line graph present in popular media.

The first step of the aggregation phase is to assess the reading level of the article's text. There is a myriad of techniques to measure the reading level of text. Much of them use machine learning techniques in order to learn text constructions and lexicalization used in different grade levels. As presented in (P. Moraes et al., 2014), simpler and well established reading level measurement techniques suffice for our scenario. The work shows that Flesh-Kincaid (Kincaid, Fishburne, Rogers, & Chissom, 1975) and SMOG (Laughlin, 1969) provide the set of information needed by the system in order to make decisions of syntactical text complexity.

After assessing the reading level of the article, the system then uses the text plan that applies to the identified reading level. Text plans define rules on Noun Phrase (NP) density and lexical choice. When describing an entity, attributes of this entity can be added to the NP as modifiers using either adjectives e.g. "*a highly volatile rising trend*", conjunctions e.g., "*the rising trend is volatile and steep*" or relative clauses e.g. "*a rising trend, which is highly volatile*". When the modifier of an NP is a Verb Phrase (VP), it is combined using a relative clause e.g., "*the line graph, which presents the number of jackets sold in 2013...*" VPs can be modified by adverbs e.g., "*the falling trend is **very** steep*". The text plans apply rules within sets of propositions that are grouped hierarchically. The system then uses the appropriate lexical items (*highly volatile vs ups and downs; conveys vs shows*) and applies the appropriate amount of aggregation in order to realize sentences.

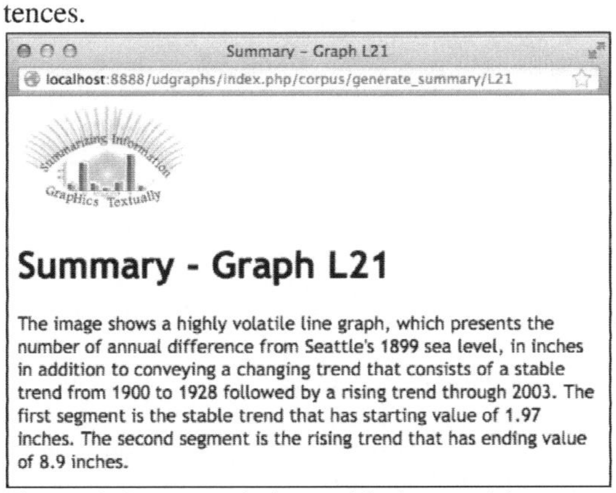

Figure 4: Pop up window with the resulting summary generated by the system.

Figure 4 and Figure 5 display the summaries generated for a user whose reading level is 11th-13th grade and 5th-7th grade respectively. From these one can see the different aggregation and lexical choice decisions made for the different reading levels. The system also includes appropriate pronominalization in order to avoid repetition of the referring expressions (P. Moraes et al., 2014).

Summary for Grades > 5 and <= 7
The image shows a line graph.
The line graph has ups and
downs. It presents the number
of annual difference from
Seattle's 1899 sea level, in
inches. It conveys a changing
trend. It consists of a stable
trend from 1900 to 1928
followed by a rising trend
through 2003. The first segment
is the stable trend. It has a
starting value of 1.97 inches.
The second segment is the
rising trend. It has an ending
value of 8.9 inches.
(SMOG 4.8)

Figure 5: Example of a summary adapted to the reading level of grades 5 to 7.

For the surface realization phase we use FUF/SURGE (Elhadad & Robin, 1999) to create the templates for realization. The template are created based on the text plans defined for a given reading level, as described above.

3 Conclusion

This paper presents the demonstration of the generation module of SIGHT. For the demo, the generation module works on a digital library that archives informational graphics collected from popular media available online. The aggregation phase of the generation module tailors the syntactical complexity of the generated text to that of the article's text in which the graphic appears.

An evaluation of the text summaries generated at different reading level is presented at (P. Moraes et al., 2014). It shows that, indeed, different users have different preferences regarding different text designs.

4 Future Work

A more automated way of defining a text plan for a given reading level is under investigation. We will explore techniques for learning how different text constructions can affect reading measures and then using these learned models when choosing an adjective over a relative clause for increasing the NP density and use of passive voice, for example.

Choosing lexical items that are classified by age is another possibility. We plan on investigating how the usage of word frequency by age/grade level (Carroll, 1972) might influence the overall generated summaries.

5 Acknowledgement

Gabriel Sina was supported by the Coordenação de Aperfeiçoamento de Pessoal de Nível Superior from Brazil CAPES – *in Portuguese*.

References

Burns, R., Carberry, S., & Elzer, S. (2010). *Visual and spatial factors in a bayesian reasoning framework for the recognition of intended messages in grouped bar charts.* Paper presented at the Proceedings of the AAAI Workshop on Visual Representations and Reasoning.

Burns, R., Carberry, S., & Schwartz, S. E. (2013). *Modeling a Graph Viewer's Effort in Recognizing Messages Conveyed by Grouped Bar Charts.* Paper presented at the UMAP.

Burns, R. J. (2013). *Automated intention recognition of grouped bar charts in multimodal documents.* University of Delaware, Ann Arbor. Retrieved from http://search.proquest.com/docview/1318643227?accountid=10457

Carroll, J. B. (1972). A New Word Frequency Book. *Elementary English, 49*(7), pp. 1070-1074.

Chester, D., & Elzer, S. (2005). *Getting computers to see information graphics so users do not have to.* Paper presented at the the Proceedings of the 15th International Symposium on Methodologies for Intelligent Systems.

Demir, S., Carberry, S., & Elzer, S. (2009). Issues in Realizing the Overall Message of a Bar Chart. In N. Nicolov, G. Angelova & R. Mitkov (Eds.), *Recent Advances in Natural Language Processing V* (pp. 311-320): John Benjamins.

Demir, S., Carberry, S., & McCoy, K. F. (2008). *Generating textual summaries of bar charts.* Paper presented at the Proceedings of the Fifth International Natural Language Generation Conference, Stroudsburg, PA, USA.

Elhadad, M., & Robin, J. (1999). SURGE: a comprehensive plug-in syntactic realization component for text generation. *Computational Linguistics*.

Elzer, S., Green, N., Carberry, S., & Hoffman, J. (2006). A Model of Perceptual Task Effort for Bar Charts and its Role in Recognizing Intention. *International Journal on User Modeling and User-Adapted Interaction, 16*(1), 1-30.

Elzer, S., Schwartz, E., Carberry, S., Chester, D., Demir, S., & Wu, P. (2007). *A Browser Extension For Providing Visually Impaired Users Access To The Content Of Bar Charts On The Web.* Paper presented at the the Proceedings of the International Conference on Web Information Systems and Technologies.

Greenbacker, C., Carberry, S., & McCoy, K. (2011, July). *A Corpus of Human-written Summaries of Line Graphs.* Paper presented at the Proceedings of the UCNLG+Eval: Language Generation and Evaluation Workshop, Edinburgh, Scotland.

Kincaid, J. P., Fishburne, R. P., Rogers, R. L., & Chissom, B. S. (1975). Derivation of New Readability Formulas (Automated Readability Index, Fog Count and Flesch Reading Ease Formula) for Navy Enlisted Personnel.

Laughlin, G. H. M. (1969). SMOG Grading-a New Readability Formula. *Journal of Reading, 12*(8), pp. 639-646.

Moraes, P., McCoy, K., & Carberry, S. (2014). *Adapting Graph Summaries to the Users' Reading Levels.* Paper presented at the Proceedings of the 8th International Natural Language Generation Conference.

Moraes, P. S., Carberry, S., & McCoy, K. (2013). *Providing access to the high-level content of line graphs from online popular media.* Paper presented at the Proceedings of the 10th International Cross-Disciplinary Conference on Web Accessibility, Rio de Janeiro, Brazil.

Page, L., Brin, S., Motwani, R., & Winograd, T. (1999). The PageRank Citation Ranking: Bringing Order to the Web: Stanford InfoLab.

Williams, S., & Reiter, E. (2005a). *Appropriate Microplanning Choices for Low-Skilled Readers.* Paper presented at the IJCAI.

Williams, S., & Reiter, E. (2005b). *Generating readable texts for readers with low basic skills.* Paper presented at the Proceedings of the 10th European Workshop on Natural Language Generation (EWNLG 2005).

Wu, P., Carberry, S., Elzer, S., & Chester, D. (2010). *Recognizing the intended message of line graphs.* Paper presented at the Proceedings of the 6th international conference on Diagrammatic representation and inference, Berlin, Heidelberg.

Two-Stage Stochastic Email Synthesizer

Yun-Nung Chen and Alexander I. Rudnicky
School of Computer Science, Carnegie Mellon University
5000 Forbes Ave., Pittsburgh, PA 15213-3891, USA
{yvchen, air}@cs.cmu.edu

Abstract

This paper presents the design and implementation details of an email synthesizer using two-stage stochastic natural language generation, where the first stage structures the emails according to sender style and topic structure, and the second stage synthesizes text content based on the particulars of an email structure element and the goals of a given communication for surface realization. The synthesized emails reflect sender style and the intent of communication, which can be further used as synthetic evidence for developing other applications.

1 Introduction

This paper focuses on synthesizing emails that reflect sender style and the intent of the communication. Such a process might be used for the generation of common messages (for example a request for a meeting without direct intervention from the sender). It can also be used in situations where naturalistic emails are needed for other applications. For instance, our email synthesizer was developed to provide emails to be used as part of synthetic evidence of insider threats for purposes of training, prototyping, and evaluating anomaly detectors (Hershkop et al., 2011).

Oh and Rudnicky (2002) showed that stochastic generation benefits from two factors: 1) it takes advantage of the practical language of a domain expert instead of the developer and 2) it restates the problem in terms of classification and labeling, where expertise is not required for developing a rule-based generation system. In the present work we investigate the use of stochastic techniques for generation of a different class of communications and whether global structures can be convincingly created. Specifically we investigate whether stochastic techniques can be used to acceptably model longer texts and individual sender characteristics in the email domain, both of which may require higher cohesion to be acceptable (Chen and Rudnicky, 2014).

Our proposed system involves two-stage stochastic generation, shown in Figure 1, in which the first stage models email structures according to sender style and topic structure (high-level generation), and the second stage synthesizes text content based on the particulars of a given communication (surface-level generation).

2 The Proposed System

The whole architecture of the proposed system is shown in left part of Figure 1, which is composed of preprocessing, first-stage generation for email organization, and second-stage generation for surface realization.

In preprocessing, we perform sentence segmentation for each email, and then manually annotate each sentence with a structure element, which is used to create a structural label sequence for each email and then to model sender style and topic structure for email organization (1st stage in the figure). The defined structural labels include *greeting*, *inform*, *request*, *suggestion*, *question*, *answer*, *regard*, *acknowledgement*, *sorry*, and *signature*. We also annotate content slots, including general classes automatically created by named entity recognition (NER) (Finkel et al., 2005) and hand-crafted topic classes, to model text content for surface realization (2nd stage in the figure). The content slots include *person*, *organization*, *location*, *time*, *money*, *percent*, and *date* (general classes), and *meeting*, *issue*, and *discussion* (topic classes).

2.1 Modeling Sender Style and Topic Structure for Email Organization

In the first stage, given the sender and the focused topic from the input, we generate the email structures by predicted sender-topic-specific mixture models, where the detailed is illustrated as be-

Proceedings of the 8th International Natural Language Generation Conference, pages 99–102,
Philadelphia, Pennsylvania, 19-21 June 2014.

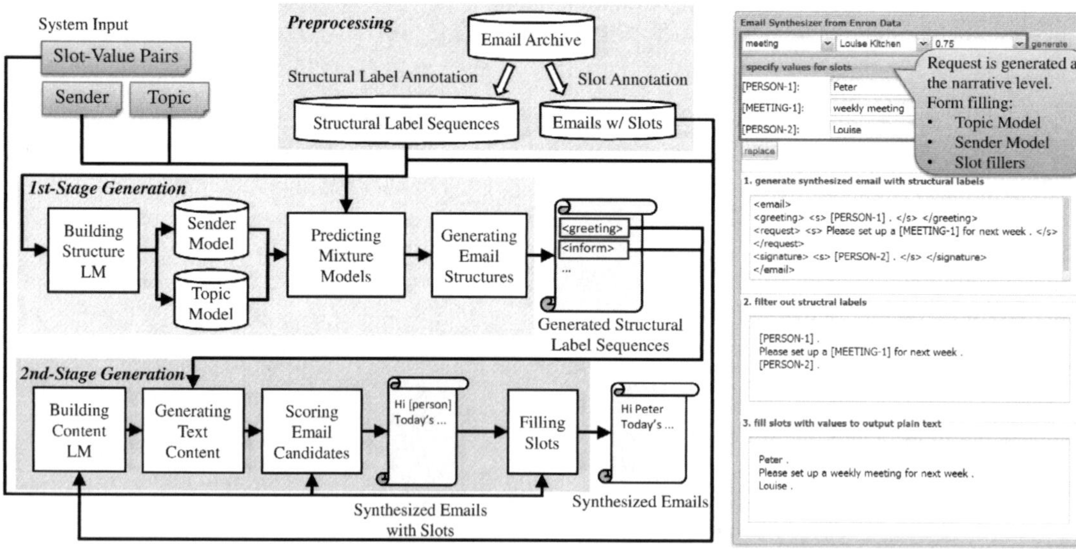

Figure 1: The system architecture (left) and the demo synthesizer (right).

low.

2.1.1 Building Structure Language Models

Based on the annotation of structural labels, each email can be transformed into a structural label sequence. Then we train a sender-specific structure model using the emails from each sender and a topic-specific model using the emails related to each topic. Here the structure models are tri-gram models with Good-Turing smoothing (Good, 1953).

2.1.2 Predicting Mixture Models

With sender-specific and topic-specific structure models, we predict the sender-topic-specific mixture models by interpolating the probabilities of two models.

2.1.3 Generating Email Structures

We generate structural label sequences randomly according to the distribution from sender-topic-specific models. Smoothed trigram models may generate any unseen trigrams based on back-off methods, resulting in more randomness. In addition, we exclude unreasonable emails that don't follow two simple rules.

1. The structural label "*greeting*" only occurs at the beginning of the email.
2. The structural label "*signature*" only occurs at the end of the email.

2.2 Surface Realization

In the second stage, our surface realizer consists of four aspects: building content language models, generating text content, scoring email candidates, and filling slots.

2.2.1 Building Content Language Models

After replacing the tokens with the slots, for each structural label, we train an unsmoothed 5-gram language model using all sentences belonging to the structural label. Here we assume that the usage of within-sentence language is independent across senders and topics, so generating the text content only considers the structural labels. Unsmoothed 5-gram language models introduce some variability in the output sentences while preventing nonsense sentences.

2.2.2 Generating Text Content

The input to surface realization is the generated structural label sequences. We use the corresponding content language model for the given structural label to generate word sequences randomly according to distribution from the language model.

Using unsmoothed 5-grams will not generate any unseen 5-grams (or smaller n-grams at the beginning and end of a sentence), avoiding generation of nonsense sentences within the 5-word window. With a structural label sequence, we can generate multiple sentences to form a synthesized email.

2.3 Scoring Email Candidates

The input to the system contains the required information that should be included in the synthesized result. For each synthesized email, we penalize it if the email 1) contains slots for which there is no provided valid value, or 2) does not have the required slots. The content generation engine stochastically generates a candidate email, scores it, and outputs it when the synthesized email with a zero penalty score.

2.4 Filling Slots

The last step is to fill slots with the appropriate values. For example, the sentence "Tomorrow's [meeting] is at [location]." becomes "Tomorrow's speech seminar is at Gates building." The right part of Figure 1 shows the process of the demo system,where based on a specific topic, a sender, and an interpolation weight, the system synthesizes an email with structural labels first and then fills slots with given slot fillers.

3 Experiments

We conduct a preliminary experiment to evaluate the proposed system. The corpus used for our experiments is the Enron Email Dataset[1], which contains a total of about 0.5M messages. We selected the data related to daily business for our use. This includes data from about 150 users, and we randomly picked 3 senders, ones who wrote many emails, and define additional 3 topic classes (meeting, discussion, issue) as topic-specific entities for the task. Each sender-specific model (across topics) or topic-specific model (across senders) is trained on 30 emails.

3.1 Evaluation of Sender Style Modeling

To evaluate the performance of sender style, 7 subjects were given 5 real emails from each sender and then 9 synthesized emails. They were asked to rate each synthesized email for each sender on a scale between 1 to 5.

With higher weight for sender-specific model when predicting mixture models, average normalized scores the corresponding senders receives account for 45%, which is above chance (33%). This suggests that sender style can be noticed by subjects. In a follow-up questionnaire, subjects indicated that their ratings were based on greeting usage, politeness, the length of email and other characteristics.

[1]https://www.cs.cmu.edu/~enron/

3.2 Evaluation of Surface Realization

We conduct a comparative evaluation of two different generation algorithms, template-based generation and stochastic generation, on the same email structures. Given a structural label, template-based generation consisted of randomly selecting an intact whole sentence with the target structural label. This could be termed sentence-level NLG, while stochastic generation is word-level NLG.

We presented 30 pairs of (sentence-, word-) synthesized emails, and 7 subjects were asked to compare the overall coherence of an email, its sentence fluency and naturalness; then select their preference. The experiments showed that word-based stochastic generation outperforms or performs as well as the template-based algorithm for all criteria (coherence, fluency, naturalness, and preference). Some subjects noted that neither email seemed human-written, perhaps an artifact of our experimental design. Nevertheless, we believe that this stochastic approach would require less effort compared to most rule-based or template-based systems in terms of knowledge engineering.

In the future, we plan to develop an automatic email structural label annotator in order to build better language models (structure language models and content language models) by increasing training data, and then improve the naturalness of synthesized emails.

4 Conclusion

This paper illustrates a design and implementation of an email synthesizer with two-stage stochastic NLG: first a structure is generated, and then text is generated for each structure element. Here sender style and topic structure can be modeled. We believe that this system can be applied to create realistic emails and could be carried out using mixtures containing additional models based on other characteristics. The proposed system shows that emails can be synthesized using a small corpus of labeled data, and the performance seems acceptable; however these models could be used to bootstrap the labeling of a larger corpus which in turn could be used to create more robust models.

Acknowledgments

The authors wish to thank Brian Lindauer and Kurt Wallnau from the Software Engineering Institute of Carnegie Mellon University for their guidance, advice, and help.

References

Yun-Nung Chen and Alexander I. Rudnicky. 2014. Two-stage stochastic natural language generation for email synthesis by modeling sender style and topic structure. In *Proceedings of the 8th International Natural Language Generation Conference*.

Jenny Rose Finkel, Trond Grenager, and Christopher Manning. 2005. Incorporating non-local information into information extraction systems by gibbs sampling. In *Proceedings of the 43rd Annual Meeting on Association for Computational Linguistics*, pages 363–370. Association for Computational Linguistics.

Irving J Good. 1953. The population frequencies of species and the estimation of population parameters. *Biometrika*, 40(3-4):237–264.

Shlomo Hershkop, Salvatore J Stolfo, Angelos D Keromytis, and Hugh Thompson. 2011. Anomaly detection at multiple scales (ADAMS).

Alice H Oh and Alexander I Rudnicky. 2002. Stochastic natural language generation for spoken dialog systems. *Computer Speech & Language*, 16(3):387–407.

A Framework for Health Behavior Change using Companionable Robots

Bandita Sarma
University of North Texas
banditasarma@my.unt.edu

Amitava Das
University of North Texas
Amitava.Das@unt.edu

Rodney D. Nielsen
University of North Texas
Rodney.Nielsen@unt.edu

Abstract

In this paper, we describe a dialogue system framework for a companionable robot, which aims to guide patients towards health behavior changes via natural language analysis and generation. The framework involves three broad stages, *rapport building and health topic identification*, *assess patient's opinion of change*, and *designing plan and closing session*. The framework uses concepts from psychology, computational linguistics, and machine learning and builds on them. One of the goals of the framework is to ensure that the Companionbot builds and maintains rapport with patients.

1 Introduction

Human beings engage in many activities or behaviors that can aggravate existing health problems or lead to new ones. Abandoning such behaviors with the help of motivational interviewing or counseling sessions is called health behavior change. Providing counseling sessions that result in behavior change is a difficult task even for expert practitioners, and hence poses a great challenge for automated dialogue systems. The process demands constant monitoring and an in-depth understanding of the patient[1]. A wrong move on the counselor's part could undo what might otherwise be a successful attempt to bring about the targeted health behavior change. This could require the counselor to return to the first stage of the process and regain the patient's trust.

In this paper, we describe a framework for a companionable robot, which can counsel its human companion and assist them in making healthier choices for a better life. In our previous work (Nielsen et al., 2010), we described an overall architecture for a companion robot capable of proactive dialogue with patients. This paper focuses on a natural language processing framework for health behavior change dialogue. Bickmore and Sidner (2006) outline a plan-based framework, COLLAGEN, based on the transtheoretical model and motivational interviewing to generate health behavior change counseling dialogue for physical activity promotion. COLLAGEN conducts a session in four steps: greeting exchange, discussion of previous day's exercise, discussion of plans for next day, and finally, farewell exchange. In addition to having similar steps, our framework also discusses in detail the natural language processing modules that are involved in judging the user's mindset at each step and guiding him/her towards making a decision on changing health behavior. In their follow up work (Bickmore et al., 2009), they discuss several issues such as minimizing repetitiveness in the behavioral, linguistic and visual aspect of the agent, establishing a therapeutic alliance between the user and the agent for a successful dialogue, maintaining continuity over multiple sessions, and the challenge of open-ended question generation. In addition to these issues, there might be verbal resistance from the patient to the suggestions by the Companionbot.

Use of telemedicine is becoming a common practice in providing remote clinical health care. It involves the use of various technologies like telephone, Facsimile, e-mail, video meetings, etc. to provide medical services. However, telemedicine is not flexible and adaptive, or when it is, it requires a human in the loop. It might also require long wait times on the patient side to receive a response from a health expert. Using companionable robots to provide guidance for health behavior change can provide greater flexibility compared to standard telemedicine practices. Bajwa (2010) described a virtual medical expert system

[1] The terms patient and user are used interchangeably throughout the paper to refer to the human using the Companionbot.

Proceedings of the 8th International Natural Language Generation Conference, pages 103–107,
Philadelphia, Pennsylvania, 19-21 June 2014.

that leverages natural language processing techniques to provide medical help to user queries from a knowledge base using pattern matching. In case the query does not have a match in the knowledge base, it is directed to an expert. The present work is along similar lines in terms of providing medical advice but in case of an unknown health condition, the Companionbot provides information through Web search. In addition to this, our framework adds the capability of generating small talk, which will help the user overcome inhibitions that might arise in talking to a robot instead of a human. The medical advice provided by the Companionbot will be in the form of suggestions rather than instructions. This is intended to make users reflect on their own choices comfortably instead of receiving instructions from the Companionbot's advice. The Nursebot project (Roy et al., 2000) discussed five different functions to assist the elderly through personal robots. One of the functions is to provide virtual telemedicine based facilities. Another robot called Paro (Kidd et al., 2006) was developed to cater to the social needs of elderly in nursing homes and was capable of generating a small set of vocal utterances in addition to limited voice recognition and body movement. Our framework, when implemented successfully, will be capable of engaging the user in a complete conversation, both casual and therapeutic.

2 Framework

The proposed dialogue system framework consists of three broad stages. The first stage aims to build rapport with the patient and identify the health topic to be discussed. The second stage involves identifying the issues and challenges the patient perceives associated with enacting relevant health behavior changes and motivating the patient to make the most appropriate change(s). The final stage summarizes the overall plans and goals, and encourages the patient to follow through. The entire process from building rapport with the patient through motivating changes in health-related behavior may span several sessions, and of course, is likely to be repeated for other behaviors.

2.1 Build rapport & identify health topic

In order to initiate a counseling session it is essential to build and maintain rapport with the patient. This helps the patient feel more comfortable with the situation, which facilitates more open communication. Reasonable rapport needs to be established in the initial stages when the Companionbot is first introduced to the patient. However, since the Companionbot is meant to be present constantly with its human companion, rapport building and maintenance is expected to be an ongoing process. Throughout both the casual and health behavior change dialogue, the Companionbot will identify the patient's interpersonal relations, health conditions and beliefs, likes and dislikes, habits, hobbies, and routines. These will be stored in a user model, which the language generation engine will exploit to engage the user in dialogue that is guided by, and infused with, personal context. A language understanding component will constantly assess the user's engagement level in the conversation. If the user seems to be disinterested at any point, a *Typical Day* strategy (Mason and Butler, 2010) is used to deal with the situation where the Companionbot will ask the user what a typical day for them is like.

When the system has achieved an adequate level of rapport, the next step is to identify a health topic of concern to the patient, so that there can be a focused discussion geared towards health behavior change. The present project will start with a small list of conditions and the behaviors that, when altered, can bring about an improvement in the condition. For example, heart disease includes diet and exercise, among others, as the associated behaviors. These conditions will be identified primarily using named-entity recognition and keyword spotting. If the Companionbot identifies heart disease as the topic, then the discussion could focus on food habits or exercise related issues.

2.2 Assess patient's opinion of change

Once a health concern is identified, the next step is to determine how important the patient thinks it is to change the associated behaviors and how confident they are about enacting those changes. This is an important stage because not all people have the same mindset regarding behavior change. Some might understand the importance of it but are not confident about achieving it while others might not consider it important at all. In order to understand the user's mindset, Mason and Butler (2010) suggest asking the user to assign cardinal values to quantify these opinions. The values may be on a scale of 0 to 10, where 0 is the lowest and

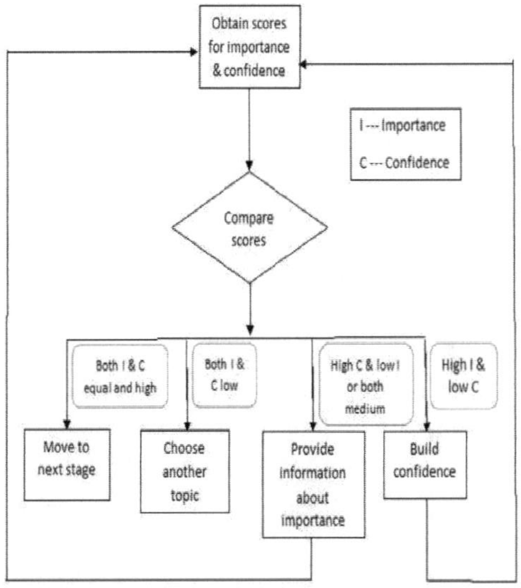

Figure 1: Block diagram for assessing patient's opinion of change

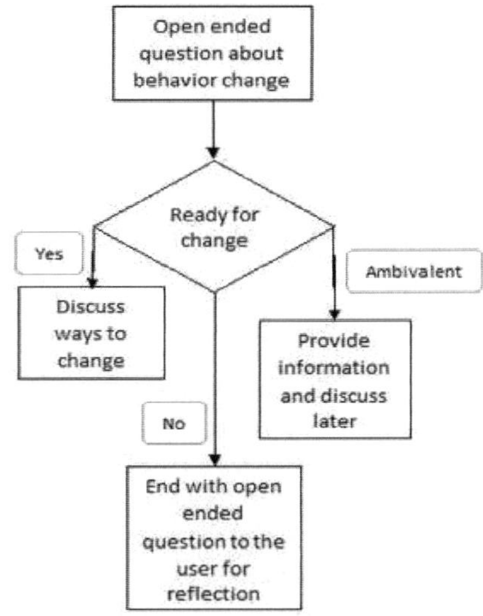

Figure 2: Block diagram for designing plan and closing the session

10 is the highest.

If there is a large difference between the user ratings of importance and confidence, the Companionbot will discuss the lower-ranked factor first (Mason and Butler, 2010). If the scores are approximately equal (e.g., the patient gives both importance and confidence a medium rating), then the Companionbot's dialogue will focus on helping the user understand the importance of the behavior change (Mason and Butler, 2010). Low values for both importance and confidence scores indicate that the user is not ready for these health behavior changes (Mason and Butler, 2010), and the Companionbot should move on to a different health topic or behavior. If both the scores are high, the Companionbot can move on to the next stage, summarizing the discussion and motivating the behavior changes. Figure 1 shows the block diagram representation for this module.

2.3 Design plan & close the session

The Companionbot moves toward concluding the conversation by asking an open-ended question regarding how the user feels about the health behavior changes that they have been discussing. A user's attitude can be categorized into one of three categories, ready for change, not ready for change, or ambivalent. If the patient is ready for change, the Companionbot will provide suggestions on how to bring about the change in the behavior in previous step by leveraging knowledge from the user model and the conversation history. There may be patients who belong to the second category and are not ready for the health behavior change. We have already discussed ways on how to tackle such a situation in Subsection 2.2. If the patient is ambivalent about changing a behavior, the Companionbot will close by providing information to help the patient reflect on the pros and cons of the health behavior change until it is appropriate to bring it up again in a future session. A knowledge base will be maintained about the behaviors associated with common and critical health conditions. Information about a health condition, which is outside the domain of current knowledge base, will be retrieved using Web search. Figure 2 shows the block diagram representation of this stage.

If a session exceeds a pre-defined time, deemed to be the limit of most patients' ability to stay adequately focused on health behavior change, or if the system recognizes that the patient is losing their focus, the Companionbot will check-in with the patient, and if appropriate, will bring the session to a close following strategies that parallel those described in the preceding paragraph.

3 Challenges

Automatic generation of dialogue becomes a particularly challenging task when its purpose is to guide people through sensitive or personal issues like health behavior change. Some patients may not like to be told what is good or bad for them. In such a case, the patient might begin resisting suggestions for change (Mason and Butler, 2010). This places the entire counseling session in a precarious position and any wrong move on the Companionbot's part could push the patient to a higher level of resistance. To mitigate this scenario, the Companionbot will include patient resistance detection in the framework. If mild resistance is detected, the discourse is automatically directed towards bringing the user back on track. Whereas if there is high resistance, the Companionbot moves on to a different topic In case the user continues resisting then the Companionbot will close the session.

For successful implementation of therapeutic dialogue systems, it is essential to ensure that they do not sound monotonous. This is possible only if the responses are generated dynamically and hardcoding is limited. During rapport building and user modeling, questions will be generated by the Companionbot from various sources like the Internet, medical forms, information provided by physicians, family members, etc. At other times, responses will be constructed using both syntactic and semantic information from the user utterances.

Since multiple sessions might be held with the user to discuss a specific behavior, it is necessary to maintain continuity between the sessions (Bickmore et al., 2009). Bickmore and Sidner (2006) advocate dedicating a part of the dialogue to reviewing prior discussions, associated actions, and patient plans, as well as discussing what the patient has done since the last session to follow though on their plans. The Companionbot maintains a detailed user model including logs of the previous sessions, which will be used to review prior discussions, plans and actions and to guide ongoing motivational interviews.

Another challenge is choosing appropriate evaluation measures to determine the system's usefulness in bringing about the desired change in the patient. The efficacy of the system will be judged by monitoring the users behavior regularly. Any noticeable changes, such as weight gain or loss and increased or decreased smoking, will be tracked. How frequently a patient interacts with the Companionbot is an implicit qualitative measure of how much they appreciate it. We also plan to use questionnaires to elicit user ratings of the system for its acceptability and quality on a Lickert scale (Lickert, 1932).

4 Conclusion

In this paper we proposed a novel framework for automatic health behavior change counseling. Successful implementation of this framework would mean that the Companionbot could be used to guide patients towards bringing changes in their behavior for a healthier life. This can reduce the long wait period in conventional telemedicine practices from the time the patients contact the remote heatlh care provider to the instance they receive the instruction (Bajwa, 2010). Since the Companionbot will be capable of small talk aimed at connecting with the user on an emotional level, we hypothesize it will be perceived as being much more natural than existing conversational robots.

References

Cory D. Kidd, Will Taggart and Sherry Turkle. 2006. *A Sociable Robot to Encourage Social Interaction among the Elderly*. IEEE International Conference on Robotics and Automation, 3972–3976.

Imran S. Bajwa. 2010. *Virtual Telemedicine Using Natural Language Processing*. International Journal of Information Technology and Web Engineering, 5(1):43–55.

Nicholas Roy, Gregory Baltus, Dieter Fox, Francine Gemperle, Jennifer Goetz, Tad Hirsch, Dimitris Margaritis, Michael Montemerlo, Joelle Pineau, Jamieson Schulte and Sebastian Thrun. 2000. *Towards Personal Service Robots for the Elderly. Workshop on Interactive Robots and Entertainment.*

Pip Mason and Christopher C. Butler. 2010. *Health Behavior Change*. Elsevier Health Sciences.

Rensis Likert. 1932. *A Technique for the Measurement of Attitudes*. Archives of Psychology, 140:1–55.

Rodney D. Nielsen, Richard Voyles, Daniel Bolanos, Mohammad H. Mahoor, Wilson D. Pace, Katie A. Siek and Wayne H. Ward. 2010. *A Platform for Human-Robot Dialog Systems Research*. In Proceedings of AAAI Fall Symposium, Dialog with Robots, 161–162.

Timothy W. Bickmore and Candace L. Sidner. 2006. *Towards Plan-based Health Behavior Change Counseling Systems*. In proceedings of AAAI Spring Symposium on Argumentation for Consumers of Healthcare.

Timothy Bickmore, Daniel Mauer, Francisco Crespo and Thomas Brown. 2008. *Negotiating Task Interruptions with Virtual Agents for Health Behavior Change*. In Proceedings of the 7th International Joint Conference on Autonomous Agents and Multiagent Systems, 1241–1244.

Timothy Bickmore, Daniel Schulman and Candace Sidner. 2009. *Issues in Designing Agents for Long Term Behavior Change*. CHI'09 Workshop on Engagement by Design.

Classifiers for data-driven deep sentence generation

Miguel Ballesteros[1], **Simon Mille**[1] **and Leo Wanner**[2,1]
[1]NLP Group, Department of Information and Communication Technologies
Pompeu Fabra University, Barcelona
[2]Catalan Institute for Research and Advanced Studies (ICREA)
<fname>.<lname>@upf.edu

Abstract

State-of-the-art statistical sentence generators deal with isomorphic structures only. Therefore, given that semantic and syntactic structures tend to differ in their topology and number of nodes, i.e., are not isomorphic, statistical generation saw so far itself confined to shallow, syntactic generation. In this paper, we present a series of fine-grained classifiers that are essential for data-driven deep sentence generation in that they handle the problem of the projection of non-isomorphic structures.

1 Introduction

Deep data-driven (or stochastic) sentence generation needs to be able to map abstract semantic structures onto syntactic structures. This has been a problem so far since both types of structures differ in their topology and number of nodes (i.e., are non-isomorphic). For instance, a truly semantic structure will not contain any functional nodes,[1] while a surface-syntactic structure or a chain of tokens in a linearized tree will contain all of them. Some state-of-the-art proposals use a rule-based module to handle the projection between non-isomorphic semantic and syntactic structures/chains of tokens, e.g., (Varges and Mellish, 2001; Belz, 2008; Bohnet et al., 2011), and some adapt the semantic structures to be isomorphic with syntactic structures (Bohnet et al., 2010). In this paper, we present two alternative stochastic approaches to the projection between non-isomorphic structures, both based on a cascade of Support Vector Machine (SVM) classifiers.[2] The first approach addresses the projection as a generic non-isomorphic graph transduction problem in terms of four classifiers for 1. identification of the (non-isomorphic) correspondences between fragments of the source and target structure, 2. generation of the nodes of the target structure, 3. generation of the dependencies between corresponding fragments of the source and target structure, and 4. generation of the internal dependencies in all fragments of the target structure. The second approach takes advantage of the linguistic knowledge about the projection of the individual linguistic token types. It replaces each of the above four classifiers by a set of classifiers, with each single classifier dealing with only one individual linguistic token type (verb, noun, adverb, etc.) or with a configuration thereof. As will be seen, the linguistic knowledge pays off: the second approach achieves considerably better results.

Since our goal is to address the challenge of the projection of non-isomorphic structures, we focus, in what follows, on this task. That is, we do not build a complete generation pipeline until the surface. This could be done, for instance, by feeding the output obtained from the projection of a semantic onto a syntactic structure to the surface realizer described in (Bohnet et al., 2010).

2 The Task

The difference in the linguistic abstraction of semantic and syntactic structures leads to divergences that impede the isomorphy between the two and make the mapping between them a challenge for statistical generation. Let us, before we come to the implementation, give some theoretical details on these structures as we picture them and on the possible approaches to the projection of a semantic structure to a syntactic one.

2.1 The Notion of semantic and syntactic structures

As semantic structure, we assume a *shallow semantic* representation that is very similar to the

[1]See, for instance, (Bouayad-Agha et al., 2012).

[2]Obviously, other machine learning techniques could also be used.

Proceedings of the 8th International Natural Language Generation Conference, pages 108–112,
Philadelphia, Pennsylvania, 19-21 June 2014.

PropBank (Babko-Malaya, 2005) and deep annotations as used in the Surface Realisation Shared Task (Belz et al., 2011): the *deep-syntactic layer* of the AnCora-UPF corpus (Mille et al., 2013).

Deep-syntactic structures (DSyntSs) do not contain any punctuation and functional nodes, i.e., governed prepositions and conjunctions, auxiliaries and determiners.[3]

As syntactic structure (in the terminology of Ancora-UPF: *surface-syntactic structures*, SSyntSs), we assume dependency trees in which the nodes are labeled by open or closed class lexemes and the edges by grammatical function relations of the type subject, oblique_object, adverbial, modifier, etc.; cf.[4] See Figure 1 for a contrastive illustration of DSyntS and SSyntS.

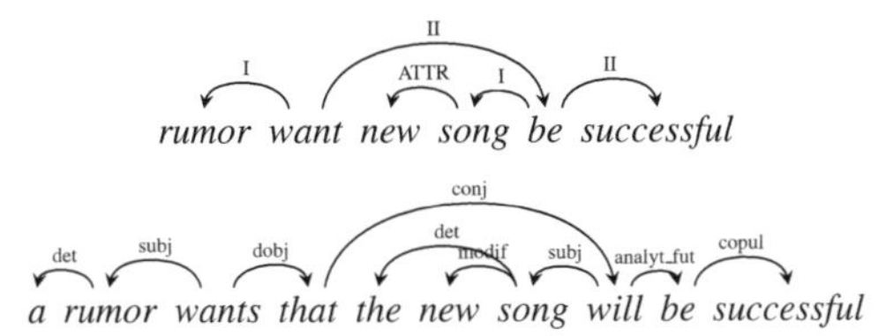

Figure 1: DSyntS (above) and SSyntS (below) of an English Sentence.

Note, however, that the proposal outlined below for the projection of non-isomorphic structures is trainable on any multi-layered treebanks where different layers are not isomorphic.

2.2 Projection of DSyntSs onto SSyntSs

In order to project a DSyntS onto its corresponding SSyntS in the course of sentence generation, the following types of actions need to be performed:

1. Project each node in the DSyntS onto its SSynS-correspondence. This correspondence can be a single node, as, e.g., *successful* → *successful*, or a subtree (*hypernode*, known as *syntagm* in linguistics), as, e.g., *song* → *the song* 'DT NN' (where 'DT' is a determiner and 'NN' a noun) or *be* → *that will be* 'IN V_{AUX} VB' (where 'IN' is a preposition, 'V_{AUX}' an auxiliary and 'VB' a full verb). In formal terms, we assume any SSyntS-correspondence to be a hypernode with a cardinality ≥ 1.

2. Generate the correct lemma for the nodes in SSyntS that do not have a 1:1 correspondence in the SSyntS (as 'DT', 'IN' and 'V_{AUX}' above).

3. Establish the dependencies within the individual SSyntS-hypernodes.

4. Establish the dependencies between the SSyntS-hypernodes (more precisely, between the nodes of different SSyntS-hypernodes) to obtain a connected SSyntS-tree.

[3]For more details on the SSyntS, see (Mille et al., 2013).

[4]DSyntSs and their corresponding SSyntSs are stored in the 14-column CoNLL'08 format.

3 Classifiers

As mentioned in the Introduction, the realization of the actions 1.– 4. can be approached either in terms of 4 generic classifiers (Section 3.1) or in terms of 4 sets of fine-grained (micro) classifiers (Section 3.2) that map one representation onto another. As also mentioned above, we realize both approaches as Support Vector Machines (SVMs).

3.1 Generic classifier approach

Each of the generic classifiers deals with one of the following tasks.

a. Hypernode Identification: Given a deep syntactic node n_d from the DSyntS, the system must find the shape of the surface hypernode (= syntagm) that corresponds to n_d in the SSyntS. The hypernode identification SVM uses the following features:

POS of n_d, POS of n_d's head, *voice*, *temp._constituency*, *finiteness*, *tense*, lemma of n_d, and n_d's dependencies.

In order to simplify the task, we define the shape of a surface hypernode as a list of surface PoS-tags. This list contains the PoS of each of the lemmas within the hypernode and a tag that signals the original deep node; for instance:

[VB(deep), V_{AUX}, IN]

b. Lemma Generation. Once the hypernodes of the SSyntS under construction have been produced, the functional nodes that have been newly introduced in the hypernodes must be assigned a lemma. The lemma generation SVM uses the following features of the deep nodes n_d in the hypernodes:

• *finiteness*, • *definiteness*, • PoS of n_d, • lemma of n_d, • PoS of the head of n_d

to select the most likely lemma.

c. Intra-hypernode Dependency Generation. Given a hypernode and its lemmas provided by the two previous stages, the dependencies (i.e., the dependency attachments and dependency labels) between the elements of the hypernode must be determined (and thus also the governor of the hypernode). For this task, the intra-hypernode dependency generation SVM uses the following features:

• lemmas included in the hypernode, • PoS-tags of the lemmas in the hypernode, • *voice* of the head h of the hypernode, • deep dependency relation to h.

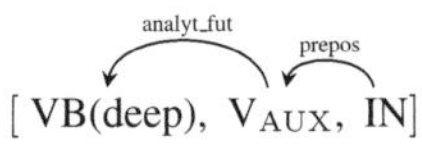

Figure 2: Internal dependency within a hypernode.

d. Inter-hypernode Dependency Generation. Once the individual hypernodes have been converted into connected dependency subtrees, the hypernodes must be connected between each other, such that we obtain a complete SSyntS. The inter-hypernode dependency generation SVM uses the following features of a hypernode s_s:

• the internal dependencies of s_s, • the head of s_s, • the lemmas of s_s, • the PoS of the dependent of the head of s_s in DSyntS

to determine for each hypernode its governor.

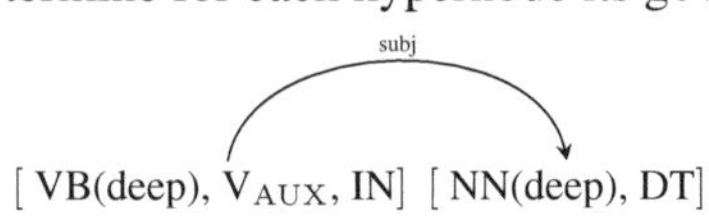

Figure 3: Surface dependencies between two hypernodes.

3.2 Implementation of sets of micro classifiers

In this alternative approach, a single classifier is foreseen for each kind of input. Thus, for the **hypernode identification module**, for each deep PoS tag (which can be one of the following four: 'N' (noun), 'V' (verb), 'Adv' (adverb), 'A' (adjective)), a separate multi-class classifier is defined. For instance, in the case of 'N', the N-classifier will use the above features to assign to the a DSynt-node with PoS 'N' the most appropriate (most likely) hypernode—in this case, [NN(deep), DT]. In a similar way, in the case of the **lemma generation module**, for each surface PoS tag, a separate classifier is defined. Thus, the DT-classifier would pick for the hypernode [NN(deep), DT] the most likely lemma for the DT-node (optimally, a determiner).

For the **intra-hypernode attachments module**, for each kind of hypernode, dynamically a separate classifier is generated.[5] In the case of the hypernode [VB(deep), V_{AUX}, IN], the corresponding classifier will create a link between the preposition and the auxiliary, and between the auxiliary and the verb, with respectively the preposition and the auxiliary as heads because it is the best link that it can find; cf. Figure 2 for illustration.

Finally, for the **inter-hypernode attachments module**, for each hypernode with a distinct internal dependency pattern, a separate classifier is dynamically derived (for our treebank, we obtained 114 different SVM classifiers because it also takes into account hypernodes with just one token). For instance, the classifier for the hypernode [NN(deep), DT] is most likely to identify as its governor V_{AUX} in the hypernode [VB(deep), V_{AUX}, IN]; cf. Figure 3.

4 Experiments and Results

In this section, we present the performance of the two approaches to DSyntS–SSyntS projection on the DSyntS- and SSynt-layers of the AnCora-UPF treebank (Mille et al., 2013).[6] Table 1 displays the results for the generic classifier for all tasks on the development and the test set, while Table 2 displays the results obtained through the sets of micro classifiers.

Dev.set	#	%
Hypernode identification	3131/3441	90.99
Lemma generation	818/936	87.39
Intra-hypernode dep. generation	545/798	68.30
Inter-hypernode dep. generation	2588/3055	84.71
Test set	#	%
Hypernode identification	5166/5887	87.75
Lemma generation	1822/2084	87.43
Intra-hypernode dep. generation	1093/1699	64.33
Inter-hypernode dep. generation	4679/5385	86.89

Table 1: Results of the evaluation of the generic classifiers for the non-isomorphic transduction.

The results show that for hypernode identification and inter-hypernode dependency generation, the results of both types of classifiers are comparable, be it on the development set or on the test set. However, thanks to the micro classifiers, with the same features, the lemma generation model based on micro classifiers improves by 4 points and the intra-hypernode dependency generation by nearly

[5]This implies that the number of classifiers varies depending on the training set, in the intra-hypernode dependency generation there are 108 SVMs.

[6]Following a classical machine learning set-up, we divided the treebank into: (i) a development set (219 sentences, 3271 tokens in the DSyntS treebank and 4953 tokens in the SSyntS treebank); (ii) a training set (3036 sentences, 57665 tokens in the DSyntS treebank and 86984 tokens in the SSyntS treebank); and a (iii) a held-out test for evaluation (258 sentences, 5641 tokens in the DSyntS treebank and 8955 tokens in the SSyntS treebank).

Dev.set	#	%
Hypernode identification	3133/3441	91.05
Lemma generation	851/936	90.92
Intra-hypernode dep. generation	767/798	96.12
Inter-hypernode dep. generation	2574/3055	84.26
Test set	#	%
Hypernode identification	5169/5886	87.82
Lemma generation	1913/2084	91.79
Intra-hypernode dep. generation	1630/1699	95.94
Inter-hypernode dep. generation	4648/5385	86.31

Table 2: Results of the evaluation of the micro classifiers for the non-isomorphic transduction.

30 points. This means that the intra-hypernode dependency generation task is too sparse to be realized as a single classifier. The micro classifiers are in this case binary, i.e., 2:1, or unary, i.e., 1:1 classifiers, which implies a tremendous reduction of the search space (and thus higher accuracy). In contrast, the single classifier is a multi-class classifier that must decide among more than 60 possible classes. Although most of these 60 classes are diferentiated by features, the differentiation is not perfect. In the case of lemma generation, we observe a similar phenomenon. In this case, the micro-classifiers are multi-class classifiers that normally have to cope with 5 different classes (lemmas in this case), while the unique classifier has to cope with around 60 different classes (or lemmas). Hypernode identification and inter-hypernode dependency generation are completely guided by the input; thus, it seems that they do not err in the same way.

Although the micro classifier approach leads to significantly better results, we believe that it can still be improved. First, the introduction of prepositions causes most errors in hypernode detection and lemma generation: when a preposition should be introduced or not and which preposition should be introduced depends exclusively on the sub-categorization frame of the governor of the deep node. A treebank of a limited size as used in our experiments simply does not contain subcategorization patterns of *all* predicative lexical items (especially of nouns)—which would be crucial. Thus, in the test set evaluation, out of the 171 lemma errors 147 are prepositions and out of the 717 errors on hypernode identification, more than 500 are due to nouns and preposition. The increase of the size of the treebank would therefore be an advantage.

Second, in the case of inter-hypernode dependency, errors are due to the labels of the dependencies more than to the attachements, and are quite distributed over the different types of configurations. The generation of these dependencies suffers from the fact that the SSyntS tag-set is very fine-grained. For instance, there are 9 different types of verbal objects in SSyntS,[7] which capture very specific syntactic properties of Spanish, such as "can the dependent can be replaced by a clitic pronoun? Can the dependent be moved away from its governor? Etc. This kind of information is not of a high relevance for generation of well-formed text. Using a more reduced (more coarse-grained) SSyntS tag set would definitely improve the quality of the projection.

5 Related work

There is an increasing amount of work on statistical sentence generation; see, e.g., (Bangalore and Rambow, 2000; Langkilde-Geary, 2002; Filippova and Strube, 2008). However, hardly any addresses the problem of the projection between non-isomorphic semantic and syntactic structures. In general, structure prediction approaches use a single classifier model (Smith, 2011). But see, e.g., (Carreras et al., 2008), who use different models to predict each part of the triplet for spinal model pruning, and (Björkelund et al., 2010; Johansson and Nugues, 2008), who use a set of classifiers for predicate identification in the context of semantic role labelling. Amalgam (Corston-Oliver et al., 2002), which maps a logical input onto sentences with intermediate syntactic (phrase-based) representation, uses language-specific decision trees in order to predict when to introduce auxiliaries, determiners, cases, etc.

6 Conclusions

We presented two alternative classifier approaches to deep generation that cope with the projection of non-isomorphic semantic and syntactic structures and argued that the micro classifier approach is more adequate. In spite of possible improvements presented in Section 4, each set of micro classifiers achieves results above 86% on the test set. For intra-hypernode dependency generation, it even reaches 95.94% .

Acknowledgments

This work has been partially funded by the European Commission under the contract number FP7-ICT-610411.

[7]There are 47 SSynt dependencies in total, to compare to the 7 dependencies in the DSyntS.

References

Olga Babko-Malaya, 2005. *Propbank Annotation Guidelines.*

Srinivas Bangalore and Owen Rambow. 2000. Exploiting a probabilistic hierarchical model for generation. In *Proceedings of the 18th International Conference on Computational Linguistics (COLING)*, pages 42–48, Saarbrücken, Germany.

Anja Belz, Michael White, Dominic Espinosa, Eric Kow, Deirdre Hogan, and Amanda Stent. 2011. The first Surface Realisation Shared Task: Overview and evaluation results. In *Proceedings of the Generation Challenges Session at the 13th European Workshop on Natural Language Generation (ENLG)*, pages 217–226, Nancy, France.

Anja Belz. 2008. Automatic generation of weather forecast texts using comprehensive probabilistic generation-space models. *Journal of Natural Language Engineering*, 14(4):431–455.

A. Björkelund, B. Bohnet, L. Hafdell, and P. Nugues. 2010. A high-performance syntactic and semantic dependency parser. In *Proceedings of the 23rd International Conference on Computational Linguistics : Demonstration Volume (COLING)*, pages 33–36, Beijing, China.

Bernd Bohnet, Leo Wanner, Simon Mille, and Alicia Burga. 2010. Broad coverage multilingual deep sentence generation with a stochastic multilevel realizer. In *Proceedings of the 23rd International Conference on Computational Linguistics (COLING)*, pages 98–106, Beijing, China.

Bernd Bohnet, Simon Mille, Benoît Favre, and Leo Wanner. 2011. StuMaBa: From deep representation to surface. In *Proceedings of the Generation Challenges Session at the 13th European Workshop on Natural Language Generation (ENLG)*, pages 232–235, Nancy, France.

Nadjet Bouayad-Agha, Gerard Casamayor, Simon Mille, and Leo Wanner. 2012. Perspective-oriented generation of football match summaries: Old tasks, new challenges. *ACM Transactions on Speech and Language Processing*, 9(2):3:1–3:31.

Xavier Carreras, Michael Collins, and Terry Koo. 2008. TAG, dynamic programming, and the perceptron for efficient, feature-rich parsing. In *Proceedings of the 12th Conference on Computational Natural Language Learning (CoNLL)*, pages 9–16, Manchester, UK.

Simon Corston-Oliver, Michael Gamon, Eric Ringger, and Robert Moore. 2002. An overview of Amalgam: A machine-learned generation module. In *Proceedings of the 2nd International Natural Language Generation Conference (INLG)*, pages 33–40, New-York, NY, USA.

Katja Filippova and Michael Strube. 2008. Sentence fusion via dependency graph compression. In *Proceedings of the 2008 Conference on Empirical Methods in Natural Language Processing (EMNLP)*, pages 177–185, Honolulu, Hawaii.

Richard Johansson and Pierre Nugues. 2008. Dependency-based Semantic Role Labeling of PropBank. In *Proceedings of the 2008 Conference on Empirical Methods in Natural Language Processing (EMNLP)*, pages 69–78, Honolulu, Hawaii.

Irene Langkilde-Geary. 2002. An empirical verification of coverage and correctness for a general-purpose sentence generator. In *Proceedings of the 2nd International Natural Language Generation Conference (INLG)*, pages 17–24, New-York, NY, USA. Citeseer.

Simon Mille, Alicia Burga, and Leo Wanner. 2013. AnCora-UPF: A multi-level annotation of Spanish. In *Proceedings of the 2nd International Conference on Dependency Linguistics (DepLing)*, pages 217–226, Prague, Czech Republic.

Noah A. Smith. 2011. *Linguistic Structure Prediction.* Synthesis Lectures on Human Language Technologies. Morgan and Claypool.

Sebastian Varges and Chris Mellish. 2001. Instance-based Natural Language Generation. In *Proceedings of the 2nd Meeting of the North American Chapter of the Association for Computational Linguistics (NAACL)*, pages 1–8, Pittsburgh, PA, USA.

Determining Content for Unknown Users: Lessons from the MinkApp Case Study

Gemma Webster, Somayajulu G. Sripada, Chris Mellish, Yolanda Melero, Koen Arts, Xavier Lambin, Rene Van Der Wal
University of Aberdeen
{gwebster, yaji.sripada, c.mellish, y.melero, k.arts, x.lambin, r.vanderwal}@abdn.ac.uk

Abstract

If an NLG system needs to be put in place as soon as possible it is not always possible to know in advance who the users of a system are or what kind of information will interest them. This paper describes the development of a system and contextualized text for unknown users. We describe the development, design and initial findings with a system for unknown users that allows the users to design their own contextualised text.

1 Introduction

Requirements of an NLG system are derived commonly by analysing a gold standard corpus. Other knowledge acquisition (KA) techniques such as interviewing experts and end-users are also frequently employed. However, when these KA studies result in only a partial specification of the system requirements or complications make carrying out a detailed user study in the time available difficult, an initial system for unknown users may need to be developed. The initial system needs to fulfil the known requirements making a number of assumptions to fill the gaps in the requirements. In this paper, we concentrate on the content determination problem for such a system.

We encountered this particular problem when producing an initial NLG system to give feedback to volunteers submitting information about signs of American Mink, an invasive species in Scotland. Our response can be viewed, on one hand, as that of exposing an early prototype for evaluation in real use. On the other hand, it can be viewed as an approach to allowing users to "design their own contextualised text". We expected that this approach would have a number of advantages. In the paper, we draw our conclusions about how this worked out in our example application.

2 Background - MinkApp

The Scottish Mink Initiative (SMI) project aims to protect native wildlife by removing breeding American Mink (an invasive species) from the North of Scotland. SMI in the form discussed here was launched in May 2011 and ran until August 2013, after which it continued but on a much smaller funding base. SMI's success and future rely on an ongoing network of volunteers from across Scotland to monitor the American mink population. During the period from 2011 to 2013, these volunteers were coordinated by 4 and later 3 full-time Mink Control officers (MCOs) who had 2.5 year fixed term contracts, had no communal offices and were geographically located across Scotland.

At present volunteers are provided with rafts to monitor American mink. Rafts are simple devices that float on water and are monitored by volunteers who regularly check a clay pad for mink footprints. In the past, volunteers in turn reported signs or lack of signs to their corresponding MCO. Now volunteers can do the same through the MinkApp website, introduced in 2012, though some choose to continue to use the previous reporting method. The data should ideally be entered roughly every 10 days; it concerns either positive or negative records from raft checks, or visual sightings of mink and actual mink captures. The records contain geographical information and a timestamp. MinkApp checks whether this data is complete and then informs the respective mink officer for that volunteer's area and enters the data into the database.

Volunteers used to receive a quarterly newsletter that had some regional specific content but was not volunteer specific. They could receive sporadic contact from their mink control officer in the form of a phone call or email. MinkApp allowed an infrastructure to be developed to provide volunteers with specific and immediate

Proceedings of the 8th International Natural Language Generation Conference, pages 113–117,
Philadelphia, Pennsylvania, 19-21 June 2014.

feedback upon submission of their observations by means of contextualised feedback text.

SMI's funding base was severely reduced in August 2013 and MinkApp has proven central to its endurance. Volunteer activities of the SMI are now supported by staff from 10 local rivers and fisheries trusts (as one of their many activities). This limited amount of staff time available could make the development of automatic personalised feedback generation vital to allow volunteers to have tailored information on the progress of the project and to keep volunteers engaged.

3 The Problem - SMI Volunteers: The Unknown Users

The nearest to a gold standard for what information to offer was the corpus of newsletters containing information on the project as a whole. However, we learned that these newsletters were often not read and we have no way of judging their level of success. These newsletters, along with emails and discussions conducted with SMI employees on their interactions with volunteers, however, gave us ideas about potential content that could be selected and indication of potential lexical structure and word use when addressing volunteers.

Although some SMI volunteers monitor mink as part of their job (e.g. gamekeepers), they could in fact be anyone with a desire to contribute to nature conservation. Volunteers are located in very disparate geographical locations across Scotland, with no set gender or age range and so volunteers' motivations, computer skills and professions are mostly unknown. Because of the range of types of people who could in principle be volunteers, they can be expected to be very varied.

It is extremely difficult to contact all volunteers as each SMI catchment is managed and organized in different ways and volunteers are contacted using different media e.g. mail, email, telephone, face-to-face. SMI is also careful to avoid attempting to contact volunteers too often, conscious that they are providing their services for free and should not be bothered unnecessarily. There is also some uncertainty about which volunteers are active, as records are often partial or out of date. It is known anecdotally from MCOs that many volunteers are unwilling to use any kind of computer system and so it is unclear what kind of people will be reached through MinkApp. Finally, most observations of mink signs that arise are "null records", i.e. records of observing no mink prints on rafts. It is not known which volunteers will be sufficiently motivated to submit "null records" and which will remain apparently inactive because they have nothing positive to report.

So, even though there was a need for automatically generated feedback *now*, there was a real question of who the readers would be and how to select the content to include in the feedback.

4 Related Work

A standard approach to establish user requirements for NLG is to assemble a corpus of human-authored texts and their associated inputs (Reiter & Dale, 2000). This can be the basis of deriving rules by hand, or one can attempt to replicate content selection rules from the corpus by machine learning (Duboue & McKeown, 2003; Konstas & Lapata, 2012). To produce a useful corpus, however, one has to know one's users or have reliable expert authors.

As first pointed out by Levine et al. (1991), an NLG system that produces *hypertext,* rather than straight text, can avoid some content selection decisions, as the user makes some of these decisions by selecting links to follow. A similar advantage applies to other adaptive hypertext systems (Brusilovsky, 2001). Another general possibility is to allow users to design aspects of the texts they receive. For instance, ICONOCLAST (Power, Scott, & Bouayad-Agha, 2003) allows users to make choices about text style. However, relatively little is known about how such approaches work 'in the wild'.

Various previous work has attempted to build models of users through observing interactions with an interface (Fischer, 2001). Alternatively, it is possible to explicitly ask questions to the user about their interests (Tintarev & Masthoff, 2008), though this requires the users to have the time and motivation to take part in an initial activity with no direct reward.

Our approach can be seen to have similarities with hypertext generation, in that we are offering alternative texts to users, and non-invasive approaches to user modelling.

5 Approach to Content Selection

To overcome the 'unknown' user and 'unknown' feedback problem it was decided to implement a relatively quick exploratory tool that could be used to help understand user requirements, provide initial evaluation of feedback content and build an understanding of user interests. To achieve these aims we developed a tool that allows users to generate their own text, selecting content from a larger set of possibilities. The information on the type of feedback generated by the user would allow us to investigate user stereotypes, their detection and the automatic adaptation of content based on their interests (Zancanaro, Kuflik, Boger, Goren-Bar, & Goldwasser, 2007).

5.1 Exploratory Tool - The Feedback Form

The feedback form (Figure 1) is displayed to users of the MinkApp system once they have submitted a raft check. The form allows the user to select which raft they wish to have their feedback generated on from a list of the rafts they manage. The users have four types of information they can select to have feedback generated on: Signs (information on signs of mink reported through raft checks), Captures (information on mink captures), My Rafts (information on their personal raft checks and submission record) and Mink Ecology (information on mink behaviour and seasonality).

Two of the four options, Signs and Captures, allow the user to select to what geographic scale they would like their feedback based on: the whole of the SMI project area, their river or their catchment – the geographical region that they report to e.g. Aberdeenshire, Tayside etc.

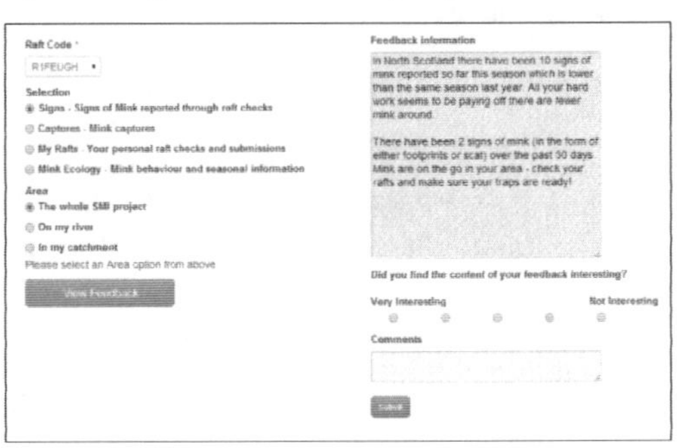

Once the user has made their selection the personalised feedback based on their choices is generated and displayed along with an option to rank how interesting they found this feedback or any comments they wish to make. The user can generate multiple texts in one session. All data from each click of an option, the generated text and user comments on the text are recorded.

5.2 Generation of the paragraphs

The structure of the text is separated out into self-contained paragraphs to allow analysis of what volunteers regularly view. For each type, the structure of the generated paragraph is determined by a simple schema:

Signs:
Neighbourhood (based on user selection) – *In the Don catchment there have been 6 signs of mink reported over the past 12 months which is higher than the previous 12 months*
Additional Information / Motivation – *Mink are coming into your area to replace captured mink. This shows your area has good ecology for mink and it is important to keep monitoring.*
Personal – *There have been no signs of mink (in the form of either footprints or scat) in the past 30 days. No signs of mink recently does not mean they are gone - remain vigilant.*

Captures:
Neighbourhood (based on user selection) – *In the Spey catchment we have trapped 5 mink over the past 12 months which is lower than the previous 12 months.*
Additional Information / Motivation – *Information available on this year's captures: An adult female mink was captured on: 2014-02-19.*

My Rafts:
Personal –*You have been very active over the past 60 days with 7 'no mink signs' reported and 2 signs of mink (in the form of either footprints or scat) reported, the last of which was logged on 14 Sep 2013 23:00:00 GMT.*
Additional Information / Motivation – *Please keep checking your raft as this evidence means there are mink in your area.*

Mink Ecology:
Temporal - *We are in the normal mink breeding season!*
Motivation – *During the breeding season female mink will defend an area covering approximately 1.5 miles.*
Additional Information - *Female mink are small enough to fit into water vole burrows which they explore in search of prey.Did you know there can be brown, black, purple, white and silver mink which reflects the colours bred for fur?*

To produce the actual content to fill the slots of the schemas, the system was designed to reason over geographical location to allow examination of the various notions of neighbourhood (Tintarev et al 2012). The system also looks at temporal trends when developing text based on the number of record submissions for a given time. The system initially looks at record submissions in the past week then opens out to a month, season and finally activity between the same seasons on different years. This use of temporal trends ensures volunteers are supplied with the most relevant (recent) mink activity information first in busy periods such as the breeding season but ensures 'cleared' areas with little mink activity are still provided with informative feedback.

6 Evaluation of the Feedback Approach

We were initially apprehensive about how much usage the feedback system would get. MinkApp was launched through the SMI newsletters, but we knew that volunteers were not always receiving or reading these. Also it turned out that the initial estimate of active volunteers was overinflated. Indeed, initially the usage of MinkApp in general was much lower than was expected. So we worked hard to promote the system, for instance asking the fisheries trusts to actively ask any volunteers they had contact with if they had heard of MinkApp and to try to use it. As a result, we did manage to increase the system usage to a level where some initial conclusions can be drawn.

MinkApp and specifically the feedback form use were monitored for 50 days (7 weeks). During this time 308 raft checks were submitted by volunteers for 98 different rafts by 44 unique users. The feedback system was used by volunteers to generate 113 different texts about 36 different rafts. 32 out of the 44 (72.7%) of all MinkApp users requested generated feedback at least once.

In 47% of the feedback form use sessions multiple texts were generated and there are some particularly interesting use patterns:

- "Regular explorer": One user accessed MinkApp seven times and generated feedback text on every use: 1 text, 3 texts, 5 texts, 5 texts, 4 texts, 2 texts and 1 text
- "Periodic explorer": One user accessed MinkApp six times and generated at least one feedback text on every second use
- "Try once only": The user who accessed MinkApp the most with eleven different sessions only generated feedback text on their first use of MinkApp.

These different patterns of use require further investigation as the number of users using MinkApp increases. The patterns can be affected by idiosyncratic factors. For instance, one volunteer informed the project coordinator that they continually selected Captures within their area as they had caught a mink and their capture had not yet been added to the system - the volunteer was using the feedback form to monitor how long it took for mink capture data to appear in MinkApp.

Of the four types of information available to volunteers Signs was the most viewed although Captures was what SMI staff had felt volunteers would be most interested in. Signs had 56.6% of the overall use and catchment was the most widely selected option for geographic area for both Signs and Captures. However there was no clearly predominant second choice for information option with Captures and My Rafts having only 2.7% of a difference within their use. Mink Ecology was the least used category, partly to do with the lack of clarity in the name 'Mink Ecology'. Signs on a local geographical scale were the most common selection for volunteers but the actual use was not clear enough to support a fixed text type or removing other options.

7 Conclusions

The results of this initial study did support the value of feedback to volunteers (more directly than we would have been able to determine in advance) with 73% of volunteers choosing to generate feedback. The feedback enabled us to offer contextualized information to volunteers quickly, without initial extensive user studies, which was very important for supporting the continuation of SMI.

The fact that the volunteer population was relatively unknown meant that there were some unpleasant surprises in terms of uptake and interest. It was necessary to make special efforts to encourage participation to get larger numbers.

When our system gets used over longer periods we might observe more meaningful patterns of behaviour.

The patterns of interest we observed were noisy and were influenced by many contextual factors meaning there was little potential yet for statistical analysis or machine learning.

8 Future Work

In-depth analysis is required as more volunteers use MinkApp and the feedback form to fully understand patterns of behaviour. Additionally qualitative studies such as interviews with volunteers could help explain use and preferences. These studies could help us improve the feedback system and text to better suit the user's needs. In the meantime, we have a working system that offers choices to users to 'generate their own text' even though we had hoped to be able to tailor to individual volunteer preferences sooner.

9 Acknowledgments

We would like to thank SMI for their on-going commitment to this research. This work is supported by the Rural Digital Economy Research Hub (EPSRC EP/G066051/1).

Reference

Arts, K., Webster, G. ., Sharma, N. ., Melero, Y. ., Mellish, C., Lambin, X., & Van der Wal, R. (2013). Capturing mink and data. Interacting with a small and dispersed environmental initiative over the introduction of digital innovation Uploader. Case study for the online platform "Framework for Responsible Research and Innovation in ICT." Retrieved from http://responsible-innovation.org.uk/torrii/resource-detail/1059

Beirne, C., & Lambin, X. (2013). Understanding the Determinants of Volunteer Retention Through Capture-Recapture Analysis: Answering Social Science Questions Using a Wildlife Ecology Toolkit. Conservation Letters, 6(6), 391–401. doi:10.1111/conl.12023

Brusilovsky, P. (2001). Adaptive Hypermedia. User Modeling and User-Adapted Interaction, 11(1-2), 87–110. doi:10.1023/A:1011143116306

Bryce, R., Oliver, M. K., Davies, L., Gray, H., Urquhart, J., & Lambin, X. (2011). Turning back the tide of American mink invasion at an unprecedented scale through community participation and adaptive management. Biological conservation, 144(1), 575–583. Retrieved from http://cat.inist.fr/?aModele=afficheN&cpsidt=23779637

Duboue, P. A., & McKeown, K. R. (2003). Statistical acquisition of content selection rules for natural language generation. In Proceedings of the 2003 conference on Empirical methods in natural language processing - (Vol. 10, pp. 121–128). Morristown, NJ, USA: Association for Computational Linguistics. doi:10.3115/1119355.1119371

Fischer, G. (2001). User Modeling in Human–Computer Interaction. User Modeling and User-Adapted Interaction, 11(1-2), 65–86. doi:10.1023/A:1011145532042

Konstas, I., & Lapata, M. (2012). Concept-to-text generation via discriminative reranking, 369–378. Retrieved from http://dl.acm.org/citation.cfm?id=2390524.2390576

Levine, J., Cawsey, A., Mellish, C., Poynter, L., Reiter, E., Tyson, P., & Walker, J. (1991). IDAS: Combining hypertext and natural language generation. In Procs of the Third European Workshop on NLG (pp. 55–62). Innsbruck, Austria.

Power, R., Scott, D., & Bouayad-Agha, N. (2003). Generating texts with style, 444–452. Retrieved from http://dl.acm.org/citation.cfm?id=1791562.1791619

Reiter, E., & Dale, R. (2000). Building Applied Natural Language Generation Systems. clt.mq.edu.au (Vol. 33.). Cambridge: Cambridge university press. Retrieved from http://clt.mq.edu.au/~rdale/publications/papers/1997/jnle97.pdf

Tintarev, N., & Masthoff, J. (2008). Adaptive Hypermedia and Adaptive Web-Based Systems. (W. Nejdl, J. Kay, P. Pu, & E. Herder, Eds.) (Vol. 5149, pp. 204–213). Berlin, Heidelberg: Springer Berlin Heidelberg. doi:10.1007/978-3-540-70987-9

Tintarev, N., Melero, Y., Sripada, S., Tait, E., Van Der Wal, R., & Mellish, C. (2012). MinkApp: generating spatio-temporal summaries for nature conservation volunteers, 17–21. Retrieved from http://dl.acm.org/citation.cfm?id=2392712.2392720

Zancanaro, M., Kuflik, T., Boger, Z., Goren-Bar, D., & Goldwasser, D. (2007). Analyzing museum visitors' behavior patterns. In C. Conati, K. McCoy, & G. Paliouras (Eds.), 11th International Conference on User Modeling (Vol. 4511, pp. 238–246). Berlin, Heidelberg: Springer Berlin Heidelberg. doi:10.1007/978-3-540-73078-1

FlowGraph2Text: Automatic Sentence Skeleton Compilation for Procedural Text Generation

†[1]Shinsuke Mori ‡[2]Hirokuni Maeta [1]Tetsuro Sasada [2]Koichiro Yoshino
[3]Atsushi Hashimoto [1]Takuya Funatomi [2]Yoko Yamakata
[1]Academic Center for Computing and Media Studies, Kyoto University
[2]Graduate School of Informatics, Kyoto University
[3]Graduate School of Law, Kyoto University
Yoshida Honmachi, Sakyo-ku, Kyoto, Japan
†forest@i.kyoto-u.ac.jp

Abstract

In this paper we describe a method for generating a procedural text given its flow graph representation. Our main idea is to automatically collect sentence skeletons from real texts by replacing the important word sequences with their type labels to form a skeleton pool. The experimental results showed that our method is feasible and has a potential to generate natural sentences.

1 Introduction

Along with computers penetrating in our daily life, the needs for the natural language generation (NLG) technology are increasing more and more. If computers understand both the meaning of a procedural text and the progression status, they can suggest us what to do next. In such situation they can show sentences describing the next instruction on a display or speak it.

On this background we propose a method for generating instruction texts from a flow graph representation for a series of procedures. Among various genres of procedural texts, we choose cooking recipes, because they are one of the most familiar procedural texts for the public. In addition, a computerized help system proposed by Hashimoto et al. (2008) called smart kitchen is becoming more and more realistic. Thus we try to generate cooking procedural texts from a formal representation for a series of preparation instructions of a dish.

As the formal representation, we adopt the flow graph representation (Hamada et al., 2000; Mori et al., 2014), in which the vertices and the arcs correspond to important objects or actions in cooking and relationships among them, respectively. We use the flow graphs as the input and the text parts as the references for evaluation.

Our generation method first automatically compiles a set of templates, which we call the skeleton pool, from a huge number of real procedural sentences. Then it decomposes the input flow graph into a sequence of subtrees that are suitable for a sentence. Finally it converts subtrees into natural language sentences.

2 Recipe Flow Graph Corpus

The input of our LNG system is the meaning representation (Mori et al., 2014) for cooking instructions in a recipe. A recipe consists of three parts: a title, an ingredient list, and sentences describing cooking instructions (see Figure 1). The meaning of the instruction sentences is represented by a directed acyclic graph (DAG) with a root (the final dish) as shown in Figure 2. Its vertices have a pair of an important word sequence in the recipe and its type called a recipe named entity (NE)[1]. And its arcs denote relationships between them. The arcs are also classified into some types. In this paper, however, we do not use arc types for text generation, because we want our system to be capable of generating sentences from flow graphs output by an automatic video recognition system[2] or those drawn by internet users.

Each vertex of a flow graph has an NE composed of a word sequence in the text and its type such as food, tool, action, etc. Table 3

‡His current affiliation is Cybozu Inc., Koraku 1-4-14, Bunkyo, Tokyo, Japan.

[1]Although the label set contains verb phrases, they are called named entities.

[2]By computer vision techniques such as (Regneri et al., 2013) we may be able to figure out what action a person takes on what objects. But it is difficult to distinguish the direct object and the indirect object, for example.

Proceedings of the 8th International Natural Language Generation Conference, pages 118–122,
Philadelphia, Pennsylvania, 19-21 June 2014.

1. 両手鍋で油を熱する。
   (In a Dutch oven, heat oil.)
   セロリと青ねぎとニンニクを加える。
   (Add celery, green onions, and garlic.)
   1 分ほど炒める。
   (Cook for about 1 minute.)
2. ブイヨンと水とマカロニと胡椒を加え
   パスタが柔らかくなるまで煮る。
   (Add broth, water, macaroni, and pepper, and simmer until the pasta is tender.)
3. 刻んだセージをまぶす。
   (Sprinkle the snipped sage.)

Figure 1: A recipe example. The sentences are one of the ideal outputs of our problem. They are also used as the reference in evaluation.

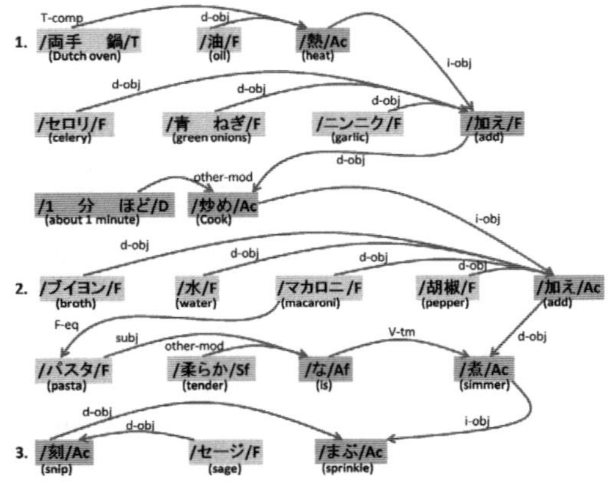

Figure 2: The flow graph of the example recipe.

lists all of the type labels along with the average numbers of occurrences in a recipe text and examples. The word sequences of verbal NEs do not include their inflectional endings. From the definition we can say that the content words are included in the flow graph representation. Thus an NLG system has to decide their order and generate the function words (including inflectional endings for verbs) to connect them to form a sentence.

Table 3: Named entity tags with average frequence per recipe.

NE tag	Meaning	Freq.
F	Food	11.87
T	Tool	3.83
D	Duration	0.67
Q	Quantity	0.79
Ac	Action by the chef	13.83
Af	Action by foods	2.04
Sf	State of foods	3.02
St	State of tools	0.30

3 Recipe Text Generation

The problem in this paper is generating a procedural text for cooking (ex. Figure 1) from a recipe flow graph (ex. Figure 2).

Our method is decomposed into two modules. In this section, we explain them in detail.

3.1 Skeleton Pool Compilation

Before the run time, we first prepare a skeleton pool. A skeleton pool is a collection of skeleton sentences, or skeletons for short, and a skeleton is a sentence in which NEs have been replaced with NE tags. The skeletons are similar to the so-called templates and the main difference is that the skeletons are automatically converted from real sentences. The following is the process to prepare a skeleton pool.

1. Crawl cooking procedural sentences from recipe sites.
2. Segment sentences into words by a word segmenter KyTea (Neubig et al., 2011). Then recognize recipe NEs by an NE recognizer PWNER (Mori et al., 2012).
3. Replace the NE instances in the sentences with NE tags.

We store skeletons with a key which is the sequence of the NE tags in the order of their occurrence.

3.2 Sentence Planning

Our sentence planner produces a sequence of subtrees each of which corresponds to a sentence. There are two conditions.

Cond. 1 Each subtree has an Ac as its root.

Cond. 2 Every vertex is included in at least one subtree.

As a strategy for enumerating subtrees given a flow graph, we choose the following algorithm.

1. search for an Ac vertex by the depth first search (DFS),
2. each time it finds an Ac, return the largest subtree which has an Ac as its root and contains only unvisited vertices.
3. set the visited-mark to the vertices contained in the returned subtree,
4. go back to 1 unless all the vertices are marked as visited.

In DFS, we choose a child vertex randomly because a recipe flow graph is unordered.

Table 1: Corpus specifications.

Usage	#Recipes	#Sent.	#NEs	#Words	#Char.
Test	40	245	1,352	4,005	7,509
NER training	360	2,813	12,101	51,847	97,911
Skeleton pool	100,000	713,524	*3,919,964	*11,988,344	22,826,496

The numbers with asterisc are estimated values on the NLP result.

Table 2: Statistical results of various skeleton pool sizes.

No. of sentences used for skeleton pool compilation	2,769 (1/256)	11,077 (1/64)	44,308 (1/16)	177,235 (1/4)	708,940 (1/1)
No. of uncovered subtrees	52	27	17	9	4
Average no. of skeletons	37.4	124.3	450.2	1598.1	5483.3
BLEU	11.19	11.25	12.86	13.12	13.76

3.3 Sentence Generation

Given a subtree sequence, our text realizer generates a sentence by the following steps.

1. Collect skeletons from the pool whose NE key matches the NE tag sequence specified by the subtree[3].
2. Select the skeleton that maximize a scoring function among collected ones. As the first trial we use the frequency of skeletons in the pool as the scoring function.
3. Replace each NE in the skeleton with the word sequence of the corresponding NE in the subtree.

4 Evaluation

We conducted experiments generating texts from flow graphs. In this section, we report the coverage and the sentence quality.

4.1 Experimental Settings

The recipe flow graph corpus (Mori et al., 2014) contains 200 recipes. We randomly selected 40 flow graphs as the test data from which we generate texts. The other 160 recipes were used to train the NE recognizer PWNER (Mori et al., 2012) with 200 more recipes that we annotated with NE tags. To compile the skeleton pool we crawled 100,000 recipes containing 713,524 sentences (see Table 1).

4.2 Skeleton Pool Coverage

First we counted the numbers of the skeletons that matches with a subtree (Step 1 in Subsection 3.3) for all the subtrees in the test set by changing the number of the recipe sentences used for the skeleton pool compilation.

Table 2 shows the numbers of subtrees that do not have any matching skeleton in the pool (uncovered subtrees) and the average number of skeletons in the pool for a subtree. From the results shown in the table we can say that when we use 100,000 recipes for the skeleton compilation, our method can generate a sentence for 98.4% subtrees. And the table says that we can halve the number of uncovered subtrees by using about four times more sentences. The average number of the skeletons says that we have enough skeletons in average to try more sophisticated scoring functions.

4.3 Text Quality

To measure the quality of generated texts, we first calculated the BLEU ($N = 4$) (Papineni et al., 2002) with taking the original recipe texts as the references. The unit in our case is a sequence of sentences for a dish. Table 2 shows the average BLEU for all the test set. The result says that the more sentences we use for the skeleton pool compilation, the better the generated sentences become.

The absolute BLEU score, however, does not tell much about the quality of generated texts. As it is well known, we can sometimes change the instruction order in dish preparation. Therefore we conducted a subjective evaluation in addition. We asked four evaluators to read 10 texts generated from 10 flow graphs and answer the following questions.

Q1. How many ungrammatical two-word sequences does the text contain?

Q2. How many ambiguous wordings do you find in the text?

Then we show the evaluators the original recipe text and asked the following question.

[3] This part is language dependent. Since Japanese is SOV language, the instance of Ac is placed at the last of the sentence to be generated. Languages of other types like English may need some rules to change the NE tag order specified by the subtree into the proper sentence element order.

Table 4: Result of text quality survey on 10 recipe texts.

	Evaluator 1			Evaluator 2			Evaluator 3			Evaluator 4		
BLEU	Q1	Q2	Q3	Q1	Q2	Q3	Q1	Q2	Q3	Q1	Q2	Q3
6.50	13	2	4	11	0	3	12	0	2	7	1	2
7.99	7	2	2	5	2	2	7	1	1	4	2	2
10.09	18	2	4	15	2	1	17	4	1	11	4	2
11.60	24	1	4	13	2	4	18	2	4	13	1	2
13.35	6	1	4	6	0	4	7	1	5	4	1	2
14.70	16	1	4	12	2	4	12	0	3	6	2	2
16.76	9	2	3	6	1	3	7	1	3	5	3	2
19.65	8	2	5	6	1	1	4	1	4	4	2	4
22.85	18	1	4	15	2	5	12	2	2	7	3	2
31.35	5	1	5	5	0	4	5	1	3	5	1	4
Ave.	12.4	1.5	3.9	9.4	1.2	3.1	10.1	1.3	2.8	6.6	2.0	2.4
PCC	−0.30	−0.46	+0.57	−0.24	−0.24	+0.36	−0.46	−0.04	+0.26	−0.29	−0.04	+0.70

PPC stands for Pearson correlation coefficient.

Q3. Will the dish be the same as the original recipe when you cook according to the generated text? Choose the one among 5: completely, 4: almost, 3: partly, 2: different, or 1: unexecutable.

Table 4 shows the result. The generated texts contain 14.5 sentences in average. The answers to Q1 tell that there are many grammatical errors. We need some mechanism that selects more appropriate skeletons. The number of ambiguous wordings, however, is very low. The reason is that the important words are given along with the subtrees. The average of the answer to Q3 is 3.05. This result says that the dish will be partly the same as the original recipe. There is a room for improvement.

Finally, let us take a look at the correlation of the result of three Qs with BLEU. The numbers of grammatical errors, i.e. the answers to Q1, has a stronger correlation with BLEU than those of Q2 asking the semantic quality. These are consistent with the intuition. The answer to Q3, asking overall text quality, has the strongest correlation with BLEU on average among all the questions. Therefore we can say that for the time being the objective evaluation by BLEU is sufficient to measure the performance of various improvements.

5 Related Work

Our method can be seen a member of template-based text generation systems (Reiter, 1995). Contrary to the ordinary template-based approach, our method first automatically compiles a set of templates, which we call skeleton pool, by running an NE tagger on the real texts. This allows us to cope with the coverage problem with keeping the advantage of the template-based approach, ability to prevent from generating incomprehensible sentence structures. The main contribution of this paper is to use an accurate NE tagger to convert sentences into skeletons, to show the coverages of the skeleton pool, and to evaluate the method in a realistic situation.

Among many applications of our method, a concrete one is the smart kitchen (Hashimoto et al., 2008), a computerized cooking help system which watches over the chef by the computer vision (CV) technologies etc. and suggests the chef the next action to be taken or a good way of doing it in a casual manner. In this application, the text generation module make a sentence from a subtree specified by the process supervision module.

There are some other interesting applications: a help system for internet users to write good sentences, machine translation of a recipe in a different language represented as a flow graph, or automatic recipe generation from a cooking video based on CV and NLP researches such as (Regneri et al., 2013; Yamakata et al., 2013; Yu and Siskind, 2013).

6 Conclusion

In this paper, we explained and evaluated our method for generating a procedural text from a flow graph representation. The experimental results showed that our method is feasible especially when we have huge number of real sentences and that some more sophistications are possible to generate more natural sentences.

Acknowledgments

This work was supported by JSPS Grants-in-Aid for Scientific Research Grant Numbers 26280084, 24240030, and 26280039.

References

Reiko Hamada, Ichiro Ide, Shuichi Sakai, and Hidehiko Tanaka. 2000. Structural analysis of cooking preparation steps in japanese. In *Proceedings of the fifth international workshop on Information retrieval with Asian languages*, number 8 in IRAL '00, pages 157–164.

Atsushi Hashimoto, Naoyuki Mori, Takuya Funatomi, Yoko Yamakata, Koh Kakusho, and Michihiko Minoh. 2008. Smart kitchen: A user centric cooking support system. In *Proceedings of the 12th Information Processing and Management of Uncertainty in Knowledge-Based Systems*, pages 848–854.

Shinsuke Mori, Tetsuro Sasada, Yoko Yamakata, and Koichiro Yoshino. 2012. A machine learning approach to recipe text processing. In *Proceedings of Cooking with Computer workshop*.

Shinsuke Mori, Hirokuni Maeta, Yoko Yamakata, and Tetsuro Sasada. 2014. Flow graph corpus from recipe texts. In *Proceedings of the Nineth International Conference on Language Resources and Evaluation*.

Graham Neubig, Yosuke Nakata, and Shinsuke Mori. 2011. Pointwise prediction for robust, adaptable japanese morphological analysis. In *Proceedings of the 49th Annual Meeting of the Association for Computational Linguistics*.

Kishore Papineni, Salim Roukos, Todd Ward, and Wei-Jing Zhu. 2002. Bleu: a method for automatic evaluation of machine translation. In *Proceedings of the 40th Annual Meeting of the Association for Computational Linguistics*, pages 311–318.

Michaela Regneri, Marcus Rohrbach, Dominikus Wetzel, Stefan Thater, Bernt Schiele, and Manfred Pinkal. 2013. Grounding action descriptions in videos. *Transactions of the Association for Computational Linguistics*, 1(Mar):25–36.

Ehud Reiter. 1995. Nlg vs. templates. In *Proceedings of the the Fifth European Workshop on Natural Language Generation*, pages 147–151.

Yoko Yamakata, Shinji Imahori, Yuichi Sugiyama, Shinsuke Mori, and Katsumi Tanaka. 2013. Feature extraction and summarization of recipes using flow graph. In *Proceedings of the 5th International Conference on Social Informatics*, LNCS 8238, pages 241–254.

Haonan Yu and Jeffrey Mark Siskind. 2013. Grounded language learning from video described with sentences. In *Proceedings of the 51st Annual Meeting of the Association for Computational Linguistics*.

Generating Annotated Graphs using the NLG Pipeline Architecture

Saad Mahamood, William Bradshaw and Ehud Reiter
Arria NLG plc
Aberdeen, Scotland, United Kingdom
{saad.mahamood, william.bradshaw, ehud.reiter}@arria.com

Abstract

The Arria NLG Engine has been extended to generate annotated graphs: data graphs that contain computer-generated textual annotations to explain phenomena in those graphs. These graphs are generated along-side text-only data summaries.

1 Introduction

Arria NLG[1] develops NLG solutions, primarily in the data-to-text area. These solutions are NLG systems, which generate textual summaries of large numeric data sets. Arria's core product is the Arria NLG Engine,[2] which is configured and customised for the needs of different clients.

Recently Arria has extended this core engine so that it can automatically produce annotated graphs, that is, data graphs that have textual annotations explaining phenomena in those graphs (see example in Figure 1). This was developed after listening to one of our customers, whose staff manually created annotated graphs and found this process to be very time-consuming. The annotated graph generation process is integrated into the NLG pipeline, and is carried out in conjunction with the generation of a textual summary of a data set.

In this short paper we summarise the relevant research background, and briefly describe what we have achieved in this area.

2 Background: Multimodality and NLG

Rich media such as web pages and electronic documents typically include several modalities in a given document. A web page, for example, can contain images, graphs, and interactive elements. Because of this there has been an interest within the NLG community in generating multimodal documents. However, basic questions remain as how best to combine and integrate multiple modalities within a given NLG application.

2.1 Annotated Graphics

Sripada and Gao (2007) conducted a small study where they showed scuba divers different possible outputs from their *ScubaText* system, including text-only, graph-only and annotated graphs. They found that divers preferred the annotated graph presentation. The ScubaText software could not in practice produce annotated graphs for arbitrary input data sets and automatically set the scale based on detected events, so this was primarily a study of user preferences.

McCoy and colleagues have been developing techniques to automatically generate textual summaries of data graphics for visually impaired users (Demier et al., 2008). This differs from our work because their goal is to replace the graph, whereas our goal is to generate an integrated text/graphics presentation.

There were several early systems in the 1990s (Wahlster et al., 1993; Feiner and McKeown, 1990, for example), which generated integrated presentations of figures and texts, but these systems focused on annotating static pictures and diagrams, not data graphics. The WIP system, which combined static diagram images and text, used a deep planning approach to produce tightly integrated multimodal documents; it is not clear how robustly this approach handled new data sets and contexts.

2.2 Embodied Conversational Agents

In recent years the challenge of combining multiple modalities such as text, speech, and/or animation has been addressed in the context of Embodied Conversational Agents or ECAs. One example is the NECA system (Krenn et al., 2002).

[1] Arria NLG plc (https://www.arria.com)
[2] For more information see: https://www.arria.com/technology-A300.php

Proceedings of the 8th International Natural Language Generation Conference, pages 123–127,
Philadelphia, Pennsylvania, 19-21 June 2014.

It allowed two embodied agents to converse with each other via spoken dialogue while being able to make gestures as well. From an architectural perspective, NECA used a pipeline architecture in some ways similar to the standard NLG data-to-text pipeline (Reiter and Dale, 2000). Document Planning is handled by the Scene Generator, which selects the dialogue content. The 'Multi-modal NLG' (M-NLG) component handles Microplanning and Surface Realisation, and also deals with specifying gestures, mood, and information structure. Thus the textual output generated by the surface realiser in the NECA M-NLG component is annotated with metadata for other modalities. In particular, information on gestures, emotions, information structure, syntactic structure and dialogue structure (Krenn et al., 2002) are also included to help inform the speech synthesis and gesture assignment modules.

2.3 Background: Psychology

The question of whether information is best presented in text or graphics is in principle largely one for cognitive psychology. Which type of presentation is most effective, and in which context? The answer of course depends on the communicative goal, the type of data being presented, the type of user, the communication medium and other contextual factors.

In particular, a number of researchers (Petre, 1995, for example) have pointed out that graphical presentations require expertise to interpret them and hence may be more appropriate for experienced users than for novices. Tufte (1983) points out that statistical graphs can be very misleading for people who are not used to interpreting them.

Alberdi et al (2001) report on a number of psychological studies on effectiveness of data visualisations which were performed with clinicians in a Neonatal Intensive Care Unit (NICU). At a high level, these studies found that visualisations were less effective and less used than had been hoped. Detailed findings include the following:

- Although consultants, junior doctors, and nurses all claimed in interviews to make heavy use of the computer system which displayed visualisations, when observed onward only senior consultants actually did so; junior doctors and nurses rarely looked at the computer screen.
- Senior consultants were much better than junior staff at distinguishing real events from noise (sensor artefacts).
- Even senior consultants could only identify 70% of key events purely from the visualisations.

Law et al (2005) followed up the above work by explicitly comparing the effectiveness of visualisations and textual summaries. The textual summaries in the experiment were manually written, but did not contain any diagnoses and instead focused on describing the data. Law et al found that clinicians at all levels made better decisions when showed the textual summaries; however at all levels they preferred the visualisations.

A similar study with computer generated summary texts produced by the Babytalk BT45 system (Portet et al., 2009), conducted by van der Meulen et al (2008), found that decision quality was best when clinicians were shown manually written summaries; computer generated texts were of similar effectiveness to visualisations. An error analysis of this study (Reiter et al., 2008) concluded that computer generated texts were much more effective in some contexts than in others.

An implication of the above studies is that in many cases the ideal strategy is to produce both text and graphics. This increases decision effectiveness (since the modalities work best in different situations), and also increases user satisfaction, since users see the modality they like as well as the one which is most effective for decision support.

2.4 Annotated Graphs in NLG Engine

We have extended our NLG Engine to generate annotated graphs as well as texts; an example output, generated by a demonstration system, is shown in figure 1. This example shows a very simple textual output; examples of more complex textual output are on the Arria website[3].

This example output shows a comparison of performance between the FTSE 100 and a given stock portfolio. The value of the FTSE 100 is used as a performance benchmark to see if a given stock portfolio is performing better or worse than compared to the stock market in general.

As can be seen in the graph in figure 1, the annotations are small text fragments, which are placed

[3]A more detailed example is given here: `https://www.arria.com/case-study-oilgas-A231.php`

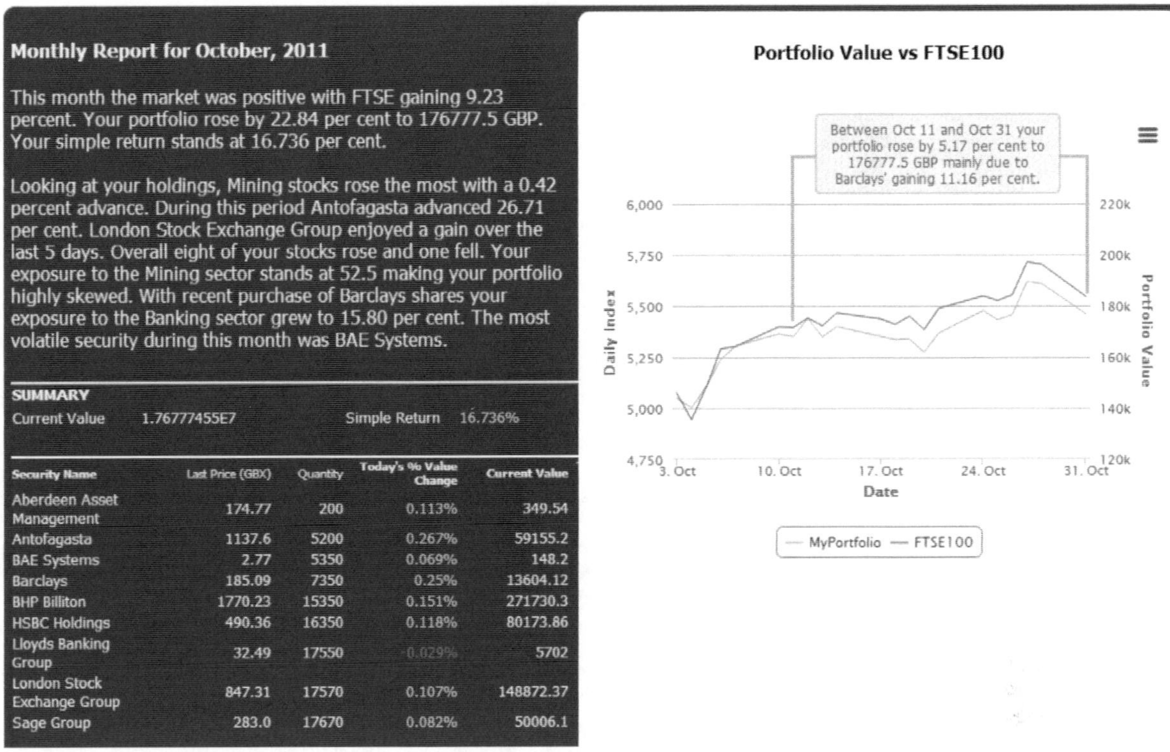

Figure 1: Combined text and annotated graph detailing the stock portfolio performance

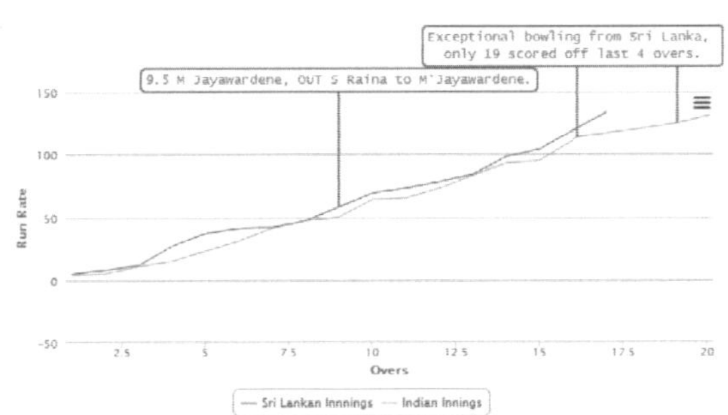

Figure 2: Graph illustrating stacking capabilities when two annotations intersect each other

on top of the graph, and are linked to the relevant events in that occur in the graph. Annotations can also be placed at the bottom of graphs and at the sides and can rearrange themselves depending on the space available. In figure 1 the range annotation used indicates the reason for the increase in the value of a given stock portfolio over a particular time period. If one or more annotations collide or intersect a stacking algorithm is used prior to presentation to rearrange the placement of colliding annotations as shown in figure 2.

Figure 3 illustrates the architecture that is used by our NLG engine. The data analysis and data interpretation modules analyse the input data and produce a set of messages which can be communicated to the user in the generated report. The document planner decides on which messages should be communicated overall, and where messages should appear (for example, situational analysis text, diagnosis text, impact text, graph annotation, or a combination of these). The document planner also decides on the type of graph used, and which data channels it displays; these data channels must include any channels which are annotated, but in some cases other channels are displayed as well.

Once document planning is complete, the visualisation planning module generates the graph design, including X and Y scale and the position of the annotations on the graph. The time range shown in the graph is largely determined by the annotation messages. In other words, the decision about what data to show on the graph is partially driven by the annotations.

The annotation microplanner and realiser generate the actual annotation texts, using special rules which are optimised for annotations (which need

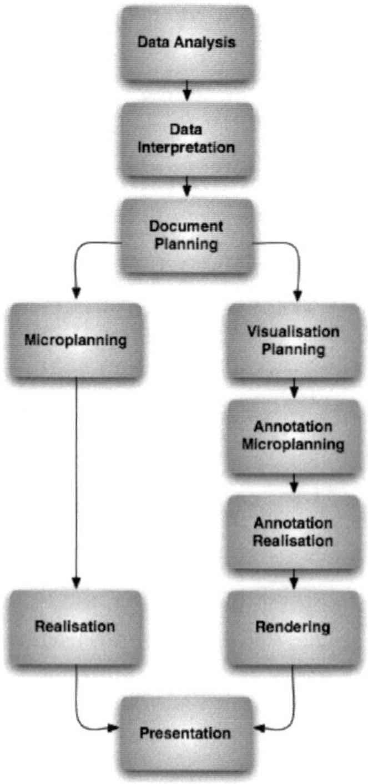

Figure 3: Pipeline architecture of the Arria NLG Engine

to be short and have different referring expressions). After this has been completed, a renderer produces the actual annotated graph. The final task lies with the presenter module, which recombines the separately generated summary text (generated by the NLG Microplanning and Realisation modules) with the annotated graphs.

3 Conclusion

Annotated graphs are a very appealing mechanism for combining text and data graphics into a single multimodal information presentation; this is shown both by the findings of Sripada and Gao (2007) and by the experiences of our customers. Amongst other benefits, we believe that annotated graphs will address some of the deficiencies in data graphics which were pointed out by Alberdi et al (2001), by helping users (especially inexperienced ones) to more easily identify key events in a graph and also to distinguish real events from sensor artefacts and other noise.

We have developed software to create annotated graphs, by modifying the standard NLG data-to-text pipeline as described above. Our clients have reacted very positively so far, and we are now exploring extensions, for example by making annotated graphs interactive.

References

E. Alberdi, J. C. Becher, K. J. Gilhooly, J. R.W. Hunter, R. H. Logie, A. Lyon, N. McIntosh, and J. Reiss. 2001. Expertise and the interpretation of computerised physiological data: Implications for the design of computerised physiological monitoring in neonatal intensive care. *International Journal of Human Computer Studies*, 55(3):191–216.

S. Demier, S. Carberry, and K. F. McCoy. 2008. Generating textual summaries of bar charts. In *Fifth International Natural Language Generation Conference (INLG 2008)*, pages 7–15. Association for Computational Linguistics.

S. Feiner and K. R. McKeown. 1990. Generating Coordinated Multimedia Explanations. In *Sixth Conference on Artificial Intelligence Applications*, volume 290-296.

B. Krenn, H. Pirker, M. Grice, S. Baumann, P. Piwek, K. van Deemter, M. Schroeder, M. Klesen, and E. Gstrein. 2002. Generation of multi-modal dialogue for a net environment. In *Proceedings of KONVENS-02*, Saarbruecken, Germany.

A. S. Law, Y. Freer, J. Hunter, R. H. Logie, N. McIntosh, and J. Quinn. 2005. A comparison of graphical and textual presentations of time series data to support medical decision making in the neonatal intensive care unit. *Journal of Clinical Monitoring and Computing*, 19(3):183–194.

M. Petre. 1995. Why Looking isn't always Seeing: Readership Skills and Graphical Programming. *Communications of the ACM*, 38:33–44.

F. Portet, E. Reiter, A. Gatt, J. Hunter, S. Sripada, Y. Freer, and C. Sykes. 2009. Automatic generation of textual summaries from neonatal intensive care data. *Artificial Intelligence*, 173(7-8):789–816.

E. Reiter and R. Dale. 2000. *Building Natural Language Generation Systems*. Cambridge University Press.

E. Reiter, A. Gatt, F. Portet, and M. van der Meulen. 2008. The Importance of Narrative and Other Lessons from an Evaluation of an NLG System that Summarises Clinical Data. *Fifth International Natural Language Generation Conference (INLG 2008)*, pages 147–155.

S. G. Sripada and F. Gao. 2007. Summarizing dive computer data: A case study in integrating textual and graphical presentations of numerical data. In *MOG 2007 Workshop on Multimodal Output Generation*, pages 149–157.

E. Tufte. 1983. *The Visual Display of Quantitative Information*. Graphics Press.

M. van der Meulen, R. Logie, Y. Freer, C. Sykes, N. McIntosh, and J. Hunter. 2008. When a graph is poorer than 100 words: A comparison of computerised natural language generation, human generated descriptions and graphical displays in neonatal intensive care. *Applied Cognitive Psychology*, 24:77–89.

W. Wahlster, E. André, W. Finkle, HJ. Profitlich, and T. Rist. 1993. Plan-based integration of natural language and graphics generation. *Artificial Intelligence*, 63:387–427.

Generating Valence Shifted Turkish Sentences

Seniz Demir
TUBITAK-BILGEM
Gebze, Kocaeli, TURKEY
seniz.demir@tubitak.gov.tr

Abstract

Valence shifting is the task of rewriting a text towards more/less positively or negatively slanted versions. This paper presents a rule-based approach to producing Turkish sentences with varying sentiment. The approach utilizes semantic relations in the Turkish and English WordNets to determine word polarities and involves the use of lexical substitution and adverbial rules to alter the sentiment of a text in the intended direction. In a user study, the effectiveness of the generation approach is evaluated on real product reviews.

1 Introduction

Language can express a content in a number of different ways with varying emotion. Emotions might equip sentences with connotations and have a powerful effect on the disposition of the hearer in a subtle way. Moreover, emotions induced through words play an important role in written and verbal communication. Sentence valence specifies the degree of emotion present in a sentence and indicates how positive or negative the sentence is. The literature has shown that the sentiment characteristics of a sentence are correlated with the valence of words the sentence contains (Guerini et al., 2008).

Valence shifting is the task of altering a text towards more/less positively or negatively slanted versions while keeping much of its semantic meaning (Gardiner and Dras, 2012). This relatively new problem has many practical uses in language based applications such as persuasive systems which are designed to influence users' behaviors. Slanting of texts can be achieved in a number of ways, the most popular of which is the lexical substitution of semantically related words with varying valences (Whitehead and Cavedon, 2010). To our knowledge, this work is the first to examine the correlation between word polarities and sentence valences in Turkish and to address the problem of valence shifting in Turkish sentences. Our methodology for determining word polarities explores the semantic relations of words within and between the Turkish and English WordNets. To alter the sentiment carried by a sentence in the intended direction, our approach utilizes word polarities and a number of hand constructed rules based on the insights gained from user studies. Two strategies, namely lexical substitution and the use of intensifiers/downtoners, are used to slant Turkish texts. An evaluation study shows the effectiveness of our approach in generating valence shifted Turkish sentences.

2 Word Polarity

Word polarity (valence) stands for the semantic orientation of a word and is one of positive, negative or neutral. Previous research has shown that it is very common to retrieve word valences from existing polarity lexicons. To our best knowledge, there is only one available Turkish word polarity lexicon (**Tr_L**) which is built in a semi-automated manner by traversing a multilingual word relatedness graph with a random walk model (Özsert and Özgür, 2013). The lexicon consists of 1398 positive (e.g., "övgü#n" (praise#n)) and 1414 negative (e.g., "anormal#a" (abnormal#a)) word entries. Although all word entries are given along with their PoS (i.e., one of noun, verb, or adjective), the lexicon neither contains word senses nor the strength of polarities.

There are a number of available English polarity lexicons. The General Inquirer lexicon (**GI_L**) annotates word entries with syntactic, semantic, and pragmatic information including its sense and PoS (Stone et al., 1966). In the MPQA_Polarity lexicon (**MPQA_L**), word entries are annotated with PoS, polarity, and the strength of polarity (i.e., strong or weak) but no sense information is

Proceedings of the 8th International Natural Language Generation Conference, pages 128–132,
Philadelphia, Pennsylvania, 19-21 June 2014.

Polarity Agreement with Tr_L	GI_L	MPQA_L	SWN_L	En_L
Positive polarity match	646	468	423	950
Negative polarity match	761	775	742	1339
No Turkish polarity & Positive English polarity	326	376	750	1177
No Turkish polarity & Negative English polarity	373	577	1019	1390

Table 1: The agreement of word polarities.

given (MPQA, 2014). The SentiWordNet lexicon **(SWN_L)**, along with PoS and sense information, annotates word entries with three sentiment scores from positivity, negativity, and objectivity perspectives (Esuli and Sebastiani, 2006)[1].

Due to the limitations of the Turkish lexicon (e.g., no adverbs exist in the lexicon), we explored ways of expanding the scope of the lexicon by taking advantage of the semantic relations between words. As described in the rest of this section, we also examined how additional polarity information can be retrieved from English polarity lexicons and applied to Turkish.

2.1 Bilingual WordNet Graph

The Turkish WordNet is fully compatible with but not as comprehensive as some other WordNets such as EuroWordNet. We represent the Turkish WordNet as a directed graph where each vertex corresponds to a word tagged with the sense and PoS information (e.g., mekan#1,n[2]). The vertices corresponding to the words that share a relation are connected with a directed edge and the edge is labeled with the kind of this relation (e.g., "synonym" or "antonym"). A monolingual graph consisting of 20343 vertices and 60164 edges is built from the Turkish WordNet. Following the same representation scheme, a monolingual graph is built from the English WordNet 2.0 which contains 177308 vertices and 786932 edges.

The Turkish and English monolingual graphs are integrated into a big bilingual graph with the use of the InterLingual Index (ILI) where words having the same meaning are connected. ILI facilitates the mapping of concepts and similar synsets between compatible WordNets. This integration enabled us to explore the agreement of word polarities between the Turkish polarity lexicon and each of the three English polarity lexicons. The first and the second rows in Table 1 show the number of cases where a Turkish-English word pair with the same ILI share a positive or a negative polarity respectively. The third and the fourth rows represent the cases where a Turkish word does not have a polarity in the Turkish lexicon whereas its English correspondent has a positive or a negative polarity in the English lexicon respectively. For instance, the word "bitmek bilmemek#a" does not have a polarity in Tr_L whereas its English correspondent "endless#a" has a negative polarity in MPQA_L.

We examined whether individual agreements between the Turkish lexicon and each English lexicon can be improved by merging all English lexicons into a single polarity lexicon **(En_L)**. During this merge, words that have different polarities in individual lexicons are omitted and the words from MPQA_L are considered as of the first sense. The final En_L lexicon consists of 9044 positive and 13890 negative words with PoS and sense information. As shown in the fourth column of Table 1, this merge improves the agreement between the Turkish and English polarity lexicons.

2.2 Detecting Word Polarity

A two-step approach is developed for determining the polarities of Turkish words. Once given a sentence, this approach first identifies prior word polarities by utilizing the information contained in polarity lexicons and then applies a set of polarity alteration rules to the sentence for finalizing polarity assignments.

To determine the polarity of a word, the presence of the word and its synonyms is first explored in the Turkish polarity lexicon. If neither the word nor any of its synonyms exists in the Tr_L lexicon, English words that have the same ILI with the Turkish word are explored in the English polarity lexicon En_L[3]. If the word polarity is still not determined, the polarity of Turkish words that share the antonym relation with the word is explored in Tr_L and the reverse of the retrieved word polarity (if any) is taken. If the use of antonym relation in Tr_L does not return a polarity, the antonym relation is explored in the En_L lexicon for the English correspondents of the Turkish word.

[1] Here, we classify a word as positive/negative if its positivity/negativity score is greater than or equal to 0.5.

[2] The noun mekan (location) is of the first sense.

[3] This enables us to benefit from English polarities shown in the third and the fourth rows of Table 1.

We hand constructed a number of polarity alteration rules that are specific to Turkish. These rules, once applied to a sentence, might alter the lexicon-based prior polarity of words. For example, the adjective "mutsuz (unhappy)" with negative polarity according to the Tr_L lexicon should be treated as positive in the sentence "Ahmet mutsuz bir çocuk değil. (Ahmet is not an unhappy child.)" since it is followed by the negative "değil (it is not)". One of our polarity alteration rules reverses the polarity of all words that immediately precede the negative "değil" in a sentence[4].

3 Sentence Valence

Our goal is to alter the sentiment of a Turkish sentence while preserving its content. This requires a means of assessing the sentiment change in the slanted versions of a sentence and beforehand computing their sentence valences. Literature has proposed different methods to calculate sentence valence using word polarities such as summing valence scores of all words in a sentence (Inkpen et al., 2004) or using the valence score of a present word with a strong valence. We first examined whether computing sentence valence by summing word polarities, a commonly used approach in English, is applicable to Turkish.

We conducted a formal experiment with 24 participants, all of which are Turkish native speakers. The participants were presented with 20 sentences and asked to classify each sentence as positive, negative, or neutral based on its content. The sentences, originally published in academic proses or newspapers, were manually selected from the Turkish National Corpus (Aksan et al., 2012). A strong attention was paid to select sentences that contain at least one word within the Tr_L lexicon. The valences of these sentences were computed by summing the word polarities as determined by our polarity detection approach[5]. Unfortunately, this straightforward approach failed to classify sentences as participants did in 13 sentences. The classifications of our approach and the participants in these cases are; positive-neutral in 6 sentences, negative-neutral in 3 sentences, neutral-negative in 2 sentences, and positive-negative in the remaining 2 sentences. For example, our approach classified the sentence "Bir simulasyon modelinin amacı bir problemi çözmek ya da çözümüne katkıda bulunmaktır. (The purpose of a simulation model is to solve a problem or to contribute to its solution.)" with a valence of +1 as positive, whereas the participants classified it as neutral.

One reason for the divergence in classifications might be the fact that our approach considers all words in the Turkish lexicon as having the same strength and of the first sense although senses are not given in the lexicon. Since this study revealed that sentence valences determined in this fashion do not correspond with valences as assigned by humans, we argue that slanting of texts cannot be assessed by considering only sentence valences.

4 Generating Valence Shifted Sentences

To explore how Turkish speakers alter the sentiment characteristics of sentences, we conducted an experiment with 19 participants where they were presented with 20 sentences and asked to generate slanted versions of these texts toward a more positive or more negative direction. The sentences along with their sentiments (i.e., positive or negative) were selected from a database of movie and product reviews. The analysis of this experiment provided a number of insights into Turkish valence shifting, the three main of which are: i) slanted versions of texts are produced via three kinds of sentential changes (lexical substitution, paraphrasing, and adverbial changes that behave as intensifiers/downtoners), ii) adverbs of certainty, probability, and quantity are often used in adverbial changes, and iii) the sentence sentiment, intended shift direction, and sentence constituents determine the kind of sentential change and where in the sentence it occurs. In this work, we limit ourselves to exploring how valence shifted Turkish sentences can be generated by lexical substitution and adverbial changes[6].

Lexical substitution of semantically related words with different polarity strengths is a popular approach in English. Since the Turkish polarity lexicon does not provide polarity strengths and our polarity detection approach assigns the same polarity to all synonym words, substituting a word

[4]Evaluating the reliability of our polarity detection approach and how well the polarity assignments coincide with human judgements is in our future work.

[5]The word polarity is +1 and -1 for positive and negative words respectively. A sentence is considered as positive if the sentence valence score>0 and as negative if the sentence valence score<0. In each sentence, less than half of the content words are annotated with a polarity.

[6]Generating slanted versions of Turkish texts by paraphrasing their content is left for future work.

with its synonym of the same strength to slant a text is not applicable in our case. We rather substitute words with other words that share either the "similar to" or "also see" relation if any of the 6 lexical substitution rules that we constructed is applicable. Below are two representative rules:

- If the intended shift is to increase the sentence valence, then substitute a word having a reverse polarity with the sentence sentiment with a word that has the same polarity with the sentence.
- If the intended shift is to decrease the sentence valence, then substitute a word having the same polarity with the sentence sentiment with a word of the same polarity once the polarity strength of the English correspondent of the substituted word is lower than that of the replaced word according to MPQA_L.

To capture adverbial changes, we constructed 10 rules whose applicability depends on sentence constituents. We classified all certainty, probability, and quantity adverbs as intensifiers or downtoners. These adverbs are either inserted, deleted, or substituted once an adverbial rule is applied to a sentence. In the current setting, the selection of which adverb will be used among all other possibilities is determined by a language model and the adverbial rules that apply to adjectives have a precedence over those that apply to verbs. Two representative rules are shown below:

- If the sentence contains only one adjective which has the same polarity with the sentence sentiment and the intended shift is to increase the sentence valence, then insert an intensifier in front of the adjective.
- If the denominative verb of the sentence is derived from an adjective which has the same polarity with the sentence sentiment and the intended shift is to increase the sentence valence, then insert an intensifier in front of the verb.

Our approach follows a straightforward strategy for shifting sentence valences. Once a sentence and the shift direction are given, the lexical substitution rules are applied in an order until a slanted version of the sentence is produced in the intended direction. If these rules do not succeed in slanting the sentence, then the adverbial rules are applied to the sentence.

To evaluate the effectiveness of our valence shifting approach, we conducted an experiment with 15 Turkish native speakers. The participants were presented with 21 sentence pairs, where one sentence is an original product review and the other sentence is its slanted version as produced by our valence shifting approach. In total, 9 adverbial and 3 lexical substitution rules were used for generating valence shifted sentences. We asked participants to specify which sentence in a pair has a higher valence according to the given sentence sentiment. Our results demonstrated that all participants agreed that our approach achieved the intended shift in 3 sentence pairs and the majority of them agreed on that in 8 of the remaining 18 sentence pairs. This evaluation study also revealed that the adverbial rules have a higher accuracy in shifting the sentence valence as compared to that of lexical substitution rules. Among the tested adverbial rules, the one, which modifies the adjective of the sentence subject if the polarity of the adjective contrasts with the sentence sentiment, did not achieve the intended valence shift. Moreover, the performance of the lexical substitution rules was observed to be higher in cases where the "similar to" relation is utilized than the cases where the "also see" relation is used. Since this initial study left many questions unexplored regarding the applicability and accuracy of all rules that we constructed, a more comprehensive study is necessary to better predict their performances.

5 Conclusion

This paper has presented our initial explorations on Turkish sentence valence and our methodology for generating valence shifted sentences in accordance with these explorations. To our knowledge, our work is the first to address the problem of valence shifting in Turkish by considering word polarities. We have presented our approach for producing slanted versions of sentences by substituting words with the use of WordNet relations and taking advantage of Turkish intensifiers and downtoners. We constructed a set of rules for specifying how and when words can be substituted or intensifiers/downtoners can be used to shift the valence of a sentence in the intended direction. In the future, we will address the task of learning polarity strengths of Turkish words and the learning of paraphrase patterns from a big collection of texts to improve the performance of our approach.

References

Yesim Aksan, Mustafa Aksan, Ahmet Koltuksuz, Taner Sezer, Umit Mersinli, Umut Ufuk, Hakan Yilmazer, Ozlem Kurtoglu, Gulsum Atasoy, Seda Oz, and Ipek Yildiz. 2012. Construction of the turkish national corpus (tnc). In *Proceedings of the Language Resources and Evaluation Conference (LREC)*, pages 3223–3227.

Andrea Esuli and Fabrizio Sebastiani. 2006. Sentiwordnet: A publicly available lexical resource for opinion mining. In *Proceedings of the Language Resources and Evaluation Conference (LREC)*, pages 417–422.

Mary Gardiner and Mak Dras. 2012. Valence shifting: Is it a valid task? In *Proceedings of the Australian Language Technology Association Workshop*, pages 42–51.

Marco Guerini, Carlo Strapparava, and Oliviero Stock. 2008. Valentino: A tool for valence shifting of natural language text. In *Proceedings of the Language Resources and Evaluation Conference (LREC)*, pages 243–246.

Diana Zaiu Inkpen, Olga Feiguina, and Graeme Hirst. 2004. Generating more-positive or more-negative text. In *Proceedings of the AAAI Spring Symposium on Exploring Attitude and Affect in Text: Theories and Applications*.

MPQA. 2014. Mpqa opinion corpus, http://mpqa.cs.pitt.edu/.

Cüneyd Murad Özsert and Arzucan Özgür. 2013. Word polarity detection using a multilingual approach. In *Proceedings of the CicLing Conference*, pages 75–82.

Philip Stone, Dexter Dunphy, Marshall Smith, and Daniel Ogilvie. 1966. *General Inquirer: A Computer Approach to Content Analysis*. MIT Press.

Simon Whitehead and Lawrence Cavedon. 2010. Generating shifting sentiment for a conversational agent. In *Proceedings of the NAACL HLT 2010 Workshop on Computational Approaches to Analysis and Generation of Emotion in Text (CAAGET)*, pages 89–97.

Latent User Models for Online River Information Tailoring

Xiwu Han[1], Somayajulu Sripada[1], Kit (CJA) Macleod[2], and Antonio A. R. Ioris[3]
Department of Computing Sciences, University of Aberdeen, UK[1]
James Hutton Institute, Aberdeen; University of Exeter, Exeter, UK[2]
School of GeoSciences, University of Edinburgh, UK[3]
{xiwuhan,yaji.sripada}@abdn.ac.uk
kit.macleod@hutton.ac.uk
a.ioris@ed.ac.uk

Abstract

This paper explores Natural Language Generation techniques for online river information tailoring. To solve the problem of unknown users, we propose 'latent models', which relate typical visitors to river web pages, river data types, and river related activities. A hierarchy is used to integrate domain knowledge and latent user knowledge, and serves as the search space for content selection, which triggers user-oriented selection rules when they visit a page. Initial feedback received from user groups indicates that the latent models deserve further research efforts.

1 Introduction

Within recent decades, access to online river information has increased exponentially thanks to great progresses in data collection and storage technologies employed by hydrological organizations worldwide (Dixon, 2010). Local residents nearby rivers and those engaged in river related activities are now much better informed and more engaged with data providers than decades ago. However, organizations such as SEPA (Scottish Environment Protection Agency), CEH (Centre for Ecology and Hydrology), EA (Environment Agency) in UK, and quite a few Canadian and Australian ones are working to improve the presentation of river information further. Many of these data providers, who are mostly government agencies, provide descriptive texts along with archived data of flow, level, flood and temperature along with their graphs and/or tables. A typical example of linguistic description from the EA website is shown below:

> The river level at Morwick is 0.65 metres. This measurement was recorded at 08:45 on 23/01/2013. The typical river level range for this location is between 0.27 metres and 2.60 metres. The highest river level recorded at this location is 6.32 metres and the river level reached 6.32 metres on 07/09/2008.[1]

The above descriptive text could vary to some extent according to different river users. For instance, it may provide information perceived as good news by farmers whilst other users e.g. canoeists or paddlers may interpret the information as bad news for their activity. Such tailored information provision promotes communication efficiency between stakeholders and the relevant government offices (Macleod et al., 2012). We explored data-to-text techniques (Reiter, 2007) in promoting online river information provision. Our engagement activities with river stakeholders showed that there could be great difficulties in specifying user groups for online river information tailoring. First, the relations between domain knowledge and user knowledge are difficult to be acquired due to domain sensitive challenges. Second, for online communication, the issue that users themselves sometimes are not sure about their tasks further hinders user modeling. This paper proposes an alternative approach of latent user models, instead of directly asking users to indicate what they are interested in.

2 User Modeling Problem

It has long been argued in NLG research that contents of generated texts should be oriented to users' tasks and existing knowledge. User models are usually employed for the tailoring task. However, user models may not be easily acquired. Reiter et al (2003a) claimed that no NLG system actually used detailed user models with non-trivial numbers of users. Most commercial

[1] http://www.environment-agency.gov.uk/homeandleisure/floods/riverlevels/120694.aspx?stationId=8143

Proceedings of the 8th International Natural Language Generation Conference, pages 133–137,
Philadelphia, Pennsylvania, 19-21 June 2014.

NLG systems would rather do with very limited user models, and examples are STOP (Reiter et al., 2003b), SUMTIME-MOUSAM (Sripada et al., 2002), and GIRL (Williams, 2002).

Recent research on user modeling falls into roughly three categories, i.e. explicit, implicit and hybrid approaches[2]. All approaches start with knowledge acquisition. Explicit models then define a finite number of user groups, and finally generate tailored texts for users to choose from, or choose to generate for a unique group at each time, e.g. (Molina, 2011 and 2012). Implicit models, e.g. (Mairesse and Walker, 2011), then construct a framework of human computer interaction to learn about the values of a finite set of features, and finally generate tailored texts according to the intersection between domain knowledge and feature values. Hybrid models, e.g. (Bouayad-Agha et al, 2012) and (Dannels et al, 2012), specify both a finite set of user groups and a human computer interaction framework, and finally classify online users into defined groups for tailored generation.

3 Latent User Models

Online river information tailoring involves a website, such as SEPA's, which provides map based (or text based) searchable river information [3]. The NLG task is to generate user-oriented texts while users are navigating the website. Both explicit and implicit user models can be employed for online river information tailoring. A finite set of user groups could be defined according to river-related activities, such as flooding, fishing, canoeing, etc. along with a set of features such as level trends, temperature ranges, etc. Then an interactive navigation mechanism could ask a user to either choose a group or tailor his/her own parameters, and relevant texts can be generated thereafter.

Unfortunately, our engagement activities with stakeholders showed that it is almost impossible to define user models using mappings from river-related activities to river data features. Furthermore, frequent users are reluctant to spend time on specifying their preferences before viewing the river information. For such an NLG task, the uncertainty comes not only from a large variety of river users and stakeholders, but also from the issue that users themselves sometimes are not sure of what data features are associated with making decisions about their activities.

Our efforts on dealing with NLG domain knowledge and user models brought about the idea of extending domain knowledge to statistically cover user knowledge, without explicitly defining user groups or implicitly modeling potential users. We argue that non-trivial number of uncertain users can be dynamically and statistically modeled by integrating a module for web mining and Google analytics into the NLG pipeline system. We regard these statistically established models as latent since they are hidden beneath the domain knowledge, and the latent variable of typical users is linked to river data types and river related activities.

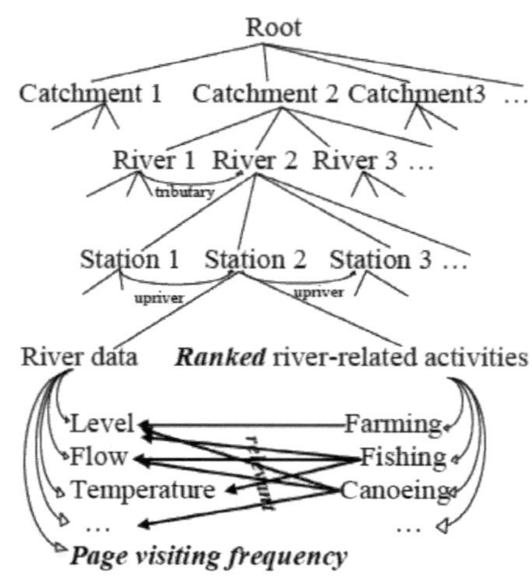

Figure 1. Domain Knowledge with Latent Models

The domain knowledge and latent user models are constructed as a whole in a hierarchical structure, as in Figure 1. We technically maintain this hierarchy as an ontology based on existing approaches e.g. (Bontcheva, 2005; Bouayad-Agha et al, 2012). The general part of the main frame was extracted from hydrology or environment websites, such as SEPA, CEH and EA, with the view that these websites were deliberately established hierarchically by manual work of domain experts in the fields of hydrology, ecology and/or geology. This part serves as the center of our domain knowledge, which starts with a root node and branches to river catchments, rivers, river stations and river data, while river data consists of water level, water flow, water temperature, etc. There are also some non-hierarchical relations embedded, namely the tributary relation between rivers, the upriver relation between river stations, and the relationship between certain river data and river related activities. In addition

[2] Note the difference between NLG and HCI user models. The former tailor the output of NLG systems, while the later tailor the systems themselves.

[3] http://sepa.org.uk/water/river_levels/river_level_data.aspx

to the time series on the status of the rivers, other information is integrated offline. Then, the domain knowledge was extended to cover potential users' knowledge and online visiting behaviors. The extended information, or the latent user models, as denoted in italic fonts in Figure 1, includes three parts, i.e. the webpage visiting frequency, the relevance degrees between certain river data and river related activities, and the ranking of popularities of river-related activities for each river station.

Our extension process includes three stages, i.e. web mining, Google analytics, and engagement activities. At first, basic and rough information about river stations was statistically gathered by using free or trial version web mining tools, such as spiders and crawlers, and corpus analysis tools. For all combinations of elements respectively from each pair of columns in Table 1, we simply count the tokens of co-occurrence within an empirical window of 10 words. For the co-occurring tokens between a given river station and related activities, the top five tokens were selected by filtering according to one threshold on co-occurrence frequencies and another threshold on frequency differences between adjacent ranked types. For the co-occurring tokens between a given activity and river data type, relevant tokens were chosen by only one threshold on the co-occurrence frequencies. Finally, the co-occurring types of river stations and river data with high frequencies were used to fine-tune the previously acquired results, supposing that some river stations seldom or never provide some types of river data.

River Stations	Related Activities	River Data Type
Aberlour	Farming	Level
Aberuchill	Fishing	Flow
Aberuthven	Canoeing	Temperature
Abington	Swimming	Width
Alford	Kayaking	Rainfall
Allnabad	Rowing	Wind
Almondell	Boating	Pollution
Alness	Research	Birds
Ancrum	Education	Animals
Anie	Hiking	Fishes
Apigill	Cycling	...
Arbroath	...	...
...	...	

Table 1. Basic Domain Knowledge for Extension

We further had the statistically acquired results complemented and modified by Google analytics data for river websites and engagement activities with domain experts and users. Google analytics provided us with webpage visiting frequencies for each hydrological station, and contributed to the ranking of river-related activity for a given station. Knowledge gathered from engagement activities, such as semi-structured interviews and focus groups, was mainly used to confirm the statistically gathered information during the first two stages (as well as refine our overall understanding of data demands, water-related activities and perception of existing communication tools). For example, flood warning information was moved up in the ranks since over 5 million people in England and Wales live and work in properties that are at risk of flooding from rivers or the sea[4] (Marsh and Hannaford, 2007). Our present research is limited to rivers in Scotland, involving 107 river catchments, 233 rivers, and 339 river stations. The webpage visiting frequencies for these stations were gathered from Google analytics data for the website of SEPA[5]. The page visiting frequency for each river station is represented by a time series with yearly periodicity, and each period includes 12 numeric elements calculated by dividing the number of monthly visiting times of the station by the total number of monthly visiting times of all river stations.

4 NLG for Online Tailoring

Our NLG pipeline system takes numeric data of a given river station as input, and outputs a tailored description for that river station. The system analyzes data of water level, flow, and temperature as similar to time series analysis tasks presented in (Turner et al., 2006). Then, the analyzed patterns are interpreted into symbolic conceptual representations, including vague expressions, which might facilitate users' understanding (van Deemter, 2010). SEPA defines normal ranges for river levels and we use these definitions in our computations to generate vague expressions. For content selection, we define five sets: $\mathbf{S} = \{s_1, s_2, \ldots\}$ the set of stations; $\mathbf{A} = \{\boldsymbol{a_1}, \boldsymbol{a_2}, \ldots\}$ the set of activities for a given station; $\mathbf{D} = \{\boldsymbol{d_1}, \boldsymbol{d_2}, \ldots\} = \{\{\boldsymbol{d_{11}}, \boldsymbol{d_{12}}, \ldots\}, \{\boldsymbol{d_{21}}, \boldsymbol{d_{22}}, \ldots\}, \ldots\}$ the set of river data sets for a given station; $\mathbf{AD} = \{\boldsymbol{a_1 d_1}, \boldsymbol{a_1 d_2}, \ldots, \boldsymbol{a_2 d_1}, \ldots\}$ where $\boldsymbol{a_i d_j}$ refers to information from the interpretation of an activity $\boldsymbol{a_i}$ under the condition of data $\boldsymbol{d_j}$; and **SAD** an overview on one station. For a river station, using the domain knowledge hierarchy, which embeds la-

[4] http://www.environment-agency.gov.uk/homeandleisure/floods/default.aspx.

[5] http://www.sepa.org.uk.

tent user models implicitly (Figure 1), we select **A** ∪ **D** ∪ **AD** ∪ **SAD** as the initial contents.

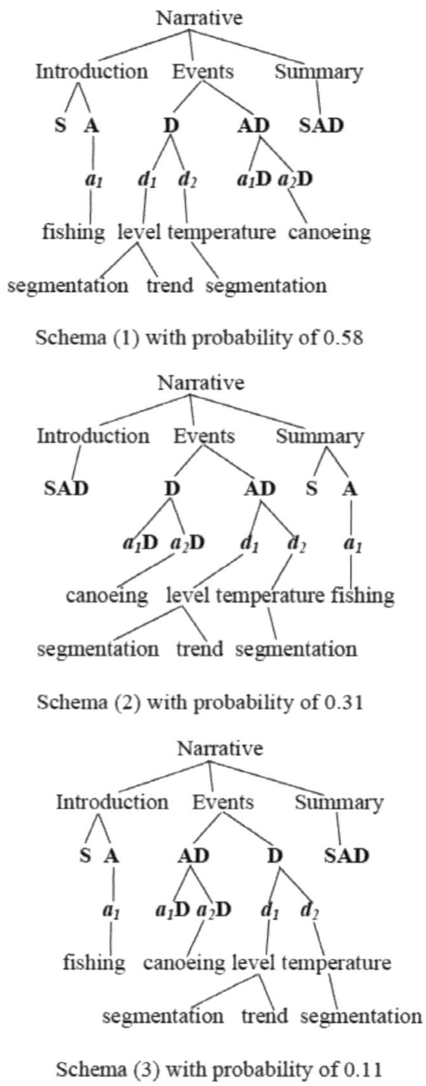

Figure 2. Statistical Schemas

A schema-based approach was employed for document planning. Each schema at the high level is made up of three components: Introduction, Events and Summary. Each of these components has its own substructure as shown in examples in Figure 4. With the estimated probabilistic distribution we generate schemas for a station based on its popular activities. We then tailor the text by randomly selecting from users' favorite vocabulary, which was acquired from online corpus for different river-related activities. Other words for structural purposes are dependent on certain schemas. Realization was performed using the simpleNLG library (Gatt and Reiter, 2009), and some generated examples are listed in Table 2.

Schema (1)	The ***Tyne at Nungate*** boasts its excellent ***salmon catches***. Now with ***medium steady*** water level and comparatively ***low water temperature***, many people want to ***fish*** some ***salmons*** in pools between the rapids or experience whitewater ***rafting*** within them, which makes the periphery of ***Nungate a hot spot***.
Schema (2)	The periphery of ***Tyne at Nungate*** poses a hot spot now, where many people are ***fishing*** or ***canoeing*** while appreciating the ***medium steady*** water level and comparatively ***low water temperature***. No wonder ***Nungate*** can boast one of the best ***salmon catching*** places.
Schema (3)	The ***Tyne at Nungate*** boasts its excellent ***salmon*** catches. Many people may now ***fish*** or ***canoe*** there thanks to the ***medium steady*** water level and comparatively ***low water temperature***, making the periphery of ***Nungate a hot spot***.

Table 2. Some Tailored NLG Examples (Italic fonts denote the tailored lexical realization)

5 Initial Feedback and Conclusion

This research is still underway and a thorough evaluation is still pending. We have received valuable feedback from small user groups. Supportive examples are: a. An overview about popular river stations can help users' further exploration of information to a significant extent; b. A general comprehension for a given river station can be more easily built up by simply reading the generated descriptions, than by solely reading the data and its related graphics; c. Along with the graphics, the generated descriptions can improve the communication efficiency by a large degree. Examples recommending further improvement/focus include: a. Schemas filled in with acquired vocabulary sometimes endow the generated document a syntactically and/or semantically unexpected flavor; b. Established users demand more linguistic varieties than new users.

Present feedback implicates that latent user models deserve further research. Our future efforts will focus on a. extending the domain knowledge to cover all river stations, b. developing generic methodology for acquiring latent user models for other online NLG tasks (e.g. generating descriptions of Census data), and c. integrating an automatic update of latent models.

Acknowledgement

This research is supported by an award from the RCUK DE programme: EP/G066051/1. The authors are also grateful to Dr. Rene van der Wal, Dr. Koen Arts, and the three anonymous reviewers for improving the quality of this paper.

References

K. Bontcheva. 2005. Generating Tailored Textual Summaries from Ontologies. *The Semantic Web: Research and Applications*, Lecture Notes in Computer Science, Vol. 3532, pages 531-545. Springer-Verlag.

N. Bouayad-Agha, G. Casamayor, Simon Mille, et al. 2012. From Ontology to NL: Generation of Multilingual User-Oriented Environmental Reports. *Natural Language Processing and Information Systems*, Lecture Notes in Computer Science Vol. 7337, pages 216-221. Springer-Verlag.

Dana Dannells, Mariana Damova, Ramona Enache and Milen Chechev. 2012. Multilingual Online Generation from Semantic Web Ontologies. *WWW 2012 – European Projects Track*, pages 239-242.

H. Dixon. 2010. Managing national hydrometric data: from data to information. *Global Change: Facing Risks and Threats to Water Resources*. Wallingford, UK, IAHS Press, pages 451-458.

A. Gatt and Ehud Reiter. 2009. Simplenlg: A Realization Engine for Practical Applications. *Proceedings ENLG-2009*, pages 90-93.

K. Macleod, S. Sripada, A. Ioris, K. Arts and R. Van der Wal. 2012. Communicating River Level Data and Information to Stakeholders with Different Interests: the Participative Development of an Interactive Online Service. *International Environmental Modeling and Software Society (iEMSs): International Congress on Environmental Modeling and Software Managing Resources of a Limited Planet*, Sixth Biennial Meeting, Leipzig, Germany. R. Seppelt, A.A. Voinov, S. Lange, D. Bankamp (Eds.) pages 33-40.

Francois Mairesse and Marilyn A. Walker. 2011. Controlling User Perceptions of Linguistic Style: Trainable Generation of Personality Traits. *Computational Linguistics*, Volume 37 Issue 3, September 2011, pages 455-488.

T. J. Marsh and J. Hannaford. 2007. *The summer 2007 floods in England and Wales – a hydrological appraisal*. Centre for Ecology & Hydrology, UK.

M. Molina. 2012. Simulating Data Journalism to Communicate Hydrological Information from Sensor Networks. *Proceedings of IBERAMIA*, pages 722-731.

M. Molina, A. Stent, and E. Parodi. 2011. Generating Automated News to Explain the Meaning of Sensor Data. In: *Gama, J., Bradley, E., Hollmén, J. (eds.) IDA 2011. LNCS*, vol. 7014, pages 282-293. Springer, Heidelberg.

Ehud Reiter, Somayajulu Sripada, and Sandra Williams. 2003a. Acquiring and Using Limited User Models in NLG. In *Proceedings of the 9th European Workshop on Natural Language Generation*, pages 13-14, Budapest, Hungary.

Ehud Reiter, Roma Robertson, and Liesl Osman. 2003b. Lessons from a failure: Generating tailored smoking cessation letters. *Artificial Intelligence*, 144(1-2), pages 41-58.

Ehud Reiter. 2007. An Architecture for Data-to-Text Systems. *Proceedings of ENLG-2007*, pages 97-104.

S. Sripada, Ehud Reiter, Jim Hunter, and Jin Yu. 2002. Segmenting time series for weather forecasting. *Applications and Innovations in Intelligent Systems X*, pages 105-118. Springer-Verlag.

R. Turner, S. Sripada, E. Reiter and I. Davy. 2006. Generating Spatio-Temporal Descriptions in Pollen Forecasts. Proceedings of EACL06 poster session, pages 163-166.

K. van Deemter. 2010. Vagueness Facilitates Search. *Proceedings of the 2009 Amsterdam Colloquium*, Springer Lecture Notes in Computer Science (LNCS). FoLLI LNAI 6042.

Sandra Williams. 2002. Natural language generation of discourse connectives for different reading levels. In *Proceedings of the 5th Annual CLUK Research Colloquium*, Leeds, UK.

Multi-adaptive Natural Language Generation using Principal Component Regression

Dimitra Gkatzia, Helen Hastie, and Oliver Lemon
School of Mathematical and Computer Sciences, Heriot-Watt University, Edinburgh
{dg106, h.hastie, o.lemon}@hw.ac.uk

Abstract

We present FeedbackGen, a system that uses a multi-adaptive approach to Natural Language Generation. With the term 'multi-adaptive', we refer to a system that is able to adapt its content to different user groups simultaneously, in our case adapting to both lecturers and students. We present a novel approach to student feedback generation, which simultaneously takes into account the preferences of lecturers and students when determining the content to be conveyed in a feedback summary. In this framework, we utilise knowledge derived from ratings on feedback summaries by extracting the most relevant features using Principal Component Regression (PCR) analysis. We then model a reward function that is used for training a Reinforcement Learning agent. Our results with students suggest that, from the students' perspective, such an approach can generate more preferable summaries than a purely lecturer-adapted approach.

1 Introduction

Summarisation of time-series data refers to the task of automatically generating reports from attributes whose values change over time. Content selection is the task of choosing what to say, i.e. what information is to be included in a report (Reiter and Dale, 2000). We consider the task of automatically generating feedback summaries for students describing their performance during the lab of a computer science module over the semester.

Various factors can influence students' learning such as difficulty of the material (Person et al., 1995), workload (Craig et al., 2004), attendance in lectures (Ames, 1992), etc. These factors change over time and can be interdependent. In addition, different stakeholders often have conflicting goals, needs and preferences, for example managers with employees, or doctors with patients and relatives, or novice and expert users. In our data, for instance, lecturers tend to comment on the hours that the student studied, whereas the students disprefer this content. In our previous work, we showed that lecturers and students have different perceptions regarding what constitutes good feedback (Gkatzia et al., 2013). Here, we present a novel approach to generation by adapting its content to two user groups simultaneously. Producing the same summary for two groups is important as it allows for shared context and meaningful further discussion and reduces development time.

2 Related Work

Previous work on NLG systems that address more than one user group employs different versions of a system for each different user group (Gatt et al., 2009; Hunter et al., 2011; Mahamood and Reiter, 2011), makes use of User Models (Janarthanam and Lemon, 2010; Thompson et al., 2004; Zukerman and Litman, 2001) or personalises the output to individual users using rules (Reiter et al., 1999). Our proposed system adapts the output to the preferences of more than one user type[1], lecturers and students, but instead of developing many different systems or using User Models that describe different users, it attempts to model the middle ground between the preferences.

In order to identify the users' preferences, we apply Principal Components Regression (PCR (Jolliffe, 1982)) analysis to two datasets that contain lecturers' and students' ratings and identify the most important variables from the principal components, which are then included in a reward function. This hand-crafted reward function is used for training an RL agent for summarisation

[1] Our approach is different to multi-objective optimisation.

Proceedings of the 8th International Natural Language Generation Conference, pages 138–142,
Philadelphia, Pennsylvania, 19-21 June 2014.

Raw Data

factors	week 2	week 3	...	week 10
marks	5	4	...	5
hours_studied	1	2	...	3
...	...	...	...	...

Trends from Data

factors	trend
(1) marks	trend_other
(2) hours_studied	trend_increasing
(3) understandability	trend_decreasing
(4) difficulty	trend_decreasing
(5) deadlines	trend_increasing
(6) health_issues	trend_other
(7) personal_issues	trend_decreasing
(8) lectures_attended	trend_other
(9) revision	trend_decreasing

Summary

> Your overall performance **was excellent** during the semester. Keep up the good work and maybe try some more challenging exercises. Your attendance was **varying** over the semester. Have a think about how to use time in lectures to improve your understanding of the material. You spent **2 hours studying the lecture material on average**. You should dedicate more time to study. You seem to find the material **easier to understand compared to the beginning of the semester**. Keep up the good work! You revised **part of** the learning material. Have a think whether revising has improved your performance.

Table 1: The table on the top left shows an example of the time-series data. The table on the bottom left shows an example of described trends. The box on the right presents a target summary.

of time-series data. Our previous work showed that when comparing RL and supervised learning in the context of student feedback generation, students preferred the output generated by the RL system (Gkatzia et al., 2014a). Therefore, here, we used RL rather than a supervised learning method. The work described here builds on work reported in (Gkatzia et al., 2014b), which uses as a reward function the average of the Lecturer-adapted and Student-adapted reward functions. However, that method seems to cancel out the preferences of the two groups whereas PCR is able to identify relevant content for both groups.

In the next section, we describe the data used, and the methodology for the multi-adaptive NLG, as well as two alternative systems. In Section 4, we describe the comparison of these three systems in a subjective evaluation and present the results in Section 5. A discussion follows in Section 6 and finally, future work is discussed in Section 7.

3 Methodology

Reinforcement Learning is a machine learning technique that defines how an agent learns to take optimal sequences of actions so as to maximize a cumulative reward (Sutton and Barto, 1998). In our framework, the task of summarisation of time-series data is modelled as a Markov Decision Process, where the decisions on content selection correspond to a sequence of actions (see Section 3.2). Temporal Difference (TD) learning (Sutton and Barto, 1990) is used for training three agents in a simulated environment to learn to make optimal content selection decisions:

1. by adapting to both groups simultaneously,
2. by adapting to lecturers,
3. by adapting to students.

3.1 The Data

For this study, the dataset described in (Gkatzia et al., 2013) was used. Table 1 presents an example of this dataset that describes a student's learning factors and an aligned feedback summary provided by a lecturer. The dataset is composed of 37 similar instances. Each instance consists of time-series information about the student's learning routine and the selected templates that lecturers used to provide feedback to this particular student. A template is a quadruple consisting of an `id`, a `factor` (bottom left of Table 1), a `reference type` (trend, week, average, other) and `surface text`. For instance, a template can be (1, marks, trend, "Your marks were <trend>over the semester"). The lexical choice for <trend>(i.e. increasing or decreasing) depends on the values of time-series data. There is a direct mapping between the values of factor and reference type and the surface text. The time-series factors are listed in Table 1.

3.2 Actions and states

The state consists of the time-series data and the number of factors which have so far been selected to be talked about (the change of the value of this variable consequently introduces a state change). In order to explore the state space the agent selects a time-series factor (e.g. marks, deadlines etc.) and then decides whether to talk about it or not, until all factors have been considered.

3.3 Reward function

The reward function is the following cumulative multivariate function:

$$Reward = a + \sum_{i=1}^{n} b_i * x_i + c * length$$

where $X = \{x_1, x_2, ..., x_n\}$ describes the chosen combinations of the factor trends observed in the time-series data and a particular template (i.e. the way of mentioning a factor). a, b and c are the correlation coefficients and $length$ describes the number of factors selected to be conveyed in the feedback summary. The value of x_i is given by the function:

$$x_i = \begin{cases} 1, & \text{the combination of a factor trend} \\ & \text{and a template type is included} \\ 0, & \text{if not.} \end{cases}$$

The coefficients represent the level of preference for a factor to be selected and the way it is conveyed in the summary. In the training phase, the agent selects a factor and then decides whether to talk about it or not. If the agent decides to refer to a factor, the selection of the template is then performed in a deterministic way, i.e. it selects the template that results in higher reward.

Each rated summary is transformed into a vector of 91 binary features. Each feature describes both (1) the trend of a factor (e.g. marks increasing, see also Table 1) and (2) the way that this factor could be conveyed in the summary (e.g. one possible way is referring to average, another possible way is referring to increasing/decreasing trend). If both conditions are met, the value of the feature is 1, otherwise 0. The 91 binary features describe all the different possible combinations. For both the Lecturer-adapted and Student-adapted systems, the reward function is derived from a linear regression analysis of the provided dataset, similarly to Walker et al. (1997) and Rieser et al. (2010).

3.3.1 Multi-adaptive Reward Function

In order to derive a reward function that finds a balance between the two above mentioned systems, we use PCR to reduce the dimensionality of the data and thus reduce the introduced noise. Through PCR we are able to reduce the number of features and identify components of factors that are deemed important to both parties to be used in the reward function.

PCR is a method that combines Principal Component Analysis (PCA) (Jolliffe, 1986) with linear regression. PCA is a technique for reducing the dataset dimensionality while keeping as much of the variance as possible. In PCR, PCA is initially performed to identify the principal components, in our case, the factors that contribute the most to the variance. Then, regression is applied to these principal components to obtain a vector of estimated coefficients. Finally, this vector is transformed back into the general linear regression equation. After performing this analysis on both datasets (students and lecturers), we choose the most important (i.e. the ones that contribute the most to the variance) *common*components or features resulting in 18 features which were used in the reward function. We then design a hand-crafted reward function taking into account this PCR analysis. The five most important features are shown in Table 2.

factor trend	way it is mentioned
(1) marks stable	average
(2) hours_studied decreasing	trend
(3) health_issues decreasing	weeks
(4) lectures_attended stable	average
(5) personal_issues increasing	trend

Table 2: The top 5 features out of the 18 selected through PCR analysis.

4 Evaluation

FeedbackGen is evaluated with real users against two alternative systems: one that adapts to lecturers' preferences and one that adapts to students' preferences. The output of the three systems is ranked by 30 computer science students from a variety of years of study. Time-series data of three students are presented on graphs to each participant, along with three feedback summaries (each one generated by a different system), in random order, and they are asked to rank them in terms of preference.

Student-adapted {Ranking: 1st*}	FeedbackGen {Ranking: 2nd*}	Lecturer-adapted {Ranking: 3rd*}
You **did well** at weeks 2, 3, 6, 8, 9 and 10, but not at weeks 4, 5 and 7. Have a think about how you were working well and try to apply it to the other labs. Your **attendance** was varying over the semester. Have a think about how to use time in lectures to improve your understanding of the material. You found the **lab exercises not very challenging**. You could try out some more advanced material and exercises. You dedicated **more time studying the lecture material** in the beginning of the semester compared to the end of the semester. Have a think about what is preventing you from studying. **Revising material** during the semester will improve your performance in the lab.	Your **overall performance** was very good during the semester. Keep up the good work and maybe try some more challenging exercises. You found **the lab exercises not very challenging**. You could try out some more advanced material and exercises. You dedicated more **time studying the lecture material** in the beginning of the semester compared to the end of the semester. Have a think about what is preventing you from studying. You have had **other deadlines** during weeks 6 and 8. You may want to plan your studying and work ahead.	Your **overall performance** was very good during the semester. Keep up the good work and maybe try some more challenging exercises. You found the lab exercises not very challenging. You could try out some more advanced material and exercises. You **dedicated more time studying** the lecture material in the beginning of the semester compared to the end of the semester. Have a think about what is preventing you from studying. You have had other deadlines during weeks 6 and 8. You may want to plan your studying and work ahead. You did not face any **health problems** during the semester. You did not face any **personal issues** during the semester.

Table 3: The table presents example outputs from the three different systems in order of highest ranked (bold signifies the chosen template content, * denotes significance with $p < 0.05$ after comparing each system with each other using Mann Whitney U test).

5 Results

Table 3 shows three summaries that have been generated by the different systems. As we can see from Table 3, students significantly prefer the output of the system that is trained for their preferences. In contrast, students significantly disprefer the system that is trained for lecturers' preferences. Finally, they rank as second the system that captures the preferences of both lecturers and students, which shows that it might be feasible to find middle ground between the preferences of two user groups. Significance testing is done using a Mann Whitney U test ($p < 0.05$), performing a pair-wise comparison.

6 Discussion

The weights derived from the linear regression analysis vary from the Lecturer-adapted function to the Student-adapted function. For instance, the lecturers' most preferred content is `hours_studied`. This, however, does not factor heavily into the student's reward function, apart from the case where `hours_studied` are decreasing or remain stable (see also Table 2).

Students like reading about `personal_issues` when the number of issues they faced was increasing over the semester. On the other hand, lecturers find it useful to give advice to all students who faced personal issues during the semester, hence`personal_issues` are included in the top 18 features (Table 2). Moreover, students seem to mostly prefer a feedback summary that mentions the understandability of the material when it increases, which is positive feedback.

As reflected in Table 2, the analysis of PCR showed that both groups found it useful to refer to the average of marks when they remain stable. In addition, both groups found understandability when it increases useful, for a variety of reasons, for example lecturers might find it useful to encourage students whereas students might prefer to receive positive feedback. Both groups also agree on `hours_studied` as described earlier. On the other hand, both groups find mentioning the students' difficulty when it decreases as positive.

7 Future Work

In the future, we plan to evaluate our methodology with lecturers and a larger sample of students across different disciplines. Moreover, we aim to port our methodology to a different domain, and try to find the middle ground between the preferences of novices and expert users when summarising medical data while providing first aid. Finally, we want to compare the methodology presented here to a multi-objective optimisation approach (Fonseca and Flemming, 1993), where the preferences of each user group will be modelled as two different optimisation functions.

Acknowledgements

The research leading to this work has received funding from the EC's FP7 programme: (FP7/2011-14) under grant agreement no. 248765 (Help4Mood).

References

Carole Ames. 1992. Classrooms: Goals, structures, and student motivation. *Journal of Educational Psychology*, 84(3):p261–71.

Scotty D. Craig, Arthur C. Graesser, Jeremiah Sullins, and Barry Gholson. 2004. Affect and learning: an exploratory look into the role of affect in learning with autotutor.

Carlos Fonseca and Peter Flemming. 1993. Genetic algorithms for multiobjective optimization: Formulation, discussion and generalization. In *5th International Conference on Genetic Algorithms*.

Albert Gatt, Francois Portet, Ehud Reiter, James Hunter, Saad Mahamood, Wendy Moncur, and Somayajulu Sripada. 2009. From data to text in the neonatal intensive care unit: Using NLG technology for decision support and information management. *AI Communications*, 22: 153-186.

Dimitra Gkatzia, Helen Hastie, Srinivasan Janarthanam, and Oliver Lemon. 2013. Generating student feedback from time-series data using Reinforcement Learning. In *14th European Workshop in Natural Language Generation (ENLG)*.

Dimitra Gkatzia, Helen Hastie, and Oliver Lemon. 2014a. Comparing multi-label classification with reinforcement learning for summarisation of time-series data. In *52nd Annual Meeting of the Association for Computational Linguistics (ACL)*.

Dimitra Gkatzia, Helen Hastie, and Oliver Lemon. 2014b. Finding Middle Ground? Multi-objective Natural Language Generation from Time-series data. In *14th Conference of the European Chapter of the Association for Computational Linguistics (EACL)*.

Jim Hunter, Yvonne Freer, Albert Gatt, Yaji Sripada, Cindy Sykes, and D Westwater. 2011. Bt-nurse: Computer generation of natural language shift summaries from complex heterogeneous medical data. *American Medical Informatics Association*, 18:621-624.

Srinivasan Janarthanam and Oliver Lemon. 2010. Adaptive referring expression generation in spoken dialogue systems: Evaluation with real users. In *11th Annual Meeting of the Special Interest Group on Discourse and Dialogue (SIGDIAL)*.

Ian T. Jolliffe. 1982. A note on the use of principal components in regression. *Journal of the Royal Statistical Society*, Series C: 31(3):300–303.

Ian Jolliffe. 1986. *Principal Component Analysis*. Springer-Verlag.

Saad Mahamood and Ehud Reiter. 2011. Generating Affective Natural Language for Parents of Neonatal Infants. In *13th European Workshop in Natural Language Generation (ENLG)*.

Natalie K. Person, Roger J. Kreuz, Rolf A. Zwaan, and Arthur C. Graesser. 1995. Pragmatics and pedagogy: Conversational rules and politeness strategies may inhibit effective tutoring. Journal of Cognition and Instruction, 13(2):161-188.

Ehud Reiter and Robert Dale. 2000. Building natural language generation systems. Cambridge University Press.

Ehud Reiter, Roma Robertson, and Liesl Osman. 1999. Types of knowledge required to personalise smoking cessation letters. Artificial Intelligence in Medicine: Proceedings of the Joint European Conference on Artificial Intelligence in Medicine and Medical Decision Making.

Verena Rieser, Oliver Lemon, and Xingkun Liu. 2010. Optimising information presentation for spoken dialogue systems. In *48th Annual Meeting of the Association for Computational Linguistics (ACL)*.

Richard Sutton and Andrew Barto. 1990. Time derivative models of pavlovian reinforcement. *Learning and Computational Neuroscience: Foundations of Adaptive Networks*, pages 497–537.

Richart Sutton and Andrew Barto. 1998. Reinforcement learning. MIT Press.

Cynthia A. Thompson, Mehmet H. Goker, and Pat Langley. 2004. A personalised system for conversational recommendations. *Journal of Artificial Intelligence Research*, 21(1).

Marilyn Walker, Diane J Litman, Candace Kamm, and Alicia Abella. 1997. PARADISE: A framework for evaluating spoken dialogue agents. In *8th conference on European chapter of the Association for Computational Linguistics (EACL)*.

Ingrid Zukerman and Diane Litman. 2001. Natural language processing and user modeling: Synergies and limitations. *In User Modeling and User-Adapted Interaction*, 11(1-2).

TBI-Doc: Generating Patient & Clinician Reports from Brain Imaging Data

Pamela Jordan[1], Nancy L. Green[2], Christopher Thomas[3], Susan Holm[1]
Learning Research & Development Center, University of Pittsburgh, Pittsburgh, PA[1]
Department of Computer Science, University of North Carolina Greensboro, Greensboro, NC[2]
Department of Computer Science, University of Pittsburgh, Pittsburgh, PA[3]
pjordan@pitt.edu, nlgreen@uncg.edu, clt29@pitt.edu,
susan.holm@gmail.com

Abstract

The TBI-Doc prototype demonstrates the feasibility of automatically producing draft case reports for a new brain imaging technology, High Definition Fiber Tracking (HDFT). Here we describe the ontology for the HDFT domain, the system architecture and our goals for future research and development.

1 Introduction

The goal of TBI-Doc is to automatically produce a draft of a traumatic brain injury (TBI) case report similar to existing expert-authored reports that interpret the results of a High Definition Fiber tracking (HDFT) procedure (Shin et al., 2012). HDFT is a new, revolutionary technology for rendering detailed images of the brain and is expected to have significant implications for TBI patients' prognosis and treatment. The typical patient for whom HDFT is indicated has suffered multiple impacts to the head over an extended period of time. Although these patients suffer significant symptoms, in most cases current imaging tools (e.g. MRI and CT) are unable to pinpoint the locations of the injuries, much less any evidence of TBI. Fortunately, HDFT is providing a wealth of details for the patient and clinician about the TBI. Unfortunately, the 25 page, expert-generated report takes up to 10 hours of effort to produce once the HDFT procedure is completed: part of the time is analysis and part is report writing.

Accordingly, TBI-Doc's success will be measured in terms of reducing the amount of human time involved in creating the final report presented to the patient and clinicians. In this paper we describe the TBI-Doc prototype which demonstrates the feasibility of the system. The main contribution at this stage of development and the focus of this paper is the ontology necessary for generating the reports and the system architecture. We conclude with our goals for future research and development.

2 The HDFT Results and Expert-Authored Case Reports

Currently HDFT produces data on 13 brain tracts. One such tract, which we focused on for the TBI-Doc prototype, is the **superior longitudinal fasciculus** (SLF) which connects regions of the frontal lobe with the parietal and temporal lobes (Fernandez-Miranda et al., 2012). The brain regions that a tract connects and the areas of the tract that appear abnormal suggest the brain functions that may be impacted (Shin et al., 2012).

To identify abnormalities, the imaging process mathematically compares the volume of the patient's right and left hemisphere for a particular tract (Shin et al., 2012) and looks for unexpected asymmetries.[1] The volume is also compared against the HDFT data of a population of individuals who have not suffered any TBI. Finally, the analyst also uses his/her knowledge of the anatomy of a healthy brain to identify abnormalities and can further characterize the density, distribution and connectivity of the fibers of the tract by visually examining a representation of it, as shown within Figure 1 for the fronto-occiptal fasciculus tract. As part of the reporting, the analyst describes the above comparisons, marks up the visual representations of the tract that illustrate his/her observations and includes graphs that represent the volume comparisons.

Because HDFT is new, currently, there are relatively few *ideal* expert-generated case reports upon which to model TBI-Doc's reports. When we began the development of TBI-Doc, an analyst had written 29 case reports but only 2-3 of these reports were considered model final reports.

[1]Some tracts normally are expected to have some asymmetries between hemispheres.

Proceedings of the 8th International Natural Language Generation Conference, pages 143–146,
Philadelphia, Pennsylvania, 19-21 June 2014. ©2014 Association for Computational Linguistics

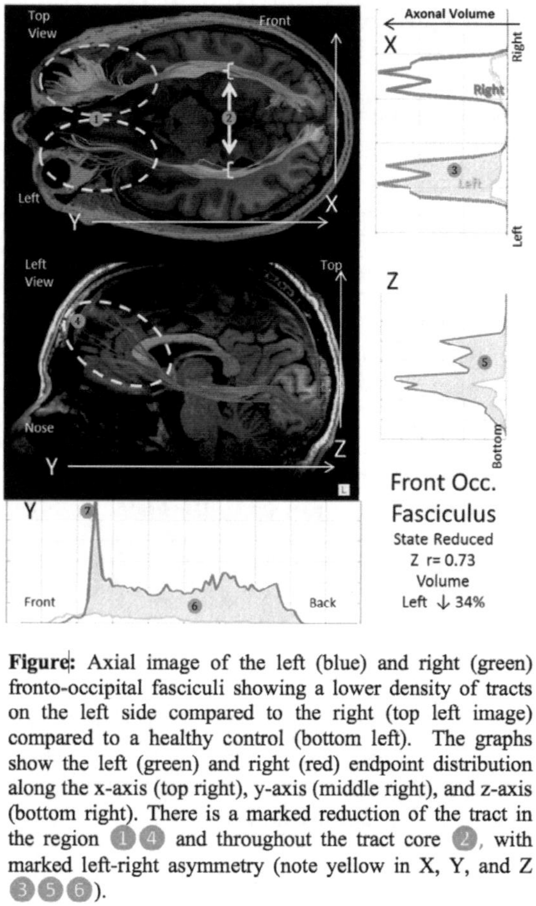

Figure 1: Tract Report Excerpt: shows HDFT images of fibers representing the FOF Tract

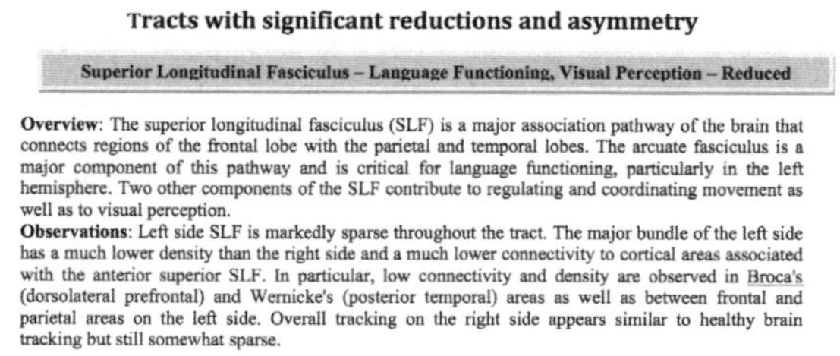

Tracts with significant reductions and asymmetry

Superior Longitudinal Fasciculus – Language Functioning, Visual Perception – Reduced

Overview: The superior longitudinal fasciculus (SLF) is a major association pathway of the brain that connects regions of the frontal lobe with the parietal and temporal lobes. The arcuate fasciculus is a major component of this pathway and is critical for language functioning, particularly in the left hemisphere. Two other components of the SLF contribute to regulating and coordinating movement as well as to visual perception.

Observations: Left side SLF is markedly sparse throughout the tract. The major bundle of the left side has a much lower density than the right side and a much lower connectivity to cortical areas associated with the anterior superior SLF. In particular, low connectivity and density are observed in Broca's (dorsolateral prefrontal) and Wernicke's (posterior temporal) areas as well as between frontal and parietal areas on the left side. Overall tracking on the right side appears similar to healthy brain tracking but still somewhat sparse.

Figure 2: Expert Observation being Modeled

The content and format of the final case report is continuing to evolve as the primary physician and nurse on the HDFT team provide feedback on the type of report they believe will be most beneficial. As of yet, there has been no feedback from patients or other types of treating clinicians (e.g. speech therapists, physical therapists, etc.) on the content and format that they find most helpful.

For the prototype we focused on modeling the tract section of one of the case reports but used the remaining reports for determining the ontology. An excerpt of the SLF tract section of that model case report is shown in Figure 2.

3 The TBI-Doc System Design

Given the existing analyst workflow, we designed the TBI-Doc system process (see Figure 3) as follows; after interpreting and manually annotating HDFT images of tracts, and creating and annotating data graphics that show quantitative HDFT results, the analyst uses TBI-Doc's graphical user interface (GUI) to provide his qualitative evaluation of the HDFT results and preferences for tailoring the report. Using the analyst's specifications provided through the TBI-Doc GUI and the annotated tract images and data graphics, TBI-Doc automatically produces a first draft of the case report. The draft is then manually reviewed and edited by the analyst before delivery. The case report is delivered to the clients as a file that can be printed on paper and viewed on a tablet.

The architecture of TBI-Doc (shown by the remainder of Figure 3) follows the standard NLG pipeline (Reiter et al., 2000) and is similar to the architecture of the healthcare-related systems described in (Green et al., 2011; Hunter et al., 2012; Scott et al., 2013). The TBI-Doc GUI represents the TBI-Doc ontology and its columns (an excerpt is shown in Table 1) cue the analyst to enter his/her qualitative judgments about the data for a tract at the region level, which is the lowest judgment level as it describes the endpoints of subsections of a tract, bundles between regions, hemisphere level and overall. The ontology was derived by analyzing existing reports to understand what is being described across all of the reports and by interviewing HDFT team members. The ontology identifies states (e.g. measures), relations (e.g. similar

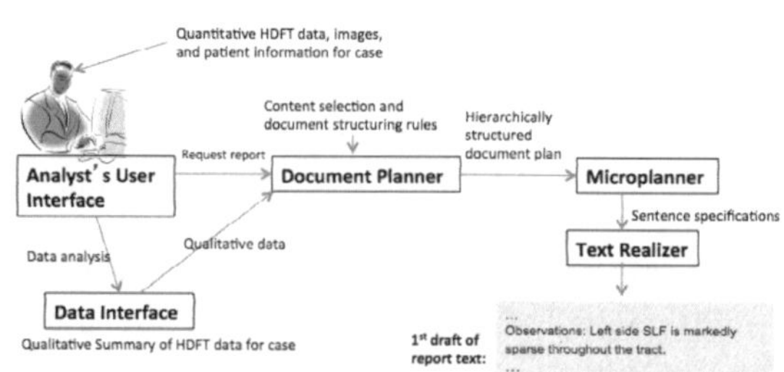

Figure 3: The TBI-Doc Process

Table 1: Example Input for SLF Tract Assessment

Tract Assessment	SPARSE						
Tract	hemi-sphere	Area Type	Area Name	Second End Point	Measure	Evaluation	Kind of Comparison
SLF	left	OverallTract	tract		density	very sparse	healthy
SLF	left	BundleBtwnRegions	DLPFC	pTemporal	density	sparse	right
SLF	left	BundleBtwnRegions	DLPFC	pTemporal	connectivity	reduced	right
SLF	left	SpecificRegion	DLPFC		connectivity	little	right
SLF	left	SpecificRegion	pTemporal		connectivity	little	right
SLF	left	SpecificRegion	DLPFC		density	sparse	right
SLF	left	SpecificRegion	pTemporal		density	sparse	right
SLF	left	BundleBtwnRegions	DLPFC	pParietal	connectivity	little	right
SLF	left	BundleBtwnRegions	DLPFC	pParietal	density	sparse	right
SLF	right	OverallTract	tract		density	normal	healthy
SLF	right	OverallTract	tract		density	some sparse	healthy

to), and entities (e.g. tract(s), regions(s), connection(s), measurements such as density) relevant to the HDFT reporting domain.

When the qualitative judgment entries or updates are complete, the analyst requests that a report be generated. The TBI-Doc Document Planner (logic implemented in Java) selects appropriate content from the database using the TBI-Doc Data Interface and adds messages constructed from that content as leaves of the Document Plan. For the parts of the report that are not dependent on values in the database, the Document Planner also adds English (canned) text as leaves of the Document Plan. The Document Planner is a set of rules for what content to select and how to order that content. For example, an abbreviated excerpt of the content selection rules follow.

```
GENERATETRACTSECTION(tract, patientId)
    GETTRACTSTATUS(tract,patientId)
    If status=reduced then
        GETTRACTFUNCTION(tract)
        GENTRACTOBSERVATION(tract,patientId)

GENTRACTOBSERVATION(tract, patientId)
  If Evaluation=reduced & TractOverall then
      GENTRACTSUMMARYSENTENCE
  ElsIf hemi not both & AreaType=OverallTract then
      GENHEMISPHERESUMMARYSENTENCE
  regions=
    GATHERREGIONS(SpecificRegion,BundleBtwnRegions)
  orderedRegions=ORDERREGIONS(regions)
  For region in orderedRegions do
      GENSENTENCE(region)
```

While there is often just a single sentence for a tract or hemisphere summary, region descriptions are generally multi-sentential. Currently the orderRegions function is designed as a default set of guidelines for ordering the region descriptions. The output of the Document Plan is then a series of predicates that represent the content to be realized. Some content, such as getTractFunction, is static and does not pass through the pipeline to the Microplanner.

The TBI-Doc Microplanner transforms the predicates output from the Document Plan into SimpleNLG sentence specifications (in Java) via a set of mapping rules. The Microplanner selects mapping rules based on the predicates to be realized and any context variables that are available. The mapping rules indicate what syntactic structures to create for a predicate and where to attach them in the sentence being built. Currently, for this demonstration prototype we have not yet addressed lexical realization and sentence aggregation. In the final step of the pipeline, SimpleNLG (Gatt and Reiter, 2009) renders the sentence specifications as English sentences. Once the pipeline is complete, the TBI-Doc Formatter combines all the sentences from SimpleNLG and the canned text into an HTML document which can then be displayed by a browser and edited via an XML editor.

Rather than implementing each of the above steps one-by-one to cover all possible cases, each step was implemented to focus on replicating the observation section of one case report. This allowed us to perform an end-to-end demonstration of the feasibility of this design. Thus many of the rules described above are incomplete for alternative pathways. TBI-Doc can currently generate from input data an observation section such as the one shown below. The judgments entered on behalf of the analyst for this demonstration are shown in Table 1 and represent what was expressed in the expert-written observations section in Figure 2:

Observations Left SLF is particularly sparse throughout the tract. The left tract from the DLPFC to the pTemporal region when compared to the right has a sparse density and a reduced connectivity. In particular little connectivity and sparse density are observed in the DLPFC and pTemporal regions as well as between the DLPFC and pParietal regions on the left. Overall the right tract appears similar to a healthy tract but still appears somewhat sparse.

4 Future Work

The current TBI-Doc is a demonstration of the feasibility of generating case reports and the main contribution of the work thus far has been to define an ontology for the HDFT domain. However, because HDFT is a new technology that is continuing to be improved rapidly and the reporting goals are still evolving, the ontology is not yet complete. Because the ontology drives the rest of the system, it follows that the rest of the system components still need more development.

For the demonstration we focused on reporting on one of the 13 existing types of brain tracts. While we anticipate that the ontology will generalize well to the other tract types, each tract type may introduce some extensions to the ontology. In addition the HDFT developers anticipate providing data on additional tract types over time.

Since knowledge acquisition is still ongoing, the Document Planner logic is still very shallow. As a result, the demonstration version of TBI-Doc is currently limited to reacting to descriptor changes and does not yet alter the document structure or intelligently alter content selection. The Microplanner currently does some context checking to select the appropriate set of transformation rules to apply but this will need expansion as the Document Planner becomes more complete. More specifically, the sentence structure needs to vary depending on the choices made by the Document Planner. In addition, lexical selection in which internal abbreviations are mapped to user preferred forms needs more work (e.g. depending on user preferences, DLPFC could map to dorsolateral prefrontal cortex and pParietal to posterior Parietal).

Our longer term interest is to explore ways to appropriately adapt the reports for different clients. A patient for whom the HDFT results indicate cognitive processing issues may find a different style of report and reading level more suitable than a supporting family member or a treating clinician. Different treating clinicians may prefer reports with different content selected. For example, a speech therapist may prefer a report that focuses on the injuries that relate to a patient's speech and language goals, while a sleep specialist may prefer a different focus.

Acknowledgments

This work was supported by US Army Combat Casualty Care Research Program contracts CDMRP PT110773 (W81XH-12-2-0140) & US Army 12342013 (W81XWH-12-2-0319). We thank Walter Schneider, Kevin Jarbo, Lauren Wagener, Will Bird & the HDFT team for their expertise and for involving us in their research.

References

Juan C Fernandez-Miranda, Sudhir Pathak, Johnathan Engh, Kevin Jarbo, Timothy Verstynen, Fang-Cheng Yeh, Yibao Wang, Arlan Mintz, Fernando Boada, Walter Schneider, et al. 2012. High-definition fiber tractography of the human brain: neuroanatomical validation and neurosurgical applications. *Neurosurgery*, 71(2):430–453.

Albert Gatt and Ehud Reiter. 2009. Simplenlg: A realisation engine for practical applications. In *Proceedings of the 12th European Workshop on Natural Language Generation*, pages 90–93. Association for Computational Linguistics.

Nancy Green, Rachael Dwight, Kanyama Navoraphan, and Brian Stadler. 2011. Natural language generation of biomedical argumentation for lay audiences. *Argument & Computation*, 2(1):23–50.

James Hunter, Yvonne Freer, Albert Gatt, Ehud Reiter, Somayajulu Sripada, and Cindy Sykes. 2012. Automatic generation of natural language nursing shift summaries in neonatal intensive care: Bt-nurse. *Artificial intelligence in medicine*, 56(3):157–172.

Ehud Reiter, Robert Dale, and Zhiwei Feng. 2000. *Building natural language generation systems*, volume 33. MIT Press.

Donia Scott, Catalina Hallett, and Rachel Fettiplace. 2013. Data-to-text summarisation of patient records: Using computer-generated summaries to access patient histories. *Patient education and counseling*, 92(2):153–159.

Samuel S Shin, Timothy Verstynen, Sudhir Pathak, Kevin Jarbo, Allison J Hricik, Megan Maserati, Sue R Beers, Ava M Puccio, Fernando E Boada, David O Okonkwo, and Walter Schneider. 2012. High-definition fiber tracking for assessment of neurological deficit in a case of traumatic brain injury: finding, visualizing, and interpreting small sites of damage: Case report. *Journal of neurosurgery*, 116(5):1062–1069.

Towards Surface Realization with CCGs Induced from Dependencies

Michael White
Department of Linguistics
The Ohio State University
Columbus, OH 43210, USA
mwhite@ling.osu.edu

Abstract

We present a novel algorithm for inducing Combinatory Categorial Grammars from dependency treebanks, along with initial experiments showing that it can be used to achieve competitive realization results using an enhanced version of the surface realization shared task data.

1 Introduction

In the first surface realization shared task (Belz et al., 2011), no grammar-based systems achieved competitive results, as input conversion turned out to be more difficult than anticipated. Since then, Narayan & Gardent (2012) have shown that grammar-based systems can be substantially improved with error mining techniques. In this paper, inspired by recent work on converting dependency treebanks (Ambati et al., 2013) and semantic parsing (Kwiatkowksi et al., 2010; Artzi and Zettlemoyer, 2013) with Combinatory Categorial Grammar (CCG), we pursue the alternative strategy of inducing a CCG from an enhanced version of the shared task dependencies, with initial experiments showing even better results.

A silver lining of the failure of grammar-based systems in the shared task is that it revealed some problems with the data. In particular, it became evident that in cases where a constituent is annotated with multiple roles in the Penn Treebank (PTB), the partial nature of Propbank annotation and the restriction to syntactic dependency trees meant that information was lost between the surface and deep representations, leading grammar-based systems to fail for good reason. For example, Figure 1 shows that with free object relatives, only one of the two roles played by *how much manufacturing strength* is captured in the deep representation, making it difficult to linearize this phrase correctly. By contrast, Figure 2 (top)

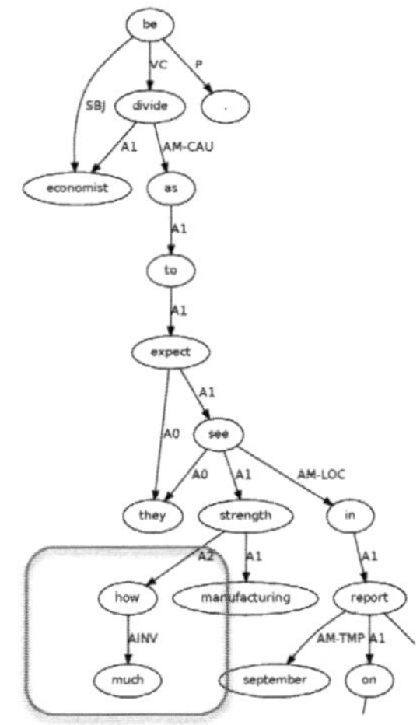

Figure 1: Shared Task Input for *Economists are divided as to [how much manufacturing strength]$_i$ they expect to see t_i in September reports on industrial production and capacity utilization , also due tomorrow* (wsj_2400.6, "deep" representation)

shows an experimental version of the shallow representation intended to capture all the syntactic dependencies in the PTB, including the additional object role played by this phrase here.[1] Including all PTB syntactic dependencies in the shallow representation makes it feasible to define a compatible CCG; at the bottom of the figure, a corresponding CCG derivation for these dependencies is shown. In the next section, we present an algorithm for inducing such derivations. In contrast to Ambati et al.'s (2013) approach, the algorithm integrates the proposal of candidate lexical categories with the derivational process, making it possible to derive categories involving unsaturated arguments, such as $\mathsf{s}_{e,\mathsf{dcl}}\backslash\mathsf{np}_x/(\mathsf{s}_{e',\mathsf{to}}\backslash\mathsf{np}_x)$; it also makes greater use of unary type-changing rules, as with Artzi & Zettlemoyer's (2013) approach.

[1]Kudos to Richard Johansson for making these enhancements available.

Proceedings of the 8th International Natural Language Generation Conference, pages 147–151,
Philadelphia, Pennsylvania, 19-21 June 2014. ©2014 Association for Computational Linguistics

Unlike their approach though, it works in a broad coverage setting, and makes use of all the combinators standardly used with CCG, including ones for type-raising.

2 Inducing CCGs from Dependencies

Pseudocode for the induction algorithm is given in Figure 3. The algorithm takes as input a set of training sentences with their gold standard dependencies. We pre-processed the dependencies to make coordinating conjunctions the head, and to include features for zero-determiners. The algorithm also makes use of a seed lexicon that specifies category projection by part of speech as well as a handful of categories for function words. For example, (1) shows how a tensed verb projects to a finite clause category, while (2) shows the usual CCG category for a determiner, which here introduces a $\langle$NMOD$\rangle$ dependency.[2]

(1) *expect* $\vdash \mathsf{s}_{e,\mathsf{dcl}} \ : \ @_e(\mathbf{expect} \wedge \langle \text{TENSE} \rangle pres)$

(2) *the* $\vdash \mathsf{np}_x/\mathsf{n}_x \ : \ @_x(\langle \text{NMOD} \rangle (d \wedge \mathbf{the}))$

The algorithm begins by instantiating the lexical categories and type-changing rules that match the input dependency graph, tracking the categories in a map (*edges*) from nodes to edges (i.e., signs with a coverage vector). It then recursively visits each node in the primary dependency tree bottom up (*combineEdges*), using a local chart (*doCombos*) at each step to combine categories for adjacent phrases in all possible ways. Along the way, it creates new categories (*extendCats* and *coordCats*) and unary rules (*applyNewUnary*). For example, when processing the node for *expect* in Figure 2, the nodes for *they* and *to* are recursively processed first, deriving the categories np_{w_9} and $s_{w_{11},to}\backslash np_{w_9}/np_{w_8}$ for *they* and *to see . . .*, respectively. The initial category for *expect* is then extended as shown in (3), which allows for composition with *to see . . .* (as well as with a category for simple application). When there are coordination relations for a coordinating conjunction (or coordinating punctuation mark), the appropriate category for combining like types is instead constructed, as in (4). Additionally, for modifiers, unary rules are instantiated and applied, e.g. the rule for noun-noun compounds in (5).

[2]In the experiments reported here, we made use of only six (non-trivial) hand-specified categories and two type-changing rules; though we anticipate adding more initial categories to handle some currently problematic cases, the vast majority of the categories in the resulting grammar can be induced automatically.

Inputs Training set of sentences with dependencies. Initial lexicon and rules. Argument and modifier relations. Derivation scoring metric. Maximum agenda size.

Definitions *edges* is a map from dependency graph nodes to their edges, where an *edge* is a CCG sign together with a coverage bitset; *agenda* is a priority queue of edges sorted by the scoring metric; *chart* manages equivalence classes of edges; see text for descriptions of auxiliary functions such as *extendCats* and *coordCats* below.

Algorithm
bestDerivs, lexcats, unaryRules ← ∅
For each item in training set:

1. *edges*[*node*] ← *instCats*(*node*), *ruleInsts*[*node*] ← *instRules*(*node*), for *node* in input graph
2. *combineEdges*(*root*), with *root* of input graph
3. *bestEdge* ← unpack(*edges*[*root*]); *bestDerivs* +← *bestEdge.sign*; *lexcats* +← abstractedCats(*bestEdge*), *unaryRules* +← abstractedRules(*bestEdge*), if *bestEdge* complete

def *combineEdges*(*node*):

1. *combineEdges*(*child*) for *child* in *node.kids*
2. *edges*[*node*] +← coordCats(*node*) if *node* has coord relations, otherwise *edges*[*node*] ← *extendCats*(*node*,*rels*) for argument *rels*
3. *agenda* ← *edges*[*node*]; *agenda* +← *edges*[*child*] for *child* in *node.kids*; *chart* ← ∅
4. While *agenda* not empty:
   (a) *next* ← *agenda.pop*
   (b) *chart* +← *next*
   (c) *doCombos*(*next*), unless *next* packed into an existing chart item
5. *edges[node]* ← chart edges for *node* filtered for maximal input coverage

def *doCombos*(*next*):

1. *agenda* +← applyUnary(*next*), if *next* is for *node*
2. For *item* in *chart*:
   (a) *agenda* +← applyBinary(*next*,*item*), if *next* is adjacent to *item*
   (b) *agenda* +← applyNewUnary(*next*,*item*), if *next* connected to *item* by a modifier relation

Outputs *bestDerivs, lexcats, unaryRules*

Figure 3: CCG Induction Algorithm

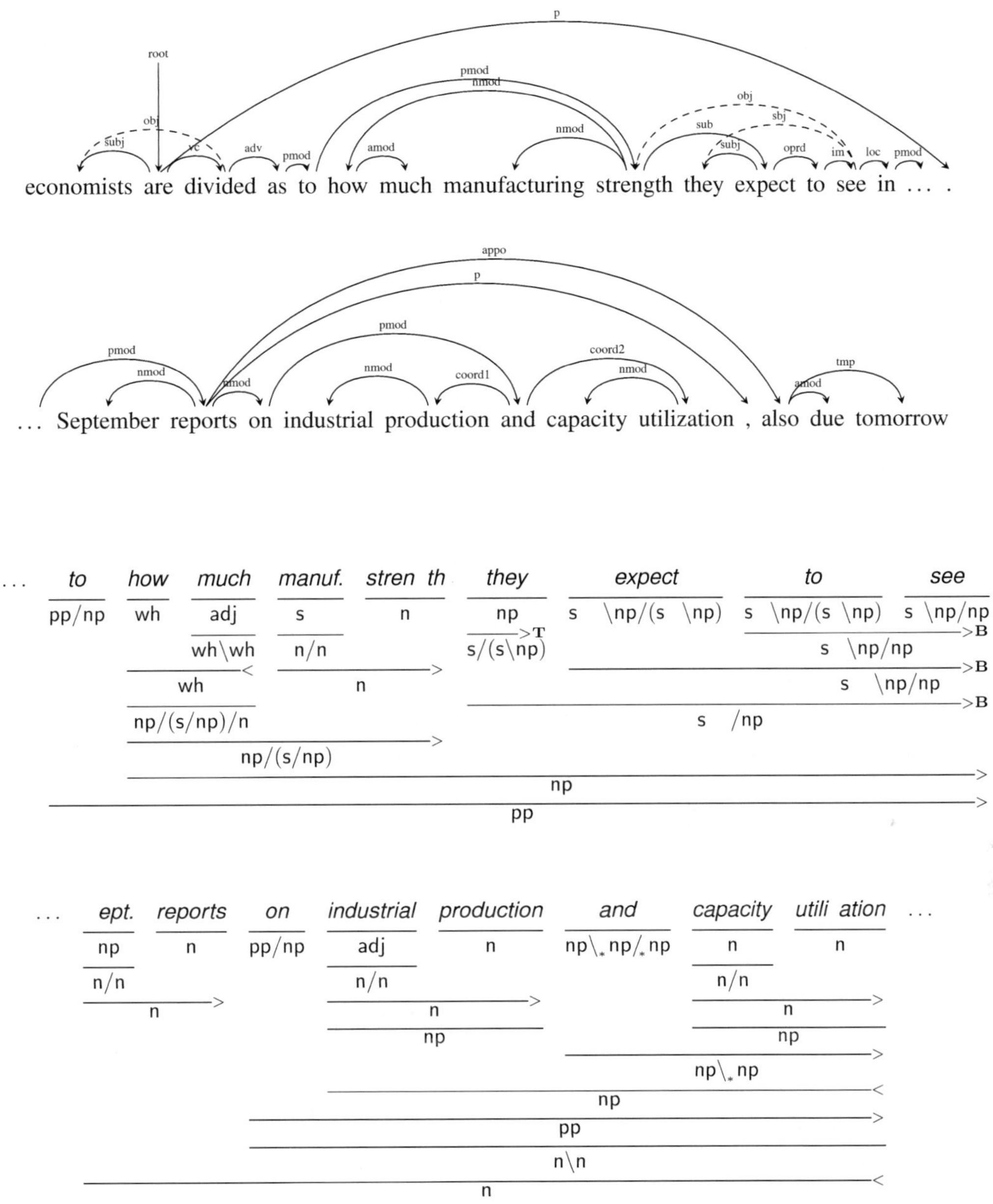

Figure 2: Augmented Syntactic Dependencies with Corresponding CCG Derivation (dashed dependencies indicate relations from additional parents beyond those in the primary tree structure)

(3) *expect* $\vdash$ $\mathsf{s}_{w_{10},\mathsf{dcl}}\backslash\mathsf{np}_{w_9}/(\mathsf{s}_{w_{11},\mathsf{to}}\backslash\mathsf{np}_{w_9})$:
$@_{w_{10}}(\textbf{expect} \wedge \langle\text{TENSE}\rangle pres \wedge$
$\langle\text{SUBJ}\rangle w_9 \wedge \langle\text{OPRED}\rangle w_{11})$

(4) *and* $\vdash$ $\mathsf{np}_{w_{19}}\backslash_{*}\mathsf{np}_{w_{18}}/_{*}\mathsf{np}_{w_{21}}$:
$@_{w_{19}}(\textbf{and} \wedge \langle\text{COORD1}\rangle w_{18} \wedge \langle\text{COORD2}\rangle w_{21})$

(5) $\mathsf{n}_{w_{20}} \Rightarrow \mathsf{n}_{w_{21}}/\mathsf{n}_{w_{21}}$: $@_{w_{21}}(\langle\text{NMOD}\rangle w_{20})$

At the end of the recursion, the lexical categories and type-changing rules are extracted from the highest-scoring derivation and added to the output sets, after first replacing indices such as w_{10} with variables.

3 Experiments and Future Work

We ran the induction algorithm over the standard PTB training sections (02–21), recovering complete derivations more than 90% of the time for most sections. Robust treatment of coordination, including argument cluster coordination and gapping, remains a known issue; other causes of derivation failures remain to be investigated. To select preferred derivations, we used a complexity metric that simply counts the number of steps and the number of slashes in the categories. We then trained a generative syntactic model (Hockenmaier and Steedman, 2002) and used it along with a composite language model to generate n-best realizations for reranking (White and Rajkumar, 2012), additionally using a large-scale (gigaword) language model. Development and test results appear in Table 1. Perhaps because of the expanded use of type-changing rules with simple lexical categories, the generative model and hypertagger (Espinosa et al., 2008) performed worse than expected. Combining the generative syntactic model and composite language model (GEN) with equal weight yielded a devtest BLEU score of only 0.4513, while discriminatively training the generative component models (GLOBAL) increased the score to 0.7679. Using all features increased the score to 0.8083, while doubling the beam size (ALL+) pushed the score to 0.8210, indicating that search errors may be an issue. Ablation results show that leaving out the large-scale language model (NO-BIGLM) and dependency-ordering features (NO-DEPORD) substantially drops the score.[3] Focusing only on the 80.5% of the sentences for which a complete derivation was found (COMPLETE) yielded a score of 0.8668. By comparison, realization with the native OpenCCG inputs (and the large-scale LM) on all sentences (NATIVE) yields a score more than five BLEU points higher, despite using inputs with more semantically-oriented relations and leaving out many function words, indicating that there is likely substantial room for improvement in the pre-processing and grammar induction process. Towards that end, we tried selecting the best derivations using several rounds of Viterbi EM with the generative syntactic model, but doing so did not improve realization quality.

Model	Exact	Complete	BLEU
Sect 00			
GEN	2.4	79.5	0.4513
GLOBAL	29.7	79.0	0.7679
NO-BIGLM	29.1	78.2	0.7757
NO-DEPORD	34.3	77.9	0.7956
ALL	35.8	78.4	0.8083
ALL+	36.4	80.5	**0.8210**
COMPLETE	44.4	-	0.8668
NATIVE	48.0	88.7	0.8793
Sect 23			
GEN	2.8	80.3	0.4560
GLOBAL	31.3	78.5	0.7675
ALL	37.6	77.2	0.8083
ALL+	38.1	80.4	**0.8260**
COMPLETE	47.0	-	0.8743
NATIVE	46.4	86.4	0.8694

Table 1: Development set (Section 00) & test set (Section 23) results, including exact match and complete derivation percentages and BLEU scores

A similar pattern is seen in the Section 23 results, with a competitive BLEU score of 0.8260 with the expanded beam, much higher than Narayan & Gardent's (2012) score of 0.675 with 38.8% coverage, the best previous score with a grammar-based system. This score still trails the shared task scores of the top statistical dependency realizers by several points (STUMABA-S at 0.8911 and DCU at 0.8575), though it exceeds the score of a purpose-built system using no external resources (ATT at 0.6701). In future work, we hope to close the gap with the top systems by integrating an improved ranking model into the induction process and resolving the remaining representational issues with problematic constructions.

Acknowledgments

Thanks to the anonymous reviewers, Richard Johansson and the University of Sydney Schwa Lab for helpful comments and discussion. This work was supported in part by NSF grants IIS-1143635 and IIS-1319318.

[3]All differences were statistically significant at $p < 0.01$ with paired bootstrap resampling (Koehn, 2004).

References

Bharat Ram Ambati, Tejaswini Deoskar, and Mark Steedman. 2013. Using CCG categories to improve Hindi dependency parsing. In *Proc. ACL*.

Yoav Artzi and Luke Zettlemoyer. 2013. Weakly supervised learning of semantic parsers for mapping instructions to actions. *TACL*, 1:49–62.

Anja Belz, Michael White, Dominic Espinosa, Eric Kow, Deirdre Hogan, and Amanda Stent. 2011. The first surface realisation shared task: Overview and evaluation results. In *Proc. ENLG*.

Dominic Espinosa, Michael White, and Dennis Mehay. 2008. Hypertagging: Supertagging for surface realization with CCG. In *Proc. ACL*.

Julia Hockenmaier and Mark Steedman. 2002. Generative models for statistical parsing with Combinatory Categorial Grammar. In *Proc. ACL*.

Philipp Koehn. 2004. Statistical significance tests for machine translation evaluation. In *Proc. EMNLP*.

Tom Kwiatkowksi, Luke Zettlemoyer, Sharon Goldwater, and Mark Steedman. 2010. Inducing probabilistic CCG grammars from logical form with higher-order unification. In *Proc. EMNLP*.

Shashi Narayan and Claire Gardent. 2012. Error mining with suspicion trees: Seeing the forest for the trees. In *Proc. COLING*.

Michael White and Rajakrishnan Rajkumar. 2012. Minimal dependency length in realization ranking. In *Proc. EMNLP*.

Two-Stage Stochastic Natural Language Generation for Email Synthesis by Modeling Sender Style and Topic Structure

Yun-Nung Chen and Alexander I. Rudnicky
School of Computer Science, Carnegie Mellon University
5000 Forbes Ave., Pittsburgh, PA 15213-3891, USA
{yvchen, air}@cs.cmu.edu

Abstract

This paper describes a two-stage process for stochastic generation of email, in which the first stage structures the emails according to sender style and topic structure (high-level generation), and the second stage synthesizes text content based on the particulars of an email element and the goals of a given communication (surface-level realization). Synthesized emails were rated in a preliminary experiment. The results indicate that sender style can be detected. In addition we found that stochastic generation performs better if applied at the word level than at an original-sentence level ("template-based") in terms of email coherence, sentence fluency, naturalness, and preference.

1 Introduction

This paper focuses on generating language for the email domain, with the goal of producing mails that reflect sender style and the intent of the communication. Such a process might be used for the generation of common messages (for example a request for a meeting without direct intervention from the sender). It can also be used in situations where naturalistic email is needed for other applications. For instance, our email generator was developed to provide emails to be used as part of synthetic evidence of insider threats for purposes of training, prototyping, and evaluating anomaly detectors (Hershkop et al., 2011).

There are two approaches to natural language generation (NLG), one focuses on generating text using templates or rules (linguistic) methods, the another uses corpus-based statistical techniques. Oh and Rudnicky (2002) showed that stochastic generation benefits from two factors: 1) it takes advantage of the practical language of a domain expert instead of the developer and 2) it restates the problem in terms of classification and labeling, where expertise is not required for developing a rule-based generation system. They found that naive listeners found such utterances as acceptable as human-generated utterances. Belz (2005) also proposed a probabilistic NLG approach to make systems more robust and components more reusable, reducing manual corpus analysis.

However, most work usually focused on well-structured documents such as news and Wikipedia, while email messages differ from them, which reflect senders' style and are more spontaneous. Lampert et al. (2009) segmented email messages into zones, including sender zones, quoted conversation zones, and boilerplate zones. This paper only models the text in the sender zone, new content from the current sender. In the present work, we investigate the use of stochastic techniques for generation of a different class of communications and whether global structures can be convincingly created in the email domain.

A lot of NLG systems are applied in dialogue systems, some of which focus on topic modeling (Sauper and Barzilay, 2009; Barzilay and Lapata, 2008; Barzilay and Lee, 2004), proposing algorithms to balance local fit of information and global coherence. However, they seldom consider to model the speaker's characteristics. Gill et al. (2012) considered sentiment such as openness and neuroticism to specify characters for dialogue generation. In stead of modeling authors' attitudes, this paper proposes the first approach of synthesizing emails by modeling their writing patterns. Specifically we investigate whether stochastic techniques can be used to acceptably model longer texts and individual speaker characteristics in the emails, both of which may require higher cohesion to be acceptable.

2 Overview of Framework

Our proposed NLG approach has three steps: preprocessing training data, modeling sender style and topic structure for email organization, followed by surface realization, shown in Figure 1.

In preprocessing, we segment sentences for each email, and label email structural elements. This is used to create a structural label sequence for each email, and then used to model sender style and topic structure for email organization (1st stage in the figure). Content slots are also annotated for surface realization (2nd stage in the figure). Details are in Section 3.

From the annotated corpus, we build sender-specific and topic-specific structure language models based on structural label sequences, and use a mixture sender-topic-specific model to stochastically generate email structure in the first stage. The process is detailed in Section 4.

Proceedings of the 8th International Natural Language Generation Conference, pages 152–156,
Philadelphia, Pennsylvania, 19-21 June 2014. ©2014 Association for Computational Linguistics

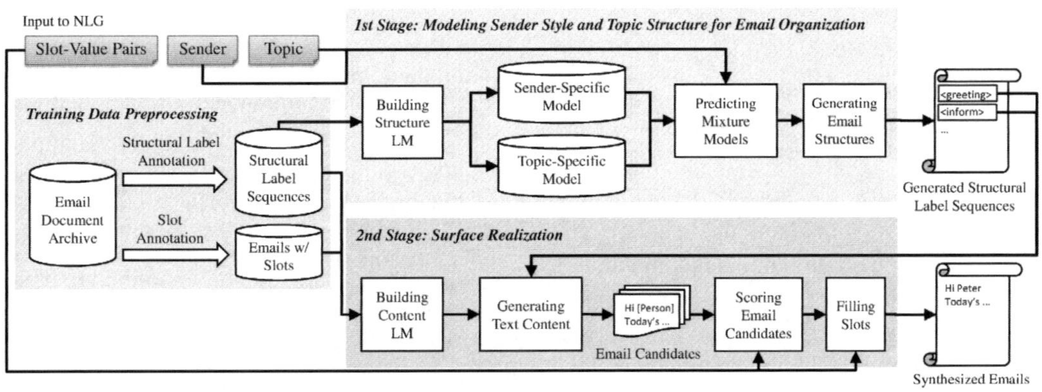

Figure 1: The proposed framework of two-stage NLG component.

In the second stage, we build a content language model for each structural element and then stochastically generate sentences using the sequence generated in the first stage. To ensure that required slot-value pairs occur in the text, candidates emails are filtered to retain only those texts that contain the desired content slots. These slots are then filled to produce the final result. Section 5 explains the process.

3 Training Data Preprocessing

To model sender style and topic structure, we annotate the data with defined structural labels in Section 3.1, and data with slots to model text content of language in Section 3.2.

3.1 Structural Label Annotation

Based on examination of the corpus, we defined 10 email structure elements:

1. *greeting*: a friendly expression or respectful phrase, typically at the start of an email.
2. *inform*: to give or impart knowledge of a fact or circumstance.
3. *request*: the act of asking for something to be given or done, especially as a favor or courtesy.
4. *suggestion*: to mention or introduce (an idea, proposition, plan, etc.) for consideration or possible action.
5. *question*: an interrogative sentence in an form, requesting information in reply.
6. *answer*: a reply or response to a question, etc.
7. *regard*: to have or show respect or concern for, usually at the end of an email.
8. *acknowledgement*: to show or express appreciation or gratitude.
9. *sorry*: express regret, compunction, sympathy, pity, etc.
10. *signature*: a sender's name usually at the end of the email.

We perform sentence segmentation using punctuation and line-breaks and then manually tag each sentence with a structure label. We exclude the header of emails for labeling. Figure 2 shows an example email with structural labels.

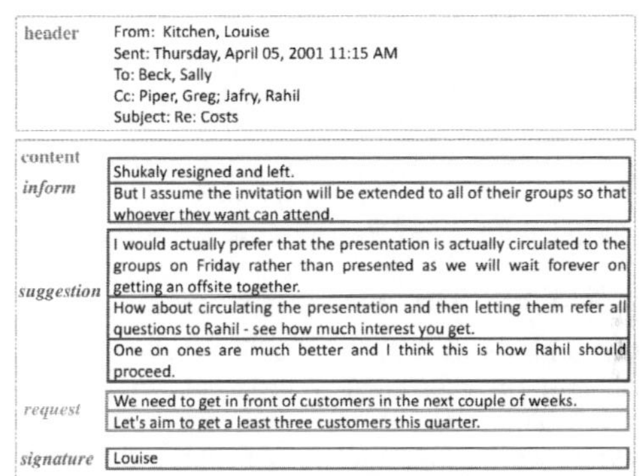

Figure 2: The email with structural labels.

3.2 Slot Annotation

The input to NLG may contain the information that needs to be included in the synthesized emails. Tokens in the corpus text corresponding to slots are replaced by slot (or concept) tokens prior to building content language models. Slots are classified into general class and topic class below.

3.2.1 General Class

We use existing named entity recognition (NER) tools for identifying general classes. Finkel et al. (2005) used CRF to label sequences of words in text that are names of things, such as person, organization, etc. There are three models trained on different data, which are a 4-class model trained for CoNLL[1], a 7-class model trained for MUC, and a 3-class model trained on both data sets for the intersection of those class sets below.

- 4-class: location, person, organization, misc
- 7-class: location, person, organization, time, money, percent, date

Considering that 3-class model performs higher accuracy and 7-class model provides better coverage, we take the union of outputs produced by 3-class and 7-class models and use the labels output by 3-class model if the two models give different results, since the 3-class model is trained on both data sets and provides better accuracy.

[1] http://www.cnts.ua.ac.be/conll2003/ner/

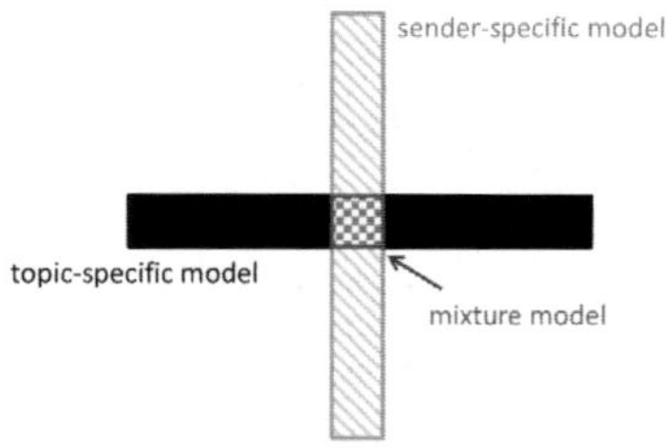

Figure 3: The visualization of the mixture model.

3.2.2 Topic Class

Many named entities cannot be recognized by a general NER, because they are topic-specific information. Accordingly we define additional entities that are part of the email domain.

4 Modeling Sender Style and Topic Structure for Email Organization

Given a target sender and topic focus specified in system input, email structures can be generated by predicted sender-topic-specific mixture models.

4.1 Building Structure Language Models

Based on the annotation of structural labels, each email can be expressed as a structural label sequence. Then we can train a sender-specific and a topic-specific structure model using the emails from each sender and the emails related to each topic respectively. Here the structure models are n-gram models with Good-Turing smoothing ($n = 3$) (Good, 1953).

4.2 Predicting Mixture Models

Using sender-specific and topic-specific structure models, we predict sender-topic-specific mixture models by interpolation:

$$P_{i,j}(l) = \alpha P_i^s(l) + (1 - \alpha) P_j^t(l), \quad (1)$$

where $P_{i,j}(l)$ is the estimated probability that the structural label l occurs from the sender i and for the topic j, $P_i^s(l)$ is the probability of the structural label l from the sender i (regardless of topics), $P_j^t(l)$ is the probability of the structural label l related to the topic j (regardless of senders), and α is the interpolation weight, balancing between sender style and topic focus. Figure 3 illustrates the mixture models combined by sender-specific and topic-specific models.

4.3 Generating Email Structure

We generate structural label sequences randomly according to the distribution from sender-topic-specific models. To generate the structural label sequences from the sender i and related to the topic j, the probability of the structural label l_k using n-gram language model is

$$P_{i,j}(l_k) = P_{i,j}(l_k \mid l_{k-1}, l_{k-2}, ..., l_{k-(n-1)}). \quad (2)$$

Since we use smoothed trigrams, we may generate unseen trigrams based on back-off methods, resulting in some undesirable randomness. We therefore exclude unreasonable emails that don't follow two simple rules.

1. The structural label "*greeting*" only occurs at the beginning of the email.
2. The structural label "*signature*" only occurs at the end of the email.

5 Surface Realization

Our surface realizer has four elements: building language models, generating text content, scoring email candidates, and filling slots.

5.1 Building Content Language Models

After replacing the tokens with slots, for each structural label, we train an unsmoothed n-gram language model using all sentences with that structural label. We make a simplifying assumption that the usage of within-sentence language can be treated as independent across senders; generating the text content only considers the structural labels. We use 5-gram to balance variability in generated sentences while minimizing nonsense sentences.

Given a structural label, we use the content language model probability directly to predict the next word. The most likely sentence is $W^* = \arg\max P(W \mid l)$, where W is a word sequence and l is a structural label. However, in order to introduce more variation, we do not look for the most likely sentence but generate each word randomly according to the distribution similar to Section 4.3 and illustrated below.

5.2 Generating Text Content

The input to surface realization is the generated structural label sequence. We use the corresponding content language model trained for the given structural label to generate word sequences randomly according to the distribution from the language model. The probability of a word w_i using the n-gram language model is

$$P(w_i) = P(w_i \mid w_{i-1}, w_{i-2}, ..., w_{i-(n-1)}, l), \quad (3)$$

where l is the input structural label. Since we build separate models for different structural labels, (3) can be written as

$$P(w_i) = P(w_i \mid w_{i-1}, w_{i-2}, ..., w_{i-(n-1)}) \quad (4)$$

using the model for l.

Using unsmoothed 5-grams will not generate any unseen 5-grams (or smaller n-grams at the beginning and end of a sentence). This precludes generation of nonsense sentences within the 5-word window. Given a generated structural label sequence, we can generate multiple sentences to create a synthesized email.

5.3 Scoring Email Candidates

The input to NLG contains the required information that needs to be in the output email, as described in Section 3.2. For each synthesized email, we penalize it if the email 1) contains slots for which there is no provided valid value, or 2) does not have the required slots.

The content generation engine stochastically generates an email candidate and scores it. If the email has a zero penalty it is passed on.

5.4 Filling Slots

The last step is to fill slots with the appropriate values. For example, the sentence "Tomorrow's [meeting] is at [location]." could become "Tomorrow's speech seminar is at Gates building."

6 Experiments

6.1 Setup

The corpus used for our experiments is the Enron Email Dataset[2], which contains a total of about 0.5M messages. We selected the data related to daily business for our use, including data from about 150 users. We randomly picked 3 senders, ones who wrote many emails, and defined additional 3 topic classes (meeting, discussion, issue) as topic-specific entities for the task. Each sender-specific model (across topics) or topic-specific model (across senders) is trained on 30 emails.

6.2 Evaluation of Sender Style Modeling

To evaluate the performance of sender style, 7 subjects were given 5 real emails from each sender and then 9 synthesized emails. They were asked to rate each synthesized email for each sender on a scale of 1 (highly confident that the email is not from the sender) to 5 (highly confident that the email is from that sender).

With $\alpha = 0.75$ in (1) for predicting mixture models (higher weight for sender-specific model), average normalized scores the corresponding senders receives account for 45%; this is above chance (which would be 33%). This suggests that sender style can be noticed by subjects, although the effect is weak, and we are in the process of designing a larger evaluation. In a follow-up questionnaire, subjects indicated that their ratings were based on greeting usage, politeness, the length of email and other characteristics.

6.3 Evaluation of Surface Realization

We conduct a comparative evaluation of two different generation algorithms, template-based generation and stochastic generation, on the same email structures. The average number of sentences in synthesized emails is 3.8, because our data is about daily business and has relatively short emails. Given a structural label, template-based generation consisted of randomly selecting an intact whole sentence with the target structural label. This could be termed sentence-level NLG, while stochastic generation is word-level NLG.

We presented 30 pairs of (sentence-, word-) synthesized emails, and 7 subjects were asked to compare the overall coherence of an email, its sentence fluency and naturalness; then select their preference. Table 1 shows subjects' preference according to the rating criteria. The word-based stochastic generation outperforms or performs as well as the template-based algorithm for all criteria, where a t-test on an email as a random variable shows no significant improvement but p-value is close to 0.05 ($p = 0.051$). Subjects indicated that emails from word-based stochastic generation are more natural; word-level generation is less likely to produce an unusual sentences from the real data; word-level generation produces more conventional sentences. Some subjects noted that neither email seemed human-written, perhaps an artifact of our experimental design. Nevertheless, we believe that this stochastic approach would require less effort compared to most rule-based or template-based systems in terms of knowledge engineering.

	Template	Stochastic	No Diff.
Coherence	36.19	**38.57**	25.24
Fluency	28.10	**40.48**	31.43
Naturalness	35.71	**45.71**	18.57
Preference	36.67	**42.86**	20.48
Overall	34.17	**41.90**	23.93

Table 1: Generation algorithm comparison (%).

7 Conclusion

This paper presents a two-stage stochastic NLG for synthesizing emails: first a structure is generated, and then text is generated for each structure element, where sender style and topic structure can be modeled. Subjects appear to notice sender style and can also tell the difference between templates using original sentences and stochastically generated sentences. We believe that this technique can be used to create realistic emails and that email generation could be carried out using mixtures containing additional models based on other characteristics. The current study shows that email can be synthesized using a small corpus of labeled data; however these models could be used to bootstrap the labeling of a larger corpus which in turn could be used to create more robust models.

Acknowledgments

The authors wish to thank Brian Lindauer and Kurt Wallnau from the Software Engineering Institute of Carnegie Mellon University for their guidance, advice, and help.

[2] https://www.cs.cmu.edu/~enron/

References

Regina Barzilay and Mirella Lapata. 2008. Modeling local coherence: An entity-based approach. *Computational Linguistics*, 34(1):1–34.

Regina Barzilay and Lillian Lee. 2004. Catching the drift: Probabilistic content models, with applications to generation and summarization. In *HLT-NAACL*, pages 113–120.

Anja Belz. 2005. Corpus-driven generation of weather forecasts. In *Proc. 3rd Corpus Linguistics Conference*.

Jenny Rose Finkel, Trond Grenager, and Christopher Manning. 2005. Incorporating non-local information into information extraction systems by gibbs sampling. In *Proc. of ACL*, pages 363–370.

Alastair J Gill, Carsten Brockmann, and Jon Oberlander. 2012. Perceptions of alignment and personality in generated dialogue. In *Proceedings of the Seventh International Natural Language Generation Conference*, pages 40–48. Association for Computational Linguistics.

Irving J Good. 1953. The population frequencies of species and the estimation of population parameters. *Biometrika*, 40(3-4):237–264.

Shlomo Hershkop, Salvatore J Stolfo, Angelos D Keromytis, and Hugh Thompson. 2011. Anomaly detection at multiple scales (ADAMS).

Andrew Lampert, Robert Dale, and Cécile Paris. 2009. Segmenting email message text into zones. In *Proceedings of the 2009 Conference on Empirical Methods in Natural Language Processing*, volume 2, pages 919–928. Association for Computational Linguistics.

Alice H Oh and Alexander I Rudnicky. 2002. Stochastic natural language generation for spoken dialog systems. *Computer Speech & Language*, 16(3):387–407.

Christina Sauper and Regina Barzilay. 2009. Automatically generating wikipedia articles: A structure-aware approach. In *Proceedings of the Joint Conference of the 47th Annual Meeting of the ACL and the 4th International Joint Conference on Natural Language Processing of the AFNLP: Volume 1-Volume 1*, pages 208–216. Association for Computational Linguistics.

Modeling Blame to Avoid Positive Face Threats in Natural Language Generation

Gordon Briggs
Human-Robot Interaction Laboratory
Tufts University
Medford, MA USA
gbriggs@cs.tufts.edu

Matthias Scheutz
Human-Robot Interaction Laboratory
Tufts University
Medford, MA USA
mscheutz@cs.tufts.edu

Abstract

Prior approaches to politeness modulation in natural language generation (NLG) often focus on manipulating factors such as the directness of requests that pertain to preserving the autonomy of the addressee (negative face threats), but do not have a systematic way of understanding potential impoliteness from inadvertently critical or blame-oriented communications (positive face threats). In this paper, we discuss ongoing work to integrate a computational model of blame to prevent inappropriate threats to positive face.

1 Introduction

When communicating with one another, people often modulate their language based on a variety of social factors. Enabling natural and human-like interactions with virtual and robotic agents may require engineering these agents to be able to demonstrate appropriate social behaviors. For instance, increasing attention is being paid to the effects of utilizing *politeness* strategies in both human-computer and human-robot dialogue interactions (Cassell and Bickmore, 2003; Torrey et al., 2013; Strait et al., 2014). This work has shown that, depending on context, the deployment of politeness strategies by artificial agents can increase human interactants' positive assessments of an agent along multiple dimensions (e.g. likeability).

However, while these studies investigated the human factors aspects of utilizing politeness strategies, they were not concerned with the natural language generation (NLG) mechanisms necessary to appropriately realize and deploy these strategies. Instead, there is a small, but growing, body of work on natural language generation architectures that seek to address this challenge (Gupta et al., 2007; Miller et al., 2008; Briggs and Scheutz, 2013). The common approach taken by these architectures is the operationalization of key factors in Brown and Levinson's seminal work on *politeness theory*, in particular, the degree to which an utterance can be considered a *face-threatening act* (FTA) (Brown and Levinson, 1987).

While this prior work demonstrates the abilities of these NLG architectures to successfully produce polite language, there remain some key challenges. Perhaps the most crucial question is: how does one calculate the degree to which an utterance is a FTA[1]? This is a complex issue, as not only is this value modulated by factors such as social distance, power, and context, but also the multifaceted nature of "face." An utterance may be polite in relation to *negative face* (i.e. the agent's autonomy), but may be quite impolite with regard to *positive face* (i.e. the agent's image and perceived character).

In this paper, we investigate the problem of modeling threats to positive face. First we discuss how prior work that has focused primarily on mitigating threats to negative face, and examine a specific example, taken from the human subject data of (Gupta et al., 2007), to show why accounting for positive face is necessary. Next, we discuss our proposed solution to begin to model threats to positive face– specifically, integrating a computational model of blame. Finally, we discuss the justification behind and limitations of this proposed approach.

2 Motivation

Brown and Levinson (1987) articulated a taxonomy of politeness strategies, distinguishing broadly between the notion of positive and negative politeness (with many distinct strategies for each). These categories of politeness correspond

[1]Less crucially, what is the appropriate notation for this value? It is denoted differently in each paper: Θ, W, and η.

Proceedings of the INLG and SIGDIAL 2014 Joint Session, pages 157–161,
Philadelphia, Pennsylvania, 19 June 2014.

to the concepts of positive and negative face, respectively. An example of a positive politeness strategy is the use of praise ("Great!"), whereas a common negative politeness strategy is the use of an *indirect speech act* (ISA), in particular, an indirect request. An example of an indirect request is the question, "Could you get me a coffee?", which avoids the autonomy-threatening direct imperative, while still potentially being construed as a request. This is an example of a conventionalized form, in which the implied request is more directly associated with the implicit form. Often considered even less of a threat to negative face are unconventionalized ISAs, which often require a deeper chain of inference to derive their implied meaning. It is primarily the modulation of the level of request indirectness that is the focus of (Gupta et al., 2007; Briggs and Scheutz, 2013).

To provide an empirical evaluation of their system, Gupta et al. (2007) asked human subjects to rate the politeness of generated requests on a five-point Likert scale in order of most rude (1) to to most polite (5). The results from (Gupta et al., 2007) for each of their politeness strategy categories are below:

1. Autonomy [3.4] (e.g. "Could you possibly do X for me?")

2. Approval [3.0] (e.g. "Could you please do X mate?")

3. Direct [2.0] (e.g. "Do X.")

4. Indirect [1.8] (e.g. "X is not done yet.")

This finding is, in some sense, counterintuitive, as unconventionalized request forms should be the least face-threatening. However, Gupta et al. (2007) briefly often an explanation, saying that the utterances generated in the indirect category sound a bit like a "complaint or sarcasm." We agree with this assessment. More precisely, while negative face is protected by the use of their unconventionalized ISAs, positive face was not.

To model whether or not utterances may be interpreted as being complaints or criticisms, we seek to determine whether or not they can be interpreted as an act of *blame*[2].

[2]What the precise ontological relationship is between concepts such as complaining, criticizing, and blaming is beyond the scope of this paper.

3 Approach

Like praise, blame (its negative counterpart) is both a cognitive and social phenomenon (Malle et al., 2012). The cognitive component pertains to the internal attitudes of an agent regarding another agent and their actions, while the social component involves the expression of these internal attitudes through communicative acts. To achieve blame-sensitivity in NLG, we need to model both these aspects. In the following sections, we briefly discuss how this could be accomplished.

3.1 Pragmatic and Belief Reasoning

Before a speaker S can determine the high-level perlocutionary effects of an utterance on an addressee (H) vis-á-vis whether or not they feel criticized or blamed, it is first necessary to determine the precise set of beliefs and intentions of the addressee upon hearing an utterance u in context c. We denote this updated set of beliefs and intentions $\Psi_H(u, c)$. Note that this set is a *model* of agent H's beliefs and intentions from the speaker S's perspective, and not necessarily equivalent to the actual belief state of agent H. In order to perform this mental modeling, we utilize a reasoning system similar to that in (Briggs and Scheutz, 2011). This pragmatic reasoning architecture utilizes a set of rules of the form:

$$[[U]]_C := \phi_1 \wedge ... \wedge \phi_n$$

where U denotes an utterance form, C denotes a set of contextual constraints that must hold, and ϕ denotes a belief update predicate. An utterance form is specified by $u = \mathit{UtteranceType}(\alpha, \beta, X, M)$, where $\mathit{UtteranceType}$ denotes the dialogue turn type (e.g. statement, y/n-question), α denotes the speaker of the utterance u, β denotes the addressee of the utterance, X denotes the surface semantics of the utterance, and M denotes a set of sentential modifiers. An example of such a pragmatic rule is found below:

$$[[\mathit{Stmt}(S, H, X, \{\})]]_\emptyset := \mathit{want}(S, \mathit{bel}(H, X))$$

which denotes that a statement by the speaker S to an addressee H that X holds should indicate that, "S wants H to believe X," in all contexts (given the empty set of contextual constraints). If this rule matches a recognized utterance (and the contextual constraints are satisfied, which is trivial in this case), then the mental model of the addressee is updated such that: $want(S, bel(H, X)) \in \Psi_H(u, c)$.

Of particular interest with regard to the Gupta et al. (2007) results, Briggs and Scheutz (2011) describe how they can use their system to understand the semantics of the adverbial modifier "yet," which they describe as being indicative of mutually understood intentionality. More accurately, "yet," is likely indicative of a belief regarding *expectation* of an action being performed or state being achieved. Therefore, a plausible pragmatic rule to interpret, "X is not done yet," could be:

$$[[Stmt(S, H, \neg done(X), \{yet\})]]_{\emptyset} := want(S, bel(H, \neg done(X))) \wedge expects(S, done(X))$$

Furthermore, in a cooperative, task-driven context, such as that described in (Gupta et al., 2007), it would not be surprising for an interactant to infer that this expectation is further indicative of a belief in a particular intention or a task-based obligation to achieve X.[3]

As such, if we consider an utterance u_d as being a standard direct request form (strategy 3), and an utterance u_y as being an indirect construction with a yet modifier (strategy 4), the following facts may hold:

$$bel(S, promised(H, S, X, t_p)) \notin \Psi_H(u_d, c)$$

$$bel(S, promised(H, S, X, t_p)) \in \Psi_H(u_y, c)$$

If S is making a request to H, there is no believed agreement to achieve X. However, if "yet," is utilized, this may indicate to H a belief that S thinks there is such an agreement.

Having calculated an updated mental model of the addressee's beliefs after hearing a candidate utterance u, we now can attempt to infer the degree to which u is interpreted as an act of criticism or blame.

3.2 Blame Modeling

Attributions of blame are influenced by several factors including, but not limited to, beliefs about an agent's intentionality, capacity, foreknowledge, obligations, and possible justifications (Malle et al., 2012). Given the centrality of intentionality in blame attribution, it is unsurprising that current computational models involve reasoning within a symbolic BDI (belief, desire, intention) framework, utilizing rules to infer an ordinal degree of blame based on the precise set of facts regarding these factors (Mao and Gratch, 2012; Tomai and Forbus, 2007). A rule that is similar to those found in these systems is:

$$bel(S, promised(H, S, X, t_p)) \wedge bel(S, \neg X) \wedge bel(S, (t > t_p)) \wedge bel(S, capable\_of(H, X)) \Rightarrow blames(S, H, high)$$

that is to say, if agent S believes agent H promised to him or her to achieve X by time t_p, and S believes X has not been achieved and the current time t is past t_p, and S believes H is capable of fulfilling this promise, then S will blame H to a high degree. Continuing our discussion regarding the perlocutionary effects of u_d and u_y, it is likely then that: $blames(S, H, high) \notin \Psi_H(u_d, c)$ and $blames(S, H, high) \in \Psi_H(u_y, c)$.

3.3 FTA Modeling

Having determined whether or not an addressee would feel criticized or blamed by a particular candidate utterance, it is then necessary to translate this assessment back into the terms of FTA-degree (the currency of the NLG system). This requires a function $\beta(\Psi)$ that maps the ordinal blame assessment of the speaker toward the hearer based on a set of beliefs Ψ, described in the previous section, to a numerical value than can be utilized to calculate the severity of the FTA (e.g. $blames(S, H, high) = 9.0$, $blames(S, H, medium) = 4.5$). For the purposes of this paper we adopt the theta-notation of Gupta et al. (2007) to denote the degree to which an utterance is a FTA. With the β function, we can then express the blame-related FTA severity of an utterance as:

$$\Theta_{blame}(u, c) = \beta_H(\Psi_H(u, c)) - \alpha(c) \cdot \beta_S(\Psi_S)$$

where β_H denotes the level of blame the speaker believes the hearer has inferred based on the addressee's belief state after hearing utterance u with context c ($\Psi_H(u, c)$)). β_S denotes the level of blame the speaker believes is appropriate given his or her current belief state. Finally, $\alpha(c)$ denotes a

[3] How precisely this reasoning is and/or ought to be performed is an important question, but is outside the scope of this paper.

multiplicative factor that models the appropriateness of blame given the current social context. For instance, independent of the objective blameworthiness of a superior, it may be inappropriate for a subordinate to criticize his or her superior in certain contexts.

Finally, then, the degree to which an utterance is a FTA is the sum of all the contributions of evaluations of possible threats to positive face and possible threats to negative face:

$$\Theta(u, c) = \sum_{p \in P} \Theta_p(u, c) + \sum_{n \in N} \Theta_n(u, c)$$

where P denotes the set of all possible threats to positive face (e.g. blame) and N denotes the set of all possible threats to negative face (e.g. directness).

We can see how this would account for the human-subject results from (Gupta et al., 2007), as conventionally indirect requests (strategies 1 and 2) would not produce large threat-value contributions from either the positive or negative FTA components. Direct requests (strategy 3) would, however, potentially produce a large Θ_N contribution, while their set of indirect requests (strategy 4) would trigger a large Θ_P contribution.

4 Discussion

Having presented an approach to avoid certain types of positive-FTAs through reasoning about blame, one may be inclined to ask some questions regarding the justification behind this approach. Why should we want to better model one highly complex social phenomenon (politeness) through the inclusion of a model of another highly complex social phenomenon (blame)? Does the integration of a computational model of blame actually add anything that would justify the effort?

At a superficial level, it does not. The criticism/blame-related threat of a specific speech act can be implicitly factored into the base FTA-degree evaluation function supplied to the system, determined by empirical data or designer-consensus as is the case of (Miller et al., 2008). However, this approach is limited in a couple ways. First, this does not account for the fact that, in addition to the set of social factors Brown and Levinson articulated, the appropriateness of an act of criticism or blame is also dependent on whether or not it is *justified*. Reasoning about whether or not an act of blame is justified requires: a computational model of blame.

Second, the inclusion of blame-reasoning within the larger scope of the entire agent architecture may enable useful behaviors both inside and outside the natural language system. There is a growing community of researchers interested in developing ethical-reasoning capabilities for autonomous agents (Wallach and Allen, 2008), and the ability to reason about blame has been proposed as one key competency for such an ethically-sensitive agent (Bello and Bringsjord, 2013). Not only is there interest in utilizing such mechanisms to influence general action-selection in autonomous agents, but there is also interest in the ability to understand and generate valid explanations and justifications for adopted courses of action in ethically-charged scenarios, which is of direct relevance to the design of NLG architectures.

While our proposed solution tackles threats to positive face that arise due to unduly critical/blame-oriented utterances, there are many different ways of threatening positive face aside from criticism/blame. These include phenomena such as the discussion of inappropriate/sensitive topics or non-cooperative behavior (e.g. purposefully ignoring an interlocutor's dialogue contribution). Indeed, empirical results show that referring to an interlocutor in a dyadic interaction using an impersonal pronoun (e.g. "someone") may constitute another such positive face threat (De Jong et al., 2008). Future work will need to be done to develop mechanisms to address these other possible threats to positive face.

5 Conclusion

Enabling politeness in NLG is a challenging problem that requires the modeling of a host of complex, social psychological factors. In this paper, we discuss ongoing work to integrate a computational model of blame to prevent inappropriate threats to positive face that can account for prior human-subject data. As an ongoing project, future work is needed to further test and evaluate this proposed approach.

Acknowledgments

We would like to thank the reviewers for their helpful feedback. This work was supported by NSF grant #111323.

References

Paul Bello and Selmer Bringsjord. 2013. On how to build a moral machine. *Topoi*, 32(2):251–266.

Gordon Briggs and Matthias Scheutz. 2011. Facilitating mental modeling in collaborative human-robot interaction through adverbial cues. In *Proceedings of the SIGDIAL 2011 Conference*, pages 239–247, Portland, Oregon, June. Association for Computational Linguistics.

Gordon Briggs and Matthias Scheutz. 2013. A hybrid architectural approach to understanding and appropriately generating indirect speech acts. In *Proceedings of the 27th AAAI Conference on Artificial Intelligence*.

Penelope Brown and Stephen C. Levinson. 1987. *Politeness: Some universals in language usage*. Cambridge University Press.

Justine Cassell and Timothy Bickmore. 2003. Negotiated collusion: Modeling social language and its relationship effects in intelligent agents. *User Modeling and User-Adapted Interaction*, 13(1-2):89–132.

Markus De Jong, Mariët Theune, and Dennis Hofs. 2008. Politeness and alignment in dialogues with a virtual guide. In *Proceedings of the 7th international joint conference on Autonomous agents and multiagent systems-Volume 1*, pages 207–214. International Foundation for Autonomous Agents and Multiagent Systems.

Swati Gupta, Marilyn A Walker, and Daniela M Romano. 2007. How rude are you?: Evaluating politeness and affect in interaction. In *Affective Computing and Intelligent Interaction*, pages 203–217. Springer.

Bertram F Malle, Steve Guglielmo, and Andrew E Monroe. 2012. Moral, cognitive, and social: The nature of blame. *Social thinking and interpersonal behavior*, 14:313.

Wenji Mao and Jonathan Gratch. 2012. Modeling social causality and responsibility judgment in multiagent interactions. *Journal of Artificial Intelligence Research*, 44(1):223–273.

Christopher A Miller, Peggy Wu, and Harry B Funk. 2008. A computational approach to etiquette: Operationalizing brown and levinson's politeness model. *Intelligent Systems, IEEE*, 23(4):28–35.

Megan Strait, Cody Canning, and Matthias Scheutz. 2014. Let me tell you! investigating the effects of robot communication strategies in advice-giving situations based on robot appearance, interaction modality and distance. In *Proceedings of the 2014 ACM/IEEE international conference on Human-robot interaction*, pages 479–486. ACM.

Emmett Tomai and Ken Forbus. 2007. Plenty of blame to go around: a qualitative approach to attribution of moral responsibility. Technical report, DTIC Document.

Cristen Torrey, Susan R Fussell, and Sara Kiesler. 2013. How a robot should give advice. In *Human-Robot Interaction (HRI), 2013 8th ACM/IEEE International Conference on*, pages 275–282. IEEE.

Wendell Wallach and Colin Allen. 2008. *Moral machines: Teaching robots right from wrong*. Oxford University Press.

Generating effective referring expressions using charts

Nikos Engonopoulos and **Alexander Koller**
University of Potsdam, Germany
{engonopo|akoller}@uni-potsdam.de

Abstract

We present a novel approach for generating effective referring expressions (REs). We define a synchronous grammar formalism that relates surface strings with the sets of objects they describe through an abstract syntactic structure. The grammars may choose to require or not that REs are distinguishing. We then show how to compute a chart that represents, in finite space, the complete (possibly infinite) set of valid REs for a target object. Finally, we propose a probability model that predicts how the listener will understand the RE, and show how to compute the most effective RE according to this model from the chart.

1 Introduction

The fundamental challenge in the generation of referring expressions (REG) is to compute an RE which is effective, i.e. understood as intended by the listener. Throughout the history of REG, we have approximated this as the problem of generating *distinguishing* REs, i.e. REs that are only satisfied by a unique individual in the domain. This has been an eminently successful approach, as documented e.g. in the overview article of Krahmer and van Deemter (2012) and a variety of recent shared tasks involving RE generation (Gatt and Belz, 2010; Belz et al., 2008; Koller et al., 2010).

Nonetheless, reducing effectiveness to uniqueness is limiting in several ways. First, in complex, real-world scenes it may not be feasible to generate fully distinguishing REs, or these may have to be exceedingly complicated. It is also not necessary to generate distinguishing REs in such situations, because listeners are very capable of taking the discourse and task context into account to resolve even ambiguous REs. Conversely, listeners can misunderstand even a distinguishing RE, so uniqueness is no guarantee for success. We propose instead to define and train a probabilistic RE resolution model $P(a|t)$, which directly captures the probability that the listener will resolve a given RE t to some object a in the domain. An RE t will then be "good enough" if $P(a^*|t)$ is very high for the intended target referent a^*.

Second, in an interactive setting like the GIVE Challenge (Koller et al., 2010), the listener may behave in a way that offers further information on how they resolved the generated RE. Engonopoulos et al. (2013) showed how an initial estimate of the distribution $P(a|t)$ can be continuously updated based on the listener's behavior, and that this can improve a system's ability to detect misunderstandings. It seems hard to achieve this in a principled way without an explicit model of $P(a|t)$.

In this paper, we present an algorithm that generates the RE t that maximizes $P(a^*|t)$, i.e. the RE that has the highest chance to be understood correctly by the listener according to the probabilistic RE resolution model. This is a challenging problem, since the algorithm must identify that RE from a potentially infinite set of valid alternatives. We achieve this by using a *chart-based* algorithm, a standard approach in parsing and realization, which has (to our knowledge) never been used in REG.

We start by defining a synchronous grammar formalism that relates surface strings to their interpretations as sets of objects in a given domain (Section 3). This formalism integrates REG with surface realization, and allows us to specify in the grammar whether REs are required to be distinguishing. We then show how to compute a chart for a given grammar and target referent in Section 4. Section 5 defines a log-linear model for $P(a|t)$, and presents a Viterbi-style algorithm for computing the RE t from the chart that maximizes $P(a^*|t)$. Section 6 concludes by discussing how to apply our algorithm to the state-of-the-art approaches of Krahmer et al. (2003) and Golland et al. (2010), and how to address a particular challenge involving cycles that arises when dealing

Proceedings of the INLG and SIGDIAL 2014 Joint Session, pages 162–171,
Philadelphia, Pennsylvania, 19 June 2014. ©2014 Association for Computational Linguistics

with probabilistic listener models.

2 Related Work

RE generation is the task of generating a natural-language expression that identifies an object to the listener. Since the beginnings of modern REG (Appelt, 1985; Dale and Reiter, 1995), this problem has been approximated as generating a *distinguishing* description, i.e. one which fits only one object in the domain and not any of the others. This perspective has made it possible to apply search-based (Kelleher and Kruijff, 2006), logic-based (Areces et al., 2008) and graph-based (Krahmer et al., 2003) methods to the problem, and overall has been one of the success stories of NLG.

However, in practice, human speakers frequently *overspecify*, i.e. they include information in an RE beyond what is necessary to make it distinguishing (Wardlow Lane and Ferreira, 2008; Koolen et al., 2011). An NLG system, too, might include redundant information in an RE to make it easier to understand for the user. Conversely, an RE that is produced by a human can often be easily resolved by the listener even if it is ambiguous. Here we present an NLG system that directly uses a probabilistic model of RE resolution, and is capable of generating ambiguous REs if it predicts that the listener will understand them.

Most existing REG algorithms focus on generating distinguishing REs, and then select the one that is *best* according to some criterion, e.g. most human-like (Krahmer et al., 2003; FitzGerald et al., 2013) or most likely to be understood (Garoufi and Koller, 2013). By contrast, Mitchell et al. (2013) describe a stochastic algorithm that computes human-like, non-relational REs that may not be distinguishing. Golland et al. (2010) are close to our proposal in spirit, in that they use a log-linear probability model of RE resolution to compute a possibly non-distinguishing RE. However, they use a trivial REG algorithm which is limited to grammars that only permit a (small) finite set of REs for each referent. This is in contrast to general REG, where there is typically an infinite set of valid REs, especially when relational REs ("the button *to the left of* the plant") are permitted.

Engonopoulos et al. (2013) describe how to update an estimate for $P(a|t)$ based on a log-linear model based on observations of the listener's behavior. They use a shallow model based on a string t and not an RE derived from a grammar, and they do not discuss how to generate the best t. The algorithm we develop here fills this gap.

Our formalism for REG can be seen as a *synchronous* grammar formalism; it simultaneously derives strings and their interpretations, connecting the two by an abstract syntactic representation. This allows performing REG and surface realization with a single algorithm, along the lines of SPUD (Stone et al., 2003) and its planning-based implementation, CRISP (Koller and Stone, 2007). Probabilistic synchronous grammars are widely used in statistical machine translation (Chiang, 2007; Graehl et al., 2008; Jones et al., 2012) and semantic parsing (Zettlemoyer and Collins, 2005; Wong and Mooney, 2007). Lu and Ng (2011) have applied such grammars to surface realization. Konstas and Lapata (2012) use related techniques for content selection and surface realization (with simple, non-recursive grammars).

Charts are standard tools for representing a large space of possible linguistic analyses compactly. Next to their use in parsing, they have also been applied to surface realization (Kay, 1996; Carroll et al., 1999; Kaplan and Wedekind, 2000). To our knowledge, ours is the first work using charts for REG. This is challenging because the input to REG is much less structured than in parsing or realization.

3 Grammars for RE generation

We define a new grammar formalism that we use for REG, which we call *semantically intepreted grammar* (SIG). SIG is a synchronous grammar formalism that relates natural language strings with the sets of objects in a given domain which they describe. It uses *regular tree grammars (RTGs)* to describe languages of *derivation trees*, which then project to strings and sets.

3.1 Derivation trees

We describe the abstract syntax of an RE by its *derivation tree*, which is a tree over some ranked signature Σ of symbols representing lexicon entries and grammatical constructions. A *(ranked) signature* is a finite set of symbols $r \in \Sigma$, each of which is assigned an *arity* $\mathsf{ar}(r) \in \mathbb{N}_0$. A tree over the signature Σ is a term $r(t_1, \ldots, t_n)$, where $r \in \Sigma$, $n = \mathsf{ar}(r)$, and $t_1, \ldots, t_n$ are trees over Σ. We write T_Σ for the set of all trees over Σ.

Fig. 1b shows an example derivation tree for the RE "the square button" over the signature $\Sigma = \{\mathit{def}|_1, \mathit{square}|_1, \mathit{button}|_0\}$, where $r|_n$ indicates that the symbol r has arity n. In term nota-

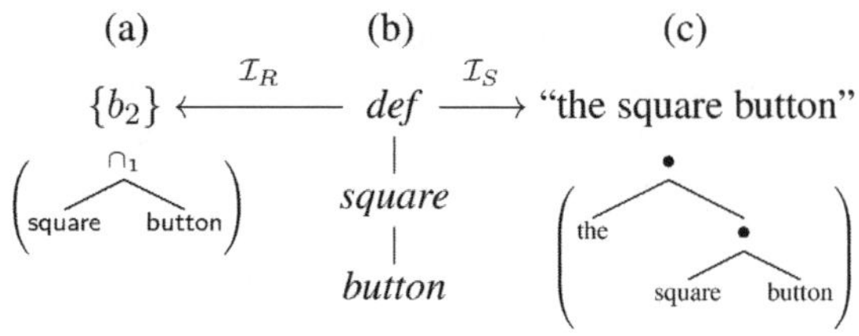

Figure 1: A SIG derivation tree (b) with its interpretations (a, c).

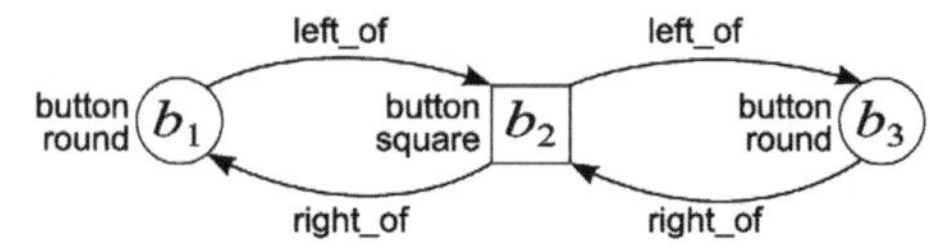

$U = \{b_1, b_2, b_3\}$ button $= \{b_1, b_2, b_3\}$
round $= \{b_1, b_3\}$ square $= \{b_2\}$
left_of $= \{\langle b_1, b_2\rangle, \langle b_2, b_3\rangle\}$
right_of $= \{\langle b_2, b_1\rangle, \langle b_3, b_2\rangle\}$

Figure 2: A simple model, illustrated as a graph.

tion, it is *def*(*square*(*button*)).

String interpretation. We *interpret* derivation trees simultaneously as strings and sets. First, let Δ be a finite alphabet, and let Δ^* be the string algebra over Δ. We define a *string interpretation* over Δ as a function $\mathcal{I}_S$ that maps each $r|_n \in \Sigma$ to a function $\mathcal{I}_S(r) : (\Delta^*)^n \to \Delta^*$. For instance, we can assign string interpretations to our example signature Σ as follows; we write $w_1 \bullet w_2$ for the concatenation of the strings w_1 and w_2.

$$\begin{aligned} \mathcal{I}_S(\textit{def})(w_1) &= \text{the} \bullet w_1 \\ \mathcal{I}_S(\textit{square})(w_1) &= \text{square} \bullet w_1 \\ \mathcal{I}_S(\textit{button}) &= \text{button} \end{aligned}$$

Since the arity of $\mathcal{I}_S(r)$ is the same as the arity of r for any $r \in \Sigma$, we can use $\mathcal{I}_S$ to recursively map derivation trees to strings. Starting at the leaves, we map the tree $r(t_1, \ldots, t_n)$ to the string $\mathcal{I}_S(r)(\mathcal{I}_S(t_1), \ldots, \mathcal{I}_S(t_n))$, where $\mathcal{I}_S(t_i)$ is the string that results from recursively applying $\mathcal{I}_S$ to the subtree t_i. In the example, the subtree *button* is mapped to the string "button". We then get the string for the subtree *square*(*button*) by concatenating this with "square", obtaining the string "square button" and so on, as shown in Fig. 1c.

Relational interpretation. We further define a *relational interpretation* $\mathcal{I}_R$, which maps each $r|_n \in \Sigma$ to a function $\mathcal{I}_R(r) : R(U)^n \to R(U)$, where $R(U)$ is a class of *relations*. We define $\mathcal{I}_R$ over some first-order *model* structure $M = \langle U, L\rangle$, where U is a finite *universe* U of individuals and L interprets a finite set of predicate symbols as relations over U. We let $R(U)$ be the set of all k-place relations over U for all $k \geq 0$. The subsets of U are the special case of $k = 1$. We write $k(R)$ for the arity of a relation $R \in R(U)$.

For the purposes of this paper, we construct $\mathcal{I}_R$ by combining the following operations:

- The denotations of the atomic predicate symbols of M; see Fig. 2 for an example.
- $\mathsf{proj}_i(R) = \{a_i \mid \langle a_1, \ldots, a_{k(R)}\rangle \in R\}$ is the projection to the i-th component; if $i > k(R)$, it evaluates to $\emptyset$.
- $R_1 \cap_i R_2 = \{\langle a_1, \ldots, a_{k(R_1)}\rangle \in R_1 \mid a_i \in R_2\}$ is the intersection on the i-th component of R_1; if $i > k(R_1)$, it evaluates to $\emptyset$.
- For any $a \in U$, $\mathsf{uniq}_a(R)$ evaluates to $\{a\}$ if $R = \{a\}$, and to $\emptyset$ otherwise.
- For any $a \in U$, $\mathsf{member}_a(R)$ evaluates to $\{a\}$ if $a \in R$, and to $\emptyset$ otherwise.

For the example, we assume that we want to generate REs over the scene shown in Fig. 2; it consists of the universe $U = \{b_1, b_2, b_3\}$ and interprets the atomic predicate symbols button, square, round, left_of, and right_of. Given this, we can assign a relational interpretation to the derivation tree in Fig. 1b using the following mappings:

$$\begin{aligned} \mathcal{I}_R(\textit{def})(R_1) &= R_1 \\ \mathcal{I}_R(\textit{square})(R_1) &= \mathsf{square} \cap_1 R_1 \\ \mathcal{I}_R(\textit{button}) &= \mathsf{button} \end{aligned}$$

We evaluate a derivation tree to a relation as we did for strings (cf. Fig. 1a). The subtree *button* maps to the denotation of the symbol button, i.e. $\{b_1, b_2, b_3\}$. The subtree *square*(*button*) evaluates to the intersection of this set with the set of square individuals, i.e. $\{b_2\}$; this is also the relational interpretation of the entire derivation tree. We thus see that "the square button" is an RE that describes the individual b_2 uniquely.

3.2 Semantically interpreted grammars

Now we define grammars that describe relations between strings and relations over U. We achieve this by combining a *regular tree grammar* (RTG, (Gécseg and Steinby, 1997; Comon et al., 2007)), describing a language of derivation trees, with a string interpretation and a relational interpretation. An RTG $G = (N, \Sigma, S, P)$ consists of a finite set N of nonterminal symbols, a ranked signature Σ, a start symbol $S \in N$, and a finite set P of production rules $A \to r(B_1, ..., B_n)$, where

$A, B_1, \ldots, B_n \in N$ and $r|_n \in \Sigma$. We say that a tree $t_2 \in T_\Sigma$ can be *derived in one step* from $t_1 \in T_\Sigma$, $t_1 \Rightarrow t_2$, if it can be obtained by replacing an occurrence of B in t_1 with t and P contains the rule $B \rightarrow t$. A tree $t_n \in T_\Sigma$ can be *derived* from t_1, $t_1 \Rightarrow^* t_n$, if there is a sequence $t_1 \Rightarrow \ldots \Rightarrow t_n$ of length $n \geq 0$. For any nonterminal A, we write $L_A(G)$ for the set of trees $t \in T_\Sigma$ with $A \Rightarrow^* t$. We simply write $L(G)$ for $L_S(G)$ and call it the *language* of G.

We define a *semantically interpreted grammar* (SIG) as a triple $\mathcal{G} = (G, \mathcal{I}_S, \mathcal{I}_R)$ of an RTG G over some signature Σ, together with a string interpretation $\mathcal{I}_S$ over some alphabet Δ and a relational interpretation $\mathcal{I}_R$ over some universe U, both of which interpret the symbols in Σ. We assume that every terminal symbol $r \in \Sigma$ occurs in at most one rule, and that the nonterminals of G are pairs A_b of a syntactic category A and a *semantic index* $b = \mathsf{ix}(A_b)$. A semantic index indicates the individual in U to which a given constituent is meant to refer, see e.g. (Kay, 1996; Stone et al., 2003). Note that SIGs can be seen as specific Interpreted Regular Tree Grammars (Koller and Kuhlmann, 2011) with a set and a string interpretation.

We ignore the start symbol of G. Instead, we say that given some individual $b \in U$ and syntactic category A, the set of *referring expressions* for b is $\mathsf{RE}_\mathcal{G}(A, b) = \{t \in L_{A_b}(G) \mid \mathcal{I}_R(t) = \{b\}\}$, i.e. we define an RE as a derivation tree that G can derive from A_b and whose relational interpretation is $\{b\}$. From t, we can read off the string $\mathcal{I}_S(t)$.[1]

3.3 An example grammar

Consider the SIG $\mathcal{G}$ in Fig. 3 for example. The grammar is written in template form. Each rule is instantiated for all semantic indices specified in the line above; e.g. the symbol round denotes the set $\{b_1, b_3\}$, therefore there are rules $N_{b_1} \rightarrow$ $round_{b_1}(N_{b_1})$ and $N_{b_3} \rightarrow round_{b_3}(N_{b_3})$. The values of $\mathcal{I}_R$ and $\mathcal{I}_S$ for each symbol are specified below the RTG rule for that symbol.

We can use $\mathcal{G}$ to generate NPs that refer to the target referent b_2 given the model shown in Fig. 2 by finding trees in $L_{\mathrm{NP}_{b_2}}(G)$ that refer to $\{b_2\}$. One such tree is $t_1 = def_{b_2}(square_{b_2}(button_{b_2}))$, a more detailed version of the tree in Fig. 1b. It can be derived by $\mathrm{NP}_{b_2} \Rightarrow def_{b_2}(\mathrm{N}_{b_2}) \Rightarrow def_{b_2}(square_{b_2}(\mathrm{N}_{b_2})) \Rightarrow t_1$. Because $\mathcal{I}_R(t_1) = \{b_2\}$, we see that $t_1 \in \mathsf{RE}_\mathcal{G}(\mathrm{NP}, b_2)$; it represents the string $\mathcal{I}_S(t_1) =$ "the square button".

$$
\begin{array}{l}
\text{for all } a \in U\text{:}\\
\mathrm{NP}_a \rightarrow def_a(\mathrm{N}_a)\\
\mathcal{I}_S(def_a)(w_1) = \text{the} \bullet w_1\\
\mathcal{I}_R(def_a)(R_1) = \mathsf{member}_a(R_1)\\[1ex]
\text{for all } a \in \mathsf{button}\text{:}\\
\mathrm{N}_a \rightarrow button_a\\
\mathcal{I}_S(button_a) = \text{button}\\
\mathcal{I}_R(button_a) = \mathsf{button}\\[1ex]
\text{for all } a \in \mathsf{round}\text{:}\\
\mathrm{N}_a \rightarrow round_a(\mathrm{N}_a)\\
\mathcal{I}_S(round_a)(w_1) = \text{round} \bullet w_1\\
\mathcal{I}_R(round_a)(R_1) = \mathsf{round} \cap_1 R_1\\[1ex]
\text{for all } a \in \mathsf{square}\text{:}\\
\mathrm{N}_a \rightarrow square_a(\mathrm{N}_a)\\
\mathcal{I}_S(square_a)(w_1) = \text{square} \bullet w_1\\
\mathcal{I}_R(square_a)(R_1) = \mathsf{square} \cap_1 R_1\\[1ex]
\text{for all } a, b \in \mathsf{left\_of}\text{:}\\
\mathrm{N}_a \rightarrow leftof_{a,b}(\mathrm{N}_a, \mathrm{NP}_b)\\
\mathcal{I}_S(leftof_{a,b})(w_1, w_2) = w_1 \bullet \text{to} \bullet \text{the} \bullet \text{left} \bullet \text{of} \bullet w_2\\
\mathcal{I}_R(leftof_{a,b})(R_1, R_2) = \mathsf{proj}_1((\mathsf{left\_of} \cap_1 R_1) \cap_2 R_2)\\[1ex]
\text{for all } a, b \in \mathsf{right\_of}\text{:}\\
\mathrm{N}_a \rightarrow rightof_{a,b}(\mathrm{N}_a, \mathrm{NP}_b)\\
\mathcal{I}_S(rightof_{a,b})(w_1, w_2) = w_1 \bullet \text{to} \bullet \text{the} \bullet \text{right} \bullet \text{of} \bullet w_2\\
\mathcal{I}_R(rightof_{a,b})(R_1, R_2) = \mathsf{proj}_1((\mathsf{right\_of} \cap_1 R_1) \cap_2 R_2)
\end{array}
$$

Figure 3: An example SIG grammar.

A second derivation tree for b_2 is $t_2 = def_{b_2}(square_{b_2}(square_{b_2}(button_{b_2})))$, corresponding to $\mathcal{I}_S(t_2) =$ "the square square button". It derives from NP_{b_2} in four steps, and has $\mathcal{I}_R(t_2) = \{b_2\}$. Even the small grammar $\mathcal{G}$ licences an infinite set of REs for b_2, all of which are semantically correct. Avoiding the generation of nonsensical REs like "the square square button" is a technical challenge to which we will return in Section 6. $\mathcal{G}$ can also derive relational REs; for instance, the derivation tree in Fig. 6 for the string "the button to the left of the square button" is in $\mathsf{RE}_\mathcal{G}(\mathrm{NP}, b_1)$.

Finally, $\mathcal{G}$ considers the non-distinguishing $t_3 = def_{b_2}(button_{b_2})$ (for "the button") a valid RE for b_2. This is because member_{b_2} will quietly project the set $\{b_1, b_2, b_3\}$ (to which $button_{b_2}$ refers) to $\{b_2\}$. As discussed in previous sections, we want to allow such non-unique REs and delegate the judgment about their quality to the probability model. It would still be straightforward, however, to impose a hard uniqueness constraint, by simply changing $\mathcal{I}_R(def_a)(R_1)$ to $\mathsf{uniq}_a(R_1)$ in Fig. 3. This would yield $\mathcal{I}_R(t_3) = \emptyset$, i.e. t_3 would no longer be in $\mathsf{RE}_\mathcal{G}(\mathrm{NP}, b_2)$.

4 Chart-based RE generation

We now present a chart-based algorithm for generating REs with SIG grammars. Charts allow us to represent all REs for a target referent compactly, and can be computed efficiently. We show in Section 5 that charts also lend themselves well to computing the most effective RE.

[1] Below, we will often write the RE as a string when the derivation tree is clear.

$$
\begin{array}{l}
\mathrm{N}_{b_1}/\{b_1,b_2,b_3\} \rightarrow \textit{button}_{b_1} \\
\mathrm{N}_{b_2}/\{b_1,b_2,b_3\} \rightarrow \textit{button}_{b_2} \\
\mathrm{N}_{b_3}/\{b_1,b_2,b_3\} \rightarrow \textit{button}_{b_3} \\
\mathrm{N}_{b_1}/\{b_1,b_3\} \rightarrow \textit{round}_{b_1}(\mathrm{N}_{b_1}/\{b_1,b_2,b_3\}) \\
\mathrm{N}_{b_3}/\{b_1,b_3\} \rightarrow \textit{round}_{b_3}(\mathrm{N}_{b_3}/\{b_1,b_2,b_3\}) \\
\mathrm{N}_{b_1}/\{b_1,b_3\} \rightarrow \textit{round}_{b_1}(\mathrm{N}_{b_1}/\{b_1,b_3\}) \\
\mathrm{N}_{b_3}/\{b_1,b_3\} \rightarrow \textit{round}_{b_3}(\mathrm{N}_{b_3}/\{b_1,b_3\}) \\
\mathrm{N}_{b_2}/\{b_2\} \rightarrow \textit{square}_{b_2}(\mathrm{N}_{b_2}/\{b_1,b_2,b_3\}) \\
\mathrm{N}_{b_2}/\{b_2\} \rightarrow \textit{square}_{b_2}(\mathrm{N}_{b_2}/\{b_2\}) \\
\mathrm{NP}_{b_2}/\{b_2\} \rightarrow \textit{def}_{b_2}(\mathrm{N}_{b_2}/\{b_1,b_2,b_3\}) \\
\mathrm{NP}_{b_2}/\{b_2\} \rightarrow \textit{def}_{b_2}(\mathrm{N}_{b_2}/\{b_2\}) \\
\mathrm{N}_{b_1}/\{b_1\} \rightarrow \textit{leftof}_{b_1,b_2}(\mathrm{N}_{b_1}/\{b_1,b_2,b_3\},\mathrm{NP}_{b_2}/\{b_2\}) \\
\mathrm{N}_{b_1}/\{b_1\} \rightarrow \textit{leftof}_{b_1,b_2}(\mathrm{N}_{b_1}/\{b_1,b_3\},\mathrm{NP}_{b_2}/\{b_2\}) \\
\mathrm{N}_{b_1}/\{b_1\} \rightarrow \textit{leftof}_{b_1,b_2}(\mathrm{N}_{b_1}/\{b_1\},\mathrm{NP}_{b_2}/\{b_2\}) \\
\mathrm{N}_{b_1}/\{b_1\} \rightarrow \textit{round}_{b_1}(\mathrm{N}_{b_1}/\{b_1\}) \\
\mathrm{NP}_{b_1}/\{b_1\} \rightarrow \textit{def}_{b_1}(\mathrm{N}_{b_1}/\{b_1,b_2,b_3\}) \\
\mathrm{NP}_{b_1}/\{b_1\} \rightarrow \textit{def}_{b_1}(\mathrm{N}_{b_1}/\{b_1,b_3\}) \\
\mathrm{NP}_{b_1}/\{b_1\} \rightarrow \textit{def}_{b_1}(\mathrm{N}_{b_1}/\{b_1\}) \\
\mathrm{N}_{b_3}/\{b_3\} \rightarrow \textit{rightof}_{b_3,b_2}(\mathrm{N}_{b_3}/\{b_1,b_2,b_3\},\mathrm{NP}_{b_2}/\{b_2\}) \\
\mathrm{N}_{b_3}/\{b_3\} \rightarrow \textit{rightof}_{b_3,b_2}(\mathrm{N}_{b_3}/\{b_1,b_3\},\mathrm{NP}_{b_2}/\{b_2\}) \\
\mathrm{N}_{b_3}/\{b_3\} \rightarrow \textit{rightof}_{b_3,b_2}(\mathrm{N}_{b_3}/\{b_3\},\mathrm{NP}_{b_2}/\{b_2\}) \\
\mathrm{N}_{b_3}/\{b_3\} \rightarrow \textit{round}_{b_3}(\mathrm{N}_{b_3}/\{b_3\}) \\
\mathrm{NP}_{b_3}/\{b_3\} \rightarrow \textit{def}_{b_3}(\mathrm{N}_{b_3}/\{b_1,b_2,b_3\}) \\
\mathrm{NP}_{b_3}/\{b_3\} \rightarrow \textit{def}_{b_3}(\mathrm{N}_{b_3}/\{b_1,b_3\}) \\
\mathrm{NP}_{b_3}/\{b_3\} \rightarrow \textit{def}_{b_3}(\mathrm{N}_{b_3}/\{b_3\}) \\
\mathrm{N}_{b_2}/\{b_2\} \rightarrow \textit{leftof}_{b_2,b_3}(\mathrm{N}_{b_2}/\{b_1,b_2,b_3\},\mathrm{NP}_{b_3}/\{b_3\}) \\
\mathrm{N}_{b_2}/\{b_2\} \rightarrow \textit{rightof}_{b_2,b_1}(\mathrm{N}_{b_2}/\{b_1,b_2,b_3\},\mathrm{NP}_{b_1}/\{b_1\}) \\
\mathrm{N}_{b_2}/\{b_2\} \rightarrow \textit{leftof}_{b_2,b_3}(\mathrm{N}_{b_2}/\{b_2\},\mathrm{NP}_{b_3}/\{b_3\}) \\
\mathrm{N}_{b_2}/\{b_2\} \rightarrow \textit{rightof}_{b_2,b_1}(\mathrm{N}_{b_2}/\{b_2\},\mathrm{NP}_{b_1}/\{b_1\})
\end{array}
$$

Figure 4: The chart for the grammar in Fig. 3.

4.1 RE generation charts

Generally speaking, a chart is a packed data structure which describes how larger syntactic representations can be recursively built from smaller ones. In applications such as parsing and surface realization, the creation of a chart is driven by the idea that we consume some input (words or semantic atoms) as we build up larger structures. The parallel to this intuition in REG is that "larger" chart entries are more precise descriptions of the target, which is a weaker constraint than input consumption. Nonetheless, we can define REG charts whose entries are packed representations for large sets of possible REs, and compute them in terms of these entries instead of RE sets.

Technically, we represent charts as RTGs over an extended set of nonterminals. A chart for generating an RE of syntactic category A for an individual $b \in U$ is an RTG $C = (N', \Sigma, S', P')$, where $N' \subseteq N \times R(U)$ and $S' = A_b/\{b\}$. Intuitively, the nonterminal $A_b/\{a_1, \dots, a_n\}$ expresses that we *intend* to generate an RE for b from A, but each RE that we can derive from the nonterminal *actually* denotes the referent set $\{a_1, \dots, a_n\}$.

A chart for the grammar in Fig. 3 is shown in Fig. 4. To generate an NP for b_2, we let its start symbol be $S' = \mathrm{NP}_{b_2}/\{b_2\}$. The rule $\mathrm{N}_{b_2}/\{b_1, b_2, b_3\} \rightarrow \textit{button}_{b_2}$ says that we can generate an RE t with $\mathcal{I}_R(t) = \{b_1, b_2, b_3\}$ from the nonterminal symbol N_{b_2} by expanding this symbol with the grammar rule $\mathrm{N}_{b_2} \rightarrow \textit{button}_{b_2}$. Similarly,

$$
\frac{\begin{array}{c} A \rightarrow r(B_1, ..., B_n) \text{ in } G \\ B_1' = B_1/R_1, ..., B_n' = B_n/R_n \text{ in } N' \end{array}}{\begin{array}{c} \text{Add } A' = A/\mathcal{I}_R(r)(R_1, ..., R_n) \text{ to } N' \\ \text{Add rule } A' \rightarrow r(B_1', ..., B_n') \text{ to } P' \end{array}}
$$

Figure 5: The chart computation algorithm.

the rule $\mathrm{N}_{b_2}/\{b_2\} \rightarrow \textit{square}_{b_2}(\mathrm{N}_{b_2}/\{b_1, b_2, b_3\})$ expresses that we can generate an RE with $\mathcal{I}_R(t) = \{b_2\}$ by expanding the nonterminal symbol N_{b_2} into $\textit{square}_{b_2}(t')$, where t' is any tree that the chart can generate from $\mathrm{N}_{b_2}/\{b_1, b_2, b_3\}$.

4.2 Computing a chart

Given a SIG $\mathcal{G}$, a syntactic category A, and a target referent b, we can compute a chart C for $\mathsf{RE}_{\mathcal{G}}(A, b)$ using the parsing schema in Fig. 5. The schema assumes that we have a rule $A \rightarrow r(B_1, \dots, B_n)$ in G; in addition, for each $1 \leq i \leq n$ it assumes that we have already added the nonterminal $B_i' = \mathrm{B}_i/R_i$ to the chart, indicating that there is a tree t_i with $B_i \Rightarrow^* t_i$ and $\mathcal{I}_R(t_i) = R_i$. Then we know that $t = r(t_1, \dots, t_n)$ can be derived from A and that $R' = \mathcal{I}_R(t) = \mathcal{I}_R(r)(R_1, \dots, R_n)$. We can therefore add the nonterminal $A' = A/R'$ and the production rule $A' \rightarrow r(B_1', \dots, B_n')$ to the chart; this rule can be used as the first step in a derivation of t from A'. We can optimize the algorithm by adding A' and the rule only if $R' \neq \emptyset$.

The algorithm terminates when it can add no more rules to the chart. Because U is finite, this always happens after a finite number of steps, even if there is an infinite set of REs. For instance, the chart in Fig. 4 describes an infinite language of REs, including "the square button", "the button to the left of the round button", "the button to the left of the button to the right of the square button", etc. Thus it represents relational REs that are nested arbitrarily deeply through a finite number of rules.

After termination, the chart contains all rules by which a nonterminal can be decomposed into other (productive) nonterminals. As a result, $L(C)$ contains exactly the REs for b of category A:

Theorem 1 *If C is a chart for the SIG $\mathcal{G}$, the syntactic category A, and the target referent b, then $L(C) = \mathsf{RE}_{\mathcal{G}}(A, b)$.*

5 Computing best referring expressions

The chart algorithm allows us to compactly represent *all* REs for the target referent. We now show how to compute the *best* RE from the chart. We present a novel probability model $P(b|t)$ for RE resolution, and take the "best" RE to be the

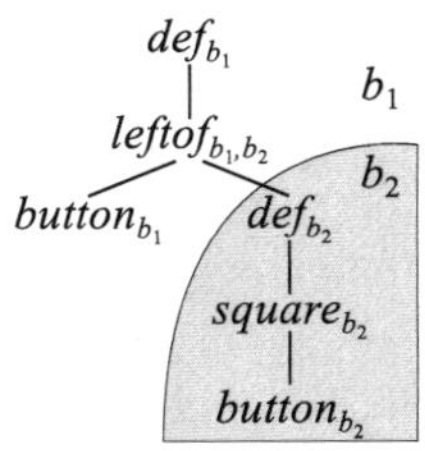

Figure 6: The derivation tree for "the button to the left of the square button".

one with the highest chance to be understood as intended. Next to the best RE itself, the algorithm also computes the entire distribution $P(b|t)$, to support later updates in an interactive setting.

Nothing in our algorithm hinges on this particular model; it can also be used with any other scoring model that satisfies a certain monotonicity condition which we spell out in Section 5.2.

5.1 A log-linear model for effective REs

We model the probability $P(b|t)$ that the listener will resolve the RE t to the object b using a log-linear model with a set of *feature functions* $f(a, t, M)$, where a is an object, t is a derivation tree, and M is the relational interpretation model.

We focus on features that only look at information that is local to a specific subtree of the RE, such as the label at the root. For instance, a feature $f_{round}(a, t', M)$ might return 1 if the root label of t' is $round_a$ and a is round in M, and 0 otherwise. Another feature $f_{def}(a, t', M)$ might return $1/k$ if t' is of the form $def_b(t'')$, $R = \mathcal{I}_R(t'')$ has k elements, and $a \in R$; and 0 otherwise. This feature counterbalances the ability of the grammar in Fig. 3 to say "the w" even when w is a non-unique description by penalizing descriptions with many possible referents through lower feature values.

When generating a relational RE, the derivation tree naturally splits into separate *regions*, each of which is meant to identify a specific object. These regions are distinguished by the semantic indices in the nonterminals that derive them; e.g., in Fig. 6, the subtree for "the square button" is an attempt to refer to b_2, whereas the RE as a whole is meant to refer to b_1. To find out how effective the RE is as a description of b_1, we evaluate the features at all nodes in the region $\mathsf{top}(t)$ containing the root of t.

Each feature function f_i is associated with a *weight* w_i. We obtain a *score tuple* $\mathsf{sc}(t')$ for some subtree t' of an RE as follows:

$$\mathsf{sc}(t') = \langle s(a_1, t', M), \ldots, s(a_m, t', M) \rangle,$$

t	b_1	b_2	b_3
"the button"	0.33	0.33	0.33
"the round button"	0.45	0.10	0.45
"the button to the left of the square button"	0.74	0.14	0.12

Figure 7: Probability distributions for some REs t.

where $U = \{a_1, \ldots, a_m\}$ and $s(a, t', M) = \sum_{i=1}^{n} w_i \cdot f_i(a, t', M)$. We then combine these into a score tuple $\mathsf{score}(t) = \sum_{u \in \mathsf{top}(t)} \mathsf{sc}(t.u)$ for the whole RE t, where $t.u$ is the subtree of t below the node u. Finally, given a score tuple $\mathrm{s} = \langle s_1, \ldots, s_m \rangle$ for t, we define the usual log-linear probability distribution as

$$P(a_i|t) = \mathsf{prob}(a_i, \mathrm{s}) = \frac{e^{s_i}}{\sum_{j=1}^{m} e^{s_j}}.$$

The *best* RE for the target referent b is then

$$\mathsf{best}_{\mathcal{G}}(A, b) = \underset{t \in \mathsf{RE}_{\mathcal{G}}(A,b)}{\arg\max}\ \mathsf{prob}(b, \mathsf{sc}(t)).$$

For illustration, we consider a number of REs for b_1 in our running example. We use f_{round} and f_{def} and let $w_{round} = w_{def} = 1$. In this case, the RE "the button" has a score tuple $\langle 1/3, 1/3, 1/3 \rangle$, which is the sum of the tuple $\langle 0, 0, 0 \rangle$ for f_{round} (since the RE does not use the "round" rule) and the tuple $\langle 1/3, 1/3, 1/3 \rangle$ for f_{def} (since "button" is three-way ambiguous in M). This yields a uniform probability distribution over U (see Fig. 7). By contrast, "the round button" gets $\langle 3/2, 0, 3/2 \rangle$, resulting in the distribution in the second line of Fig. 7. This RE is judged better than "the button" because it assigns a higher probability to b_1.

Relational REs involve derivation trees with multiple regions, only the top one of which is directly counted for $P(b|t)$ (see Fig. 6). We incorporate the quality of the other regions through appropriate features. In the example, we use a feature $f_{leftof}(a, t', M) = \sum_{b:\langle a,b \rangle \in \mathsf{left\_of}} P(b|t'')$, where t'' is the second subtree of t'. This feature computes the probability that the referent to which the listener resolves t'' is actually to the right of a, and will thus take a high value if t'' is a good RE for b_2. Assuming a probability distribution of $P(b_2|t') = 0.78$ and $P(b_1|t') = P(b_3|t') = 0.11$ for t' ="the square button", we get the tuple $\langle 0.78, 0.11, 0 \rangle$ for f_{leftof}, yielding the third line of Fig. 7 for $w_{leftof} = 1$.

5.2 Computing the best RE

We compute $\mathsf{best}_G(A, b)$ from the chart by adapting the Viterbi algorithm. Our key data structure assigns a score tuple $\mathbf{is}(A')$ to each nonterminal A' in the chart. Intuitively, if the semantic index of A' is b, then $\mathbf{is}(A')$ is the score tuple $\mathsf{sc}(t)$ for the tree $t \in L_{A'}(C)$ which maximizes $P(b|t)$. We also record this best tree as $\mathsf{bt}(A')$. Thus the algorithm is correct if, after running it, we obtain $\mathsf{best}_G(A, b) = \mathsf{bt}(\mathrm{A}_b/\{b\})$.

As is standard in chart algorithms, we limit our attention to features whose values can be computed bottom-up by local operations. Specifically, we assume that if $A' \to r(B'_1, \ldots, B'_n)$ is a rule in the chart and t_i is the best RE for B'_i for all i, then the best RE for A' that can be built using this rule is $r(t_1, \ldots, t_n)$. This means that features must be *monotonic*, i.e. that the RE that seemed locally best for B'_i leads to the best RE overall.

Under this assumption, we can compute $\mathbf{is}(A')$ and $\mathsf{bt}(A')$ bottom-up as shown in Fig. 8. We iterate over all nonterminals A' in the chart in a fixed linear order, which we call the *evaluation order*. Then we compute $\mathbf{is}(A')$ and $\mathsf{bt}(A')$ by maximizing over the rules for A'. Assume that the best RE for A' can be constructed using the rule $A' \to r(B'_1, \ldots, B'_n)$. Then if, at the time we evaluate A', we have fully evaluated all the B'_i in the sense that $\mathsf{bt}(B'_i)$ is actually the best RE for B'_i, the algorithm will assign the best RE for A' to $\mathsf{bt}(A')$, and its score tuple to $\mathbf{is}(A')$. Thus, if we call an evaluation order *exact* if the nonterminals on the right-hand side of each rule in the chart come before the nonterminal on the left-hand side, we can inductively prove the following theorem:

Theorem 2 *If the evaluation order is exact, then for every nonterminal A' in the chart, we obtain* $\mathsf{bt}(A') = \arg\max_{t \in L_{A'}(C)} P(\mathsf{ix}(A')|t)$ *and* $\mathbf{is}(A') = \mathsf{sc}(\mathsf{bt}(A'))$.

In other words, the algorithm is correct if the evaluation order is exact. If it is not, we might compute a sub-optimal RE as $\mathsf{bt}(A')$, which underestimates $\mathbf{is}(A')$. The choice of evaluation order is thus crucial.

6 Evaluating charts with cycles

It remains to show how we can determine an exact evaluation order for a given chart. One way to think about the problem is to consider the *ordering graph* $O(C)$ of the chart C (see Fig. 9 for an example). This is a directed graph whose nodes

for nonterminals A' in evaluation order **do**
  for rules **r** of the form $A' \to r(B'_1, \ldots, B'_n)$ **do**
    $a = \mathsf{ix}(A')$
    $t' = r(\mathsf{bt}(B'_1), \ldots, \mathsf{bt}(B'_n))$
    $\mathbf{s} = \mathsf{sc}(t') + \sum_{i=1,\ \mathsf{ix}(B'_i)=a}^{n} \mathbf{is}(B'_i)$
    if $\mathsf{prob}(a, \mathbf{s}) > \mathsf{prob}(a, \mathbf{is}(A'))$ **then**
      $\mathbf{is}(A') = \mathbf{s}$
      $\mathsf{bt}(A') = t'$

Figure 8: Computing the best RE.

are the nonterminals of the chart; for each rule $A' \to r(B'_1, \ldots, B'_n)$ in C, it has an edge from B'_i to A' for each i. If this graph is acyclic, we can simply compute a topological sort of $O(C)$ to bring the nodes into a linear order in which each B'_i precedes A'. This is enough to evaluate charts using certain simpler models. For instance, we can apply our REG algorithm to the log-linear model of Golland et al. (2010). Because they only generate REs with a bounded number of relations, their grammars effectively only describe finite languages. In such a case, our charts are always acyclic, and therefore a topological sort of $O(C)$ yields an exact evaluation order.

This simple approach will not work with grammars that allow arbitrary recursion, as they can lead to charts with cycles (indicating an infinite set of valid REs). E.g. the chart in Fig. 4 contains a rule $\mathrm{N}_{b_2}/\{b_2\} \to \mathit{square}_{b_2}(\mathrm{N}_{b_2}/\{b_2\})$ (shown in Fig. 9), which can be used to construct the RE t' = "the square square button" in addition to the RE t = "the square button". Such cycles can be *increasing* with respect to a log-linear probability model, i.e. the model considers t' a better RE than t. Indeed, t has a score tuple of $\langle 0, 2, 0\rangle$, giving $P(b_2|t) = 0.78$. By contrast, t' has a score tuple of $\langle 0, 3, 0\rangle$, thus $P(b_2|t') = 0.91$. This can be continued indefinitely, with each addition of "square" increasing the probability of being resolved to b_2. Thus, there is no best RE for b_2; every RE can be improved by adding another copy of "square".

In such a situation, it is a challenge to even compute *any* score for every nonterminal without running into infinite loops. We can achieve this by decomposing $O(C)$ into its strongly connected components (SCCs), i.e. the maximal subgraphs in which each node is reachable from any other node. We then consider the *component graph* $O'(C)$; its nodes are the SCCs of $O(C)$, and it has an edge from c_1 to c_2 if $O(C)$ has an edge from some node in c_1 to some node in c_2. $O'(C)$ is acyclic by construction, so we can compute a topological

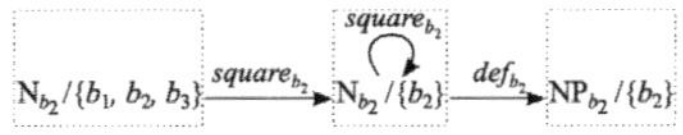

Figure 9: A fragment of the ordering graph for the chart in Fig. 4. Dotted boxes mark SCCs.

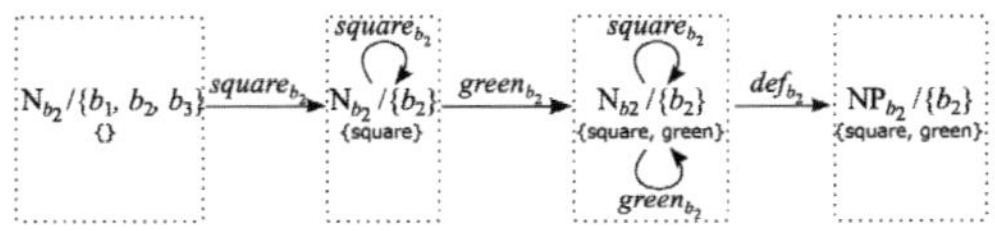

Figure 10: A fragment of a chart ordering graph for a grammar with enriched nonterminals.

sort and order all nonterminals from earlier SCCs before all nonterminals from later SCCs. Within each SCC, we order the nonterminals in the order in which they were discovered by the algorithm in Fig. 5. This yields a linear order on nonterminals, which at least ensures that by the time we evaluate a nonterminal A', there is at least one rule for A' whose right-hand nonterminals have all been evaluated; so $\mathbf{is}(A')$ gets at least *some* value.

In our example, we obtain the order $\mathrm{N}_{b_2}/\{b_1, b_2, b_3\}$, $\mathrm{N}_{b_2}/\{b_2\}$, $\mathrm{NP}_{b_2}/\{b_2\}$. The rule $\mathrm{N}_{b_2}/\{b_2\} \rightarrow \textit{square}_{b_2}(\mathrm{N}_{b_2}/\{b_2\})$ will thus not be considered in the evaluation of $\mathrm{N}_{b_2}/\{b_2\}$, and the algorithm returns "the square button". The algorithm computes optimal REs for acyclic charts, and also for charts where all cycles are *decreasing*, i.e. using the rules in the cycle make the RE worse. This enables us, for instance, to encode the REG problem of Krahmer et al. (2003) into ours by using a feature that evaluates the rule for each attribute to its (negative) cost according to the Krahmer model. Krahmer et al. assume that every attribute has positive cost, and is only used if it is necessary to make the RE distinguishing. Thus all cycles in the chart are decreasing.

One limitation of the algorithm is that it does not overspecify. Suppose that we extend the example model in Fig. 2 with a color predicate $\mathsf{green} = \{b_2\}$. We might then want to prefer "the green square button" over "the square button" because it is easier to understand. But since all square objects (i.e. $\{b_2\}$) are also green, using "green" does not change the denotation of the RE, i.e. it is represented by a loop from $\mathrm{N}_{b_2}/\{b_2\}$ to $\mathrm{N}_{b_2}/\{b_2\}$, which is skipped by the algorithm. One idea could be to *break* such cycles by the careful use of a richer set of nonterminals in the grammar; e.g., they might record the set of all attributes that were used in the RE. Our example rule would then become $\mathrm{N}_{b_2}/\{b_2\}/\{square, green\} \rightarrow \textit{green}_{b_2}(\mathrm{N}_{b_2}/\{b_2\}/\{square\})$, which the algorithm can make use of (see Fig. 10).

7 Conclusion

We have shown how to generate REs using charts. Based on an algorithm for computing a chart of all valid REs, we showed how to compute the RE that maximizes the probability of being understood as the target referent. Our algorithm integrates REG with surface realization. It generates distinguishing REs if this is specified in the grammar; otherwise, it computes the best RE without regard to uniqueness, using features that prefer unambiguous REs as part of the probability model.

Our algorithm can be applied to earlier models of REG, and in these cases is guaranteed to compute optimal REs. The probability model we introduced here is more powerful, and may not admit "best" REs. We have shown how the algorithm can still do something reasonable in such cases, but this point deserves attention in future research, especially with respect to overspecification.

We evaluated the performance of our chart algorithm on a number of randomly sampled input scenes from the GIVE Challenge, which contained 24 objects on average. Our implementation is based on the IRTG tool available at `irtg.googlecode.com`. While in the worst case the chart computation is exponential in the input size, in practice runtimes did not exceed 60 ms for the grammar shown in Fig. 3.

We have focused here on *computing* best REs given a probability model. We have left *training* the model and evaluating it on real-world data for future work. Because our probability model focuses on effectiveness for the listener, rather than human-likeness, our immediate next step is to train it on an interaction corpus which records the reactions of human listeners to system-generated REs. A further avenue of research is to deliberately generate succinct but ambiguous REs when the model predicts them to be easily understood. We will explore ways of achieving this by combining the effectiveness model presented here with a language model that prefers succinct REs.

Acknowledgments. We thank Emiel Krahmer, Stephan Oepen, Konstantina Garoufi, Martín Villalba and the anonymous reviewers for their useful comments and discussions. The authors were supported by the SFB 632 "Information Structure".

References

Douglas E. Appelt. 1985. *Planning English sentences*. Cambridge University Press.

Carlos Areces, Alexander Koller, and Kristina Striegnitz. 2008. Referring expressions as formulas of description logic. In *Proceedings of the 5th International Natural Language Generation Conference (INLG)*.

Anja Belz, Eric Kow, Jette Viethen, and Albert Gatt. 2008. The GREC challenge 2008: Overview and evaluation results. In *Proceedings of the 5th International Conference on Natural Language Generation (INLG)*.

John Carroll, Ann Copestake, Dan Flickinger, and Victor Poznanski. 1999. An efficient chart generator for (semi-)lexicalist grammars. In *Proceedings of the 7th European Workshop on Natural Language Generation*.

David Chiang. 2007. Hierarchical phrase-based translation. *Computational Linguistics*, 33(2):201–228.

Hubert Comon, Max Dauchet, Rémi Gilleron, Christof Löding, Florent Jacquemard, Denis Lugiez, Sophie Tison, and Marc Tommasi. 2007. Tree automata techniques and applications. Available on `http://tata.gforge.inria.fr/`.

Robert Dale and Ehud Reiter. 1995. Computational interpretations of the Gricean Maxims in the generation of referring expressions. *Cognitive Science*, 19(2):233–263.

Nikos Engonopoulos, Martin Villalba, Ivan Titov, and Alexander Koller. 2013. Predicting the resolution of referring expressions from user behavior. In *Proceedings of the Conference on Empirical Methods in Natural Language Processing (EMNLP)*, Seattle.

Nicholas FitzGerald, Yoav Artzi, and Luke Zettlemoyer. 2013. Learning distributions over logical forms for referring expression generation. In *Proceedings of the Conference on Empirical Methods in Natural Language Processing*.

Konstantina Garoufi and Alexander Koller. 2013. Generation of effective referring expressions in situated context. *Language and Cognitive Processes*.

Albert Gatt and Anja Belz. 2010. Introducing shared task evaluation to NLG: The TUNA shared task evaluation challenges. In E. Krahmer and M. Theune, editors, *Empirical Methods in Natural Language Generation*, number 5790 in LNCS, pages 264–293. Springer.

Ferenc Gécseg and Magnus Steinby. 1997. Tree languages. In G. Rozenberg and A. Salomaa, editors, *Handbook of Formal Languages*, volume 3, chapter 1, pages 1–68. Springer-Verlag.

Dave Golland, Percy Liang, and Dan Klein. 2010. A game-theoretic approach to generating spatial descriptions. In *Proceedings of the 2010 Conference on Empirical Methods in Natural Language Processing (EMNLP)*.

Jonathan Graehl, Kevin Knight, and Jonathan May. 2008. Training tree transducers. *Computational Linguistics*, 34(3).

B. Jones, J. Andreas, D. Bauer, K.-M. Hermann, and K. Knight. 2012. Semantics-based machine translation with hyperedge replacement grammars. In *Proceedings of COLING*.

Ron Kaplan and Jürgen Wedekind. 2000. LFG generation produces context-free languages. In *Proceedings of the 18th COLING*.

Martin Kay. 1996. Chart generation. In *Proceedings of the 34th ACL*.

John Kelleher and Geert-Jan Kruijff. 2006. Incremental generation of spatial referring expressions in situated dialogue. In *In Proceedings of Coling-ACL '06, Sydney Australia*.

Alexander Koller and Marco Kuhlmann. 2011. A generalized view on parsing and translation. In *Proceedings of the 12th International Conference on Parsing Technologies*, pages 2–13. Association for Computational Linguistics.

Alexander Koller and Matthew Stone. 2007. Sentence generation as a planning problem. In *Proceedings of the 45th Annual Meeting of the Association of Computational Linguistics (ACL)*.

Alexander Koller, Kristina Striegnitz, Donna Byron, Justine Cassell, Robert Dale, Johanna Moore, and Jon Oberlander. 2010. The First Challenge on Generating Instructions in Virtual Environments. In E. Krahmer and M. Theune, editors, *Empirical Methods in Natural Language Generation*, number 5790 in LNAI, pages 337–361. Springer.

Yannis Konstas and Mirella Lapata. 2012. Concept-to-text generation via discriminative reranking. In *Proceedings of the 50th ACL*.

Ruud Koolen, Albert Gatt, Martijn Goudbeek, and Emiel Krahmer. 2011. Factors causing overspecification in definite descriptions. *Journal of Pragmatics*, 43:3231–3250.

Emiel Krahmer and Kees van Deemter. 2012. Computational generation of referring expressions: A survey. *Computational Linguistics*, 38(1):173–218.

Emiel Krahmer, Sebastiaan van Erk, and André Verleg. 2003. Graph-based generation of referring expressions. *Computational Linguistics*, 29(1):53–72.

Wei Lu and Hwee Tou Ng. 2011. A probabilistic forest-to-string model for language generation from typed lambda calculus expressions. In *Proceedings of EMNLP*.

Margaret Mitchell, Kees van Deemter, and Ehud Reiter. 2013. Generating expressions that refer to visible objects. In *Proceedings of NAACL-HLT*, pages 1174–1184.

Matthew Stone, Christine Doran, Bonnie Webber, Tonia Bleam, and Martha Palmer. 2003. Microplanning with communicative intentions: The SPUD system. *Computational Intelligence*, 19(4):311–381.

Liane Wardlow Lane and Victor Ferreira. 2008. Speaker-external versus speaker-internal forces on utterance form: Do cognitive demands override threats to referential success? *Journal of Experimental Psychology: Learning, Memory, and Cognition*, 34:1466–1481.

Yuk Wah Wong and Raymond J. Mooney. 2007. Learning synchronous grammars for semantic parsing with lambda calculus. In *Proceedings of the 45th ACL*.

Luke S. Zettlemoyer and Michael Collins. 2005. Learning to map sentences to logical form: Structured classification with probabilistic categorial grammars. In *Proceedings of the 21st Conference on Uncertainty in Artificial Intelligence (UAI)*.

Crowdsourcing Language Generation Templates for Dialogue Systems

Margaret Mitchell
Microsoft Research
Redmond, WA USA
memitc@microsoft.com

Dan Bohus
Microsoft Research
Redmond, WA USA
dbohus@microsoft.com

Ece Kamar
Microsoft Research
Redmond, WA USA
eckamar@microsoft.com

Abstract

We explore the use of crowdsourcing to generate natural language in spoken dialogue systems. We introduce a methodology to elicit novel templates from the crowd based on a dialogue seed corpus, and investigate the effect that the amount of surrounding dialogue context has on the generation task. Evaluation is performed both with a crowd and with a system developer to assess the naturalness and suitability of the elicited phrases. Results indicate that the crowd is able to provide reasonable and diverse templates within this methodology. More work is necessary before elicited templates can be automatically plugged into the system.

1 Introduction

A common approach for natural language generation in task-oriented spoken dialogue systems is template-based generation: a set of templates is manually constructed by system developers, and instantiated with slot values at runtime. When the set of templates is limited, frequent interactions with the system can quickly become repetitive, and the naturalness of the interaction is lost.

In this work, we propose and investigate a methodology for developing a corpus of natural language generation templates for a spoken dialogue system via crowdsourcing. We use an existing dialogue system that generates utterances from templates, and explore how well a crowd can generate reliable paraphrases given snippets from the system's original dialogues. By utilizing dialogue data collected from interactions with an existing system, we can begin to learn different ways to converse while controlling the crowd to stay within the scope of the original system. The proposed approach aims to leverage the system's existing capabilities together with the power of the crowd to expand the system's natural language repertoire and create richer interactions.

Our methodology begins with an existing corpus of dialogues, extracted from a spoken dialogue system that gives directions in a building. Further details on this system are given in §4.1. The extracted dialogue corpus contains phrases the system has generated, and crowd-workers construct alternates for these phrases, which can be plugged back into the system as *crowd templates*. We investigate via crowdsourcing the effect of the amount of surrounding context provided to workers on the perceived meaning, naturalness, and diversity of the alternates they produce, and study the acceptability of these alternates from a system developer viewpoint. Our results indicate that the crowd provides reasonable and diverse templates with this methodology. The developer evaluation suggests that additional work is necessary before we can automatically plug crowdsourced templates directly into the system.

We begin by discussing related work in §2. In §3, we detail the proposed methodology. In §4, we describe the experimental setup and results. Directions for future work are discussed in §5.

2 Related Work

Online crowdsourcing has gained popularity in recent years because it provides easy and cheap programmatic access to human intelligence. Researchers have proposed using crowdsourcing for a diverse set of natural language processing tasks, including paired data collection for training machine translation systems (Zaidan and Callison-Burch, 2011), evaluation of NLP systems (Callison-Burch and Dredze, 2010) and speech transcriptions (Parent and Eskenazi, 2010). A popular task targeting language diversity is paraphrase generation, which aims at collecting diverse phrases while preserving the original meaning. Crowdsourcing paraphrase generation has

Proceedings of the INLG and SIGDIAL 2014 Joint Session, pages 172–180,
Philadelphia, Pennsylvania, 19 June 2014.

been studied for the purposes of plagiarism detection (Burrows and Stein, 2013), machine translation (Buzek et al., 2010), and expanding language models used in mobile applications (Han and Ju, 2013). Automated and crowd-based methods have been proposed for evaluating paraphrases generated by the crowd (Denkowski and Lavie, 2010; Tschirsich and Hintz, 2013). Researchers have proposed workflows to increase the diversity of language collected with crowd-based paraphrase generation (Negri et al., 2012) and for reducing the language bias in generation by initiating generation with visual input (Chen and Dolan, 2011). While paraphrase generation typically aims to preserve the meaning of a phrase without considering its use beyond the sentence level, we focus on collecting diverse language to be used directly in a dialogue system in a way that agrees with the full dialogue context.

Manually authoring dialogue systems has been identified as a challenging and time-consuming task (Ward and Pellom, 1999), motivating researchers to explore opportunities to use the crowd to improve and evaluate dialogue systems. Wang et al. (2012) proposed methods to acquire corpora for NLP systems using semantic forms as seeds, and for analyzing the quality of the collected corpora. Liu et al. (2010) used crowdsourcing for free-form language generation and for semantic labeling, with the goal of generating language corpora for new domains. Crowd-workers contribute to dialogue generation in real-time in the Chorus system by providing input about what the system should say next (Lasecki et al., 2013). Crowdsourcing has also been used with some success for dialogue system evaluation (Jurčíček et al., 2011).

Previous work on increasing language diversity in dialogue systems with crowdsourcing has focused on learning about diversity in user input to improve components such as speech recognition and language understanding (e.g., Wang et al. (2012)). Instead, our work focuses on adding diversity to system outputs. Mairesse et al. (2010) followed a similar approach to the work reported here, using crowdsourcing to collect paraphrases for a dialogue system in the restaurant domain. However, the focus of the Mairesse et al. work was on training an NLG module using this data. Our work focuses on crowdsourcing techniques to extract relevant paraphrases, examining the effect of context on their suitability and generalizability.

3 Methodology

Our methodology for developing natural language generation templates is illustrated by the pipeline in Figure 1. This pipeline is designed for dialogue systems that use a template-based natural language generation component. It assumes that the given system has an initial set of language generation templates that have been manually authored, and expands from there. The initial system is used to collect a corpus of dialogues, which we will refer to as the **dialogue seed corpus**, through interactions with users. Based on the dialogue seed corpus, we automatically construct a set of **generation HITs**, web-based crowdsourcing tasks that are used to elicit paraphrases from crowd-workers for instantiated system templates. A generation HIT displays one of the system turns extracted from a system dialogue, with a phrase highlighted, and different amounts of surrounding context in different conditions. The worker is asked to replace the phrase with another one that keeps the same meaning and the coherence of the interaction. If slots are marked in the original, they must be preserved by the worker, which allows us to easily convert the elicited paraphrases to crowd templates. Once a corpus of crowd templates are collected in this fashion, a system developer may filter and decide which to add as viable alternatives to the system's existing list of language generation templates (top path in the pipeline from Figure 1).

We also construct a set of **evaluation HITs** and post them to the crowd to assess the suitability and relative naturalness of the crowd templates (bottom path in the pipeline from Figure 1.) We study how the scores obtained in this crowd-evaluation may be used to help filter the set of new templates that are presented as candidates to the system developer. In the following subsections, we describe each of the pipeline components in detail.

3.1 Dialogue Seed Corpus

We assume as a starting point an existing dialogue system that uses a template-based language generation component. The system uses a set of templates T, which are instantiated with slots filled to generate system phrases. A system turn may contain one or more such phrases connected together. For instance, in the dialogue fragments shown in Figure 2, the template *"Sorry, that was [Place] you wanted, right?"* generates at runtime *"Sorry, that was Ernestine Patrick's office you wanted,*

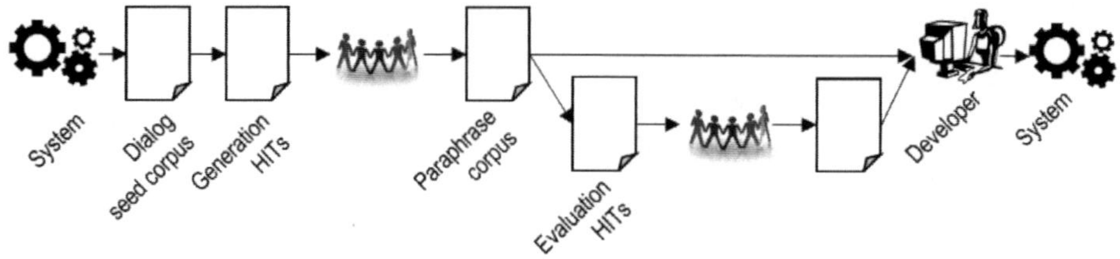

Figure 1: Pipeline for crowd-based development of natural language generation templates.

right?". Statistics on the dialogue seed corpus used in this study are provided in §4.2.

The proposed methodology does not require transcriptions of user utterances in the dialogue seed corpus; instead, it utilizes the recognition results for each user turn. The primary reason behind this choice is that a dialogue that contains recognized user turns may be more coherent than one that contains transcripts and can be generated automatically, as the dialogue manager generates system responses based on the recognition results. However, turn-overtaking issues and recognition problems sometimes resulted in incoherent dialogue interactions. Improving speech recognition remains an area for future work.

3.2 Generation HITs

We use the dialogue seed corpus to produce generation HITs to elicit paraphrases for system phrases from crowd-workers. In the simplest form, a generation HIT might present a single system phrase to the worker. We hypothesize that the surrounding context may be an important factor in facilitating the construction of appropriate paraphrases, affecting their diversity, naturalness, generalizability, etc.; we therefore investigate the effect of presenting varying amounts of dialogue context to the worker.

Specifically, given a system phrase corresponding to a template t instantiated in a dialogue, we investigate six different dialogue context conditions. A phrase in a condition presented to a crowd-worker will be referred to as a **seed**, p. Examples of seeds in each condition are illustrated in Figure 2. In the first condition, denoted $Phrase$, a seed is presented to the worker in isolation. In the second condition, denoted **S**, the entire system turn containing p is presented to the worker, with p highlighted. In the next 4 conditions, denoted su**S**, su**S**u, $susu$**S**, $susu$**S**u, seeds are presented in increasingly larger contexts including one or two previous system and user turns (denoted with lowercase 's' and 'u' in the encoding

Condition: Phrase
Prompt:
Sorry, that was ***Ernestine Patrick 's office*** you wanted, correct?

Condition: S
Prompt:
System: I'm sorry! I still didn't get that. Sorry, that was ***Ernestine Patrick 's office*** you wanted, correct?

Condition: suS
Prompt:
System: Pardon me?
User: ... no
System: I'm sorry! I still didn't get that. Sorry, that was ***Ernestine Patrick 's office*** you wanted, correct?

Condition: suSu
Prompt:
System: Pardon me?
User: ... no
System: I'm sorry! I still didn't get that. Sorry, that was ***Ernestine Patrick 's office*** you wanted, correct?
User: ... no

Condition: susuS
Prompt:
System: You said Ernestine Patrick 's office , right?
User: nop ...
System: Pardon me?
User: ... no
System: I'm sorry! I still didn't get that. Sorry, that was ***Ernestine Patrick 's office*** you wanted, correct?

Condition: susuSu
Prompt:
System: You said Ernestine Patrick 's office , right?
User: nop ...
System: Pardon me?
User: ... no
System: I'm sorry! I still didn't get that. Sorry, that was ***Ernestine Patrick 's office*** you wanted, correct?
User: ... no

Figure 2: Generation HIT excerpts in six different context conditions (w/o instructions, examples).

above), followed by the system turn **S** that contains the highlighted seed p, followed in two conditions ($susu$**S**u and su**S**u) by another user turn. Not all context conditions are applicable for each instantiated template, e.g., conditions that require previous context, such as su**S**, cannot be constructed for phrases appearing in the first system turn. We follow a between-subjects design, such that each worker works on only a single condition.

Each generation HIT elicits a paraphrase for a seed. The HIT additionally contains instructions and examples of what workers are expected to do and not to do.[1] We instruct workers to read the dialogue presented and rephrase the highlighted phrase (seed) so as to preserve the meaning and the cohesion of the interaction. To identify slots accurately in the crowd-generated paraphrases, we mark slot values in the given seed with bold italics and instruct workers to keep this portion exactly the same in their paraphrases (see Figure 2). These paraphrases are then turned into **crowd templates** following 3 basic steps: (1) Spelling error correction; (2) Normalization;[2] and (3) Replacing filled slots in the worker's paraphrase with the slot name. We ask workers to provide paraphrases (in English) that differ from the original phrase more substantially than by punctuation changes, and implement controls to ensure that workers enter slot values.

In completing the generation tasks, the crowd produces a corpus of paraphrases, one paraphrase for each seed. For example, *"I apologize, are you looking for Ernestine Patrick's office?"*, is a paraphrase for the highlighted seed shown in Figure 2. As we have asked the workers not to alter slot values, crowd templates can easily be recovered, e.g., *"I apologize, are you looking for [Place]?"*

3.3 Evaluation HITs

A good crowd template must minimally satisfy two criteria: (1) It should maintain the meaning of the original template; and (2) It should sound natural in *any* dialogue context where the original template was used by the dialogue manager, i.e., it should generalize well, beyond the specifics of the dialogue from which it was elicited.

To assess crowd template quality, we construct evaluation HITs for each crowd template. Instantiated versions of the original template and the crowd template are displayed as options A and B (with randomized assignment) and highlighted as part of the entire dialogue in which the original template was used (see Figure 3). In this **in-context (IC)** evaluation HIT, the worker is asked whether the instantiated crowd template has the same meaning as the original, and which is more natural. In addition, because the original dialogues

[1] Instructions available at m-mitchell.com/corpora.html.

[2] We normalize capitalization, and add punctuation identical to the seed when no punctuation was provided.

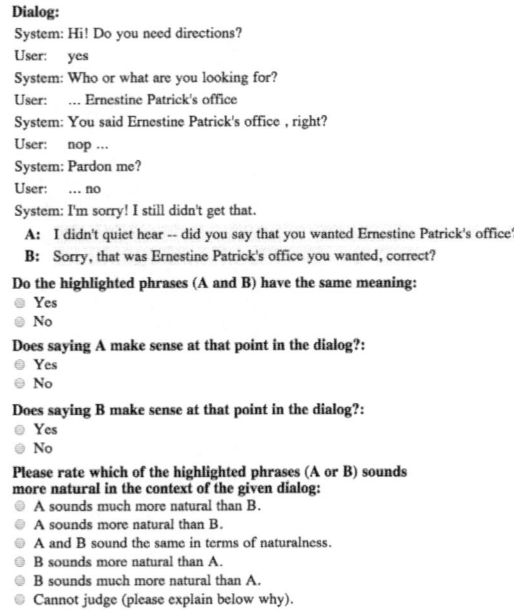

Dialog:
System: Hi! Do you need directions?
User: yes
System: Who or what are you looking for?
User: ... Ernestine Patrick's office
System: You said Ernestine Patrick's office , right?
User: nop ...
System: Pardon me?
User: ... no
System: I'm sorry! I still didn't get that.
A: I didn't quiet hear -- did you say that you wanted Ernestine Patrick's office?
B: Sorry, that was Ernestine Patrick's office you wanted, correct?

Do the highlighted phrases (A and B) have the same meaning:
- Yes
- No

Does saying A make sense at that point in the dialog?:
- Yes
- No

Does saying B make sense at that point in the dialog?:
- Yes
- No

Please rate which of the highlighted phrases (A or B) sounds more natural in the context of the given dialog:
- A sounds much more natural than B.
- A sounds more natural than B.
- A and B sound the same in terms of naturalness.
- B sounds more natural than A.
- B sounds much more natural than A.
- Cannot judge (please explain below why).

Figure 3: Example evaluation HIT excerpt.

were sometimes incoherent (see §3.1), we also asked the evaluation workers to judge whether the given phrases made sense in the given context.

Finally, in order to assess how well the crowd template generalizes across different dialogues, we use a second, **out-of-context (OOC)** evaluation HIT. For each crowd template, we randomly selected a new dialogue where the template t appeared. The out-of-context evaluation HIT presents the instantiated original template and crowd template in this new dialogue. The crowd-workers thus assess the crowd template in a dialogue context different from the one in which it was collected. We describe the evaluation HITs in further detail in §4.

3.4 Developer Filtering

While a crowd-based evaluation can provide insights into the quality of the crowd templates, ultimately, whether or not a template is appropriate for use in the dialogue system depends on many other factors (e.g., register, style, expectations, system goals, etc.). The last step in the proposed methodology is therefore a manual inspection of the crowd templates by a system developer, who assesses which are acceptable for use in the system without changes.

Figure 4: Directions Robot system.

Cond.	Crowd Generation				Crowd Eval.	
	# Gen HITs (× 3)	# w	Time/ HIT (sec)	# Uniq. Para.	# Eval HITs (× 5)	Time/ HIT (sec)
Phrase	767	26	34.7	1181	1126	29.4
S	860	28	30.8	1330	1260	39.2
suS	541	26	33.3	1019	772	30.5
suSu	265	24	38.8	531	392	32.6
susuS	360	24	41.0	745	572	32.3
susuSu	296	28	42.9	602	440	34.4
Total	3089	-	-	5408	4562	-
Average	-	26	36.9	-	-	33.1

Table 1: Statistics for the crowd-based generation and evaluation processes. Each generation HIT was seen by 3 unique workers and each evaluation HIT was seen by 5 unique workers. #w represents number of workers. For evaluation, #w = 231.

4 Experiments and Results

We now describe our experiments and results. We aim to discover whether *there is an effect of the amount of surrounding context on perceived crowd template naturalness*. We additionally explore whether the crowd template retains the meaning of the original template, whether they both make sense in the given context, and the diversity of the templates that the crowd produced for each template type. We report results when the templates are instantiated *in-context*, in the original dialogue; and *out-of-context*, in a new dialogue. We first describe the experimental test-bed and the corpora used and collected below.

4.1 Experimental Platform

The test-bed for our experiments is Directions Robot, a situated dialogue system that provides directions to peoples' offices, conference rooms, and other locations in our building (Bohus et al., 2014). The system couples a Nao humanoid robot with a software infrastructure for multimodal, physically situated dialogue (Bohus and Horvitz, 2009) and has been deployed for several months in an open space, in front of the elevator bank on the 3rd floor of our building (see Figure 4). While some of the interactions are need-based, e.g., visitors coming to the building for meetings, many are also driven by curiosity about the robot.

The Directions Robot utilizes rule-based natural language generation, with one component for giving directions based on computed paths, and another component with 38 templates for the rest of the dialogue. Our experimentation focuses on these 38 templates. As the example shown in Figure 2 illustrates, slots are dynamically filled in at run-time, based on the dialogue history.

We conducted our experiments on a general-purpose crowdsourcing marketplace, the Universal Human Relevance System (UHRS).[3] The marketplace connects human intelligence tasks with a large population of workers across the globe. It provides controls for selecting the country of residence and native languages for workers, and for limiting the maximum number of tasks that can be done by a single worker.

4.2 Crowd-based Generation

Dialogue seed corpus We used 167 dialogues collected with the robot over a period of one week (5 business days) as the dialogue seed corpus. The number of turns in these dialogues (including system and user) ranges from 1 to 41, with a mean of 10 turns. 30 of the 38 templates (79%) appeared in this corpus.

Generation HITs We used the dialogue seed corpus to construct generation HITs, as described in §3.2. In a pilot study, we found that for every 10 instances of a template submitted to the crowd, we received approximately 6 unique paraphrases in return, with slightly different ratios for each of the six conditions. We used the ratios observed for each condition in the pilot study to down-sample the number of instances we created for each template seen more than 10 times in the corpus. The total number of generation HITs resulting for each condition is shown in Table 1.

Crowd generation process Statistics on crowd generation are shown in Table 1. Each worker could complete at most 1/6 of the total HITs for that condition. We paid 3 cents for each genera-

[3]This is a Microsoft-internal crowdsourcing platform.

tion HIT, and each HIT was completed by 3 unique workers. From this set, we removed corrupt responses, and all paraphrases for a generation HIT where at least one of the 3 workers did not correctly write the slot values. This yielded a total of 9123 paraphrases, with 5408 unique paraphrases.

4.3 Crowd-based Evaluation

Evaluation HITs To keep the crowd evaluation tractable, we randomly sampled 25% of the paraphrases generated for all conditions to produce evaluation HITs. We excluded paraphrases from seeds that did not receive paraphrases from all 3 workers or were missing required slots. As discussed in §3, paraphrases were converted to crowd templates, and each crowd template was instantiated in the original dialogue, *in-context* (IC) and in a randomly selected *out-of-context* (OOC) dialogue. The OOC templates were instantiated with slots relevant to the chosen dialogue. This process yielded 2281 paraphrases, placed into each of the two contexts.

Crowd evaluation process As discussed in §3.3, instantiated templates (crowd and original) were displayed as options A and B, with randomized assignment (see Figure 3). Workers were asked to judge whether the original and the crowd template had the same meaning, and whether they made sense in the dialogue context. Workers then rated which was more natural on a 5-point ordinal scale ranging from -2 to 2, where a -2 rating marked that the original was much more natural than the crowd template. Statistics on the judgments collected in the evaluation HITs are shown in Table 1. Workers were paid 7 cents for each HIT. Each worker could complete at most 5% of all HITs, and each HIT was completed by 5 unique workers.

Outlier elimination One challenge with crowdsourced evaluations is noise introduced by spammers. While questions with known answers may be used to detect spammers in objective tasks, the subjective nature of our evaluation tasks makes this difficult: a worker who does not agree with the majority may simply have different opinions about the paraphrase meaning or naturalness. Instead of spam detection, we therefore seek to identify and eliminate outliers; in addition, as previously discussed, each HIT was performed by 5 workers, in an effort to increase robustness.

We focused attention on workers who performed at least 20 HITs (151 of 230 workers, covering 98% of the total number of HITs). Since we randomized the A/B assignment of instantiated original templates and crowd templates, we expect to see a symmetric distribution over the relative naturalness scores of all judgments produced by a worker. To identify workers violating this expectation, we computed a score that reflected the symmetry of the histogram of the naturalness votes for each worker. We considered as outliers 6 workers that were more than $z=1.96$ standard deviations away from the mean on this metric (corresponding to a 95% confidence interval). Secondly, we computed a score that reflected the percentage of tasks where a worker was in a minority, i.e., had the single opposing vote to the other workers on the *same meaning* question. We eliminated 4 workers, who fell in the top 97.5 percentile of this distribution. We corroborated these analyses with a visual inspection of scatterplots showing these two metrics against the number of tasks performed by each judge.[4] As one worker failed on both criteria, overall, 9 workers (covering 9% of all judgements) were considered outliers and their responses were excluded.

4.4 Crowd Evaluation Results

Meaning and Sense Across conditions, we find that most crowd templates are evaluated as having the *same meaning* as the original and *making sense* by the majority of workers. Evaluation percentages are shown in Table 2, and are around 90% across the board. This suggests that in most cases, the generation task yields crowd templates that meet the goal of preserving the meaning of the original template.

Naturalness To evaluate whether the amount of surrounding context has an effect on the perceived naturalness of a paraphrase relative to the original phrase, we use a Kruskal-Wallis (KW) test on the mean scores for each of the paraphrases, setting our significance level to .05. A Kruskal-Wallis test is a non-parametric test useful for significance testing when the independent variable is categorical and the data is not assumed to be normally distributed. We find that there is an effect of condition on the relative naturalness score (KW chi-squared = 15.9156, df = 5, $p = 0.007$) when crowd

[4]Scatterplots available at m-mitchell.com/corpora.html.

Cond.	Crowd Evaluation								Developer Evaluation		
	% Same Meaning		% Makes Sense		Avg. Relative Naturalness		Avg. D-score		% Dev. Accepted		Avg. D-score
	IC	**OOC**	**IC**	**OOC**	**IC**	**OOC**	**IC**	**OOC**	**All**	**Seen>1**	
Phrase	92	91	90	90	-.54 (.66)	-.50 (.61)	.67	.67	37	67	.30
S	91	89	88	88	-.50 (.65)	-.47 (.66)	.68	.64	35	53	.29
suS	84	87	85	87	**-.37** (.65)	**-.37** (.61)	.70	.70	40	63	.41
suSu	88	85	**95**	88	-.48 (.62)	-.43 (.61)	.76	.71	38	50	.39
susuS	**94**	**94**	91	**94**	-.43 (.70)	-.39 (.67)	**.81**	**.80**	38	**78**	.34
susuSu	91	89	92	86	-.40 (.61)	-.38 (.66)	.73	.74	**45**	67	**.42**

Table 2: % same meaning, % makes sense, and average relative naturalness (standard deviation in parentheses), measured in-context (IC) and out-of-context (OOC); crowd-based and developer-based diversity score (D-score); developer acceptance rate computed over all templates, and those seen more than once. The $susuS$ condition yields the most diverse templates using crowd-based metrics; removing templates seen once in the evaluation corpus, this condition has the highest acceptance in the developer evaluation.

templates are evaluated in-context, but not out-of-context (KW chi-squared = 9.4102, df = 5, p-value = 0.09378). Average relative naturalness scores in each condition are shown in Table 2.

Diversity We also assess the diversity of the templates elicited from the crowd, based on the evaluation set. Specifically, we calculate a diversity score (D-score) for each template type t. We calculate this score as the number of unique crowd template types for t voted to make sense and have the same meaning as the original by the majority, divided by the total number of seeds for t with evaluated crowd templates. More formally, let P be the original template instantiations that have evaluated crowd templates, M the set of unique crowd template types voted as having the *same meaning* as the original template by the majority of workers, and S the set of unique crowd template types voted as *making sense* in the dialogue by the majority of workers. Then:

$$\text{D-score}(t) = \frac{|M \cap S|}{|P|}$$

The average diversity scores across all templates for each condition are shown in Table 2. We find the templates that yield the most diverse crowd templates include `WL_Retry` *"Where are you trying to get to in this building?"* and `OK_Help`, *"Okay, I think I can help you with that"*, which have a diversity rating of 1.0 in several conditions: for each template instance we instantiate (i.e., each generation HIT), we get a new, unique crowd template back. Example crowd templates for the `OK_Help` category include *"I believe I can help you find that"* and *"I can help you ok"*. The templates with the least diversity are those for `Hi`, which has a D-score around 0.2 in the S and $Phrase$ conditions.

4.5 Developer Acceptability Results

For the set of crowd templates used in the crowd-based evaluation process, one of the system developers[5] provided binary judgments on whether each template could be added (without making any changes) to the system or not. The developer had access to the original template, extensive knowledge about the system and domain, and the way in which each of these templates are used.

Results indicate that the developer retained 487 of the 1493 unique crowd templates that were used in crowd-evaluation (33%). A breakdown of this acceptance rate by condition is shown in Table 2. When we eliminate templates seen only once in the evaluation corpus, acceptability increases, at the expense of recall. We additionally calculate a diversity score from those templates accepted by the developer, which is simply the number of crowd template types accepted by the developer, divided by the total number of seeds used to elicit the crowd templates in the developer's evaluation, for each template type t.

The developer evaluation revealed a wide range of reasons for excluding crowd templates. Some of the most common were lack of grammaticality, length (some paraphrases were too long/short), stylistic mismatch with the system, and incorrect punctuation. Other reasons included register issues, e.g., too casual/presumptive/impolite, issues of specificity, e.g., template was too general, and issues of incompatibility with the dialogue state and turn construction process. Overall, the developer interview highlighted very specific system

[5]The developer was not an author of this paper.

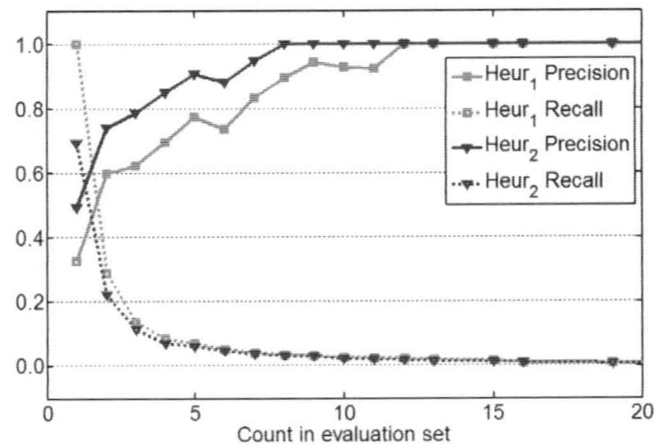

Figure 5: Precision and recall for heuristics.

and domain knowledge in the selection process.

4.6 Crowd-based Evaluation and Developer Acceptability

We now turn to an investigation of whether statistics from the crowd-based generation and evaluation processes can be used to automatically filter crowd templates. Specifically, we look at two heuristics, with results plotted in Figure 5. These heuristics are applied across the evaluation corpus, collating data from all conditions. The first heuristic, $Heur_1$, uses a simple threshold on the number of times a crowd template occurred in the evaluation corpus.[6] We hypothesize that more frequent paraphrases are more likely to be acceptable to the developer, and in fact, as we increase the frequency threshold, precision increases and recall decreases.

The second heuristic, $Heur_2$, combines the threshold on counts with additional scores collected in the out-of-context crowd-evaluation: It only considers templates with an aggregated judgment on the *same meaning* question greater than 50% (i.e., the majority of the crowd thought the paraphrase had the same meaning as the original), and with an aggregated relative naturalness score above the overall mean. As Figure 5 illustrates, different tradeoffs between precision and recall can be achieved via these heuristics, and by varying the count threshold.

These results indicate that developer filtering remains a necessary step for adding new dialogue system templates, as the filtering process cannot yet be replaced by the crowd-evaluation. This is not surprising since the evaluation HITs did not express all the different factors that we found the developer took into account when selecting templates, such as style decisions and how phrases are combined in the system to form a dialogue. Future work may consider expanding evaluation HITs to reflect some of these aspects. By using signals acquired through crowd generation and evaluation, we should be able to reduce the load for the developer by presenting a smaller and more precise candidate list at the expense of reductions in recall.

[6]Since the evaluation corpus randomly sampled 25% of the generation HITs output, this is a proxy for the frequency with which that template was generated by the crowd.

5 Discussion

We proposed and investigated a methodology for developing a corpus of natural language generation templates for a spoken dialogue system via crowdsourcing. We investigated the effect of the context we provided to the workers on the perceived meaning, naturalness, and diversity of the alternates obtained, and evaluated the acceptability of these alternates from a system developer viewpoint.

Our results show that the crowd is able to provide suitable and diverse paraphrases within this methodology, which can then be converted into crowd templates. However, more work is necessary before elicited crowd templates can be plugged directly into a system.

In future work, we hope to continue this process and investigate using features from the crowd and judgments from system developers in a machine learning paradigm to automatically identify crowd templates that can be directly added to the dialogue system. We would also like to extend beyond paraphrasing single templates to entire system turns. With appropriate controls and feature weighting, we may be able to further expand dialogue capabilities using the combined knowledge of the crowd. We expect that by eliciting language templates from multiple people, as opposed to a few developers, the approach may help converge towards a more natural distribution of alternative phrasings in a dialogue. Finally, future work should also investigate the end-to-end effects of introducing crowd elicited templates on the interactions with the user.

Acknowledgments

Thanks to members of the ASI group, Chit W. Saw, Jason Williams, and anonymous reviewers for help and feedback with this research.

References

D. Bohus and E. Horvitz. 2009. Dialog in the open world: Platform and applications. *Proceedings of ICMI'2009.*

Dan Bohus, C. W. Saw, and Eric Horvitz. 2014. Directions robot: In-the-wild experiences and lessons learned. *Proceedings of AAMAS'2014.*

Martin Potthast Burrows, Steven and Benno Stein. 2013. Paraphrase acquisition via crowdsourcing and machine learning. *ACM Transactions on Intelligent Systems and Technology (TIST)*, 43.

Olivia Buzek, Philip Resnik, and Benjamin B. Bederson. 2010. Error driven paraphrase annotation using mechanical turk. *Proceedings of the NAACL HLT 2010 Workshop on Creating Speech and Language Data with Amazon's Mechanical Turk.*

Chris Callison-Burch and Mark Dredze. 2010. Creating speech and language data with amazon's mechanical turk. *Proceedings of the NAACL HLT 2010 Workshop on Creating Speech and Language Data with Amazon's Mechanical Turk.*

David L. Chen and William B. Dolan. 2011. Collecting highly parallel data for paraphrase evaluation. *Proceedings of the 49th Annual Meeting of the Association for Computational Linguistics: Human Language Technologies-Volume 1.*

Michael Denkowski and Alon Lavie. 2010. Exploring normalization techniques for human judgments of machine translation adequacy collected using amazon mechanical turk. *Proceedings of the NAACL HLT 2010 Workshop on Creating Speech and Language Data with Amazon's Mechanical Turk.*

Matthai Philipose Han, Seungyeop and Yun-Cheng Ju. 2013. Nlify: lightweight spoken natural language interfaces via exhaustive paraphrasing. *Proceedings of the 2013 ACM international joint conference on Pervasive and ubiquitous computing.*

Filip Jurčíček, Simon Keizer, Milica Gašić, Frančois Mairesse, Blaise Thomson, Kai Yu, and Steve Young. 2011. Real user evaluation of spoken dialogue systems using amazon mechanical turk. *Proceedings of INTERSPEECH*, 11.

Walter S. Lasecki, Rachel Wesley, Jeffrey Nichols, Anand Kulkarni, James F. Allen, and Jeffrey P. Bigham. 2013. Chorus: a crowd-powered conversational assistant. *Proceedings of the 26th annual ACM symposium on User interface software and technology.*

Sean Liu, Stephanie Seneff, and James Glass. 2010. A collective data generation method for speech language models. *Spoken Language Technology Workshop (SLT), IEEE.*

François Mairesse, Milica Gašić, Filip Jurčíček, Simon Keizer, Blaise Thomson, Kai Yu, and Steve Young. 2010. Phrase-based statistical language generation using graphical models and active learning. *Proceedings of the 48th Annual Meeting of the Association for Computational Linguistics.*

Matteo Negri, Yashar Mehdad, Alessandro Marchetti, Danilo Giampiccolo, and Luisa Bentivogli. 2012. Chinese whispers: Cooperative paraphrase acquisition. *Proceedings of LREC.*

Gabriel Parent and Maxine Eskenazi. 2010. Toward better crowdsourced transcription: Transcription of a year of the let's go bus information system data. *Spoken Language Technology Workshop (SLT), IEEE.*

Martin Tschirsich and Gerold Hintz. 2013. Leveraging crowdsourcing for paraphrase recognition. *LAW VII & ID*, 205.

William Yang Wang, Dan Bohus, Ece Kamar, and Eric Horvitz. 2012. Crowdsourcing the acquisition of natural language corpora: Methods and observations. *Spoken Language Technology Workshop (SLT), IEEE.*

W. Ward and B. Pellom. 1999. The cu communicator system. *Proceedings of IEEE ASRU.*

Omar F. Zaidan and Chris Callison-Burch. 2011. Crowdsourcing translation: Professional quality from non-professionals. *Proceedings of the 49th Annual Meeting of the Association for Computational Linguistics: Human Language Technologies-Volume 1.*

Author Index